Symbols, Selves, and Social Reality

A SYMBOLIC INTERACTIONIST APPROACH TO SOCIAL PSYCHOLOGY AND SOCIOLOGY

~

THIRD EDITION

KENT L. SANDSTROM
UNIVERSITY OF NORTHERN IOWA
DANIEL D. MARTIN
UNIVERSITY OF MINNESOTA–DULUTH
GARY ALAN FINE
NORTHWESTERN UNIVERSITY

New York   Oxford
OXFORD UNIVERSITY PRESS
2010

Oxford University Press, Inc., publishes works that further Oxford University's
objective of excellence in research, scholarship, and education.

Oxford New York
Auckland   Cape Town   Dar es Salaam   Hong Kong   Karachi
Kuala Lumpur   Madrid   Melbourne   Mexico City   Nairobi
New Delhi   Shanghai   Taipei   Toronto

With offices in
Argentina   Austria   Brazil   Chile   Czech Republic   France   Greece
Guatemala   Hungary   Italy   Japan   Poland   Portugal   Singapore
South Korea   Switzerland   Thailand   Turkey   Ukraine   Vietnam

Copyright © 2010 by Oxford University Press, Inc.
Previous editions copyright Roxbury Publishing Company: 2006, 2003

Published by Oxford University Press, Inc.
198 Madison Avenue, New York, New York 10016

http://www.oup.com

Oxford is a registered trademark of Oxford University Press

Library of Congress Cataloging-in-Publication Data
Sandstrom, Kent L.
Symbols, selves, and social reality : a symbolic interactionist approach to social psychology
and sociology / Kent L. Sandstrom, Daniel D. Martin, Gary Alan Fine.—3rd ed.
   p. cm.
Includes bibliographical references and index.
ISBN 978-0-19-538566-3 (alk. paper)
1. Symbolic interactionism. 2. Social psychology. I. Martin, Daniel D. II. Fine, Gary Alan.
III. Title.
HM499.S26 2010
302—dc22   2008050500

Printed in the United States of America
on acid-free paper

CONTENTS

~

CHAPTER SIX: ROLE TAKING, ROLE MAKING, AND THE COORDINATION OF ACTION 145

CHAPTER SEVEN: THE POLITICS OF SOCIAL REALITY: CONSTRUCTING AND NEGOTIATING DEVIANCE 170

CHAPTER EIGHT: COLLECTIVE BEHAVIOR AND SOCIAL MOVEMENTS   203

PREFACE

~

We have written *Symbols, Selves, and Social Reality* with the conviction that education should be a personally relevant, thought-provoking, and enjoyable endeavor—an endeavor that enables its participants to think critically and imaginatively about "reality" and to participate in the transformation of their social world. Guided by this conviction, we have designed the book to help students reflect critically on the everyday social realities they experience and to recognize how these realities are humanly created and transformed.

Our book is intended for social psychology courses within the discipline of sociology. It is designed to introduce students to the perspective of symbolic interactionism within the framework of a one-semester course.

Symbols, Selves, and Social Reality will be best utilized in courses such as "Self and Society," "Society and the Individual," "Social Psychology," "Microsociology," and "Symbolic Interactionism." However, it could also be used effectively in courses such as "Contemporary Social Theory" and "Introduction to Sociology."

DISTINCTIVE FEATURES OF OUR TEXT

This book differs from other texts on symbolic interactionism in several important respects. First, it offers a more empirical focus. Competing texts feature relatively abstract delineations of the core tenets and concepts of symbolic interactionism. Our book links discussion of the central premises and concepts of symbolic interactionism more closely to pertinent research, including several ethnographic studies conducted by its authors. In doing so, *Symbols, Selves, and Social Reality* provides more illustrative examples and excerpts from recent interactionist-oriented studies than other texts.

Second, our text places greater emphasis on topics that are inherently interesting to undergraduate students, such as gender- and race-related issues. For instance, in addressing the topics of socialization and self-development, the book includes an in-depth discussion of how individuals acquire and sustain gendered identities. Moreover, when discussing the processes of person perception and impression management, our book considers how and why these processes are shaped by gender- and race-related dynamics.

Third, *Symbols, Selves, and Social Reality* features an entire chapter on collective action and offers timely and engaging analyses of topics such as rumor, riots, panics, and the narrative elements of social movements.

Fourth, our text includes more pedagogical tools than its competitors. At the end of each chapter, we provide: (1) a summary of key points and concepts; (2) a glossary of key terms; (3) a list of suggested readings; and (4) questions that instructors can use for class discussion or assignments.

In addition, the book features boxed illustrations of points we make in the narrative. For example, the chapter on symbols and perception includes an excerpt from a recent interactionist analysis of how the human sense of smell is informed and influenced by social meanings and expectations. Also, the chapter on socialization includes an excerpt from a study of how children learn and reinforce gender boundaries as they play in the "gender transgression zone," and the chapter on the self includes a featured discussion of how people present and negotiate identities in "cybersexual" interactions. Furthermore, the chapter on deviance includes a boxed excerpt that illustrates how people defined as "deviant" challenge and transform stigmatizing labels.

Finally, *Symbols, Selves, and Social Reality* offers a discussion of how symbolic interactionism is related to and different from other social psychological perspectives; how it is linked to the new perspectives emerging in sociology during the past couple of decades; and how it offers a distinctive understanding of the self, social interaction, and social organization.

NEW TO THIS EDITION

The third edition of *Symbols, Selves, and Social Reality* covers a broader range of topics than the first two editions; it includes a new chapter on "the interactionist toolkit"—the methods, strategies, and perspectives interactionists draw upon as they conduct research. Based on suggestions received from reviewers, this edition also includes several new discussions. These discussions focus on topics such as the impact of Internet technologies

on interaction and self-presentation, the social construction of 9/11 and the problem of terrorism, the narrative elements of social movements, the social shaping and management of odors, the nature and application of grounded theory, and the personal relevance of symbolic interactionism. In addition to incorporating these new discussions, we have changed this edition of *Symbols, Selves, and Social Reality* by reducing the number of highlighted concepts, condensing the chapter summaries, relocating the section on theoretical perspectives to the beginning of the book, and removing a chapter that focused on interactionism's future. In making these changes, we have tried to ensure that *Symbols, Selves, and Social Reality* continues to be useful, engaging, and accessible to students.

CONCLUDING THOUGHTS FOR INSTRUCTORS

We hope this book will be a helpful resource in offering an enriching and engaging course for your students. We believe that it conveys interactionist ideas and approaches in a way that will capture student interest. Most crucially, we believe the book will help you encourage students to grapple with challenging ideas and questions, to think more critically about their social worlds, and to gain greater insight into themselves and their social experiences.

ACKNOWLEDGMENTS

~

A book is always a collective creation, and, as authors, we recognize how much we benefited from the support and labor of others. We would like to thank the following colleagues for the helpful comments and suggestions they provided as reviewers: Patricia Adler (University of Colorado); Peter Adler (University of Denver); John Eric Baugher (University of Southern Maine); James Beggan (University of Louisville); Spencer Cahill (University of South Florida); Kathy Charmaz (Sonoma State University); Martha Copp (East Tennessee State); Karla Erickson (Grinnell College); Andrea Fontana (University of Nevada, Las Vegas); Mary J. Gallant (Rowan University); Mary Ann Groves (Manhattan College): Peter M. Hall (University of Missouri); Michael Katovich (Texas Christian University); Lyn H. Lofland (University of California, Davis); David Maines (Oakland University); John Bryce Merrill (University of Colorado–Boulder); Dan E. Miller (University of Dayton); Jodi O'Brien (Seattle University); Stan Saxton (deceased); David Snow (University of California, Irvine); Angela Yancik (University of Dayton); John Eric Baugher (University of Southern Maine); James Beggan (University of Louisville); John Bryce Merrill (University of Colorado–Boulder); Karla Erickson (Grinnell College); and J. Patrick Williams (Arkansas State University).

We also want to thank Ron Berger, Kathy Charmaz, William Clohesy, Vicki Kessler, Chris Mullins, Sherith Pankratz, Nate Sandstrom, Phil Sandstrom, Whitney Laemmli, Lori Wiebold, and Janelle Wilson for the support and encouragement they provided to us in the writing and production of this text book.

ABOUT THE AUTHORS

~

Kent L. Sandstrom (Ph.D., University of Minnesota) is Professor of Sociology at the University of Northern Iowa and Co-Editor of the *Journal of Contemporary Ethnography*. He has won the Outstanding Teaching Award and the Professional Service Award at the University of Northern Iowa. He has also received the Herbert Blumer Award from the Society for the Study of Symbolic Interaction and the President's Special Award from the Midwest Sociological Society. He teaches courses in social psychology, medical sociology, qualitative methods, and introductory sociology.

Daniel D. Martin (Ph.D., University of Minnesota) is a sociology professor at the University of Minnesota–Duluth, where he teaches courses in social movements, the sociology of community, organizations and antiglobalization, and applied research. He is the recipient of the Panhellenic Association Outstanding Professor Award and the Honored Professor Award. He is presently working on a book titled *The Politics of Sorrow: Race, Class and Identity,* looking at the experiences of families mobilizing around issues of child homicide.

Gary Alan Fine (Ph.D., Social Psychology, Harvard University) is John Evans Professor of Sociology at Northwestern University. He is the former president of the Society for the Study of Symbolic Interaction. His books *Morel Tales: The Culture of Mushrooming* (1998) and *Authors of the Storm: Meteorology and the Culture of Prediction* (2007) each received the Charles Horton Cooley Award from the Society for the Study of Symbolic Interaction for the best work in sociology, and he received the George Herbert Mead Award from the Society for the Study of Symbolic Interaction for lifetime achievement in 2003. He teaches classes in social psychology, qualitative methodology, class and culture, and collective memory.

CHAPTER ONE

~

THE MEANING OF SYMBOLIC INTERACTIONISM

Reality is infused with possibility.
—John Dewey

Things are rarely as simple as they seem. Even children's play is not merely child's play. Consider Little League baseball. As anyone who has taken part in this activity can attest, Little League can be a placid, pastoral preserve in which children engage in a sweet rite of spring. On other occasions, though, Little League can be a fiery cauldron of adult emotions and rivalries. Players can become hostile, coaches manipulative, and fans abusive. The meaning of Little League, then, can vary dramatically. For some parents, Little League represents a proving ground for children they see as future all-stars. For some coaches, Little League serves as a classroom where they can teach children important life lessons, such as the value of teamwork, sportsmanship, and competition. And for some children, Little League is simply a place where they can learn how to play baseball and "hang out" with friends. Yet for most children, Little League comes to represent far more than a context for play; it becomes a venue for "serious" business—a business in which they learn the values and expectations of the adult world, along with the competing demands of pre-adolescent culture.[1]

When we think of Little League baseball, as well as other routine activities and experiences, we usually do not think of how our understandings are relative. We believe the world around us to be largely the same as our interpretations of it. We presume that we see "reality." We look at people, objects, and events and assume that their meaning and significance are easily discerned and that others will agree with us. In most cases, this assumption is not a problem. A desk is only a desk; what else could it be? A book is a book. A tree is a tree. A beautiful piece of sculpture is just that, as is a piece of garbage. This view, crucial for the conduct of our everyday lives, serves us well. Typically the things around us have a straightforward meaning, or at least we act as if they do.

While we rely on this belief in objective reality, this does not mean that things are always what they seem or that everyone's understandings are the same. We all know that members of different groups can see the same event or behavior in very different ways. For instance, fans cheering for one Little League team will see a pitch as a "strike," while fans of the opposing team will see it as a "ball." Similarly, one set of fans will see a close

1

play at first base as a "hit," while the other set will see it as an "out." Because of this, we give certain people, such as umpires, the power to be arbiters of disputed or ambiguous events. Although the umpires may be as wrong in their interpretations as the fans supporting either team, we give them the power to define what really happened. Ultimately, social life depends on judgments about the nature of the world.

Within the field of social psychology, the perspective of symbolic interactionism has traditionally been the one most concerned with the meanings that people give to actions and events and with understanding how these meanings are constructed and negotiated. In turn, this perspective has provided the best known and most elaborately developed explanation of the connection between individual perception and social organization. It stresses that people create, negotiate, and change social meanings through the process of interaction. In the interactionist view, then, people have considerable power in shaping social reality. Through interacting with one another, they not only create meanings, but also build and maintain social order.

THE ORIGINS AND DEVELOPMENT OF SYMBOLIC INTERACTIONISM

Symbolic interactionism is a perspective in sociology that places meaning, interaction, and human agency at the center of understanding social life. This perspective grew out of the American philosophical tradition of pragmatism, an approach developed in the late nineteenth century in the writings of Charles S. Peirce, William James, and John Dewey. These thinkers challenged the mechanistic worldview and dualistic assumptions of classical rationalism, the philosophy that had dominated Western thought since the seventeenth century.[2]

Drawing on the ideas of a broad range of scholars, including G. W. F. Hegel, Charles Darwin, David Hume, and Johann Fichte, the pragmatists developed a philosophical perspective that offered a unifying view of all facets of the human condition—mental and physical, subjective and objective, individual and social. In formulating this philosophy, the pragmatists developed an approach that was a direct revolt against classical rationalism. This approach differed sharply from rationalism in its assumptions about (1) the nature of reality; (2) the nature of the human knower; (3) the relationship between facts, values, truth, and knowledge; and (4) the role of science. In the following discussion we briefly highlight the pragmatists' key ideas regarding these themes because they serve as the backdrop for the symbolic interactionist perspective that informs this book.

The Nature of Reality. The pragmatists rejected the rationalist view of "reality" as fixed, ready made, and waiting to be discovered. By contrast, they conceived of reality as dynamic, unfinished, and always in the making. As John Dewey asserted, reality has multiple natures and possibilities, and it is open to many interpretations.[3] In turn, human beings cannot meaningfully discuss a naked or uninterpreted objective reality. It is not that things in themselves are unattainable to our knowledge, but rather that they can have a variety of possible meanings. Moreover, they do not reveal these meanings to us. What a specific thing means is problematic. Its meaning becomes shaped and reshaped in the course of its interaction with other things, particularly with human "knowers." An object can take on new and different meanings as people encounter and interact with it in new ways. Consider, for example, a beer can. If it is full of beer and handed to you at a party, you are likely to define it as a source of fun, refreshment, or intoxication. On the other hand, if it is empty and it was left on your living room floor by your "lazy" roommate, you may see it as a symbol of irresponsibility and a source of irritation.

The Nature of the Human Knower. The pragmatists challenged the rationalists' "spectator theory of knowledge," which viewed the worlds of mind and matter as distinct and which saw knowledge as a way to represent the inner nature of an objective, external world as correctly as possible. The pragmatists also rejected the rationalist notion that we, as human beings, are passive knowers who intuit the nature and meaning of things from a distance, drawing on logical principles or "thought forms" that exist in a separate metaphysical realm. By contrast, the pragmatists argued that we acquire knowledge through our ongoing experiences, which consist of active exchanges with our physical and social environment. We do not observe things passively or objectively—that is, independent of our social positions and relationships or with complete skepticism about our own beliefs.[4] Indeed, pragmatists such as Charles Peirce and John Dewey suggested that it would be self-deceptive for us to try to do so. In a related vein, Peirce and Dewey emphasized that the worlds of mind and matter are not distinct; instead, they are vitally linked through human action. It is through activity that we select, measure, handle, and ultimately come to know objects in the world around us. Knowing is thus a process of "doing and making" that we engage in when we need to transform objects into objects of knowledge.[5] This need most often arises when we encounter a problem (or felt difficulty) that interferes with our ongoing actions. Most important, as John Dewey posited, we establish the "meaning" of objects through our practical skills, symbolic abilities, and manipulative powers. Put simply, we give meanings to things based on how we respond to them.[6] To make this clear, let us draw again on the example of the beer can. If you respond to the can by opening its top and drinking the fluid in it, you are defining it as something that holds a beverage to be consumed. Or, if you shake the can vigorously and then hand it to a friend in another room, you may be defining it as a "surprise" or as "payback" for a similar action. Of course, there are many more options. For instance, if you respond to the beer can by picking it up and turning it in for a refund at a local recycling center, you are defining it as a prospective source of cash.

The Relative Nature of Truth and the Linkage of Facts, Values, and Action. In line with their belief that we create meaning and reality, the pragmatists claimed that facts are not "out there" to be discovered by scientists or other human inquirers. Instead, scientists—like all people— actively carve facts out of reality depending on their own interests and purposes. Thus, questions of fact cannot be raised without corresponding questions of value. Based on this observation, the pragmatists proposed that scientific inquiry and the search for truth are moral activities. In support of these claims, they pointed out that all judgments of truth involve a practical and evaluative judgment, that the verification of truth refers to a process of determining value, and that the criterion of truth is the realization of some kind of value.[7] In elaborating on these themes, the pragmatists argued that the truth of an idea or statement depends on its practical consequences. An idea is true (and thus "good") if it works— that is, if it enables people to adapt successfully to the requirements of a given situation. As William James proposed, truth "is the name of whatever proves itself to be good in the way of belief, and good, too, for definite assignable reasons."[8] According to the pragmatist view, then, truth is not an absolute phenomenon. Rather, it is relative to the needs and interests of particular individuals and groups. We create the truth as we test out the usefulness of various ideas through our ongoing actions. Moreover, the "truth" of an idea or belief endures only as long as it allows us to adapt effectively to our circumstances.

The Progressive Role of Science. While recognizing the relative and socially constructed nature of truth, even in scientific guise, the pragmatists believed strongly in the possibility of human progress facilitated by a scientifically informed process of social reconstruction. In contrast to the rationalists, pragmatist thinkers argued that philosophy could not and should not seek timeless, absolute truths. Instead, it should become engaged with the world and its problems, seeking and applying knowledge that would help us to improve our current circumstances. The pragmatists did not see knowledge as something that should exist for its own sake. Rather, it should exist for the sake of doing[9]—that is, it should allow us to solve problems and engage in creative and adaptive activity that in some way rearranges the world.[10] In general, the pragmatists' action-oriented and instrumentalist tendencies led them to emphasize the potential applications and consequences of scientific inquiry and knowledge. They believed that knowledge was a key resource for problem solving and that science should enable us to resolve the issues we face and to take part in action that promotes the public good.[12]

PRAGMATISM AND SOCIOLOGY: THE CONTRIBUTIONS OF GEORGE HERBERT MEAD

Pragmatist philosophy entered into sociology most directly through the writings and teachings of George Herbert Mead (1863–1931). Mead, a distinguished professor at the University of Chicago, taught a social psychology course as a member of the philosophy department. His best known book, *Mind, Self, and Society*, emerged out of student transcriptions of lecture notes for that course. Published in 1934, the book became a critical text in the development of symbolic interactionism.

Mead sought to translate pragmatist thought into a theory and method for the social sciences. In doing so he drew not only on the ideas of the pragmatist founders, such as Charles Peirce and William James, but also on the philosophical concepts of G. W. F. Hegel, the psychological insights of Wilhelm Wundt, the sociological analyses of Charles Horton Cooley and James Mark Baldwin, and the evolutionary theory of Charles Darwin. Mead derived his greatest inspiration, however, from the works of John Dewey, his friend and colleague at the University of Chicago. Building on Dewey's groundbreaking ideas, Mead developed a profoundly sociological account of human consciousness and behavior—an account that explained how these phenomena emerge through the processes of interaction and communication.

Mead emphasized that we, as human beings, are distinct from other creatures because we have the capacity for language and thus can think, reason, communicate, and coordinate our actions with others. While these abilities rely on certain biological characteristics, Mead suggested that we have evolved in a way that has freed us from some of the constraints of other animals and allowed us to create social worlds apart from the demands of nature. Guided by this assumption of emergence, Mead focused his analyses on the unique character and consequences of the human ability to use language.

Mead stressed that the symbolic nature of human behavior and communication make them distinctive. Unlike animals who respond to one another largely through instinctive gestures, such as growls, hisses, nips, or chirps, humans communicate through exchanging symbols. When people use words or gestures that call forth the same meaning for others as they do for themselves, they use **significant symbols**.[13] According to Mead, most interactions among human beings are based on the exchange of significant symbols. As a result, these interactions require people to engage in a complex process of interpretation. When two individuals engage in a conversation, they have to make sense of each other's words and behaviors, reflecting on questions such as: What's the meaning of this situation? What does this other person want from me? What do I want from him or her? How is this person likely to act toward me? What will happen if our desires or actions clash? Will we get into a serious conflict? If we do, what consequences will this have for our future interactions? And, how will it affect my interactions with others?

The Importance of Significant Symbols. As Mead noted, significant symbols are important for several reasons. First, they allow us to exchange shared meanings with others and communicate effectively with them. Second, they enable us to anticipate how others are likely to act in a situation and to coordinate our actions with theirs. For example, at a funeral service most Americans share the understanding that "the deceased" refers to the dead person lying in a casket. They also understand that they should respond in a solemn and respectful way to "the deceased" and his or her surviving family members. These understandings allow everyone at a funeral to coordinate their actions smoothly, even in the midst of a highly emotional event.

Funeral home personnel, of course, often take the lead in showing respect for the deceased, maintaining a physical distance of two to three feet from the casket and refraining from making any adjustments to the casketed body while in view of others. They also refrain from making coarse, sarcastic, or humorous comments that would challenge people's understanding that a solemn event is taking place. Overall, the funeral home staff take great care to act and talk in ways that convey respect for the deceased and concern for grieving survivors.

When interacting with one another outside of public view, however, funeral home personnel may act toward "the deceased" in a much different way, using very different significant symbols to communicate with one another and coordinate their actions. For instance, they may refer to the corpse as a "cold one" (or frozen body), a "floater" (or a body that floated to the surface after a drowning), or "Mr. Crispy" (a body recovered from a fire). They may also describe the embalming of the corpse as "pickling" and the caskets as "stuffing boxes" or "stove pipes." Through using these significant symbols, the funeral home staff can distance themselves from especially difficult aspects of the work they share, thereby reducing or relieving some of the discomfort it evokes.[14]

The Social Origins and Dynamics of Mind. In highlighting the role that language and significant symbols play in human behavior, Mead offered a crucial contribution to sociological thought—a theory of the social origins of the human mind.

Drawing on the insights of John Dewey, Mead regarded the mind as an active and ongoing process, not a reactive or unchanging structure. Through creating and exchanging significant symbols, people make and interpret meaning. They also engage in "minded" behavior. For Mead, mind does not refer to an inner psychic world separated from society. Instead, it describes a behavioral process consisting of self-interaction and reflection based on social symbols.

Mead recognized that the emergence of the mind depends on a certain level of physiological development in the central nervous system and cerebral cortex. A mind cannot arise without a highly developed brain. Yet a highly developed brain is not sufficient to make a mind. The emergence of mind depends importantly on social factors. As human beings we develop the capacity for mind through our involvement in society, or interaction with others.[15] Through these interactions we acquire the ability to interpret and use significant symbols.

As Mead revealed, we typically develop a mind as infants because we have to adjust and adapt to a social world of organized, symbolic action—a world of rules, roles, relationships, and institutions. We must learn to use and interpret significant symbols so that we can understand this complex world, communicate with others, and satisfy our impulses and desires. According to Mead, we do this through the crucial process of "taking the role of the other." By placing ourselves in the position of others and looking at the world through their eyes, we learn what things mean. We come to see objects—trees, cats, students, beer, restaurants, ourselves—as others do and to name these objects in ways that call out the same responses in others as they do in us. Through this process we develop the capacity to think or converse with ourselves. That is, by addressing ourselves from the standpoint of others, we acquire a system of shared meanings that allows us to define things and engage in internal conversations (or "thinking"). It is these conversations that constitute the mind.

In addition to explaining how the mind emerges through the social process of role taking, Mead emphasized its importance for the maintenance of society. It is through mind, the process of interacting or conversing with ourselves, that we interpret the meanings of others' words and gestures and anticipate their actions. Mind allows us to assume the perspectives of others, understand their overt and covert behaviors, imagine alternative responses to these behaviors, and fit our actions together with theirs. For instance, when seeing a family standing by their car on the shoulder of a highway and waving at passersby, we implicitly put ourselves in their place, infer that they need help because their car has broken down, and consider different courses of action, such as pulling over to assist them. Most significantly, by using our minds in this way we effectively engage in joint and meaningful action with other individuals. This process makes society possible.

The Processual and Creative Nature of Human Action. In developing his theory of mind, along with his analyses of society and selfhood, Mead highlighted a second key theme: *process*. Mead proposed that all of the key elements of human behavior—consciousness, activity, interaction, role taking, selfhood, and society—are continuously in flux, not static or fixed. Moreover, they arise out of the process of communication and become sustained and transformed through this process.

A third theme that Mead accentuated in his theory was *agency*, or free will. Mead's image of human beings differed sharply from those held by the instinctivist and behaviorist social psychologies that prevailed at the time. Mead saw people as active and creative agents who shape their own worlds and behavior. He believed that human behavior is far too complex to be explained by theories that emphasize instincts or reflex-like responses to "stimuli." Mead was particularly critical of the behaviorist explanations developed by his colleague and friend, John Watson. Watson proposed that social psychologists did not have to pay

attention to the mind, or internal mental events, to understand human conduct. Instead, they needed to concentrate on what they could directly observe: overt physical behavior and the environmental stimuli associated with that behavior.

While Mead had sympathy for an approach that emphasized behavior, he thought that Watson made a critical mistake in excluding mental events or "subjective behavior." Although subjective behavior is not directly observable, Mead argued that it is essential to human conduct. Since people are symbolic creatures, they can interpret and talk about their inner experiences, such as their thoughts or desires, making them observable, if only indirectly. In elaborating this point, Mead criticized Watson (and his behaviorist allies) for focusing too narrowly on the individual. The action of individuals—not just their observable behaviors but also their internal conduct, such as thinking, assessing, and planning—must be analyzed within a social context. A person's behavior is rarely disconnected from the behavior of others. In stressing these themes Mead distinguished his own approach to human conduct, sometimes referred to as *social behaviorism*, from the behaviorism of Watson and others that focused on action, ignoring internal processes. Mead illustrated how people's behavior, including the behavior of mind, arises from adaptation and adjustment to social interaction and can only be understood in relation to this interaction. Most crucially, he demonstrated how and why behaviorists failed to account for the social character of the human act. To understand the complete social act, a social psychologist must understand the dynamics of mind. Because people possess minds, they can invent, discover, initiate, and construct new realities and lines of action. They do not simply "react" to stimuli or biological impulses; rather, they are active and self-conscious agents who use symbols to create objects, designate meanings, define situations, and plan lines of action. In so doing, they actively construct the reality of their environment and exercise a measure of control over it.

Mead's ideas significantly extended social psychological understanding of human consciousness and behavior. Building on pragmatist insights, Mead developed a comprehensive theory that explained human thought and conduct in sociological terms. In later chapters we will discuss Mead's ideas and contributions at greater length, particularly his accounts of the development of the self and the coordination of social action. In the following section, however, we shift our attention to how Mead's scholarly work contributed to the rise of symbolic interactionism and shaped its guiding assumptions.

The Emergence of Symbolic Interactionism

Mead's ideas about human behavior had a profound impact on many of his students, notably Herbert Blumer, a former professional football player who eventually became a prominent sociologist at the University of California at Berkeley and president of the American Sociological Association. Blumer's compilation of writings, *Symbolic Interactionism*, became widely acknowledged as the major statement of the symbolic interactionist perspective.[16] Historically, Mead and Blumer belonged to a group of other early sociologists, such as W. I. Thomas, Robert Park, and Everett Hughes, who were addressing related issues. Because most of these scholars were affiliated with the University of Chicago, symbolic interactionism is sometimes known as the Chicago School of sociology, even though a related school eventually developed at the University of Iowa.

Ironically, symbolic interactionism did not initially go by that name. Herbert Blumer unintentionally applied that label to the perspective in 1937 when writing an essay on social psychology for a social science textbook.[17] In that essay, Blumer emphasized how Mead's work offered a basis for a new social psychological approach that synthesized and transcended the dominant approaches of the time. Blumer referred to this approach as symbolic interactionism, and he

clearly recognized Mead as being its founder. Yet Blumer also drew heavily on the insights of other theorists and, according to some critics, developed a perspective that differed in important respects from Mead's "social behaviorism."[18]

Regardless of whether Blumer merely extended Mead's ideas or took them in new directions, he credited Mead with being the originator of the interactionist perspective. But Blumer also served as a key founder of this approach. In addition to writing major works that described and applied the core tenets of symbolic interactionism, he and one of his colleagues, Everett Hughes, had a major influence on a cohort of graduate students they taught at the University of Chicago in the 1940s and early 1950s. These students, including such notable scholars as Howard Becker, Fred Davis, Elliot Friedson, Erving Goffman, Joseph Gusfield, Helena Lopata, Tamotsu Shibutani, Gregory Stone, Anselm Strauss, and Ralph Turner, further refined and developed the symbolic interactionist perspective. They have since become recognized as the Second Chicago School.[19]

GUIDING ASSUMPTIONS OF THE SYMBOLIC INTERACTIONIST PERSPECTIVE

Like the advocates of other social psychological theories, symbolic interactionists regularly debate with one another about core beliefs, theoretical interpretations, and the appropriateness of various research topics and methods. Despite their areas of disagreement, however, interactionists share some common outlooks and assumptions. Central to their perspective are the following three premises laid out by Herbert Blumer:

> The first premise is that human beings act toward things on the basis of the meanings those things have for them.... The second premise is that the meaning of such things is derived from, or arises out of, the social

interaction that one has with one's fellows. The third premise is that these meanings are handled in, and modified through, an interpretive process used by the person in dealing with the things he [or she] encounters.[20]

In his first premise, Blumer suggests that if we wish to understand human behavior we must know how people define those things—objects, events, individuals, groups, structures—they encounter in their environment. These things do not have an inherent or unvarying meaning. Rather, their meanings differ depending on how we define and respond to them. For instance, the thing we call "paper" will have a different meaning depending on whether we identify it as something to read, write on, buy things with, or fly across a room. Take a clean piece of paper, crumple it and toss it on the floor, and the "paper" becomes "trash." In the same way, another person will mean different things to us and call out different responses depending on whether we define him or her as mugger, lover, criminal, cop, rival, or friend. The crucial factor, then, is how we define, or give meaning to, the things we encounter because that will shape our actions toward them.

Blumer's second premise indicates where these meanings come from—*social interactions*. We are not born knowing the meanings of things. Nor do we learn these meanings simply through individual experiences. Instead, we learn what things mean through our interactions with other people. For example, in the United States we learn what a "baseball" means through taking part in a team game that consists of pitchers, batters, fielders, hits, runs, walks, outs, and innings. As we play this game with others, including friends, parents, and coaches, we quickly discover that a baseball is something you're supposed to hit if you're a "batter," throw if you're a "pitcher," or catch and tag others with if you're a "fielder." Before we find out these things, a baseball does not have a self-evident meaning. We learn that it is something to hit, throw, catch, and tag runners with through observing how others act with respect to it.

In his third premise, Blumer makes the crucial point that the meanings of the things we encounter are altered through our understandings of these things. While acknowledging that the meaning of a thing is formed through social interaction, Blumer stresses that we should not see a person's use of that meaning as automatic. Instead, the use of meanings by an individual occurs through interpretation and self-reflection. As Blumer argued, interpretation is not an unthinking application of previously established social meanings. Instead, it is a formative process in which we use meanings as instruments to guide and choose our actions.[21]

In essence, then, while acknowledging that social definitions guide action, Blumer stressed that the interpretive process involves more than a reflex-like application of these definitions. When we find ourselves in a situation, we must decide which of the many things present in that situation are relevant. We have to determine which objects or actions we need to give meaning and which we can neglect. Moreover, we must figure out which of the many meanings that can be attributed to a thing are the appropriate ones in this context. For example, if you are at a party, you have to decide what meanings to give to the actions of a person who interests you across the room. Let's imagine that the person glances at you and smiles briefly before sipping a drink and looking away. As someone who is interested in this person, you would ask yourself: Why did he or she smile at me? Does he or she think I'm attractive? Does he or she want to meet me? Or, is he or she just being polite? How should I react to his or her behavior in this situation? Should I go over there and say hello? Or, should I just stay here for awhile so that he or she won't see me as too "eager" or "aggressive"?

As this example illustrates, we learn that the same actions (or objects) can have a variety of meanings, and, as we decide how to respond appropriately in a given situation, we have to determine which of these meanings best applies. Unfortunately, when we find ourselves in some situations, particularly new and ambiguous ones, we discover that no established meanings apply. As a result, we must be flexible enough to learn or devise new meanings. We have this flexibility because we handle the things we encounter through a dynamic and creative process of interpretation. This process allows us to generate new or different meanings and to adjust our actions accordingly.

While Blumer's three premises set the boundaries of symbolic interactionism and serve as its cornerstones, several other implicit assumptions inform and guide this perspective, providing it with its philosophical foundations. These assumptions include:

1. *Human beings are unique creatures because of their ability to use symbols.* Following their pragmatist forebears, symbolic interactionists stress the significance of people's symbolic capacities. Because we use and rely upon symbols, we do not usually respond to stimuli in a direct or automatic way; instead, we give meanings to stimuli and then act in terms of these meanings. Our behavior is distinctively different from that of other animals, who act more often based on instincts or reflexes. While we engage in some reflex-based actions, we typically decide how to act based on how we interpret the stimuli we encounter in a given context. In other words, we respond to things—objects, events, people, or experiences—based on the meanings we attribute to those things.

   As Blumer emphasized, things do not have an intrinsic meaning. Rather, the meanings of things derive from and emerge through social interaction. We learn what things mean as we interact with others. In doing so, we rely heavily on **language**, a system of symbols shared by members of a social world and used for the purposes of communication and representation. Guided by language and the processes of communication and role taking it facilitates, we learn how to define and act

toward the objects, events, and experiences that make up our environment. In essence, we learn to see and respond to symbolically mediated realities—realities that have names, such as man, woman, book, professor, house, and neighborhood. These realities are socially constructed.

2. *People become distinctively human through interaction.* Through social interaction, we learn to use symbols, to think and make plans, to take the perspective of others, to develop a sense of self, and to participate in complex forms of communication and social organization. Interactionists do not believe that we are born human. Instead, they argue that we develop into distinctively human beings only as we interact with others. Interactionists acknowledge that we are born with certain kinds of biological "hardware" (e.g., a highly developed nervous system) that give us the potential to become fully human, but they contend that involvement in society is essential for the realization of this potential.

3. *People are conscious, self-reflexive beings who shape their own behavior.* The most important capacities that we develop through involvement in social interaction are the "mind" and the "self." As Mead observed, we form minds and selves through the processes of communication and role taking. That is, we develop the capacity to see and respond to ourselves as objects and thus to interact with ourselves, or think. Because we can think, we have a significant element of choice and autonomy in formulating our actions. Through thinking, we actively shape the meaning of the things in our world, accepting them, rejecting them, or changing them in accord with how we define and act toward them.

   For example, we can define a dandelion as a tasty source of food, rather than a noxious "weed," and eat its leaves in a dinner salad, as some Europeans do. Similarly, we can define a "nerdy" classmate as an interesting source of information, rather than as a boring bookworm, and form a rewarding friendship with him or her. Thus, our behavior toward the stimuli and objects we confront in our environment is not determined. Rather, it is formulated by us based on which stimuli and objects we take into account and how we define them.

In making this assertion, interactionists embrace a voluntaristic image of human behavior. They suggest that people exercise a notable degree of choice and freedom in their actions. At the same time, interactionists understand that a variety of social factors, such as language, culture, race, class, and gender, constrain our interpretations and behavior. Thus, interactionists can be characterized as "soft determinists"; they presume that people's actions are influenced but not determined by social constraints or other forces.[22]

4. *People are purposive creatures who act in and toward situations.* According to interactionists, we don't "release" our behavior, like tension in a spring, in response to biological drives, psychological needs, or social expectations. Rather, we act toward situations. In other words, we build up and construct our behavior based on the meaning we give to the situation in which we find ourselves. For instance, we will react very differently to a college class we are taking based on whether we define it as "something we have to get through" or as "a great class." Of course, the meaning that we give to a particular situation, such as a class, emerges out of our ongoing interactions. That is, we define the situation and decide how to act toward it through taking account of the unfolding intentions, actions, and expressions of others. We thus derive, negotiate, and establish our "definitions of a situation" through processes of symbolic interaction.

As we negotiate and establish a definition of a situation, we also determine what goals we should pursue in that situation. We are purposive in our thoughts and actions; we plan and select lines of behavior that we believe will lead

to our desired ends. Of course, our beliefs and predictions can be wrong; we do not necessarily act wisely or correctly. Nor do we always pursue goals in a clear-cut or single-minded way. Once we begin acting, we may encounter obstacles and contingencies that block or distract us from our original goals and direct us toward new ones. Our actions and intentions, then, are dynamic and emergent.

5. *Society consists of people engaging in symbolic interaction.* Interactionists differ from other social psychologists in their view of society and the relationship between society and the individual. Following Blumer, interactionists conceive of society as a fluid but structured process that consists of individuals interacting with one another. This process is grounded in individuals' abilities to assume each other's perspectives (to "role take"), to adjust and coordinate their unfolding acts, and to interpret and communicate these acts. In emphasizing that society consists of people acting and interacting symbolically, interactionists part company with the psychologically oriented theories that see society as existing primarily "in our heads," either in the form of reward histories or socially shaped cognitions. Interactionists also depart from sociologically oriented perspectives that conceive of society as an entity that exists independently of individuals, dictating our actions through imposed rules, roles, statuses, or structures. We are born into a preexisting society that sets the framework for our actions through patterns of meaning and reward, but we also shape our identities and behaviors as we make plans, seek goals, and interact with others in specific situations. We do not have to reproduce the society or social meanings we inherit.[23] Through our interactions with others we have the power to give new meanings to things, including ourselves, and to reshape or transform society. Society and its structures are human products; they are rooted in the joint acts we engage in with others.

In general, when discussing the relationship between the individual and society, interactionists assert that these two phenomena cannot be meaningfully separated. Both are part of an ongoing process of interaction, and both are mutually constructed in and through this interaction.[24] As Charles Horton Cooley observed, society and the individual are not distinct things, but instead are "flip sides of the same coin."[25] People acquire and realize their individuality (or selfhood) through interaction and, at the same time, maintain and alter society.

6. *Emotions are central to meaning, behavior, and the self.* Interactionists highlight the importance of emotions in shaping people's actions, interactions, and self-concepts. While other sociologists have often bracketed or disregarded emotions, relegating them to the realm of psychology or biology, interactionists stress that our feelings and emotional displays are profoundly social in their origins and expression. They are shaped by "feeling rules"—social guidelines for how we should feel in particular situations.[26] Based on the feeling rules that apply in a given situation, we engage in various forms of emotion work, suppressing or calling forth specific feelings that fit with group expectations. For instance, at a wedding we typically call forth and display feelings of joy and celebration, while at a funeral we experience and display feelings of sorrow, even if we do not feel close to the deceased.

Interactionists emphasize that different groups and organizations have differing emotional cultures and feeling rules; they expect their members to experience particular emotions and to display them appropriately. In turn, interactionists examine not only what objects mean to us in a given situation, but also how we *feel* about them, how we manage and express those feelings, and whether our feelings and emotional displays fit with the norms of our group.

Interactionists also recognize that emotion is a central aspect of the self. Indeed, as Cooley noted, our most powerful feelings are attached to our images of self. It is these feelings about self that give form to our agency, or choices about what to do, in our interactions. That is, we decide how to act with cherished self-images in mind (e.g., images of self as funny, cool, responsible, or attractive), and we consider what implications our actions will have for these images. When our self-images are threatened or undermined by what unfolds in an interaction, we usually react by doing some kind of remedial work. In part, this is to repair the interaction, thereby helping it to proceed smoothly, but it is also to sustain positive self-feelings and a coherent self-concept.

7. *The "social act" should be the fundamental unit of social psychological analysis.* Interactionists contend that the social act, or what Blumer referred to as joint action, is the central concern of social psychology. A social act refers to behavior that in some way takes account of others and is guided by what they do; it is formulated so that it fits together with the behavior of another person, group, or social organization. It also depends on and emerges through communication and interpretation. This definition covers a diverse array of human action, ranging from a handshake, a kiss, a wink, and a fistfight, to a lecture, a beer bash, a soccer game, and a religious revival. Whenever we orient ourselves to others and their actions, regardless of whether we are trying to hurt them, help them, convert them, or destroy them, we are engaging in a social act. We are aligning and fitting together our lines of behavior with theirs. In doing so we may be acting as individuals or as representatives of a group or organization, such as a church, university, corporation, or government.

In focusing on social acts, interactionists are not limited to examining the behavior of individuals or even small groups. They also consider the social conduct of crowds,

Box 1–1 THE NATURE OF JOINT ACTION

Interactionists stress that social life consists of joint action, or what people do together. In analyzing joint action, interactionists emphasize three of its key features. First, it is often routine and repetitive. In most situations, such as a classroom or a movie theater, people are guided by a firm understanding of how they ought to act and how others will act. They draw on a set of shared and ready-made meanings, such as the roles of student, professor, or moviegoer, when choosing and forming lines of action. Hence, many of their actions are relatively unproblematic and fit into preestablished and recurrent patterns. This does not mean, however, that these actions do not involve processes of definition and interpretation. Even in the case of preestablished and repetitive social acts, such as attending a class or watching a movie, people have to build up and align their lines of action through processes of designation and interpretation.[1] Their routine actions are not automatic; they simply flow out of commonly accepted and stable meanings.

A second key feature of joint action is that it is typically linked to a larger and complex network of actions. Take a seemingly simple act: you buy a bag of potato chips from a clerk at the local 7–11. This act is tied to and dependent on the diverse actions of a broad range of people and organizations, including the farmer who raised the potatoes, the trucking company that transported the potatoes to a factory, the factory workers who transformed the potatoes into chips, the stockholders who provide capital, and the store manager who purchased the chips from a wholesaler so that they, in turn, could be sold to you as a customer.

A third feature of joint action is that it is connected to previous contexts and forms of conduct. As Blumer noted, "...any instance of joint action, whether newly formed or long established, has necessarily arisen out of a background of previous actions of participants."[2] The individuals or groups involved in developing a joint action, such as a college course, bring to that development the sets of meanings and interpretive schemes they have acquired through their prior social experiences. Thus, the specific course that students create together with their professor will emerge out of, and be influenced by, the understandings and expectations that they have picked up through their past experiences, particularly their experiences in other college courses.

Overall, interactionists propose that joint acts are built up over time, have careers, and are subject to unforeseen contingencies and changes. When a social act, such as a classroom lecture, assumes a patterned, recurrent, and orderly character, this is due not to internalized norms or system requirements, but to the common social definitions that underlie it. These definitions are not necessarily or automatically reproduced. They are subject to challenge and disruptive contingencies as well as to acceptance and affirmation. When individuals or groups take part in joint acts, regardless of how routine, they may encounter surprises, misunderstandings, problems, or conflicts that require them to alter their guiding definitions and ongoing actions. Their joint acts, then, have a contingent nature and are potentially open to change at any time, as illustrated by a lecture that gets sidetracked because a student asks a provocative question or because a professor loses his or her train of thought.

---

1. Herbert Blumer, *Symbolic Interactionism: Perspective and Method* (Englewood Cliffs, NJ: Prentice-Hall, 1969), p. 18.
2. Ibid., p. 20.

industries, political parties, school systems, hospitals, religious cults, therapeutic organizations, occupational groups, social movements, and the mass media.[27] Inspired by Herbert Blumer, they regard the domain of social psychology—and, more generally, social science—as "constituted precisely by the study of joint action and the collectivities that engage in joint action."[28]

8. *Sociological methods should enable researchers to grasp people's meanings.* As noted earlier, symbolic interactionists emphasize the significance of the fact that people, as symbolic creatures, act on the basis of the meanings they give to things in their world. In turn, interactionists believe it is essential to understand those meanings, seeing them from the point of view of the individuals or groups under study. To develop this insider's view, researchers need to empathize with, or "take the role of," the individuals or groups they are studying. They also need to observe and interact with these individuals or groups in a natural and unobtrusive way. This "naturalistic" approach enables researchers to learn how people define, construct, and act toward the "realities" that constitute their everyday worlds.

Taken together, these assumptions serve as the philosophical underpinnings of a symbolic interactionist view of (1) the nature of human action and society, (2) the relationship between society and the individual, (3) the centrality of emotion to the self and social life, (4) the importance of the social act, and (5) the appropriateness of naturalistic methods for studying human conduct. In identifying and describing these assumptions, we have not tried to provide an exhaustive list that would be embraced by all symbolic interactionists. Instead, we have tried to describe some of the basic and irreducible principles that inform the thought of most interactionists. In doing so we have not meant to imply that interactionists don't disagree and debate about these principles. They clearly do. We will refer to some of these disagreements and debates later in the book. Meanwhile,

in the concluding section of this chapter, we will focus on how symbolic interactionism can be a useful and beneficial perspective for you.

HOW IS SYMBOLIC INTERACTIONISM RELEVANT AND BENEFICIAL TO YOU?

As you have read this chapter, you may have thought: "A lot of this stuff is interesting, but why should I care about symbolic interactionism? How is this perspective useful or beneficial to me?" These are certainly legitimate questions. We think that interactionism can benefit you in at least two important ways. First, it can help you to gain a better understanding of how and why you think, feel, and act in the ways that you do. In a related vein, it can enhance your understanding of your "self" and the nature and consequences of your personal "agency." Second, it can give you helpful insights into how your actions are affected by others and how you also affect them, particularly as you engage in joint actions with them

Understanding Yourself and Your Choices[29]

As we will demonstrate in subsequent chapters of this book, through drawing on interactionist theory you can gain a deeper understanding of how and why you think, feel, and act in particular ways. For instance, through learning about the importance of symbols and meanings in shaping human thoughts, feelings, and behavior, you can recognize how the language and meanings that you have learned direct your perceptions, emotions, and actions in various situations. You can also better understand how and why you have come to define yourself in certain ways and how these self-definitions guide your actions in different contexts.

Because of the emphasis it places on the social nature and roots of the self, interactionism can clearly enhance your knowledge of how your images of self have emerged through and been shaped by your interactions with others. It can also help you to understand why your conceptions and expressions of self often change in different situations, particularly as you respond to shifts taking place in your ongoing interactions and relationships.

Perhaps most crucially, symbolic interactionism can help you to better understand the intricate dialogue and interaction that takes place between your "self" and the larger society as you think, feel, and act. Interactionism differs from many other psychological and sociological theories because it stresses that you, like other people, have the capacity for freedom, or **agency**, as you act toward situations and respond to social demands. Interactionism, however, does not think or talk about freedom in the same way that many Americans do.[30] That is, it does not talk about freedom in a language of "individual choices" that separates these choices from the larger society or social structures in which they occur. Rather, interactionism recognizes that freedom is always linked with social structure and constraint. You make choices but these choices are always conditioned by your social experiences and relationships, and they are made within situations characterized by various forms of social control.

Consider a "choice" made by most women in the United States—whether or not to shave their legs. The vast majority of American women opt to shave their legs, but why do they engage in this behavior? If we asked them, most would suggest that it is a matter of personal choice, saying something like: "It makes me feel better" or "I think it makes my legs look better."[31] Unfortunately, these answers don't acknowledge or reveal how the women's "choices" are shaped by their social context or relationships—why it makes them feel better or feel as if they look better. By adopting an interactionist perspective, you can recognize that these choices are profoundly influenced by how the women think others would react to them if they didn't shave. As Michael Schwalbe has

noted, you could reveal this by asking women, "If shaving your legs is a personal decision, why do so many women in our culture make the same choice?" Their answers would suggest the influence exerted by others, as reflected in comments such as, "If you didn't shave your legs, people would stare at you and think you were weird" or "People might think you were a lesbian" or "Guys wouldn't think you were very sexy."[32] Each of these answers illustrate that women's decision to shave their legs is not really a personal matter; instead, it is a "choice" shaped by the anticipated reactions of others.

One of the merits of interactionism is that it can help you recognize that often you do not exercise as much agency, or freedom, in making decisions as you might imagine. At the same time, however, interactionism helps you remember that your choices and actions are not strictly dictated by cultural expectations or the reactions of others. Because you have the ability to think and use symbols, you have an important element of freedom as you interact with others and formulate your actions. You can improvise to some degree as you negotiate identities, define situations, and perform roles (such as student, friend, or employee) in your everyday interactions. In turn, you can resist, avoid, or overcome some of the constraints you face in various situations.

This capacity for agency comes with a burden. It means that you must bear a lot of responsibility for your behavior, whether it involves shaving your legs, attending class, driving a car, or investing in the stock market. You cannot simply say: "Society makes me do this." Rather, you are called to develop an informed sense of agency; that is, you must ask yourself why you are making these (or other) choices and what consequences result from them.

Understanding Joint Action

As noted earlier in the chapter, interactionism also stresses that social life consists of joint action, or what people do together. In analyzing joint action, interactionism offers a double vision: it recognizes that (1) we are all individuals and (2) we are all stand-ins, or representatives, of groups, classes, and other social categories. This fact has important ethical implications.[33] It means that everything we do has consequences for others and that what we do together can be for good or for ill; that is, it can help to make the world a more just and enjoyable place or it can reproduce harmful social arrangements.

Interactionism is thus relevant for you because it calls you to be conscious not only of how your actions are influenced by others but also of how you influence them, particularly as you engage in joint actions with them. Guided by an interactionist perspective, you will recognize that you need to consider the privileges you derive, as well as the harm you incur, through your actions and interactions. You will also recognize that you need to take responsibility for these consequences. This means that you will not only have to work on your attitudes but also change your practices. More specifically, it means that you will need to bring yourself at times into difficult interactions with others—in the workplace, at school, at home, and elsewhere—to learn more about the consequences of your actions and to find out how to engage in more just social practices. In some cases, it might also mean joining with others, perhaps even in a social movement, to work for changes in society or in social policy.

Interactionism, then, has personal relevance for you in that it can help you gain a deeper understanding of how your "choices" and actions are influenced by your social interactions, and vice versa. In the process, interactionism can offer you useful insights into yourself, your relationships, and the larger social world. It can thus help you to live a more mindful, engaged, and rewarding life.

SUMMARY

- Symbolic interactionism has a rich intellectual history. It emerged out of the philosophical tradition of pragmatism, which itself drew on a variety of philosophies. The pragmatist thinker who served as a key founder of symbolic interactionism was George Herbert Mead. Drawing on the ideas of John Dewey and the other pragmatist founders, Mead formulated a "naturalistic" theory of human thought and behavior—a theory that understood and explained these phenomena as products of natural rather than supernatural processes, specifically the processes of interaction and communication. One of Mead's most distinctive contributions was his theory of how people develop "minds" through role taking, or assuming the perspectives of others. This process is facilitated by the human capacity to use language and communicate through significant symbols. As we learn to take the role of others and use significant symbols, we acquire the ability to think or converse with ourselves. We develop a mind. This allows us to consciously formulate our behavior and to adjust it to the behavior of others, making society possible.

- Guided by Mead's insights, Herbert Blumer, along with a number of his colleagues and students at the University of Chicago, developed symbolic interactionism into a major social psychological perspective. In formulating this perspective, Blumer emphasized that it had three guiding premises: (1) people act toward things on the basis of the meanings those things have for them; (2) these meanings derive from their interactions with others; and (3) these meanings are handled in, and sustained or altered through, the interpretive process that people use as they deal with the things they encounter.

- While these three premises set the broad parameters of symbolic interactionism, a number of other assumptions serve as its philosophical underpinnings. Chief among them are the beliefs that people are unique creatures because of their symbolic capacities and that society consists of people interacting

symbolically. Along with harboring these assumptions, interactionists contend that people are self-reflexive beings who actively shape their own behavior while acting purposively in and toward situations.

- In conclusion, symbolic interactionism stresses that you, as a human being, have the ability to think and use symbols and, thus, exercise an important element of freedom as you interact with others and formulate your actions. Your freedom, however, is not unlimited. Instead, it is conditioned by your social experiences, contexts, and relationships. It also comes with the price of responsibility. As you exercise your freedom and decide how to act, you need to consider not only how your choices are affected by others, but also how they will affect others. Finally, interactionism stresses the importance of understanding your "social acts." These acts include a broad range of behaviors, such as making roles, defining situations, forming impressions, presenting selves, negotiating identities, managing emotions, transmitting rumors, and building social movements. In the remaining chapters of this book we describe and analyze such acts, drawing on the relevant insights of symbolic interactionism as well as other, related theoretical perspectives.

GLOSSARY OF KEY TERMS

Agency The ability to make choices and exercise a measure of control over one's actions.

Language A system of symbols we share with other members of our social worlds and use for the purposes of communication and representation. These symbols have standardized meanings and catalog events, objects, and relations in the world.

Meaning The purpose or significance of something. Interactionists propose that the meaning of a thing is determined by how we respond to and make use of it.

Mind A process of mental activity consisting of self-interaction that is based on socially acquired symbols. This process arises when we face a problem in a given situation.

Pragmatism A theoretical perspective in philosophy, originally developed by Charles Sanders Peirce, which proposes that the meanings of objects, concepts, and propositions reside in their possible consequences for our experiences and practices. In contrast to rationalists, pragmatists claim that "reality" is something that we shape and come to know through our active interventions in the environment. The reality of objects is determined by how we make use of them in a given situation.

Role Taking The process through which we see ourselves (as objects) from the standpoint of others and thereby coordinate our actions with theirs.

Significant Symbol A word or gesture that has a shared meaning to an individual and others; that is, it calls forth the same response in the person using it as it does in others.

Social Act Behavior that in some way takes account of others and is guided by what they do; it is formulated so that it fits

	together with the behavior of another person, group, or social organization. It depends on and emerges through processes of communication and interpretation.
Symbolic Interactionism	A theoretical perspective that emphasizes how people interpret, act toward, and thereby give meaning to objects, events, and situations around them. This perspective highlights how human meanings and actions arise out of the social processes of interpretation, communication, and role taking.

QUESTIONS FOR REFLECTION OR ASSIGNMENT

1. According to pragmatist philosophers, what is the nature of "reality"? What is the nature of "truth"? Can facts be separated from values? What do you think of these pragmatist views? Do you generally agree or disagree with them? Why?

2. How does pragmatist philosophy inform some of the key assumptions of symbolic interactionism? What links exist between the pragmatists' beliefs about the role of science and symbolic interactionists' beliefs about the role of social psychology?

3. According to symbolic interactionists, what is "meaning"? Why is it so central to human behavior and interaction? How do people come to give meaning to their own actions and to the actions of others?

4. How can symbolic interactionism be relevant to you? Why should you bother to learn about it? Do you see yourself as having "agency," or the ability to shape your own actions? If so, how is this agency related to your ability to use symbols and construct social meanings?

SUGGESTED READINGS FOR FURTHER STUDY

Blumer, Herbert. *Symbolic Interactionism: Perspective and Method* (Englewood Cliffs, NJ: Prentice-Hall, 1969).

Maines, David. *The Faultline of Consciousness: A View of Interactionism in Sociology* (New York: Aldine de Gruyter, 2001).

Mead, George Herbert. *Mind, Self, and Society* (Chicago: University of Chicago Press, 1934).

O'Brien, Jodi. *The Production of Reality*, 4th ed. (Thousand Oaks, CA: Pine Forge Press, 2005).

Reynolds, Larry and Nancy Herman-Kinney, eds. *Handbook of Symbolic Interactionism* (Lanham, MA:AltaMira Press, 2003).

Strauss, Anselm L. *Continual Permutations of Action* (Chicago: Aldine, 1993).

ENDNOTES

[1] Gary Alan Fine, *With the Boys: Little League Baseball and Preadolescent Culture* (Chicago: University of Chicago Press, 1987).

[2] Dmitri N. Shalin, "The Pragmatic Origins of Symbolic Interactionism and the Crisis of Classical Science," *Studies in Symbolic Interaction* 12, 1991, p. 226.

[3] Dmitri N. Shalin, "Pragmatism and Social Interactionism," *American Sociological Review* 51, 1986, p. 11.

[4] Dmitri N. Shalin, "The Pragmatic Origins of Symbolic Interactionism and the Crisis of Classical Science," (Note 2), p. 226.

[5] R. W. Sleeper, *The Necessity of Pragmatism* (New Haven, CT: Yale University Press, 1986); see also Eugene Halton, "Pragmatism," in George Ritzer, ed. *Encyclopedia of Social Theory.* (Thousand Oaks, CA: Sage, 2004).

[6] Richard Bernstein, *Praxis and Action* (Philadelphia: University of Pennsylvania Press, 1971).

[7] John D. Goheen and John L. Mothershead, Jr., eds., *Collected Papers of C. I. Lewis* (Stanford, CA: Stanford University Press, 1970), p. 280; see also H. S. Thayer, *Meaning and Action* (Indianapolis, IN: Bobbs-Merrill, 1968).

[8] William James, *Pragmatism: A New Name for Some Old Ways of Thinking* (New York: Longmans Green, 1907), p. 50.

[9] Dmitri N. Shalin, "Pragmatism and Social Interactionism," (Note 2), p. 11.

[10] John Dewey, *John Dewey: The Early Works*, vol. 3 (Carbondale: Southern Illinois Press, 1969).

[11] John Dewey, *The Public and Its Problems* (New York: Holt, [1927] 1954); John Dewey, *Individualism, Old and New* (New York: Capricorn Books, [1929] 1962).

[12] See John Baldwin, *George Herbert Mead: A Unifying Theory for Sociology*, Sage University Paper Series on Masters of Social Theory, vol. 6 (Beverly Hills, CA: Sage, 1987); Larry T. Reynolds, "Intellectual Antecedents," in Nancy J. Herman and Larry T. Reynolds, *Symbolic Interaction: An Introduction to Social Psychology* (Dix Hills, NY: General Hall, Inc., 1993); and Norman Denzin, "Prophetic Pragmatism and the Postmodern: A Comment on Maines," *Symbolic Interaction* 19, 1996, pp. 341–356.

[13] George Herbert Mead, *Mind, Self, and Society* (Chicago: University of Chicago Press, 1934), p. 141.

[14] Peter Adler and Patricia Adler, "Symbolic Interactionism," in Jack D. Douglas, Patricia Adler, Peter Adler, Andrea Fontana, C. Robert Freeman, and Joseph A. Kotarba, eds., *Introduction to the Sociologies of Everyday Life* (Boston: Allyn and Bacon, 1980), pp. 31–32.

[15] See Herbert Blumer, *Symbolic Interactionism: Perspective and Method* (Englewood Cliffs, NJ: Prentice-Hall, 1969).

[16] Ronny E. Turner and Charles Edgley, "Death as Theater: A Dramaturgical Analysis of the American Funeral," *Sociology and Social Research* 60, 1976, pp. 377–392.

[17] Herbert Blumer, "Social Psychology," in Emerson Schmidt, ed., *Man and Society* (New York: Prentice-Hall, 1937).

[18] See Clark McPhail and Cynthia Rexroat, "Mead vs. Blumer: The Divergent Perspectives of Social Behaviorism and Symbolic Interactionism," *American Sociological Review* 44, 1979, pp. 449–467; J. David Lewis and Richard L. Smith, *American Sociology and Pragmatism* (Chicago: University of Chicago Press, 1980).

[19] Gary Alan Fine, ed., *A Second Chicago School? The Development of a Postwar American Sociology* (Chicago: University of Chicago Press, 1995).

[20] Herbert Blumer, *Symbolic Interactionism*, (Note 15), p. 2.

[21] Ibid., p. 5.

[22] Jerome Manis and Bernard Meltzer, *Symbolic Interaction: A Reader in Social Psychology*, 3rd ed. (Boston, MA: Allyn and Bacon, 1978), p. 8.

[23] John Hewitt, *Self and Society*, 7th ed. (Boston, MA: Allyn and Bacon, 1997), p. 23.

[24] Dmitri Shalin, "Pragmatism and Social Interactionism," (Note 2).

[25] Charles Horton Cooley, *Human Nature and the Social Order* (New York: Charles Scribner and Sons, [1902] 1964), pp. 36–37.

[26] Arlie Hochschild, *The Managed Heart* (Berkeley: University of California Press, 1983).

[27] For examples of this type of interactionist analysis, see David Altheide, *Terrorism and the Politics of Fear*. (Lanham, MA: AltaMira Press, 2006) and *Creating Fear: News and the Construction of Crisis*. (New York: Aldine, 2002); Robert Benford and Scott M. Hunt, "Dramaturgy and Social Movements: The Social Construction and Communication of Power," *Sociological Inquiry* 62, 1992, pp. 36–55; Harvey Farberman, "A Criminogenic Market Structure: The Automobile Industry," *The Sociological Quarterly* 16, 1975, pp. 438–456; Norman Denzin, "Notes on the Criminogenic Hypothesis: A Case Study of the American Liquor Industry," *American Sociological Review* 42, 1977, pp. 905–920; Peter M. Hall, "A Symbolic Interactionist Analysis of Politics," *Sociological Inquiry* 42, 1972, pp. 35–75; Peter M. Hall, "Interactionism and the Study of Social Organization," *The Sociological Quarterly* 28, 1987, pp. 1–22; Sherryl Kleinman, *Opposing Ambitions: Gender and Identity in an Alternative Organization* (Chicago: University of Chicago Press, 1996);

Anselm Strauss, *Negotiations* (San Francisco: Jossey-Bass, 1978); David A. Snow, E. Burke Rochford, Jr., Steven K. Worden, and Robert D. Benford, "Frame Alignment Processes, Micro-mobilization and Movement Participation," *American Sociological Review* 51, 1986, pp. 464–481.

[28] Herbert Blumer, *Symbolic Interactionism*, (Note 15), p. 17.

[29] This section draws on ideas shared by Sherryl Kleinman in an unpublished manuscript titled "Towards a Feminist Interactionism."

[30] For an engaging analysis of the two competing views of freedom embraced by Americans, see George Lakeoff, *Whose Freedom?: The Battle over America's Most Important Idea* (New York: Farrar, Straus, and Giroux, 2006).

[31] See Michael Schwalbe, *The Sociologically Examined Life: Pieces of the Conversation*, 2nd ed. (Mountain View, CA: Mayfield, 2001), p. 73.

[32] Ibid.

[33] Sherryl Kleinman, "Towards a Feminist Interactionism," (Note 29).

CHAPTER TWO

~

THE INTERACTIONIST TOOLKIT: METHODS, STRATEGIES, AND RELEVANT PERSPECTIVES

Have you ever wondered why you think, feel, or act in a particular way? For instance, do you wonder why you like or dislike a specific politician or political party? Or, do you wonder why you get along so well with some of your family members and so poorly with others? Or, perhaps, do you wonder why it has been relatively easy or difficult for you to be involved in romantic relationships? If you want to find an answer to any of these questions, or to similar ones, you could clearly benefit from doing some research. That is, you could benefit from gathering and analyzing data in a systematic way. While these data might not give you the precise answers you are looking for, they will undoubtedly offer you some helpful insights and information.

Of course, research is not always easy or convenient. It can cost time, money, and a great deal of effort. Moreover, it can be difficult to figure out how to design a study in a way that will provide answers to your questions. Imagine that you want to gain a better understanding of your dating experiences, so you decide to study the dating relationships of students at your university. How would you begin your research? Which students or student groups would you choose to study? How would you recruit or select them to participate in your study? Once they agreed to take part in your research, how would you study them? For

instance, would you mail them a survey, interview them in person, or observe them in "dating scenes," such as a club or a bar? If you decide to base your study on face-to-face interviews, how, when, and where would you conduct them? Also, how many students would you interview and how much time would you spend with them? What questions would you ask? How would you analyze or make sense of the data you gathered?

Researchers routinely have to ask and answer these types of questions. The answers they provide depend largely on the assumptions they have about how research is best conducted and what types of data are most useful, meaningful, or valid. In the following section, we will discuss how symbolic interactionists conduct research. In so doing, we will highlight their key assumptions about how researchers can best study and understand human behavior. We will also explain why most interactionist scholars use research strategies, such as participant observation, that differ notably from more traditional scientific approaches.

METHODOLOGICAL TRADITIONS AND PRACTICES

We social scientists always, implicitly or explicitly, attribute a point of view to the people whose actions we analyze. We *always*, for instance, describe the meanings the people we have studied give to the events they participate in, so the only question is not whether we should do that, but how accurately we do it...The nearer we get to the conditions in which [people] actually attribute meanings to objects and events, the more accurate our description of those events will be.

—Howard Becker, *Tricks of the Trade*

Most social psychological theories are grounded in traditions that stress the merits of the scientific method, even though research on scientific practice has found that this method is often violated in the name of commonsense understandings. Developed originally in the physical sciences, the scientific method specifies that researchers should begin their studies by defining a problem that warrants investigation. Next, they should draw on existing theories to formulate a set of hypotheses pertaining to that problem. Finally, researchers should test the plausibility of these hypotheses by holding them up against data gathered through quantitative research methods, such as lab experiments, survey questionnaires, structured interviews, or computer simulations. By following these procedures, social psychological researchers can develop a sophisticated or comprehensive understanding of human behavior.

For the most part, symbolic interactionists question the wisdom of using this conventional scientific approach to study human conduct. As we noted in Chapter One, interactionists propose that if you want to develop an adequate understanding of human behavior, you need to put yourself in the position of those engaging in this behavior so you can understand what meanings they attribute to it. This approach requires the application of a humanistic methodology, referred to as **naturalistic inquiry**.[1] This methodology is called "naturalistic" because it focuses on people's behavior in natural social settings and

advocates the use of informal and unobtrusive techniques to acquire a first-hand understanding of this behavior.

According to Herbert Blumer, naturalistic inquiry has two key phases: exploration and inspection.[2] During the exploration phase, the researcher familiarizes himself or herself with a topic of concern by becoming immersed in a specific social world, such as a gang or a bar, focusing on how members of that world experience it and negotiate relationships in it. In adopting this approach, the researcher tries to be sensitive to the perspectives and understandings of those studied, even if they are members of an unpopular or "deviant" group. As a result, he or she relies heavily on qualitative research methods, such as in-depth interviews, life histories, personal document analysis, and, ideally, participant observation (or ethnography).

When using the method of ethnography, a researcher joins the people he or she is studying in their routine activities, observing them in an unobtrusive but systematic way and letting them say in their own words why they are doing what they do. Like a newcomer in any social situation, the ethnographic researcher must learn the roles that apply in the group or context being studied, thereby gauging "where things and people are, the niceties of rank and privilege, who expects him [or her] to do what, at what time, for how long; what the rules are—which ones can or must be broken, which followed to the letter."[3] While learning these roles and rules, the researcher keeps a set of field notes, which serve as a detailed record of what he or she observes. These notes contain descriptive information about the patterns of meaning, action, and interaction that characterize the group or setting being investigated. For instance, if the researcher is studying a gang, the notes may include information about where the gang meets, how it is organized, how members interact with one another, what roles and activities they engage in regularly, what rules they live by, and how they recruit new members. Some of this information will be directly pertinent to the researcher's primary interests or questions, while some will be less relevant. Most important, through field notes an interactionist researcher produces a detailed description of key features of the group he or she is studying, whether that group is a gang, a sorority, a police department, or a city council. This description includes details about the group's settings and interactions as well as lengthy narratives and personal stories provided by the group's members.

Following this phase of exploratory data gathering, the researcher engages in systematic **inspection** of the substantive data he or she has gathered, such as field notes, interview transcripts, or personal documents. In scrutinizing these data, the researcher does not adhere to the conventional mode of scientific inquiry with its emphasis on testing hypotheses, operationalizing concepts, and framing analyses within pre-existing theory. By contrast, the interactionist researcher closely evaluates whatever concepts or elements are used for analysis (e.g., class, status, or social mobility). He or she does so by examining the empirical instances covered by a given concept in a number of different ways, observing them from multiple angles. When taking part in inspection, the researcher engages in a creative and imaginative process that enables him or her to think about things in new ways. He or she is not restricted to preestablished, routine, or prescribed protocols or theoretical frameworks. Instead, he or she is guided by "sensitizing concepts," which offer "a general sense of reference and guidance in approaching empirical instances," "suggest directions along which to look," and "rest on a general sense of what is relevant."[4]

Many interactionist researchers rely on a method called **grounded theory** as they gather, inspect, and analyze data.[5] When guided by this methodological approach, researchers begin to code and analyze data as soon as they collect it. That is, they engage in the processes of collecting and analyzing data simultaneously,

working back and forth between these processes to develop theoretical explanations of the data they are gathering. In doing so, the practitioners of grounded theory take part in several key analytic steps, including open and focused coding, memo writing, theoretical sampling, and creating and linking theoretical categories. (See Box 2-1 for more a detailed description of each of these steps.) Through engaging in these strategies, interactionist researchers try to build rich, inductive understandings of the empirical worlds they are studying. Typically this understanding is presented in written form as an ethnographic text or a detailed description of the patterns of meaning and action that characterize a particular group, setting, or social world. At the same time, this ethnographic description draws on, refines, and improves sensitizing concepts, thereby extending existing theory as well as offering insight into the dynamics of a specific group or setting. Ultimately, then, by drawing on grounded theory methods, interactionists try to produce analyses that provide in-depth *understanding* of a group or social world, derived in part from the words and meanings of participants in that group or social world. At the same time, they strive to develop broader-based *explanations*, emerging out of the dialogue of data and theory, which reveal key patterns and processes that characterize social life.

CHANGING DIRECTIONS IN INTERACTIONIST ETHNOGRAPHY

Ethnography has changed considerably in practice and orientation over the past three decades, and this change has been self-consciously recognized by interactionists and other analysts. Two changes have had major consequences for interactionist ethnographies: greater emphasis on theory in directing ethnographic observation and writing and greater self-awareness of the role of the ethnographer as both author and witness.[6]

Box 2–1 CONSTRUCTING GROUNDED THEORY

Kathy Charmaz

The term, grounded theory, refers to a set of methods for conducting the research process and the product of this process, the resulting theoretical analysis of an empirical problem. As a specific methodological approach, grounded theory refers to a set of systematic guidelines for data gathering, coding, and analysis, particularly to generate middle-range theories. Grounded theory methods are distinctive in that data collection and analysis proceed simultaneously and each informs the other. From the beginning of the research process, the researcher analyzes the data and identifies analytic leads and tentative categories to develop through further data collection. A grounded theory of a studied topic starts with concrete data and ends with rendering them in an explanatory theory.

Applying Grounded Theory

Coding Data. For grounded theorists, the analytic process begins with very early and close coding of the data collected. This coding has two phases: open and focused. In open coding, researchers treat data analytically and discover what they see in it. They scrutinize the data through analyzing and coding each line of text. This line-by-line coding keeps researchers open to fresh ideas and thus reduces their inclinations to force the data into preconceived categories. Such active analytic involvement fosters developing theoretical sensitivity because researchers begin to ask analytic questions of the data. Grounded theorists ask a fundamental question: What is happening here? But rather than merely describing action, they seek to identify its phases, preconditions, properties, and purposes. They also strive to analyze the basic social or social psychological processes in the setting they are studying.

The strategy of initial coding forces researchers to think about small bits of data and to interpret them—immediately. Through coding, researchers take a new perspective on the data and view them from varied angles. Line-by-line coding loosens whatever taken-for-granted assumptions researchers may have shared with study participants and prompts taking their meanings, actions, and worlds as problematic objects of study. This close scrutiny of data prepares researchers to compare pieces of data. Thus, they compare statements or actions from one individual, different incidents, experiences of varied participants, and similar events at different points in time.

Initial coding guides focused or selective coding. After examining the initial codes, researchers look for both the most frequent codes and those that provide the most useful conceptual handles on the data. They adopt these codes for focused coding. Focused codes provide analytic tools for handling large amounts of data; reevaluating earlier data for implicit meanings, statements, and actions; and, subsequently, generating categories in the emerging theory.

Memo Writing. Memo writing is the pivotal, intermediate stage between coding and writing the first draft of the report. Through writing memos, researchers develop their analyses in narrative form and move descriptive material into analytic statements. In the early stages of research, memo writing consists of examining initial codes, defining them, taking them apart, and looking for assumptions, meanings, and actions imbedded in them as well as relationships between codes. Early memos are useful to discuss hunches, note ambiguities, raise questions, clarify ideas, and compare data with data.

These memos also advance the analysis because they prompt researchers to spell out which comparisons between data are the most telling and how and why they are. Such comparisons help researchers to define fundamental aspects of participants' worlds and actions and to view them as processes. Subsequently, they can decide which processes are most significant to study and then explore and describe them in memos. Writing memos becomes a way of studying data. Researchers can then pursue the most interesting leads in their data through further data collection and analysis.

Memo writing enables researchers to define and delineate their emerging theoretical categories. Then they write later memos to develop these categories and to ascertain how they fit together. They compare data with the relevant category, as well as category to category. Writing progressively more theoretical memos during their studies increases researchers' analytic competence in interpreting the data as well as their confidence in the interpretations.

By making memos increasingly more analytic with full coverage of each category, researchers gain a handle on how they fit into the studied process. Then they minimize what can pose a major obstacle: how to integrate the analysis into a coherent framework.

Theoretical Sampling. As researchers write memos that describe and refine their codes and categories, they discern gaps that require further data collection. Subsequently, they engage in theoretical sampling, which means gathering further, more specific data to illuminate, extend, or refine theoretical categories and make them more precise. Thus, the researcher's emerging theory directs this sampling, not the proportional representation of population traits. With skillful use of this sampling, researchers can fill gaps in their emerging theoretical categories, answer unresolved questions, clarify conditions under which the category holds, and describe consequences of the category. Most crucially, through theoretical sampling, researchers make their categories more precise, their memos more useful, and their study more firmly grounded in the data.

Constructing and Linking Theoretical Categories. Coding, memo writing, and theoretical sampling progressively lead researchers to construct theoretical categories that explain the studied process or phenomena. Some categories arise directly from open coding, such as research participants' telling statements. Researchers successively infer other categories as their analyses become more abstract and include a greater range of codes.

Grounded theorists invoke the saturation of core categories as the criterion for ending data collection. But what does that mean? And whose definition of saturation should be adopted? If the categories are concrete and limited, then saturation occurs quickly. Some studies that claim to be grounded theories are neither well grounded nor theoretical; their categories lack explanatory power, and the relationships between them are either unimportant or already established.

For a grounded theory to have explanatory power, its theoretical categories should be abstract, explicit, and integrated with other categories. Thus, grounded theorists complete the following tasks: locating the context(s) in which the category is relevant; defining each category; delineating its fundamental properties; specifying the conditions under which the category exists or changes; designating where, when, and how the category is related to other categories; and identifying the consequences of these relationships. These analytic endeavors produce a fresh theoretical understanding of the studied process.

For many years ethnography was a technique to obtain descriptive material—to discover what was "really" happening in a previously unexplored social setting. Ethnographers chose to study an interesting but unexamined group, hung out with them for a while, recorded their activities, and then wrote a detailed description. Because ethnography was characterized by this descriptive, "you were there" focus, it was unjustly, if somewhat understandably, criticized as little more than glorified journalism. Its emphasis on careful description of a different (or exotic) cultural context was useful for compiling information but led many analysts to feel dissatisfied with the lack of theoretical development that resulted.

During the 1980s, interactionists, along with other qualitative sociologists, began to produce more theoretically grounded ethnographies. A prominent example was Arlie Hochschild's award-winning book *The Managed Heart*, which examined how flight attendants are socialized to handle and display emotion in their workplace.[7] Hochschild's analysis failed as a descriptive ethnography; that is, it offered the reader little insight into the work routines of flight attendants. Instead, Hochschild wrote a theoretically oriented ethnography that highlighted the key forms of emotional labor performed by flight attendants. She excluded material extraneous to her central argument that flight attendants are required to do a great deal of emotion work, structured by feeling rules that reflect the demands of a service industry and the effects of gender inequality. Also, unlike many descriptive ethnographers, Hochschild based her analyses on a number of observations drawn from other sources that addressed her theoretical interest in how and why intimate feelings have become commercialized in modern societies.

Since the 1980s, even more "traditional" interactionist ethnographies that offer descriptive narratives have become more self-consciously theoretical. For example, in a detailed investigation of fantasy gaming, Gary Alan Fine applied and expanded Erving Goffman's model of frame analysis. Fine examined how the self is constructed and negotiated when individuals must operate within several social frames simultaneously (e.g., character, player, and person).[8] In a more recent project, Fine investigated the National Weather Service not only to study how meteorologists forecast the weather but also, on a broader level, to understand how futures are produced and how scientific knowledge is shaped by group culture and organizational demands. Through this research Fine demonstrated how weather forecasting is not simply a matter of reading natural events—weather forecasts are as influenced by social and cultural factors, such as work routines and occupational cultures, as they are by approaching storm clouds.[9]

A traditional issue in ethnographic research is the role of the observer, both in drawing theoretical conclusions and in describing the situation. In recent years ethnographers have moved away from the secret or "covert" observation that had characterized some ethnography. Covert observation was designed to gain access to settings that an outsider could not have penetrated (such as the inner circles of drug dealing, power politics, or corporate decision making), but it was also an attempt to observe groups from the inside without creating the biases that result when people know they are being studied. Now researchers are more likely to admit their roles, but they still use their own experiences and emotions to make sense of the thoughts, feelings, and actions of those they investigate. For instance, in his study of fantasy gamers, Fine recorded his experiences as a player and a referee: his boredom, exhaustion, and reactions to aggressive and sexual content in the games. He didn't claim that he was a typical player, but he understood that his reactions were "real" and captured some important things about the games. Similarly, when Sherryl Kleinman studied Renewal, a holistic health care center, she recorded how she felt as she observed the inequalities between male and female staff. Kleinman's record of her feelings, which included anger, showed her that something was wrong with how Renewal staff members constructed alleged facts, such as their claim that they "were all equal." Indeed, Kleinman's anger enabled her to see that even though the male staff members were "nice" and thoughtful in many ways, and even though the female members felt okay about serving as caretakers for the men, gender-based exploitation was taking place.[10]

In a related vein, some interactionists use a more radical and emotionally attuned method they call **autoethnography**, which refers to the study of oneself or one's own experiences. This method was commonly employed by scholars, such as Charles Horton Cooley, in the early 1900s, but it has recently regained currency among ethnographers. One of the scholars who has championed the resurrection of autoethnography is Carolyn Ellis. She wrote detailed notes on the illness and eventual death of her romantic partner in an effort to examine how individuals (starting with herself) experience and address grief, loss, and serious illness.[11] This "introspective" form of ethnography has triggered controversy among interactionists because it makes study of the self primary and relies on no "objective" external measures. Ellis's analyses, along with the works of other autoethnographers, are driven by the goal of emotional evocation rather than "objectivity." They strive to engage readers personally, moving them to resonate with the sorrows and triumphs of others and, in so doing, to *feel* a sense of caring, desire, or connection (see Box 2-2). In emphasizing the goal of evocation, autoethnographers are guided by a practical as well as emotional orientation. That is, they seek to help readers not only resonate with the experiences of others, but also use these experiences to reflect upon their own lives, thereby enhancing their ability to make sense of themselves and the world around them. In addition to pursuing

Box 2-2 AUTOETHNOGRAPHY: ESSAYING THE PERSONAL TO SEE THE SOCIAL

Autoethnographers examine their own lived experiences of events, interactions, or relationships as their "primary data." In doing so, they try to move toward general, sociologically informed conclusions, but they do not write these conclusions in the dispassionate third-person voice that typically characterizes social scientific research—a voice that keeps readers at a distance. Instead, autoethnographers write in an emotionally evocative first-person voice that invites readers to come close and experience a particular social reality for themselves.

To illustrate this approach, we share the following excerpt from Lisa Tillman-Healy's autoethnography of her experiences of bulimia. In this excerpt Tillman-Healy draws on three narrative voices to describe her first attempt to tell a lover about her bulimic behavior.

My First Confession

My cheek presses against his chest. His breathing shifts over from consciousness to sleep.

Do it, Lisa. Don't wait.

"Douglas?" my strained voice calls out.

"Umhmm"

"There's something I need to tell you."

Probably not a good opening line.

"What's that?" he asks.

"I know I should have told you this before, and I hope you won't be upset that I didn't."

Deep breath. Swallow. It's okay. You're doing fine.

"What is it?" he asks, more insistent this time.

Looooong pause. "Lisa, what is it?"

He's getting nervous. Spit it out.

"Oh, god. Douglas. I don't…I…shit!"

You've come too far. Don't fall apart. Just say it, Lisa. Say the words.

"To one degree or another…I have been…bulimic."

Fuck! I hate the sound of that word.

"…since I was 15."

It's out there. You said it.

He pulls me closer: "Who knows about this?"

"A few old friends and some people I go to school with."

"Your family?"

Oh God. Here we go.

"No, I haven't told them."

Boom!

"Jesus," he says.

No kidding.

"Well, how bad is it now?"

"It's been much worse."

"That's not what I asked."

"It's not that bad."

Liar.

"Have you done it since you met me?"

If you only knew.

"A couple of times, but I don't want you to be concerned."

Oh, please. Please be concerned.

"You must know what that does to your body."

Believe me, I know. I know everything.

"I'm really glad you told me," he says as I start to cry.

"I love you, Lisa. Tell me how I can help you. Please."

You just did. You can't imagine how much.

He pulls me close, stroking my hair until I go to sleep.

I am 22 years old.

In writing this self-story, Tillman-Healy invites us as readers to understand what bulimia means to those who live with it daily. Drawing on personal experience and "sociopoetic" prose, she pulls us away from "the abstractions and categories that fill traditional research on eating disorders and into the experience, to help us engage how bulimia feels" (p. 104). Moreover, in writing other segments of her autoethnography, Tillman-Healy links her personal struggles with bulimia to the "culture of thinness" that prevails in the United States and helps us see how her experiences are an outgrowth of this culture. She thereby challenges us to understand how we are implicated in creating and reproducing the problem of bulimia.

Source: Lisa Tillman-Healy, "A Secret Life in a Culture of Thinness: Reflections on Body, Food, and Bulimia," in Carolyn Ellis and Arthur Bochner, eds., *Composing Ethnography: Alternative Forms of Qualitative Writing* (Walnut Creek, CA: Alta Mira Press, 1996), pp. 76–10.

these aims, autoethnographers propose that a more general sociological understanding can emerge from a self-reflexive reading of one's own feelings and experiences.[12] They thereby imply that we must rediscover the introspectionism of early twentieth-century psychologists, a tradition undermined by the rise of behaviorist methods and perspectives.

Along with resurrecting and refining authoethnography, interactionist researchers have developed or extended a variety of other ethnographic methods, including narrative analysis, discourse analysis, situational analysis, active interviewing, postmodern interviewing, life history interviewing, action research, conversation analysis, grounded theory, and ethnographic content analysis.[13] These methods have emerged out of interactionists' critical questioning of conventional science and its assumptions that researchers simply and straightforwardly report the "reality" or "facts" that they observe. When using these methods, interactionist ethnographers remain aware of the central role that they, like other researchers, play in interpreting and constructing the realities presented in their analyses. That is, they recognize that their observations and analyses do not capture "objective" truth or reality; instead, they are shaped and mediated by their own values, experiences, backgrounds, and social positions.

Many interactionist researchers also recognize that the words and stories that their informants share with them are not simply reports of the truth of these individuals' lives or experiences. Indeed, interactionists view a research interview as a social encounter that itself produces many features of the data collected. In turn, when using a method such as narrative analysis, interactionist researchers do not presume that peoples' words or stories speak for themselves. Moreover, if they are "interpretive interactionists," they do not seek to uncover the truth of the stories others tell them. Rather, they examine how individuals craft these narratives, focusing on the rhetorical formulas, strategies, or styles they use in telling them. In the process,

these researchers seek to understand how the people they are studying use culturally available resources to construct their stories. For instance, when analyzing the stories shared by persons dealing with cancer, HIV/AIDS, or anorexia, an interpretive interactionist might highlight how these individuals draw upon and reiterate prominent cultural stories that emphasize the positive self-changes that can result from grappling with a life challenge such as an eating disorder or serious illness.

Ultimately, unlike the ethnographers who merely want to describe the perspective of others or those who rely solely on their own interpretations or experiences, most contemporary interactionist ethnographers strive for a mix—they want their interpretation and theorizing to be attuned to and informed by the understandings of the members of the social world they are studying, but they also want to push beyond these understandings to provide broader theoretical insights as they write up their analyses. In turn, their ethnographic texts highlight the words and understandings of their informants while also framing these words and understandings within the theoretical perspective provided by symbolic interactionism.

ALTERNATIVES TO ETHNOGRAPHY: THE IOWA SCHOOL AND CONVENTIONAL SCIENTIFIC METHODS

Although the majority of interactionists rely on ethnographic research techniques, some prefer more traditional scientific methods. These analysts were once labeled as members of the Iowa School of symbolic interactionism, a school founded in the 1950s by Manford Kuhn, a professor of sociology at the University of Iowa, and prominent through the 1960s and 1970s. This school emerged out of Kuhn's dissatisfaction with what he defined as the "conjectural and deductive orientation" of the work of Mead, Dewey, and other founders of interactionism.[14] In contrast to Herbert Blumer and others associated with the Chicago School, Kuhn sought to develop a set of theoretical generalizations derived from the thought of the interactionist founders but rigorously tested through standard methods of empirical research, including experimental and survey research.

Kuhn presumed that those inspired by interactionist ideas could develop a more adequate explanation of human behavior if they used conventional methods, which would enable them to better attain the research ideals of uniformity and replicability. Kuhn also believed that the use of standard procedures would help interactionist-oriented analysts discover generic principles or "laws" that applied to all human beings across different situations.[15] One of his first methodological tasks was to develop a standardized instrument to measure the self, which he called the Twenty Statements Test (TST). The TST simply requests that respondents write 20 replies to the question: "Who am I?" Based on this instrument, Kuhn and his students claimed that they could directly gauge the contents of people's "self-attitudes," which they saw as a crucial force in human behavior. They also proposed that they could effectively test and operationalize some of the ambiguous aspects of Mead's theoretical notions regarding the self.

Kuhn and his students started an alternative and more quantitative tradition within symbolic interactionism. This Iowa School tradition has promoted studies that fit into the mold of conventional social scientific research. The analysts who conduct these studies formulate and test hypotheses, operationalize concepts, gather data through questionnaires and structured interviews, and use advanced statistical techniques to analyze these data.[16] Some even develop theories filled with mathematical equations and terminology.

In concluding our brief discussion of the Iowa School tradition and its differences from the Chicago School, we want to add an important caveat. While we have referred to the division that analysts commonly draw between the Iowa and Chicago traditions, this division is somewhat misleading. Today neither Iowa nor Chicago is a center for this kind of research, and the division was never as sharp as this categorization suggests. It is more useful to see interactionism as consisting of two major streams of research carried on at a variety of institutions, including training centers such as the University of Indiana, the University of Minnesota, and the University of California at San Diego. Some interactionists focus on the importance of the self, guided by the questions: "Who are we?" and "How did we come to be that way?" These analysts seek to better measure and conceptualize the nature and development of the human self. In doing so, they often rely on quantitative research methods, such as surveys and questionnaires. Other interactionists concentrate on the dynamics of the situation, looking outward rather than inward to understand how social life and relationships shape our actions. These theorists orient their research efforts toward identifying interaction processes and revealing how groups create meaning. They also use ethnographic methods. The first approach is distinctively "social psychological" in orientation, with a heavily cognitive emphasis, and grounded more clearly in the central concerns of Mead. By contrast, the second approach is "micro-sociological," with strong ties to social and cultural anthropology and a focus on "behavior," not attitudes or cognitions. While both of these approaches have been categorized as symbolic interactionism, they have coexisted rather uneasily. Traditionally, it was claimed that scholars affiliated with the Iowa School have emphasized the understanding of the self-concept, while those identified with the Chicago School and its fieldwork tradition have stressed settings and situations. This distinction no longer holds true (and never was very true), not simply because interactionism has little presence at either Chicago or Iowa but also because some of those trained as Chicago interactionists deal with the self-concept and some of those associated with the Iowa School, especially the New Iowa School and the work of Carl Couch, have become more interested in the structure of situations and interaction processes.

Finally, although most interactionists prefer to use qualitative methods when they conduct research, many agree with Herbert Blumer, who favored "the use of any research method when the research problem warranted such use" and who opposed "the wholesale and inappropriate use of any single method, whether it is a survey, experiment, or ethnography."[17] Many interactionists also agree that it is appropriate for interactionists to use quantitative methods and statistical analyses as long as they recognize that it is people, not variables, who think and do things and that "social causality does not lie in variables or statistical models but in interpretive processes as people individually or jointly define situations and act within them."[18]

RELATED SOCIAL PSYCHOLOGICAL PERSPECTIVES

Symbolic interactionism (SI) is, of course, only one of many prominent perspectives in the field of social psychology. Even within the discipline of sociology, social psychology is rooted in several theoretical traditions, including not only interactionism but also exchange theory, social cognition theory, phenomenology, ethnomethodology, and dramaturgical analysis. Each of these traditions addresses central questions about the nature of human perception, action, and interaction, but each asks somewhat different questions and, correspondingly, provides distinctive answers. Many scholars draw on more than one of these traditions as they conduct their research and develop analyses. They regard the traditions as complementary rather than irreconcilably opposed to one another. Through adopting such a stance, these analysts benefit in two ways: They broaden their research orientations, and they develop richer and more comprehensive explanations of what they observe.

In the following section, we consider four of the leading perspectives in sociological social psychology: dramaturgical theory, exchange theory, social cognition theory, and ethnomethodology. In doing so, we briefly highlight each theory's origins and core assumptions. We also point out its most notable strengths and weaknesses, particularly from the vantage point of symbolic interactionism.

Dramaturgical Theory

Of all the perspectives in social psychology, dramaturgical theory has the closest kinship to symbolic interactionism. Like interactionism, it highlights the role of interaction in the shaping of human behavior. Unlike interactionism, however, dramaturgical theory is not as concerned with people's thoughts and interpretations as it is with how people manipulate their actions and appearances in their daily interactions. Dramaturgical theory also focuses much of its attention on the dynamics and rituals of face-to-face interaction.

The dramaturgical approach developed out of the insights that Erving Goffman provided in his book *The Presentation of Self in Everyday Life*.[19] Goffman believed that we could better understand how people play roles and construct social structure if we thought of them as actors on a stage. People put on masks and performances, and they do so to manage the impressions that others have of them. Borrowing from the ideas of Kenneth Burke, a prominent literary critic, and Gregory Bateson, a prominent anthropologist, Goffman broadened the dramatic metaphor by arguing that social life could be usefully examined in terms of scenes, acts, audiences, scripts, and regions. *Scenes* refer to the situations in which interaction takes place. *Acts* include the sequences of behavior or role performance that unfold in a scene. *Audiences* consist of the people who observe this behavior. *Scripts* include the communications that take place between actors, and *regions* include the front stage and backstage areas of role performances.

Goffman used situations such as dating to illustrate the utility of dramaturgical theory. A couple on a first date typically, and often anxiously, tries to impress each other with their personal attractiveness, behavioral adeptness, and interpersonal savvy. Before going out on the date, they may spend a great deal of time primping and preening to look their best. Goffman referred to the location for this preparation as a "backstage," because like the actor putting on makeup and a costume, it is the region where a person prepares for a public performance, such as talking and dancing with one's date at a party. Of course, what is a backstage region for one person, such as the young man, may be a "front stage" area for another, such as the sister or roommate of the young woman going on the date. Most crucially, Goffman's basic premise was that we try to manage the impressions that others have of us, perhaps most obviously in the early phases of a dating relationship, but also as we go through our daily rounds. Goffman identified and revealed the techniques that we use to stage convincing self-presentations and role performances so that all who participate in a situation will feel comfortable. According to Goffman, our goal is to realize desired selves while also making interaction flow harmoniously, and we do so with the understanding that others will collaborate with us, or engage in "teamwork."

In general, Goffman's dramaturgical analyses drew attention to the conventions, or implicit cultural understandings, that influence everyday, face-to-face interactions. His work also revealed how we actively participate in creating particular interpretations, role performances, and social structures. According to Goffman, our definitions of situations and role behaviors are not dictated by larger cultural scripts. Instead, these scripts provide us with "rough drafts" for action. We often have room to innovate in our role performances, or at least to choose among various behavioral options, as we try to attain our personal goals. Most important, as we fashion role performances and manage others' impressions in our daily interactions, we continually reconstruct the social order, legitimate the parts we play in it, and make it "real" to ourselves and others.

In highlighting these themes, dramaturgical theory offers many useful contributions to social psychology. For symbolic interactionists, this theory's most significant contribution is its revelation of how the theatrical metaphor can help us to better understand the dynamics of people's interactions and gain entrance to their firsthand experience of social life. In addition, as we will highlight in Chapter Five, dramaturgical theory suggests that people's selves are dramatic effects; that is, they are established, not reflected, in social interaction, particularly through performances and stage work. It also illustrates how individuals define situations through their interactions with others and how their definitions of situations serve as the source of their unfolding "motives" and role performances.[20]

Despite having these important virtues, dramaturgical theory also has some drawbacks. First, it tries to account for people's behavior in theatrical concepts that do not derive from their lived experience or reflect the meanings they give to their behavior and interactions. Second, some dramaturgical theorists become so interested in applying the theatrical metaphor to the behavior they are studying that they lose sight of other important aspects of this behavior. At times, they even seem to mistake the metaphor for the underlying behavior. The metaphor is, as Goffman himself notes, only a scaffolding erected to help us study and understand our behavior—it is not the behavior itself. Third, dramaturgical theorists often present an overly static and superficial portrayal of the interaction process. In focusing on the rules and rituals of face-to-face interaction, they gloss over some of its more dynamic and negotiated features. Fourth, dramaturgical theorists offer a hollow image of the self, focusing on the strategies people use to manage impressions and present personal "fronts" but failing to provide a theory of the self that takes part in these activities. Finally, dramaturgical theorists generally present ahistorical accounts of interaction and social life. In turn, their analyses have shed little light on how roles, identities, and self-presentations have been constructed and negotiated in previous eras, or how people are socialized into these roles.[21]

Exchange Theory

Exchange theory has established a solid tradition within both psychology, emerging out of the work of John Thibaut and Harold Kelly, and sociology, growing out of the analyses of George Homans, Peter Blau, Richard Emerson, and Karen Cook.[22] This theory has become increasingly popular during the past three decades, as illustrated by its rapidly growing prominence in social psychological journals.

As a tradition, exchange theory has synthesized the principles of classical economics with the principles of behaviorism, one of the leading perspectives in psychology. In line with behaviorism, exchange theory assumes that people are hedonistic or pleasure-seeking creatures, maximizing their satisfactions. It also regards a person's prior history of rewards and punishments as important for predicting his or her future actions. That is, exchange theory proposes that an individual will be more or less likely to engage in a given behavior based on the rewards or punishments he or she has received for acting similarly in the past.

While embracing these two core principles of behaviorism, exchange theory differs from this perspective in a number of important ways. First, rather than focusing on the behavior of individuals, exchange theory highlights the interactions that occur between individuals. Its key unit of analysis is the exchange relationship, or the series of transactions that take place between two or more people over time. Exchange theory argues that people enter into relationships in order to meet their needs and acquire valued rewards. Within these relationships, they engage in exchanges that are comparable to economic transactions, and the individuals behave in light of their assessments of

outcomes. For instance, people exchange various personal resources (knowledge, status, physical attractiveness, emotional skills, a sense of humor) for desired rewards, such as a good grade, a desirable job, an enjoyable friendship, or an exciting date. Thus, while the resources people exchange may be material, they can also include nonmaterial and social rewards such as love, esteem, approval, and respect. Regardless of the specific resources they exchange, individuals are trying to get "the best possible deal." Whether buying a car, forming a friendship, or negotiating a date, they consider whether the exchange in question will bring them a profitable payoff or whether they can get a better deal with a different exchange partner.

In accord with these assumptions, a second way that exchange theory differs from behaviorism is in its belief that people are "rational" beings. As a result, exchange theory is considered to be part of a family of approaches labeled *rational choice theory*. According to exchange theory, we engage in a kind of mental bookkeeping as we choose lines of behavior, weighing the costs and benefits of various alternatives and opting for the one we expect to provide the greatest profit or net reward. Of course, exchange theory recognizes that we are not always well informed and that we can misjudge the consequences of our actions. What matters most in our choices is how we perceive things. We will choose to take part in those actions we think will be most rewarding to us, based on our view of the relative costs and benefits of available alternatives as well as our assessments of how likely we are to realize a desired outcome.

A third way exchange theory differs from behaviorism is that it incorporates social structure into its analyses of people's actions and interactions.[23] In contrast to behaviorism, which reduces social factors to reinforcement histories and has no real theory of society, exchange theory offers a more developed conception of society and its impact. Exchange theory sees society as consisting of two or more people who exchange resources that have mutual value. It also suggests that the structure of society is determined by the availability of resources and by who controls those resources.[24] For example, if you own land with a spring-fed reservoir in an area where there is little water, your neighbors will want to exchange something they own for some of your water. One may offer you a piece of finely crafted furniture for the water. Another may offer you beautiful rugs. If you don't need new furniture but you do need nice floor coverings, it would be rational for you to exchange the water with the neighbor who makes rugs. Most important, your interactions with others in the community will be based on structural factors, such as the law of supply and demand, and your control over resources. In essence, the inequalities that exist in the distribution of valued resources will shape the nature of your social exchanges and relationships. Some exchange theorists even go so far as to claim that such seemingly psychological attributes as your "personality traits" are actually outcomes of the patterns of interdependence that characterize your relationships and the problems of exchange that flow from these patterns.[25]

From the viewpoint of symbolic interactionism, exchange theory has some admirable strengths. It provides a useful explanation of how and why people maintain relationships and create stability in their lives. As people exchange valued resources, they become mutually dependent and start to expect that rewarding exchanges will continue. They subsequently commit themselves to sustaining those relationships that provide them with more rewards than costs. This behavior accounts for the continuity and order they experience in many of their daily relationships.

In addition to offering an explanation of the stability of relationships, exchange theory contends that people engage in constructive mental processes as they act toward others and the world around them.[26] To evaluate costs and benefits and adjust their actions accordingly, individuals have to be able to imagine the alternatives available to them, anticipate the reactions of others, and exercise control over their own unfolding conduct. By highlighting

these points, exchange theory, like symbolic interactionism, recognizes that human behavior is rooted in a complex set of cognitive processes.

Unlike interactionism, however, exchange theory does not emphasize the importance of people's symbolic abilities, nor does it offer a detailed theory of the self. While presuming that individuals exercise self-control over their conduct, exchange theory does not explain how the self develops or how it serves to guide and regulate behavior. Moreover, exchange theory is rooted in a reductionist psychology that accounts for all human behavior in terms of a single motive—the pursuit of personal advantage, however defined. Symbolic interactionists challenge the validity of such an assumption, grounded in the unlikely claim that everyone is concerned primarily with economic benefit. They contend that human motivation is much more diverse, complex, and social.[27] According to interactionists, people do not always or necessarily act on calculations of maximizing benefits. In various contexts, they may act in altruistic ways or in ways that incur more personal costs than benefits.

Finally, drawing on the insights of feminist critics, some interactionists criticize exchange theory for having a "masculine bias."[28] They point out that this theory assumes that human beings develop an individualistic and rationally oriented self, which may be truer for men than women, particularly in Western industrial societies. In contrast to men, women tend to form more connective and emotionally oriented selves that value empathy, intimacy, and caring relationships. Thus, by stressing that people are motivated only by self-oriented and rational interests rather than relational and emotional concerns, exchange theory ignores and devalues motives that may be more characteristic of women.

Social Cognition Theory and Cognitive Sociology

Social cognition theory offers an different analysis of human perception and behavior from exchange theory. It focuses attention on cognition—people's thought processes, or conscious mental activities, and their consequences for social behavior. This approach emerged in the early part of the twentieth century through the work of psychologists such as James Mark Baldwin and sociologists such as W. I. Thomas and Florian Znaniecki. It became more firmly established in social psychology, however, through the research of Kurt Lewin, who developed "field theory" in the 1930s, and Fritz Heider, who formulated "balance theory" in the 1940s—both attempts to understand how individuals made sense of conflicting and contradictory information.

Following in the tradition of their founders, contemporary social cognition theorists stress that we cannot understand people's behavior without concentrating on how they structure and process information. According to these theorists, people process information through mental structures, or *schemas*, that selectively receive and organize it. These structures, which we acquire through our social groups, serve as templates for interpreting stimuli and experiences. Schemas simplify and give coherence to our perceptions, enable us to fill in the gaps in the information we get from the environment, and help us make sense of otherwise vague or confusing situations.[29] Our schemas allow us to provide order and meaning to a world of complex stimuli, both in the physical and social realms.

In stressing the influence of mental structures and thought processes in human behavior, social cognition theorists, like symbolic interactionists, challenge the "stimulus-response" model of behaviorism. They highlight how people's actions cannot be explained as simply conditioned and unreflective responses to stimuli. Instead, they point out our behavior emerges out of selective interpretations of the stimuli we encounter. We respond to a given stimulus based on how we make sense of it. This interpretive process, referred to as social cognition, is guided by preexisting schemas. These schemas direct us to pay attention to certain information, to code and store this information in specific ways, to recall it when needed, and

to use it appropriately as we experience a stimulus and formulate a behavioral response.

In addition to challenging the stimulus-response model of behaviorism, social cognition theory offers insights that undermine a key tenet of exchange theory: the assumption that humans engage in rational thought and action. In a variety of research projects, social cognition theorists have demonstrated that individuals often do not think or behave in ways that appear rational. For instance, when asked to identify their preferences in items such as panty hose and fabrics, many people did not provide rational or logically consistent responses. After selecting item A in a choice between A and B, and B in a choice between B and C, they frequently opted for C when asked to choose between A and C. This choice violated the principle of transitivity, one of the key assumptions of rationality.[30]

Overall, social cognition theory has made a number of important contributions to social psychology. Its key contributions, particularly from a symbolic interactionist viewpoint, are its accounts of (1) how social categories affect the processes of thought and interpretation and (2) how these processes inform and guide the formulation of behavior. But, while recognizing these contributions, interactionists also point to the limitations of social cognition theory. They criticize this perspective most strongly for its inadequate conception of society. As Kollock and O'Brien have noted, social cognition theory implies that "society" is something that exists "out there," independent of people but able to shape and direct their thoughts.[31] This theory is primarily focused on the individual's internal processes and does not offer many ideas about what society is, how it operates, or even how it gets inside people's minds to influence their cognitions. Along with these problems, social cognition theory tends to give so much priority to people's thought processes that it neglects their behavior and the impact of their social interactions. Until this theory develops a more sophisticated conception of the relationship between thought, action, and interaction, it will not be able to explain how people's behavior results in socially structured patterns.

Fortunately, the insights of social cognition theory have been extended and refined by the work of "cognitive sociologists" such as Eviatar Zerubavel and Karen Cerulo.[32] These analysts have demonstrated how cultural beliefs and social structures systematically pattern our perceptions of objects, events, time, places, and other people. They have also revealed how the perceptual filters we acquire through our culture and social interactions institutionalize specific "ways of seeing," directing us to pay attention to some stimuli while "turning a blind eye" to others.[33] Moreover, these theorists have shown how the systems of classification and discrimination that guide our perceptions, such as our perceptions of racial, ethnic, and gender groups, are shaped by the power relations that exist among various segments of a society.

Ethnomethodology

Ethnomethodology has its roots in the philosophical tradition of phenomenology, founded by the German philosopher Edmund Husserl. Within sociology, phenomenologists have focused attention on the subjective viewpoints of individuals and the forms of consciousness or knowledge they take for granted in their social lives. Phenomenologists also explore how people use such knowledge as a basis of their existence. Like phenomenologists, ethnomethodologists are concerned with the perspectives of individuals or, more specifically, with how they perceive and act in the world as they see it. Ethnomethodologists are most interested, however, in the methods that people use to produce meaning in social settings and to render these settings "as if" they were clear and orderly. As West and Zimmerman have observed, ethnomethodology focuses on "how members of society go about the task of seeing, describing, and explaining order in the world in which they live."[34]

The founder of ethnomethodology, Harold Garfinkel, challenged the dominant sociological view, which emphasized that social order was rooted in people's internalization of shared cultural norms and values. Garfinkel instead proposed that each new situation "posed constraints of its own, and that the key to social order was to document those constraints" and the social practices that produced and sustained them.[35] Garfinkel thus focused his attention on the observable methods that people use to construct recognizable social order. In doing so, he believed that he was fulfilling Emile Durkheim's call for sociologists to focus on social practices and the phenomena of ordinary society, particularly those habits and assumptions "so obscure that they cannot be expressed in words, yet so powerful that they dominate" our lives.[36]

Garfinkel and other ethnomethodologists emphasize that social reality has a precarious foundation. People live under the illusion that they share meanings with others and act on the basis of that illusion. But all that people really share is the assumption that their meanings are shared. This works well as long as we don't ask too many questions about the "background assumptions" that guide us. Ironically, then, ethnomethodologists suggest that it is our lack of communication that serves as the basis of meaning and order. We get along by tacitly accepting each other's explanations of what we are doing and why. We also learn that we should not raise too many questions about "what everyone knows." Those who raise such questions pay a costly price in their interactions.

Guided by these premises, many ethnomethodologists begin their investigations by refusing to assume that social meaning or order "really" exists. They contend that social psychologists should consider how people construct interpretations of meaning and order and act as if these things exist in their everyday interactions. More specifically, ethnomethodologists propose that social psychologists should focus on the rules and methods that people use to make sense of what they do and to accomplish a sense of order. In an effort to reveal these rules and methods, ethnomethodologists adopt research strategies that raise questions of how people manage their everyday interactions. At times, these strategies consist of violating taken-for-granted assumptions or disrupting established routines, thereby creating "breaches" in social order. For instance, ethnomethodologists sometimes engage in "reverse bargaining," insisting that they wish to pay more for an item than the price marked on it. At other times, these researchers treat the remarks of others as literal, answering a routine question such as "How are you?" with a detailed medical report and observing the chaos that results. By using such strategies—what some call "Candid Camera sociology"—ethnomethodologists try to gain a fresh perspective on the "obvious" aspects of how people see, describe, and explain reality (see Box 2-3).

In responding to ethnomethodology, symbolic interactionists acknowledge the insights it offers about how people construct the illusion of meaning and order in their social lives. As ethnomethodologists have illustrated, people use a variety of means to convince themselves and others that they share common outlooks and understandings when in actuality they do

---

Box 2-3 "WHAT DO YOU MEAN?": AN EXERCISE IN ETHNOMETHODOLOGY

Harold Garfinkel designed and conducted a number of "breaching experiments" that deliberately interrupted the normal patterns of conversation between people. In one of these experiments, Garfinkel instructed his students to challenge every statement made by selected subjects, asking them "What do you mean?" after they made each statement. The result was a series of conversations characterized by the following pattern:

Subject: I had a flat tire.

Experimenter: What do you mean, you had a flat tire?

Subject: (appears momentarily stunned and then replies in a hostile manner) What do you mean, "What do you mean?" A flat tire is a flat tire. That is what I meant. Nothing special. What a crazy question!

Through this and related experiments, Garfinkel and his students revealed some of the implicit methods that we use in constructing order and consensus in routine conversations. One of these methods, the et cetera principle, was violated in the above experiment, leading the subject to become agitated and hostile. In most of our conversations, we abide by the et cetera principle, meaning that we "wait for" or "fill in" information that we need to make sense of others' comments or actions. We agree not to disrupt our conversations with them by asking them questions such as "What do you mean?"—questions that would disrupt the flow of interaction and challenge the sense of order or reality that exists in that situation.

Most important, Garfinkel and his students demonstrated how, in any interaction, there are certain background features, such as the et cetera principle, that all of us are expected to understand and abide by so that we can conduct our "common conversational affairs without interference" (p. 42). These features, or folk methods, guide many of our everyday conversations and are a crucial part of our joint efforts to create the perception that an external social order exists. If you want to gain a better understanding of how we create this perception, try asking your roommates or family members "What do you mean?" after each of their statements. Be prepared to end this experiment quickly, though. As an ethnomethodologist, you will discover that when you breach routines, and the sense of order they sustain, you will often provoke negative reactions.

Source: Harold Garfinkel, *Studies in Ethnomethodology* (Englewood Cliffs, NJ: Prentice-Hall, 1967.

not. In addition to revealing how people create the illusion of order, ethnomethodologists have insightfully demonstrated how they can escape from social structural constraints by using words and methods that make it seem as if they have abided by norms when in fact they have not.[37] Perhaps most crucially, ethnomethodologists have offered a view that specifies the nitty-gritty details of social order, showing how it is established through people's everyday practices.

While appreciating the insights provided by ethnomethodology, symbolic interactionists criticize it for its tendency to ignore the impact that audiences and situations have on people's interpretations. Some interactionists also object to the tendency of ethnomethodologists to reduce almost everything that people do to the production of fictitious order. By adopting this approach, ethnomethodologists overlook a variety of important issues, such as how and why people decide to act, how they develop and negotiate selves, and how their ongoing interactions affect their behavior.[38]

EMERGING VOICES AND PERSPECTIVES WITHIN INTERACTIONISM

While interactionism differs in significant ways from other social psychological perspectives, such as exchange theory, interactionist scholars often draw upon these perspectives in making sense of people's actions and interactions. They also incorporate and become influenced by insights offered by other important theoretical perspectives. Indeed, interactionists have developed a broader range of research interests and analyses in recent years, in part because of the influence of three other perspectives that have gained greater prominence in sociology: feminism, conflict theory, and postmodernism. In the discussion that follows, we briefly discuss each of these perspectives, focusing on how they have influenced interactionism and pushed it in new directions.

Feminism

Feminist theorists stress that gender is an organizing principle of social life, not only in micro-level settings such as the home or schoolyard, but also in macro-level institutions such as governments, religious organizations, and the global economy. Feminists also emphasize how gender is a social construction rather than a biological phenomenon—that is, they point out how notions such as "femininity" and "masculinity" vary across history and cultures and are learned, sustained, and transformed through people's ongoing activities and relationships. More recently, "standpoint feminists" have stressed that investigations of women's experiences of inequality should consider how this experience intersects with other forms of discrimination, including racism, heterosexism, classism, and colonialism. These analysts focus attention on how gender-based oppression does not operate independently of oppression grounded in race/ethnicity, sexual orientation, social class, nationality, religion, or disability. Instead, these forms of discrimination link up with one another to form a system of multiple oppressions.

Since the 1980s, interactionists have become increasingly aware of the concerns and assumptions they share with feminist theorists. For instance, like feminists, they regard gender as a set of social meanings, relationships, and practices through which sex differences are made salient. Moreover, like feminists, they focus attention on how we learn and perform gender roles and identities and how we reproduce the "reality" of gender through cultural beliefs, social arrangements, and interpersonal relationships.[39]

In general, interactionist researchers have drawn upon and extended feminist theory through their analyses of how people "do gender" through routine practices and how everyday practices maintain or disrupt gender inequalities. In an intriguing set of studies, Candace West and Don Zimmerman blended feminist analysis with interactionist (and ethnomethodological) insights to explain how gender is performed and sustained, both individually and institutionally, through micro-level conversations and relations (e.g., through how women and men talk, what they talk about, how often they talk, where and when they talk, how often they interrupt others, and so on).[40] West and Zimmerman pointed out that these performances of gender are influenced but not determined by structural factors; that is, women and men have some room to make choices and exercise agency as they enact gender performances. In turn, they have the ability to change or undermine the gender order.

Other interactionist studies have focused attention on how gender inequalities are called forth and reproduced in workplaces or institutional settings, particularly through the division of emotional labor. For example, in her study of a personal wellness center, Sherryl Kleinman used the interactionist concepts of emotion work, moral identity, and symbolic interaction to analyze how gender inequality was both concealed and reproduced in the relationships and emotional displays that characterized this setting. In a related vein, a number of feminist-oriented interactionists have offered revealing insights into how organizations manufacture feelings and control expressions of emotion.[41] Based on research in a variety of sites, including airlines, law firms, police departments, alternative health care clinics, and weight loss associations, these scholars have illustrated how organizations require women to engage in devalued forms of emotion work, thereby perpetuating their subordination and reproducing gender inequality for corporate benefit.

While sharing areas of concern and agreement, feminist and interactionists also have points of tension. A key source of tension is feminism's commitment to liberation-oriented research and social practice. Feminists often feel disenchanted with the less "radical" methodological and political stances characterizing interactionism as a whole. Unlike many mainstream interactionists, feminists do not regard research and theory as merely avenues for understanding social reality. Instead, they see research and theory as liberating

social practices that ought to contribute to the elimination of gender inequality and oppression.

Conflict Theory

Conflict theory has a long history, especially among European scholars, but it became more prominent in the United States during the 1960s because of larger political changes and social movements that provoked dissatisfaction with the functionalist perspective that dominated American sociology in the 1950s. Conflict theory cannot be summarized easily because it has many variants. However, all of these variants emphasize that societies are characterized by patterns of inequality that lead less powerful groups to become aware of their interest in changing social arrangements through mobilizing for conflict.[42]

Those conflict theorists who draw heavily on Karl Marx's ideas focus on how social conditions and relationships, particularly the economic organization of a society, shape people's outlooks and actions. When analyzing a capitalist society, these theorists emphasize that the capitalist mode of production gives rise to two key classes: the *bourgeoisie* (or "haves") and the *proletariat* (or "have nots"). The "haves" possess a great deal of power because they own and control the means of production, or the means through which people make a living, such as land, factories, or businesses. The "have nots," by contrast, must sell their labor to make a living and meet their basic needs.

In general, Marxian-based conflict theorists stress that social life is characterized by conflict between the "haves" and "have nots." This conflict is rooted in competition for scarce resources, such as food, clothing, shelter, money, and leisure. Obviously, the "haves" hold a distinct advantage in this conflict because they have more access to and control over these resources. Moreover, they often control the key means of communication in modern capitalist societies, such as the mass media, and they use these media to convince the "have nots" that privileged people deserve the power they have and that current social arrangements work out to the advantage of everyone.

Conflict theorists direct much of their research attention toward the struggles for power that take place between privileged and less powerful groups, not only as they try to control access to material resources, but also to shape dominant beliefs and cultural practices. In turn, conflict theorists examine how the privileged try to exercise control over oppressed groups, such as by passing laws that serve their interests and criminalize the forms of dissent or behavior more often engaged in by "have nots." Conflict theorists also investigate how the oppressed try to resist or challenge the control of elites, particularly by mobilizing themselves to engage in collective action, such as a strike, a social movement, or a revolution.

Guided by Marx's vision, many conflict theorists believe that the central reason for doing social theory and research is not merely to understand the world but to change it, particularly in ways that promote justice and liberation.[43] In turn, like feminists, they criticize traditional interactionists for their failure to commit to more advocacy-oriented forms of theory and research. They also criticize the interactionist perspective for its failure to focus greater attention on how economic structures, power relations, and class inequalities shape people's interactions and identities.

Yet, while interactionists have not examined economic, political, and class-related factors in as much as detail as conflict theorists, they have not ignored these factors. During the past three decades, interactionists have explored a number of topics connected to power and economics—topics such as inequality, ideology, agency, collective action, and the shaping of consciousness.[44] Also, in recent years interactionists have done more extensive research on political power, conflict, and negotiation, especially while examining the construction of deviance and social problems. Because we will highlight this research in Chapter Seven, we will not describe it in detail here.

Most importantly, interactionists have incorporated and gone beyond conflict theory approaches in analyzing broader social changes affecting U.S. society, such as the "medicalization of deviance" and the emergence of drug scares.[45] In examining these changes, interactionists have highlighted how various groups use metaphorical images and rhetorical strategies to define certain behaviors or issues as problematic and to build consensus that action needs to be taken to constrain the actions of others.[46] In the process, interactionists have integrated macro-sociological questions more fully into their analyses and developed the foundations for a "critical interactionist" approach to social life.

Perhaps the best example of critical interactionism is found in the work of Michael Schwalbe, who has blended the insights of Karl Marx and George Herbert Mead in studying identity work, the labor process, and the reproduction of inequality. Recently, Schwalbe and his associates have identified four generic social processes through which inequalities are created and sustained.[47] These include *oppressive othering* (how powerful groups seek and sustain advantage through defining members of less powerful groups as inferior); *boundary maintenance* (how dominant groups protect their economic and cultural privileges by maintaining boundaries between themselves and subordinate groups); *emotion management* (how groups suppress or manage potentially destabilizing feelings, such as anger, resentment, sympathy, and despair); and *subordinate adaptations* (how members of subordinate groups adapt to their unequal status and, in some cases, reproduce it.) These four social processes provide links between local, everyday interactions and larger structural inequalities.

Peter Hall has also integrated Marxist and interactionist perspectives in analyzing power, politics, and the organization of the policy process. Hall has examined how politicians, including U.S. presidents, manage impressions and manipulate symbols to "reassure" the public, promote the public's quiescence, and discourage people's participation in the political process.[48] In his investigations of policy making, particularly in the educational arena, Hall has revealed how and why the organizational context of policy (or the structural conditions within which policy is made) shapes and mediates the policy process.[49]

Postmodernism

Over the past three decades, the most significant challenges to social theory and mainstream interactionism have been posed by postmodern theorists. These scholars emphasize that we live in a new and profoundly different world—a world characterized by the rise of a consumption-oriented society, the growth of information technologies and culture industries, the transformation of images into commodities, the increased diversity of social worlds, the fragmentation of individual selves, and the crumbling of dominant values such as the importance of progress. As we grapple with these characteristics of postmodern society, we feel as if the world around us is constantly in a state of flux.[50]

Postmodern theorists seek to help us make sense of this unique historical and social situation. Within the orbit of symbolic interactionism, these theorists have formulated an approach they refer to as *interpretive interactionism*—an approach that draws on feminist, neo-Marxist, and other critical perspectives. According to postmodern interactionists, the theories and studies of traditional interactionism (as well as traditional sociology) need to be questioned because they play directly into the hands of the elites who want to preserve the status quo and protect their power and privilege.[51]

While challenging the intellectual agenda of traditional interactionism, postmodern interactionists share some of its central assumptions and emphases. For instance, they share interactionism's suspicion of positivism and scientism, emphasizing that all social science is value-laden because it is shaped by the interests and social positions of the individuals who produce it. In addition, postmodernists embrace interactionism's emphasis on interpretive and qualitative

research. They also make language and information technology central to their analyses.

Through their analyses, postmodern interactionists have extended the interactionist perspective in several intriguing ways. For instance, they have highlighted how the meanings of postmodern society "are mediated and filtered through existing systems of interpretation," which are profoundly influenced by larger cultural institutions, such as the mass media, the economy, university systems, and popular culture.[52] Second, postmodern interactionists have introduced a variety of concepts, such as the "saturated self," "hyper-reality" (or mass media depictions of reality), and systems of discourse, that have reshaped interactionist and sociological thought. Third, they have highlighted how writing or "representation" is a central part of data collection and analysis.[53] Through writing, researchers do not simply "tell the facts" of their research findings; instead, they create representations of their data—representations that convey its "reality" to readers. Finally, as we will highlight in Chapter Five, postmodern interactionists have provided insightful analyses of the changing nature and experience of the self in highly electronic and industrialized societies.

Yet, while postmodern theory has offered some promising insights into interactionism, a number of traditional interactionists see it as fundamentally flawed. According to these scholars, postmodern interactionism has many failings, including being unscientific and inattentive to empirical reality, having a flawed theory of history, and having an overly political and moralistic agenda.[54] In turn, they believe that efforts to make interactionism more postmodern in orientation are leading it down an intellectual dead end.

In responding to these critiques, postmodern interactionists, led by Norman Denzin, have urged their mainstream colleagues to return to the spirit of the early pragmatist philosophers, embracing their openness to innovation, their nuanced and antireductionist understandings of social life, and their concern with promoting progressive social reforms. By taking this step, interactionists could synthesize some of the ideas of pragmatism and postmodernism, thereby developing a new and more critical perspective that merges interactionist theory with the pursuit of progressive political and social changes.[55]

SUMMARY

- Following Blumer, interactionists emphasize that people are self-reflexive beings who actively shape their own behavior based on the meanings they give to things, including themselves. As a result, interactionists think it is essential to get inside people's worlds of meaning and experience these worlds as they do. To develop this insider's perspective, interactionists empathize with, or "take the role of," the individuals or groups they study. They typically do so by using methods that allow them to observe and interact with these individuals or groups in their natural social settings. This enables them to acquire a deeper understanding of how social actors define, construct, and act toward the "realities" of their everyday lives.
- Some interactionists rely on more conventional scientific procedures and quantitative measures, such as surveys, experiments, or questionnaires. Following Manford Kuhn and the tradition of the Iowa School, they seek to develop theoretical generalizations that draw on interactionist ideas but are rigorously tested through standard methods of empirical research. Unlike their more ethnographically oriented counterparts, these interactionists strive to produce findings and explanations that attain the conventional scientific ideals of reliability and replicability.
- Overall, interactionist scholars are not as divided by methodology as they are by their research emphases. Two streams of interactionist research are prevalent. One of these streams seeks to better conceptualize and measure the nature and development of the human self and its consequences for our outlooks and behavior. The other research stream focuses more attention on the dynamics of situations, emphasizing how the characteristics of our contexts and interactions shape our thoughts, feelings, and actions.
- While this book highlights the theoretical perspective of symbolic interactionism, we recognize that it is only one of many approaches that sociologically-minded social psychologists draw upon as they try to understand human behavior. Other valuable approaches include dramaturgical theory, exchange theory, social cognition theory, and ethnomethodology. Although interactionism shares some assumptions with each of these perspectives, it also diverges from them in significant ways.
- Interactionism does not exist in a theoretical vacuum. In addition to influencing and being influenced by the above perspectives, it has had a productive dialogue with other prominent social theories, such as feminism, conflict theory, and postmodernism. Through this dialogue, interactionism has extended the scope and boundaries of its analyses, developing explanations that offer new and more comprehensive understandings of social life and human behavior. We will highlight a number of these explanations in the chapters that follow.

GLOSSARY OF KEY TERMS

Autoethnography   An emerging research method used by some symbolic interactionists. It consists of an "introspective" form of ethnography that makes study of the "self" central to sociological understanding. Those who practice autoethnography believe that deeper social psychological understanding can emerge from a self-reflexive and sociologically informed reading of one's own life.

Conflict Theory

A sociological perspective that focuses on the inequalities and struggles for power that characterize societies, especially modern capitalist societies. This conflict takes place primarily between members of two key classes, the *bourgeoisie* (or "haves") and the *proletariat* (or "have nots"), and it is rooted in their competition for scarce resources, such as food, clothing, shelter, money, and leisure.

Dramaturgical Theory

A social psychological perspective that studies human behavior and social interaction in terms of the analogy of the theater. This perspective is closely related to symbolic interactionism. Drawing on the groundbreaking ideas of Erving Goffman, dramaturgical theorists focus on how people manipulate various aspects of themselves and their settings to influence how others define and respond to them.

Ethnography

A research method in which an investigator systematically but unobtrusively observes a group or setting while joining participants in their routine activities. Some analysts use the terms "participant observation" and "ethnography" interchangeably.

Ethnomethodology

A social psychological perspective that focuses on the methods we use to create and maintain a sense of order and structure in our everyday interactions. thnomethodologists also consider how we produce meaning and construct interpretations of social interaction.

Exchange Theory

A social psychological perspective that assumes we are motivated by a desire to maximize rewards and minimize costs. Guided by this desire, we will choose to engage in those behaviors and relationships that lead to the greatest personal profit (rewards minus costs) relative to other available alternatives.

Grounded Theory

A methodological approach commonly used by interactionist researchers to collect, inspect, and analyze data. When guided by this approach, researchers engage in the processes of collecting and analyzing data simultaneously, working back and forth between these processes to develop theoretical explanations of the data they are gathering. In doing so, researchers take part in open and focused coding, memo writing, theoretical sampling, and creating and linking theoretical categories.

Feminism   A theoretical perspective that focuses attention on how gender is socially constructed and how it serves as an organizing principle of social life on both micro- and macro-levels. Feminists also advocate for social, political, economic, and legal changes that would promote greater justice for women and greater equality between women and men.

Naturalistic Inquiry   The qualitative methodology used by most symbolic interactionists. When using it, researchers focus on people's behavior in natural social settings and rely on informal and unobtrusive techniques to gain a first-hand understanding of this behavior. Naturalistic inquiry consists of two phases: (1) exploration, a beginning phase in which the researcher becomes immersed in a specific social world, focusing on how members of that world experience it and interact with one another; and (2) inspection, the phase in which the researcher systematically analyzes the qualitative data he or she has gathered. These data may consist of field notes, interview transcripts, or personal documents.

Postmodernism   A theoretical perspective that emphasizes that we live in a new and profoundly different world—a world characterized by the rise of a consumption-oriented society, the growth of information technologies and culture industries, the transformation of images into commodities, the increased diversity of social worlds, and the crumbling of dominant values such as the importance of progress. Postmodern theorists stress that as we grapple with these characteristics of postmodern society, we feel as if the world around us is constantly in a state of flux and we find it difficult to sustain a stable or coherent sense of self.

Social Cognition Theory   A social psychological perspective that claims we can best understand human behavior by concentrating on how we structure and process information from the environment. According to this perspective, we process information through mental structures, or schemas, that give coherence to our perceptions, allow us to fill in the gaps in the information we get from the environment, and help us to make sense of otherwise vague or confusing situations.

QUESTIONS FOR REFLECTION AND ASSIGNMENT

1. Why do symbolic interactionists tend to rely on "participant observation" more than any other research methods? What does this method enable them to include (or highlight) in their analyses? Why do some interactionists rely heavily on the method called "autoethnography"? What is involved in using this method? What are some of its strengths and limitations?
2. Why do symbolic interactionists place so much emphasis on interpretation in analyzing human action and interaction? How does this differentiate them from other theoretical perspectives in social psychology?
3. Which of the social psychological perspectives discussed in this chapter do you find most useful for understanding your own thoughts, feelings, and actions? What underlying assumptions does this perspective have about (1) the bases of human action and (2) the nature of the relationship between individuals and society? How does it help you to have a deeper understanding of yourself and your relationship to society?
4. Dramaturgical theory has been described as a "close cousin" to symbolic interactionism. How is it similar to interactionism? How does it differ? What (if any) shortcomings do you think characterize dramaturgical theory? Does it share any assumptions with other perspectives highlighted in this chapter?
5. In your view, what is one of the unique methodological or theoretical contributions of symbolic interactionism? Why do you see this contribution as unique? Has it led you to look

at research or theory (or yourself) differently? If so, how?

SUGGESTED READINGS FOR FURTHER STUDY

Becker, Howard. *Tricks of the Trade: How to Think about Your Research While You're Doing It* (Chicago, IL: University of Chicago Press, 1998).

Charmaz, Kathy. *Constructing Grounded Theory: A Practical Guide Through Qualitative Analysis* (Thousand Oaks, CA: Sage, 2006).

Denzin, Norman K. and Yvonne Lincoln, eds. *Handbook of Qualitative Research*, 2nd ed. (Thousand Oaks, CA: Sage Publications, 2000).

Ellis, Carolyn. *The Ethnographic "I": A Methodological Novel about Autoethnography* (Lanham, MD: Alta Mira Press, 2004).

Lemert, Charles. *Postmodernism Is Not What You Think* (Boulder, CO: Paradigm Publishers, 2005).

Ulmer, Jeffery and Mindy Wilson. "The Potential Contributions of Quantitative Research to Symbolic Interactionism," *Symbolic Interaction* 26 (4), 2003, pp. 531–552.

ENDNOTES

[1] Herbert Blumer, *Symbolic Interactionism: Perspective and Method* (Englewood Cliffs, NJ: Prentice-Hall, 1969), pp. 40–47.

[2] Ibid.

[3] Blanche Geer, Jack Haas, Charles ViVona, Stephen Miller, Clyde Wood, and Howard S. Becker, "Learning the Ropes: Situational Learning in Four Occupational Training Programs," in Irwin Deutscher and Elizabeth Thompson, eds., *Among the People: Encounters with the Poor* (New York: Basic Books, 1968), p. 209.

[4] Herbert Blumer, *Symbolic Interactionism*, (Note 1), p. 148.

5 The original and classic explication of grounded theory can be found in Barney G. Glaser and Anselm L. Strauss, *The Discovery of Grounded Theory* (Chicago: Aldine, 1967). Subsequently, different variants of this approach have emerged, including those with a more "objectivist" slant and those with a more "constructivist" orientation. For a description of these variants as well as an eloquent articulation of the constructivist approach embraced by the authors of this text, see Kathy Charmaz, *Constructing Grounded Theory: A Practical Guide Through Qualitative Analysis* (London: Sage, 2006).

6 James Clifford and George Marcus, *Writing Culture* (Berkeley: University of California Press, 1986); John VanMaanen, "Trade Secrets: On Writing Ethnography," in Richard H. Brown, ed., *Postmodern Representations* (Urbana: University of Illinois Press, 1995), pp. 60–79.

7 Arlie Hochschild, *The Managed Heart* (Berkeley, CA: University of California Press, 1983.)

8 Gary Alan Fine, *Shared Fantasy: Role Playing Games as Social Worlds* (Chicago: University of Chicago Press, 1983).

9 Gary Alan Fine, *Authors of the Storm: Meteorologists and the Culture of Prediction* (Chicago: University of Chicago Press, 2007).

10 Sherryl Kleinman, *Opposing Ambitions: Gender and Identity in an Alternative Organization* (Chicago: University of Chicago Press, 1996).

11 Carolyn Ellis, *Final Negotiations* (Philadelphia: Temple University Press, 1995).

12 Carolyn Ellis, "Sociological Introspection and Emotional Experience," *Symbolic Interaction* 14, 1991, pp. 23–50; Carolyn Ellis and Arthur Bochner, "Taking Ethnography Into the 21st Century," *Journal of Contemporary Ethnography* 25, 1996, pp. 3–5.

13 Because this book focuses on interactionist theory and concepts rather than ethnographic methods, we chose not to provide a more detailed discussion of the methods we list here. For those students who want to learn more about these methods, we recommend Norman Denzin and Yvonne Lincoln, eds. *Handbook of Qualitative Research,* 2nd ed.

(Thousand Oaks, CA: Sage Publications, 2000). We also want to note that there are many forms of narrative analysis. Some focus attention on the group effects of narratives rather than the formulas through which individuals construct them. For illuminating discussion of a more group-oriented version of narrative sociology, see David Maines, *The Faultline of Consciousness: A View of Interactionism in Sociology* (New York: Aldine de Gruyter, 2001.)

14 Manfred H. Kuhn, "Major Trends in Symbolic Interaction Theory in the Past Twenty-Five Years," *The Sociological Quarterly* 5, 1964, p. 70.

15 Peter Adler and Patricia Adler, "Symbolic Interactionism," in Jack D. Douglas, Patricia Adler, Peter Adler, Andrea Fontana, C. Robert Freeman, and Joseph A. Kotarba, eds., *Introduction to the Sociologies of Everyday Life* (Boston: Allyn and Bacon, 1980).

16 David R. Heise, "Affect Control Theory: Concepts and Model," *Journal of Mathematical Sociology* 13 (1–2), 1987, pp. 1–33; Jerold Heiss, *The Social Psychology of Interaction* (New Brunswick, NJ: Prentice-Hall, 1981).

17 David R. Maines, "Herbert Blumer and the Possibility of Science in the Practice of Sociology," *Journal of Contemporary Ethnography* 18, 1989, p. 174.

18 Jeffery Ulmer and Mindy Wilson. "The Potential Contributions of Quantitative Research to Symbolic Interactionism," *Symbolic Interaction* 26 (4), 2003, pp. 531–552.

19 Erving Goffman, *The Presentation of Self in Everyday Life* (New York: Doubleday, 1959).

20 Dennis Brissett and Charles Edgley, eds., *Life as Theater: A Dramaturgical Sourcebook*, 2nd ed. (Chicago: Aldine Press, 1990).

21 Alfred R. Lindesmith, Anselm L. Strauss, and Norman K. Denzin, *Social Psychology*, 7th ed. (Englewood Cliffs, NJ: Prentice-Hall, 1993), p. 19.

22 J. W. Thibaut and Harold H. Kelly, *The Social Psychology of Groups* (New York: Wiley, 1959); George Homans, *Social Behavior: Its Elementary Forms* (New York: Harcourt, 1961); Peter Blau,

Exchange and Power in Social Life (New York: Wiley, 1964); Richard M. Emerson, "Power-Dependence Relations," *American Sociological Review* 27, 1962, pp. 31–41.

23 Judith A. Howard, *Gendered Selves, Gendered Situations* (Thousand Oaks, CA: Sage, 1997).

24 Jodi O'Brien and Peter Kollock, *The Production of Reality*, 2nd ed. (Thousand Oaks, CA: Pine Forge Press, 1997).

25 See Harold H. Kelly, "Personal Relationships: Their Nature and Significance," in R. Gilmour and S. Duck, eds., *The Emerging Field of Personal Relationships* (Hillsdale, NJ: Erlbaum, 1986), p. 15.

26 Alfred R. Lindesmith, Anselm L. Strauss, and Norman K. Denzin, *Social Psychology*, (Note 21), p. 16.

27 John Hewitt, *Self and Society*. 7th ed. (Boston, MA: Allyn and Bacon, 1997), p. 15.

28 See Alfred R. Lindesmith, Anselm L. Strauss, and Norman K. Denzin, *Social Psychology*, (Note 21); Judith A. Howard, *Gendered Selves, Gendered Situations*, (Note 23).

29 James Wiggins, Beverly Wiggins, and James Vander Zanden, *Social Psychology*, 5th ed. (New York: McGraw-Hill, 1995).

30 Jodi O'Brien and Peter Kollock, *The Production of Reality*, 2nd ed. (Thousand Oaks, CA: Sage, 1997), p. 26.

31 Ibid., p. 27.

32 See Eviatar Zerubavel, *The Elephant in the Room: Silence and Denial in Everyday Life* (New York: Oxford University Press, 2006) and *Social Mindscapes: An Invitation to Cognitive Sociology* (Cambridge, MA: Harvard University Press, 1997); Karen Cerulo, *Culture in Mind: Toward a Sociology of Culture and Cognition.* (New York: Routledge, 2002); Aaron Cicourel, *Cognitive Sociology: Language and Meaning in Social Interaction* (New York: Free Press, 1974).

33 Karen A. Cerulo, "Cognitive Sociology," in G. Ritzer, ed., *Encyclopedia of Social Theory*. Vol 1. (Thousands Oaks, CA: Sage Press, 2003), pp. 107–111.

34 Candace West and Don Zimmerman, "Doing Gender," *Gender and Society* 1, 1987, pp. 125–151.

35 Anne W. Rawls, "Harold Garfinkel," in G. Ritzer, ed., *Encyclopedia of Social Theory*. Vol. 1 (Thousands Oaks, CA: Sage Press, 2003), p. 303.

36 Emile Durkheim, *The Division of Labor in Society* (New York: MacMilan, [1893] 1933), p. 362.

37 Mary Gallant and Sherryl Kleinman, "Symbolic Interactionism vs. Ethnomethodology," *Symbolic Interaction* 6, 1983, pp. 1–18.

38 John Hewitt, *Self and Society*, 7th ed. (Boston: Allyn and Bacon), p. 18.

39 Barbara Laslett and Johanna Brenner, "Gender and Social Reproduction: Historical Perspectives," *Annual Review of Sociology* 15, 1989, pp. 381–404.

40 Candace West and Don H. Zimmerman, "Doing Gender," *Gender and Society* 1, 1987, pp. 125–151; Candace West and Don H. Zimmerman, "Small Insults: A Study of Interruptions in Cross-Sex Conversations Between Unacquainted Persons," in B. Thorne, N. Henley, and C. Kramarae, eds., *Language, Gender, and Society* (Rowley, MA: Newbury House, 1983), pp. 102–117.

41 See, for example, Arlie Hochschild, *The Commercialization of Intimate Life: Notes from Home and Work* (Berkeley, CA: University of California Press, 2003); Jennifer Pierce, *Gender Trials: Emotional Lives in Contemporary Law Firms* (Berkeley, CA: University of California Press, 1995); Sherryl Kleinman, *Opposing Ambitions: Gender and Identity in an Alternative Organization* (Chicago: University of Chicago Press, 1996); Daniel D. Martin, "Organizational Approaches to Shame: Management, Announcement, and Contestation," *The Sociological Quarterly* 41, 2000, pp. 125–150.

42 Jonathan H. Turner, "Conflict Theory," in George Ritzer, ed. *Encyclopedia of Social Theory, Vol. 1* (Thousand Oaks, CA: Sage, 2005), pp. 134–139.

43 Erik Ohlin Wright, "Explanation and Emancipation in Marxism and Feminism," *Sociological Theory* 11, 1993, pp. 39–54.

44 Michael Schwalbe, Sandra Godwin, Daphne Holden, Douglas Schrock, Shealy Thompson, and Michele Wolkomir, "Generic Processes in the Reproduction of Inequality: An Interactionist Theory," *Social Forces* 79, 2000, pp. 419–452; Gary Alan Fine and Kent Sandstrom, "Ideology in Action: A Pragmatic Approach to a Contested Concept," *Sociological Theory* 11, 1993, pp. 21–38; T. R. Young, *The Drama of Social Life* (New Brunswick, NJ: Transaction Publishers, 1990); Michael Schwalbe, "The Elements of Inequality," *Contemporary Sociology*, November 2000. For many years, Larry Reynolds has also explored topics pertinent to power and inequality from a "critical interactionist" perspective. See, for example, Larry T. Reynolds, *Self-Analytical Sociology* (Rockport, TX: Magner Publishing, 2000).

45 Peter Conrad and Joseph Schneider, *Deviance and Medicalization* (St. Louis, MO: Mosby, 1980); Joel Best, ed. *Images of Issues* (New York: Aldine, 1989).

46 See Joel Best, ed. *Images of Issues* (Note 45) and Joel Best, *Threatened Children: Rhetoric and Concern about Child-Victims* (Chicago: University of Chicago Press, 1993).

47 Michael Schwalbe, et al., "Generic Processes in the Reproduction of Inequality: An Interactionist Theory," (Note 44).

48 See Peter M. Hall, "A Symbolic Interactionist Analysis of Politics," *Sociological Inquiry* 42, 1972, pp. 35–75; Peter M. Hall, "The Presidency and Impression Management," *Studies in Symbolic Interaction* 2, 1979, pp. 283–305.

49 Peter M. Hall, "Meta-Power, Social Organization, and the Shaping of Social Action," *Symbolic Interaction* 20, 1997, pp. 397–418.

50 Norman Denzin, "Prophetic Pragmatism and the Postmodern: A Comment on Maines," *Symbolic Interaction* 19, 1996, pp. 341–356.

51 Ibid., p. 349.

52 Norman Denzin, "Postmodernism," in George Ritzer, ed. *Encyclopedia of Social Theory*, Vol. 2 (Thousand Oaks, CA: Sage, 2005), p. 582.

53 See David Maines, "On Postmodernism, Pragmatism, and Plasterers: Some Interactionist Thoughts and Queries," *Symbolic Interaction* 19, 1996, pp. 323–340; Gil Richard Musolf, "Some Recent Directions in Symbolic Interactionism," in Larry T. Reynolds, ed., *Interactionism: Exposition and Critique*, 3rd ed. (Dix Hills, NY: General Hall, 1983), pp. 231–283; David Snow and Calvin Morrill, "Ironies, Puzzles, and Contradictions in Denzin and Lincoln's Vision of Qualitative Research," *Journal of Contemporary Ethnography* 22, 1995, pp. 358–362.

54 Norman Denzin, "Prophetic Pragmatism and the Postmodern," (Note 50).

55 David Maines, *The Faultline of Consciousness: A View of Interactionism in Sociology* (New York: Aldine de Gruyter, 2001), p. 240.

CHAPTER THREE

~

PEOPLE AS SYMBOL MAKERS AND USERS: LANGUAGE AND THE CREATION OF REALITY

"This probably sounds strange," Bill announced, "but for me AIDS has been more of a blessing than a curse. Of course, there are days when I don't feel like that—days when my face breaks out in a terrible rash, my legs ache for hours, and I can hardly get out of bed. But, overall, I'd have to say that living with AIDS has been a beneficial and even spiritual experience for me. It's really changed me! For example, it's helped me to see what's truly important in life and what isn't. And it's given me a stronger sense of freedom— freedom to accept my limits and enjoy life. I don't worry so much about pleasing other people anymore. I do more of the things that I really want to do. Like I go outside with my dog for a couple of hours and just sit out in the grass with him, and I don't worry about it because that's something I enjoy doing—it's relaxing and life giving. And no one expects me to explain why I took the time to do that. So, I feel freed up from normal pressures and expectations. I guess that's been one of the 'blessings' of AIDS. Another blessing is that it's led me to appreciate the opportunities that each day brings.... I've learned, you know, to feel grateful for each day really—for the sun, the trees, everything.

And that gives me a more intense experience of life. There's times when it even comes off as feeling high—like a high from drugs or something like that, except it's not from that. It's just from being so immersed in life—there's a high in that for me!"[1]

How could anyone define the "reality" of AIDS like Bill does? How could he see and experience a potentially life-threatening illness as a blessing and source of freedom? These questions cannot be answered adequately by theories that emphasize reward exchanges, cognitive schemas, strategies of impression management, or patterns of inequality. To explain Bill's experience of AIDS, one must recognize the symbolic aspects of human behavior. More specifically, one must appreciate how Bill's experience is shaped by the meanings that he gives to this illness. These meanings are not intrinsic to AIDS or the physical symptoms it evokes. Rather, they are conferred on the illness through the *social* processes of interpretation, communication, and interaction. In the following discussion, we elaborate on this point by focusing on how people give meaning to realities such as AIDS. In doing so, we highlight the symbolic nature of human experience and action.

CREATING AND TRANSFORMING REALITY

All human behavior consists of, or is dependent upon, the use of symbols. Human behavior is symbolic behavior; symbolic behavior is human behavior. The symbol is the universe of humanity.

—Leslie A. White

Compared with other animals, we find ourselves in a unique situation as human beings. We do not live directly in a state of nature, nor do we see "reality" nakedly. As the philosopher Suzanne Langer observed, human perception consists of the continuous creation and re-creation of images and symbols.[2] Our only means of taking in the world of objects and people around us is through continually re-creating them. In other words, we convert our experiences into images and symbols. Our brains do not simply record or relay what is going on "outside" or "inside" of us. Instead, when processing information or sensations, our brains act like giant, symbolic transformers, changing virtually everything that passes through them into a stream of symbols.[3]

According to Langer, this tendency for our brains to act like symbolic transformers is a crucial feature of our experience as human beings. It allows us to have a "constructive" rather than passive relationship to our environment. We do not simply react to things that exist in the world around us. Nor do we see these things "in the raw." Instead, we transform and interpret them through a symbolizing process.[4] Thus, as we participate in the process of perception—the process of making sense of stimuli in our environment—we rely on our capacity to create and use symbols. Through this capacity we transform the stimuli that bombard us, such as a cluster of stars on a clear night, into a coherent and meaningful pattern—in this case, a pattern we call the Big Dipper.

Sensation

Sensation is the result of the activity *of the [human] organism, and is produced, not received...*
—John Dewey

Throughout our lives we are barraged by a flood of sensory experiences. We swim in a sea of sensation. Consider this very moment. Your attention is (we hope) focused on this book and the words you are reading in this sentence. But pause for a moment and think of all the other things you are experiencing. For instance, what else are you seeing besides this page and sentence? Are you seeing what's above, below, and to the sides of the page? Are you periodically glancing up to see what else is around you? Are you being affected by anything besides visual images? For instance, are you hearing any noises or smelling any odors? Do you feel any pressures on your body, such as the touch of your fingers on the book, your back on a chair, your elbows on a table, or your feet on the floor? After briefly paying attention to what's going on around you, you can recognize that you are being bombarded with stimuli.

If we remained at the level of sensation, we would soon be overwhelmed. Our world would lack continuity or coherence. Life would be a booming, buzzing confusion of lights, sounds, smells, colors, and movements. We would bounce from one experience to another with little if any direction or purpose. We would not be able to organize our sensory experiences into broader patterns or configurations. Our perceptions, then, are not merely a matter of sensation; they also involve interpretation.[5] Our senses provide us with the raw data to arrive at meaning.

As commonly recognized, we rely on five major senses as we interact with and gather information from our environment: sight, hearing, taste, smell, and touch. When any of these senses are stimulated, as when the receptors in our ears respond to sound waves emitted by a roaring engine, they transmit a message to the brain, which processes this input. Each sense can be aroused by external stimuli, as when we are moved by a beautiful sunset, refreshed by a cool breeze, or, less pleasantly, repulsed by the smell of manure. Our senses can also be aroused by stimuli that come from sources within us, as when we feel a pang of hunger, a flash of pain, or a surge of sexual desire.

Most important, we do not react passively to our environment. We actively seek out stimuli through our bodily senses. For instance, we move our head, eyes, hands, and body to explore the sensations of light, sound, and contact that surround us.[6] In this process, we extract information about our sensations and select what is relevant. We turn toward or away from shades of light. We turn toward or away from various noises, such as a whispering voice or an exploding firecracker. We sniff for pleasant odors and hold our nose at unpleasant odors in the air around us. We feel physical objects, enjoying their texture, evaluating how we can use them, and gauging their potential dangers. Our senses, then, do not merely receive stimuli; they actively seek out stimuli until they achieve a clearer understanding of their nature.[7]

Box 3-1 THE SOCIAL SHAPING OF PERCEPTION: THE CASE OF ODOR

In an intriguing study, Dennis Waskul and Philip Vannini demonstrated how one of our most powerful senses—smell—is informed and influenced by social meanings and expectations. Based on their analysis of journals kept by 23 graduate students, Waskul and Vannini insightfully reveal how the act of smelling, or olfaction, "intersects with social, cultural, and moral order" (p. 53). In doing so, they highlight three themes. First, to sense a smell, such as the smell of freshly baked cookies, is to make sense of it. That is, the act of smelling "is commonly marked by somatic work, a process whereby a somatic perception undergoes a reflexive interpretation" (p. 58). For instance, when we smell freshly baked bread we will make sense of that smell in terms of our relevant memories, associations, and relationships. As Frank (age 45), one of Waskul and Vannini's respondents, remarked:

> One of my favorite smells is that of fresh baked bread. It reminds me of many things, including my grandmother, my mother, my brother, and I making numerous loaves to get ready for winter in Alberta. It has associated with it thoughts of a warm kitchen, [and] important people in my life (p. 58).

In a related vein, we may perceive a smell as noxious or unpleasant, even if it is generally regarded as neutral or sweet-smelling, because we link it to negative memories or interactions. As Beth (age 29) observed:

> Right now I would say [I dislike the smell of] Spray and Wash because I recently had a very bad and sickly night that involved imbibing large quantities of red wine. By "accident," I spilled a glass of red wine on the white carpet in the office of my parent's house. They were away on vacation at the time and so I drunkenly panicked tried my best to clean it up....To make a long story short, my brain has linked the two smells (red wine and Spray and Wash), and my sickly drunken state together to create an instant gag reflex at the smell of Spray and Wash (pp. 60-61).

Second, Waskul and Vannini reveal how our sense of smell, like other perceptions, is structured by somatic rules grounded in cultural expectations:

> The management of odor is common and widespread, observable in almost every body everywhere. In Anglo-phone North America, odor is traditionally something to be eliminated or produced—on (and in) the body, the home, at work, automobiles, our communities—by use of air fresheners, deodorants, breath mints, fans, ventilation, air purification systems, pollution laws. Even the mere mention of odors in a conversation, especially body odors, is a delicate subject and it is not uncommon to find ourselves occasionally

ignoring or denying the presence of uncontrollable, bad odors out of both a sense of tactfulness and taboo. Adherence to the olfaction rules of moral odor/moral order represent more than the folkways of a culture and more than a matter of manners, politeness, and etiquette. As testified by "scent free" work and public space regulations, violations of olfaction rules are of potential legal concern and the production of inappropriate odor can be cause for civil litigation...(p. 56).

Put simply, in North American cultures we have a multitude of olfactory rules that tell us how we should or should not smell and where, when, and why we should exude particular odors. These rules not only structure how we act but also how we interpret and evaluate smells—and the people or things that emit them. As Waskul and Vannini emphasize, there is a direct link between "moral order" and "moral odor." An odorous body is regarded as being an offensive body and "failure to adhere to somatic rules and maintain expected olfactory impressions is potentially stigmatizing" (p. 66). Jackie (age 36) demonstrated this link when she wrote, "It is important to control or manipulate odor on your body so that you are not judged based on poor body odor. Strong or bad body odor can be taken as a sign of being unclean or sloppy" (p. 63). Similarly, Susan (age 25) confessed, "I find myself judging people negatively when they smell bad in some way—be it their breath, or something else. I don't usually notice if their smell is just normal or pleasant, but I definitely notice when it isn't" (p. 66).

Finally, Waskul and Vannini insightfully reveal how odor, because of its moral meanings, is a central component of our daily identity work and interpersonal rituals. As they note, "odor is a 'sign vehicle'[1] we manipulate and manage on bodies and in environments in an effort to convey desired impressions." The respondents in their study, like most of us, took great care to regulate their bodily odors and to remedy any undesirable scents, including bathroom odors, when they occurred. Olfactory work, or the management of their bodily aromas, thus became a key concern in their presentations of self. In turn, they took great pains to "smell nice" and to avoid experiences of "olfactory abjection," or moments when they had a rank and embarrassing stench. Women were particularly vigilant in this regard, and they more actively engaged in "active somatic surveillance which is, of course, a somatic social control" (p. 68). As Waskul and Vannini observe, this gendered pattern is directly connected to "the sociocultural and political structures of both sense-making and the somatic rules that structure them...."

1. See Erving Goffman, *The Presentation of Self in Everyday Life* (New York: Doubleday, 1959).

Source: Dennis Waskul and Philip Vannini, "Smell, Odor, and Somatic Work: Sense-Making and Sensory Management," *Social Psychology Quarterly* 71(1), 2008, pp. 53–71.

Conceptualization and Categorization

We understand our sensory experiences through grouping them into units, categories, or concepts, based on their similarities. We thereby engage in the process of *conceptualization*. That is, we experience the world in terms of concepts—regularized ways of thinking about real or imagined objects and events. These concepts enable us to picture "things" in our world, to describe or represent these things to ourselves and one another, and to grasp their meaning.[8] We use concepts because we are "cognitive misers" and we want to find relatively simple ways to deal with the stimuli picked up by our senses. By sorting these stimuli into related and manageable units and giving them labels, we recode their contents into summary categories—categories such as *red, tall, dark, beer, roommate, professor,* and *dorm room.* By using these and other categories, we simplify and generalize the world—we chunk and cluster its elements into meaningful concepts. For example, we look into the sky and register a collection of light waves striking our retinas as "blue"; we bite into a candy bar and interpret thousands of transmissions from our taste buds as "sweet"; we walk up to a person in a store and recode the range of sensations she emits into "friendly-looking clerk." Through condensing and transforming our perceptions into these categories, we simplify the abundance of stimuli and information available to us. We organize our experiences.

At the same time, we bring order, continuity, and predictability into our perceptual world. Through plugging various stimuli into categories, we can link our present sensations to past sets of experience and perceptual organization. We can view an object or event as the same object or event despite the fact that it changes during each moment and from various perspectives. For example, we can recognize an event that shifts back and forth from one person lecturing to several people exchanging ideas as a "social psychology course." We can also treat a number of objects that differ in a few ways, such as cars, vans, and trucks, as essentially similar "vehicles." Through this ability to categorize objects, we can reduce the anxiety we would feel in an otherwise disordered and ambiguous world of stimuli.

Conceptualization allows us to sort and organize stimuli in a meaningful and orderly way. Through this process we actively attune ourselves to certain stimuli while ignoring others. We lump or group stimuli together and then respond to these groups as if they were objects. The key point is that we do not respond to the world "as it is." It does not have an inherent meaning. Instead, as human beings we actively slice up the world and organize it into concepts—plants and animals, fruits and vegetables, cities and villages—that allow us to give it meaning and see it as orderly. Although this is an intricate process, it seems fairly simple because many of the concepts we rely on are supplied by the groups to which we belong. We learn these concepts as we learn the language and culture of our society.[9]

Symbols, Signs, and Meanings

Human experience takes on distinctive characteristics because people respond not only to signs but also to symbols. A **sign** is directly connected to an object or event and calls forth a fixed or habitual response. Its meaning is associated with its physical form and can be grasped through the senses. For instance, dark clouds are a sign of rain and smoke is a sign of fire. Both animals and people can make sense of and respond to these signs. Symbols, however, are a uniquely human phenomenon. Roughly speaking, symbols are something that people create and use to stand for something else. A powerful example is a flag. People use a colored rectangle of cloth to stand for a nation and its guiding principles. This cloth evokes passionate sentiments—pride, loyalty, patriotism, and, for some, disgust or animosity. Another example of a symbol is a hug. In our society a hug is widely regarded as a symbol of affection; thus, the willingness of one person to hug another is seen as an expression of his or her caring for that person. Among the various sets of symbols, the most important are linguistic symbols, those combinations of spoken sounds or written marks that are used for all meanings. A **symbol**, then, is any object, gesture, or word that becomes an abstract representation of something else. Whatever it represents constitutes its meaning.

In most cases, the association between a symbol and the meanings it represents are arbitrary. The meanings designated by a symbol have no intrinsic relationship to the object it describes; the meanings are generally a matter of convention.

Therefore, the meaning of a symbol cannot be discerned by examining the nature of the symbol itself. Think, for example, of the word *rose*. There is nothing inherent in this combination of four letters that would necessitate or even suggest it as a representation for a particular plant. The word has no color, smell, or thorns. Nor does it have anything in its spoken or printed form that would lead one to automatically think of the flower it describes. We conjure up an image of a velvety and sweet-smelling flower when hearing the word "rose" only because we have learned to make this association since childhood. We could just as easily have learned to call a rose "by any other name." Of course, if we had been born in a non–English-speaking country, such as Romania, a rose would not be a rose to us—it would be a *trandafir*.

The Importance of Symbols

Our ability to use symbols has several important implications for our experience and activity. First, because symbols are abstractions, their use allows us to transcend our immediate environments and to have experiences that are not rooted in the here and now. We do not simply respond to the stimuli that arouse our senses in our current situation. We interpret these stimuli and respond to them in terms of our images of the past, present, and future, as well as our images of what is good, right, or important. In essence, we respond to stimuli of our own creation—that is, stimuli provided by the shadowy world of symbols. Thus we act within and toward a world that we have a major part in creating, a world that is inherently abstract rather than concrete, a world of symbols that in some senses is imaginary.[10]

To understand this point, think of the abstract concepts that guide people's outlooks and actions, such as equality, justice, freedom, love, and honesty. At bottom, these are humanly created symbols. They do not exist "in nature" or have a material reality. But most of us tend to respond to them as if they are representations of essential truths about the world that should guide our actions.

Even in situations that have a physical character, such as sporting events, people are guided by and respond to symbolic realities. For example, athletes know that coaches stress the concepts of hustle, sportsmanship, and teamwork. These concepts are real only in terms of the representations that players and coaches make of them. Coaches presume that they can gauge "hustle" through observing the behavior and demeanor of their players. If a player displays a high level of effort, he or she is hustling. "Sportsmanship" is behavior that accords with certain moral standards of fair play and thoughtfulness. When a player behaves "properly" in an instance when improper behavior is possible, we have witnessed sportsmanship. If his or her team, having just lost a hard-fought game, graciously congratulates their opponents, they are seen as demonstrating sportsmanship. Likewise, "teamwork" is not the act of a single player but depends on the relationship among players. A single action doesn't demonstrate teamwork, but two or more coordinated actions (such as a throw, a catch, and a tag) do. Hustle, sportsmanship, and teamwork are not objective behaviors but rather depend on symbolic interpretations within the context of a sports event.

In addition to allowing us to transcend our immediate environment, symbols allow us to remember, imagine, plan, and have vicarious experiences.[11] Whenever we remember things, imagine things, or make plans to do things, we rely on and manipulate symbols. We also use symbols to have vicarious experiences. These experiences allow us to learn about the world and understand others' experiences through observation; we do not have to experience everything ourselves in order to understand it. This ability is important not only for our individual and collective survival but also for another distinctive human characteristic: the transmission of culture.

Symbols provide the mechanism by which we create and acquire **culture**, or the ways of thinking, feeling, and acting that characterize our society. Interactionists believe that it is through communication, or symbolic interaction, that we learn, create, and pass on culture. The boundaries of the spread of culture are linked to the boundaries of effective communication.[12] This point is important in that groups develop their own symbol systems, which come to exemplify how people are expected to think, feel, and behave. Every group develops its own **idioculture**, or system of shared knowledge, beliefs, sentiments, and behaviors that serves as a frame of reference and basis of interaction for group members.[13] Nicknames serve as a case in point. Often they characterize members of the group to each other and demonstrate that the individuals truly belong. Further, these nicknames are frequently connected to a particular group itself. In Gary Alan Fine's research on Little League baseball, many of the players had team nicknames that reflected their position on the team. One boy, for instance, was called "Maniac," both a linguistic play on his last name and an indicator that he often threw the ball wildly. The next year this same boy became the starting third baseman, his throwing skills improved, and his teammates started calling him "Main Eye."

Finally, the most crucial implication of symbols is that they provide us with templates for categorizing our experiences and placing them within a larger frame of reference. Without symbols, we cannot give meaningful form to what is happening around us, and our understandings of the world have a hit-or-miss quality. We combine and cluster symbols to form concepts that we use to sort our sensory experiences into orderly social categories. These categories often take the form of *names*—names that have shared meanings for the members of a culture. Through using these names, we come to "know" the world around us.

Naming "Reality" and Creating Meaningful Objects

As Anselm Strauss has observed, people act toward objects in light of the names they give to these objects.[14] Naming is an integral part of human cognition. In naming an object, we classify and give meaning to it, thereby evaluating it and calling forth action toward it. The name organizes our perceptions and serves as a basis for our subsequent behavior; that is, it intervenes between the "stimulus" provided by the object and our "response" to it. In other words, we respond to the name that we give to the object and not to the essence of the object itself.

Take the example of a green, $2\frac{1}{2}'' \times 6''$ rectangular piece of paper with Andrew Jackson's picture on it. Call it "money" or, more specifically, a "twenty-dollar bill." Based on this name, you immediately know how to act toward it. You know that you can use it at a store or business to purchase goods or services, such as groceries, clothing, or a haircut. And you know this because you have learned the meaning that the name "money" calls forth in our society. This meaning is not inherent to green, $2\frac{1}{2}'' \times 6''$ rectangular pieces of paper, as demonstrated by the fact that it is also granted to silver and copper circular-shaped pieces of metal. Instead, it emerges out of a shared agreement about what the objects we call "money" represent and how we should act toward them.

As another example of how we respond to things based on the names we give them, imagine a situation that involves you interacting with an unnamed person. It's late at night and you're walking across campus on your own. After you walk through a passageway between two buildings, you suddenly hear footsteps about 50 feet behind you. Feeling somewhat nervous, you glance backward and see a large male figure in the shadows. You pick up your pace. The man behind you matches your speed and even starts to gain on you. You tentatively name (or categorize) this man as a potential "mugger" or "rapist," and panic wells up within you. In turn, as he draws steadily closer to you, you prepare to run, yell, or defend yourself. Just as you're about to take defensive action, the man behind you calls out your name and says, "Hey, I've been trying to catch up with you since you walked between those buildings back there! I was going to yell 'wait up' but I wasn't sure it was you until now. Anyway, I was wondering if you'd like to walk back to the dorm together." As you hear these words, you quickly recognize that it is one of your friends who has been walking behind you. In that moment he is transformed from "mugger" or "rapist" into "thoughtful friend." Your response to him shifts accordingly. Your feelings of anxiety dissipate and you feel relaxed and reassured. You respond warmly rather than with a scream or a punch.

What these examples illustrate is that we formulate lines of action within and through the symbolic processes of naming and categorization. We use these processes to give meanings to things around us and to our actions as well as those of others. In other words, when we engage in the processes of naming and categorization, we transform things, events, and actions into **social objects**, or objects that have shared meaning. These objects call out a common mode of response in us.

According to interactionists, meaning is a socially created phenomenon. As such, it has three key features. First, it is extrinsic; that is, it is not a quality innate to particular objects. Instead, it is conferred on those objects "from the outside" based on how they are named and their intended use. Second, the meaning of objects is not fixed but varies with time, culture, situation, and the people acting toward them. For example, a bank is a different social object to student loan seekers, to its managers and employees, and to potential bank robbers. Each acts differently toward the bank, and, consequently, to each it is a different object with a different meaning. This point leads us to the third important feature of meaning: it emerges and is transformed through our communication with others as we learn from them how to define the meaning of an object and as we offer our own meaningful view of that object. Think, for instance, of how we learn the meaning of an upright middle finger in the United States. We observe the anger or upset feelings that others convey when they raise this finger or have it displayed toward them. In turn, we quickly learn that raising one's middle finger toward others, or "flipping them off," is not a kind gesture, nor is it meant to tell them to look up in the air. Instead, we learn that this is a lewd and hostile gesture that conveys feelings of anger and tells others that we wish them harm (ironically, through engaging in sexual activity). Most important, what this example demonstrates is that meaning emerges and becomes established through the process of social interaction. The establishment of meaning through this process is essential because human action requires symbolization. Without meaning, we do not know how to act toward the "things" around us—including others and ourselves. To name "things" is not only to know them but also to know how to *respond* to them. The names, or symbolic categories, we attribute to things represent knowledge, communication, and action.

LANGUAGE, NAMING, AND THE CONSTRUCTION OF REALITY

Given the emphasis that interactionists place on symbols and the process of communication, they accord a special place to language. Language is the key medium through which people share meanings and construct "reality." As we noted in Chapter One, language is a system of symbols that members of a culture use for representation and communication. Hence, language is the source of the symbols we use to give meanings to objects, events, or people and to convey these meanings to ourselves and others.

Language serves as the foundation for the development of the most important kind of symbols: words. Words have a unique and almost magical quality—they have meaning not only on their own but also when joined with others. In addition, words serve as the basis for other symbols.[15] While people often use other modes of communication, such as gestures, facial expressions, and postures, these expressions become meaningful to us through words. For instance, in

Box 3–2 THE POWER OF NAMES: NORTH DAKOTA AND PALMETTO BUGS

In the following excerpt, Dave Barry, a humorist writer, offers a comical and obviously exaggerated illustration of how names (and the meanings they reflect) powerfully influence our perceptions and actions.

North Dakota is talking about changing its name. I frankly didn't know you could do that. I thought states' names were decreed by the Bible or something. In fact, as a child I believed that when Columbus arrived in North America, the states' names were actually, physically written on the continent, in gigantic letters, the way they were on maps. I still think this would be a good idea, because if an airplane's navigational system failed, the pilot should just look out the window and see exactly where the plane was. ("OK, there's a huge 'W' down there, so we're over Wyoming. Or, Wisconsin.")

But apparently states can change their names, and some North Dakotans want to change "North Dakota." Specifically, they don't like the word "North," which connotes a certain northness. In the words of North Dakota's former governor, Ed Schafer: "People have such an instant thing about how North Dakota is cold and snowy and flat."

We should heed the words of the former governor, and not just because the letters in "Ed Schafer" can be rearranged to spell "Shed Farce." The truth is when we think about North Dakota, which is not often, we picture it having the same year-round climate as Uranus.

…That's how powerful a name can be.

I'll give you another example. I live in Florida, where we have BIG cockroaches.

Q.: How big are they?

A.: They are so big that, when they back up, they are required by federal law to emit warning beeps.

These cockroaches could harm Florida's image. But we Floridians solved that problem by giving them a new name, "palmetto bugs," which makes them sound cute and harmless. So when a guest walks into a Florida kitchen and screams at the sight of an insect the size of Charles Barkley, we say: "Don't worry! It's just a palmetto bug!" And then we and our guest have a hearty laugh, because we know there's nothing to worry about, as long as we do not make any sudden moves toward the palmetto bug's sandwich.

So changing names is a sound idea, an idea based on the scientific principle that underlies the field of marketing, which is: People are stupid. Marketing experts know that if you call something by a different name, PEOPLE WILL BELIEVE IT'S A DIFFERENT THING. That's how "undertakers" became "funeral directors." That's how "trailers" became "manufactured housing." That's how "We're putting you on hold for the next decade" became "Your call is important to us."

And that's why some North Dakotans want to give their state a new name, a name that will give the state a more positive, inviting, and forward-looking image. That name is: "Palmetto Bug." No, seriously, they want to drop the "North" and call the state, simply, "Dakota." I think this change is brilliant, and could also work for other states with image problems. New Jersey, for example, should call itself, simply, "New."

Be advised that "Dakota" is not the first shrewd marketing concept thought up by North Dakotans. Are you familiar with Grand Forks, ND? No? It's located just west of East Grand Forks, MN. According to a letter I received from a Grand Forks resident who asked to remain nameless ("I have to live here," he wrote), these cities decided they needed to improve their image, and the result was—get ready—"The Grand Cities."

The Grand Cities, needless to say, have a website (grand-cities.net), where you can read sentences about The Grand Cities written in Marketing Speak.... Here's an actual quote: "It's the intersection of earth and sky. It's a glimpse of what lies ahead. It's hope, anticipation, and curiosity reaching out to you in mysterious ways. Timeless. Endless. Always enriching your soul. Here, where the earth meets the sky, the Grand Cities of Grand Forks, North Dakota, and East Grand Forks, Minnesota."

Doesn't that just make you want to cancel your trip to Paris or Rome and head for the Grand Cities? As a resident of Florida ("Where the earth meets the water, and forms mud") I am definitely planning to go to Dakota. I want to know what they're smoking up there.

Source: Dave Barry, "North Dakota Wants Its Place in the Sun," *Waterloo-Cedar Falls Courier*, August 12, 2001, p. C1. Reprinted by permission of Tribune Media Service.

our culture a red light at an intersection means "Stop!"; a side-to-side turning of the head means "No!"; a waved hand toward an arriving friend means "Hi!"; and a police siren means "Pull over to the side of the road!"

Words facilitate our ability to communicate and share meanings. To understand this fact, try the following exercise. Approach several friends and tell them something about yourself without using any spoken or written words. Try to let them know what you are going to do this weekend. If this task seems too difficult, try letting them know what day it is. Obviously, without using words you face a challenging task. That is part of the amusement of the game of charades. Even if you are adept at using nonverbal gestures, you could probably communicate much more easily and accurately with your friends through relying on spoken or written words.

Overall, words are important because they offer shared names or categories through which we give meanings to our experiences and share these meanings. Words have their fullest impact and significance in relationship to other words within a language. As a part of the structure of language, words frame our conceptions and understandings of the world and guide our actions toward it.

Although words facilitate our ability to communicate and act, they do not necessarily make it *easy* for us to interact with others. The words we use are often ambiguous, and they may lead us to experience gaps or difficulties in our conversations with others. As an example, consider the following exchanges between a mother and her teenage daughter:

Daughter: Mom, can I take the car for a while to see my friends?

Mother: Okay, but don't be out too late—it's a school night and I need to use the car sometime to go to the grocery store.

Daughter: Okay, that's no problem. I'll see you later.

The daughter returns four hours later, at 10:30 p.m.

Daughter: Hi, Mom, I just wanted to let you know I'm home and the car is back.

Mother: [Angrily] Where the heck have you been? I told you not to be out too late!

Daughter: [Defensively] I wasn't out late—it's only 10:30! I don't go to bed until midnight!

Mother: But it's a school night; you should be in earlier than that!

Daughter: Well, you didn't tell me a time. You just said that I shouldn't be out too late. 10:30 is not late!

Mother:	Well, I did tell you that I needed the car sometime tonight to go grocery shopping.
Daughter:	Yeah, and I brought it back for you. You can go shopping now. The grocery store is open until midnight.
Mother:	It's too late for me to go grocery shopping now! It's 10:30 and I'm tired.
Daughter:	Well, I don't see how that's my fault.
Mother:	Oh, go to your room! I don't know why you can't listen to me better!

As this dialogue illustrates, the words we use do not always have a straightforward meaning; nor are they always interpreted in the way we intend them. Instead of leading to shared understanding and effective interaction, a number of the words we use, such as "awhile," "later," and "sometime," have imprecise meanings and can lead to misinterpretations that result in frustrating or ineffective interaction. Thus, even when we use the same words as others, we do not necessarily "speak the same language" (and interact smoothly with them), as most parents and teenagers can attest.

In addition to containing abstract and arbitrary symbols known as "words," human languages have another essential feature: grammar or *syntax*. Syntax is a set of rules for combining symbols to produce more extended meaning. Syntax allows us to indicate who is talking or acting, when something happened, to ask a question, to disagree, to speak about things that haven't happened yet or could never happen, to construct alternative visions of what might happen if we do this or, on the other hand, do that. In other words, syntax enables us to use symbols to *think* and to communicate thoughts to others.

The Necessity of Language

What would have happen to us as children if we were not exposed to an existing language? Would we invent a language of our own? As far as researchers can tell, the answer is no. This is a fascinating question for social psychologists and philosophers because it is linked to the question of what it means to be human. It is a challenging question to answer, however, because it is difficult, if not impossible, to take care of an infant's physical needs without also interacting with it in some kind of language. There are, of course, accounts of "wild children"—or children who have for unusual reasons lived to late childhood—without being spoken to. These children are reported to be lacking in many human qualities and, unless taught a language, cannot take care of their own needs for food or shelter. (See, for example, Susan Curtiss's book entitled *Genie: A Psycholinguistic Study of a Modern-Day "Wild Child."*[16])

Some evidence about the importance of language comes from studies of otherwise normal children who are born deaf and have not been exposed to a language with a visual basis, such as one of the sign languages. These children also seem to have difficulties with what we think of as basic human activities, such as thinking, learning, or forming relationships with other people. By contrast, deaf children who do learn a sign language do not have such difficulties.[17] The impact of language on a deaf child's cognitions and behaviors are poignantly illustrated in the story of Helen Keller, a well-known American in the early to mid-twentieth century. She was both blind and deaf as the result of a severe illness that she suffered when she was less than two years old, before she had learned to talk. Ms. Keller began to learn language at the age of seven, after her parents hired a teacher who was trained to work with deaf children. Ms. Keller eventually graduated from college and became a writer, lecturer, and advocate for the rights of persons with disabilities. In the following excerpt from her autobiography, she describes the intense feelings she experienced when learning language and, in turn, acquiring the power to name things:

> The most important day I remember in all my life is the one on which my teacher, Anne Mansfield Sullivan, came to me. I am filled with wonder when I consider the immeasurable contrast between the two lives which

it connects. It was the third of March, 1887, three months before I was seven years old.

The morning after my teacher came she led me into her room and gave me a doll. When I had played with it a little while, Miss Sullivan slowly spelled into my hand the word "d-o-l-l". I was at once interested in this finger play and tried to imitate it. When I finally succeeded in making the letters correctly I was flushed with childish pleasure and pride. Running downstairs to my mother I held up my hand and made the letters for doll. I did not know that I was spelling a word or even that words existed; I was simply making my fingers go in monkey-like imitation. In the days that followed I learned to spell in this uncomprehending way a great many words, among them *pin, hat, cup,* and a few verbs like *sit, stand,* and *walk.* But my teacher had been with me several weeks before I understood that everything has a name.

One day, while I was playing with my new doll, Miss Sullivan put my big rag doll into my lap also, spelled "d-o-l-l" and tried to make me understand that "d-o-l-l" applied to both. I became impatient with her repeated attempts and, seizing the new doll, I dashed it upon the floor. I was keenly delighted when I felt the fragments of the broken doll at my feet. Neither sorrow nor regret followed my passionate outburst. I had not loved the doll, in the still, dark world in which I lived there was no strong sentiment or tenderness. I felt my teacher sweep the fragments to one side of the hearth, and I had a sense of satisfaction that the cause of my discomfort was removed. She brought me my hat, and I knew I was going out into the warm sunshine. This thought, if a wordless sensation may be called a thought, made me hop and skip with pleasure.

We walked down the path to the well-house, attracted by the fragrance of the honeysuckle with which it was covered. Some one was drawing water and my teacher placed my hand under the spout. As the cool stream gushed over one hand she spelled into the other the word *water,* first slowly, then rapidly.

I stood still, my whole attention fixed upon the motions of her fingers. Suddenly I felt a misty consciousness as of something forgotten—a thrill of returning thought; and somehow the mystery of language was revealed to me. I knew then that "w-a-t-e-r" meant the wonderful cool something that was flowing over my hand. That living word awakened my soul, gave it light, hope, joy, set it free! There were barriers still, it is true, but barriers that could in time be swept away. I left the well-house eager to learn, everything had a name, and each name gave birth to a new thought. As we returned to the house every object I touched seemed to quiver with life. That was because I saw everything with a strange, new sight that had come to me. On entering the door I remembered the doll I had broken. I felt my way to the hearth and picked up the pieces. I tried vainly to put them together. Then my eyes filled with tears; for I realized what I had done and for the first time I felt repentance and sorrow.

I learned a great many new words that day. I do not remember what they all were; but I do know that *mother, father, sister, teacher,* were among them—words that were to make the world blossom for me. It would have been difficult to find a happier child than I was as I lay in my crib at the close of the eventful day and lived over the joys it had brought me, and for the first time longed for a new day to come.[18]

As Helen Keller's story reveals, our genetically acquired capacity to learn a symbolic language can only be activated through its use in interaction with other humans. Moreover, we rely on language to realize our full human capacities for thinking, acting, and forming relationships with others.

Language, Naming, and Our Constructions of Others

To illustrate how language structures our perceptions of the world, let's look at how people think of and act toward one another. In general, we make sense of each other in roughly the same way we make sense of other social objects: we pick up sensory "data," sort and organize these data through naming or applying categories to it, and use these categories to interpret each other's meaning. We thereby engage in the process of **social cognition**.

Social cognition takes place whenever we come into contact with others. During our encounters, we actively seek and gather information about each other. This information is vital if we are to engage in effective interaction. Without having information about one another, we cannot determine each other's "meaning" and thus will not know how to act toward each other. The result is embarrassing, awkward, or alienating interaction. Think of what happens when someone stops to chat with you and, try as you might, you just can't remember who she is. Until you can name and place this person, you'll feel uncomfortable talking with her. You might act as if you know her, but you'll feel uncertain about what to say and how to behave. Without knowing her identity, you won't know how best to relate to her.

Processing Information About Others: Forming Impressions Through Stereotypes. As we interact with others, particularly those we know little about, we quickly form an impression, or overall mental picture, of them. We do so by considering and piecing together a number of highly perceptible cues and clues we glean from their appearance and behavior. The meanings that we give to these cues or clues may be modified as we evaluate them in terms of other information we acquire about an individual. In most cases, we develop a more or less coherent impression of others by making inferences based on their social and physical attributes, apparent character traits, and verbal and nonverbal expressions.

In developing an impression of others, we often "fill in the gaps." We do so by drawing on prototypes. A prototype is a mental image, or schema, that we use to represent a typical set of features that exemplify an object or person. For instance, the idea of a church calls up the prototype of a building with a sanctuary, cross, organ, and pews. We draw on a variety of such prototypes in our experiences and interactions with others. They offer us a fuzzy and schematic guide for assessing people.[19] One example is the prototype "extrovert." When labeling someone as extroverted, we assume that person to be outgoing, boisterous, friendly, and loud, even if some of these traits are not evident. This example shows how we fill in the gaps about a person's characteristics and behavior in a way that goes beyond the information we can gather at the immediate moment. Apparently, we make such inferences spontaneously so that we can make sense of the information we gather about other people. We also store these inferences in our memories.

One important form of prototype is the stereotype. A **stereotype** is a mental image that attributes a common set of characteristics to members of a particular group or social category. In popular thinking, stereotypes are understood as hostile and inaccurate attitudes that rigid people hold toward members of "minority" groups. This characterization is, however, overly narrow. Stereotypes are not necessarily negative or false beliefs. Nor are they necessarily directed toward members of oppressed groups or held only by rigid people. All of us rely on stereotypes to some degree in our everyday lives. They are an outgrowth of our inclination to simplify the world through naming it or putting it into summary categories.

In coining the word "stereotype," Walter Lippman, an influential journalist and political commentator, defined it as an oversimplified picture of the world. Lippman observed that the world is characterized by "so much subtlety, so much variety, so many permutations and combinations...we have to construct it on a simpler model before we can manage with it."[20] Stereotypes provide us with these models. They enable us to avoid the strain involved in evaluating every reaction of every person we interact with, moment by moment, as we participate in social encounters. Drawing on stereotypes, we group individuals into categories based on some characteristics, such as their age, gender, or job status, while simultaneously disregarding other characteristics. Doing so enables us to make rapid decisions based on minimal information about others. Stereotypes, then, allow us to assess others quickly, to anticipate their actions, and to plan our own actions accordingly.

Of course, even though stereotypes offer the advantages of convenience and efficiency, they have significant drawbacks. One major drawback is their unreliability. Because stereotypes are generalizations, they distort, overlook, or disregard potentially significant information about others. When we use a stereotype, we are prone to exaggerate or neglect important details about a person and thus to operate on the basis of false or misleading assumptions. We may subsequently make the mistake of assuming that a person has characteristics that, in fact, he or she does not possess, or we may fail to see the actual characteristics that a person possesses. In addition, we may subtly "push" the person into acting in ways that reflect our expectations rather than their attributes.[21]

In summary, stereotypes are useful and necessary human tools, but they can be blunt and sometimes harmful. While they enable us to deal with the ambiguous "realities" of the others we encounter, they can also lead us to overlook their important features. Stereotypes can therefore blind and constrain as well as guide and enable us. Nevertheless, given our tendency to carve up the world into simple and distinct categories, stereotypes remain part of our everyday thinking and action. By allowing us to group information into identifiable categories, they make impression formation and information processing more efficient. Our lives would be incredibly chaotic if we couldn't categorize people quickly in terms of their attributes. In the following section, we consider the salience of stereotypes in the process through which we interpret the prominent attributes of others, form impressions of them, and assign them social identities.

Forming Impressions of Character Traits. As Solomon Asch revealed in landmark studies conducted more than fifty years ago, people form distinct impressions of one another within a short period of time. Asch illustrated how we use small amounts of information about others to make stereotypical inferences about their implicit personality traits. We do this based on our assumptions that people have basic traits that form consistent patterns. For example, we assume that an "industrious" person is also likely to be "skillful" and "intelligent," while a "lazy" person is not apt to have these traits, at least to the same degree.[22]

In addition to making inferences about the consistency of traits, we tend to organize traits in particular ways. We regard some traits as more influential and salient than others; these central traits serve to inform our overall perceptions of a person, influencing the meaning or connotation of the other traits we see him or her possessing. For instance, compare the description of a person as "warm and determined" to that of "cold and determined." Does the connotation of the trait determined change from one description to the other?

Asch discovered that changing "warm" to "cold" in a list of traits about a person drastically altered other people's perceptions of that person. Changing other traits on the list had much less effect. Based on this finding, Asch identified a person's perceived level of warmth as a **central organizing trait**[23]—a trait that has the greatest impact on the overall impression we form of him or her. In a related vein, he also concluded that different types of information about a person's character traits have different effects on the formation and organization of impressions.

In the years since Asch conducted his research, other cognitive social psychologists have further investigated the importance of various traits in the impression-formation process. They have discovered that the centrality of a trait depends on the nature of the judgment we are making. "Warmth" is central when we assess another person's sociability, but "bluntness" becomes the most salient trait when we consider another person's honesty.[24] Most important, through their studies Asch and other cognitive social psychologists have demonstrated how the character traits we infer about others not only shape our impressions of them but also influence the social identities we attribute to them.

When assigning others a social identity, we name and place them as a social object. Thus, a **social identity** is a mental category we use to locate a person in relation to others, highlighting how he or she is similar to and different from these others. It can consist of a single characteristic, such as being a woman, an environmentalist, or a Republican, or it can consist of a cluster of traits and statuses, such as being a tall, outgoing, Hispanic man who is a Democrat. We assign a social identity to others based on the information we glean from their appearance, actions, and social context.

While appreciating the insights that cognitive psychologists have offered into the identity attribution process, symbolic interactionists critique them for unduly emphasizing the importance of character traits in this process. As people gather information about and assign identities to others, they focus their attention on a number of other features, including social statuses, physical attributes, moods and emotions, and patterns of speech. In addition, individuals negotiate and alter the identities they attribute to others as they communicate with them. People rarely if ever give meaning to others through considering a list of static traits, except when asked to do so in a social psychology experiment. Instead, they give meaning to others through actively gathering information about them through an ongoing and ever-evolving process of interaction.

In the following discussion we highlight how people gather and make use of information about others' social attributes as they come into their presence. We also consider how this information-gathering process is influenced by prevailing stereotypes about gender, age, ethnicity, and physical appearances.

Identifying Others Based on Social Statuses. In our everyday interactions, we are influenced by cultural beliefs about what we can expect from people with particular attributes. We acquire these beliefs through a variety of social sources, including parents, relatives, friends, and the mass media. These sources teach us what it means to be young or old, male or female, Christian or Muslim, white or nonwhite. They also teach us, directly or indirectly, how to act toward people who occupy these statuses. We do not enter into interactions with others free of biases. We bring along a set of cultural preconceptions (or stereotypes) about how people with particular attributes are likely to act and how we in turn should act toward them.

Some attributes, such as gender, age, and ethnicity, are particularly likely to activate stereotypical beliefs. For many people, these characteristics override any other features. For instance, when a woman becomes a minister, others often put her gender ahead of her profession. They relate to her first as a woman and second as a minister. In such a case, gender becomes a *master status*—a status that powerfully affects how others define and interact with an individual.

The information provided by master statuses such as gender, ethnicity, and age is so taken for granted that we can easily overlook its impact on our interactions. We become more aware of its significance when we are confronted by situations where it is not available. This was nicely highlighted some years back by the androgynous character, Pat, on NBC's *Saturday Night Live*. As the other characters humorously demonstrated in their interactions with Pat, life becomes complicated when we do not know someone else's gender. We cannot give that person a clear-cut meaning and, consequently, do not know how to relate to him or her. We feel confused, uncomfortable, and perhaps even annoyed.

Identifying Others Based on Gender. As noted above, gender is a key status we take into account as we develop impressions of others and gauge their meaning for us. Once we know a person's gender, we often make a number of inferences about how he or she is likely to think, feel, and act.

While these inferences have changed somewhat over the past few decades in the United States, some patterns of belief have persisted. In general, Americans tend to perceive men and women in terms of a number of stereotypical beliefs about gender-related character traits, role behaviors, physical characteristics, and work roles. Various studies have documented how people form distinctively different impressions of others based on their gender.[25] These studies demonstrate that, despite the important changes provoked by the women's movement, gender images continue to shape our perceptions of and relationships to others in our everyday interactions. Although many strongly believe in the equality of men and women, we are still influenced by underlying stereotypes that encourage us to think of men and women in terms of disparate and unequal categories. Because of the influences of these stereotypes, we give different meanings to very similar actions and expressions presented to us by men and women. This process of attributing different meanings and identities to men and women imposes restrictive limits on both genders, but it has particularly burdensome consequences for women in our society.

 Identifying Others Based on Age and Ethnicity. In addition to considering how gender stereotypes influence our perceptions of and relationships with others, social psychologists have focused attention on the related impact of age and ethnicity. Like gender, these two social characteristics are "priority attributes," or attributes that we take into account in almost all situations as we make decisions about the kinds of people others are, the kinds of actions they are most likely to engage in, and the beliefs and attitudes they are most likely to hold. We use people's age and ethnicity as important templates in deciding how we might act appropriately in our contacts with them.

Age is clearly a prominent characteristic that guides our images of others. In our society we place people into a variety of age-related categories, such as baby, child, teenager, adult, and senior citizen. These categories call forth different social expectations. When encountering children, we expect them to be active, playful, happy, and carefree. When interacting with adolescents, we expect them to be moody, reserved, rebellious, and independent. When coming into contact with elderly people, we expect them to be sickly, depressed, senile, and slow moving or, on the more positive side, to be serene, wise, and nurturing. Regardless of which stereotypes we adopt, we define and form impressions of others in terms of the generalized expectations activated by their perceived age.

We also form stereotypical impressions and expectations of others based on their ethnic status. Ethnic stereotypes are the most widely researched form of stereotype, probably because they have limiting and harmful effects on our social appraisals and relationships. In comparison to gender and age-based stereotypes, ethnic stereotypes vary more dramatically across cultures and historical periods. Recent research indicates that ethnic stereotypes have changed substantially in the United States during the past sixty-five years. In this process of change, a number of negative stereotypes have become less pervasive. Regrettably, however, some negative ethnic stereotypes have persisted and continue to have a strong influence on Americans' perceptions and interactions.[26]

In addition to revealing the persistence of negative stereotypes, social psychologists have uncovered the emergence of a more subtle and implicit form of prejudice toward ethnic groups, particularly African Americans. Some have described this orientation as "unconscious racism,"[27] while others refer to it as "modern racism" or "symbolic racism."[28] Those who hold this type of prejudice stress the value of equal opportunity and often regard themselves as fervently antiracist. However, they believe that African Americans now have equal opportunities and only fail to succeed because they lack motivation, individualism, and deferred gratification.[29] They also believe that African Americans stay in low-paid positions because they do not work hard enough to succeed or have come to believe that others are prejudiced against them. Finally, they frequently view African Americans as overly demanding and militant and as seeking to implement policies of reverse discrimination or quotas.

In sum, although ethnic stereotypes have changed significantly over the past few decades, they cannot help but have a powerful influence on the judgments we make about others. When a person becomes identified as Jewish, Middle Eastern, Hispanic, Native American, or Asian American, he or she is presumed to have a certain set of characteristics. Even when we consciously reject ethnic stereotypes or we belong to an ethnic or racial minority, ethnic stereotypes often continue to affect our interpretations of others on a semiconscious level.[30] They encourage us to see certain aspects of others' behavior or appearances and to disregard others as we interact with them. Unfortunately, these attitudes pose major difficulties for the millions of Americans who are the targets of such stereotypes. They become understood in terms of relatively rigid categories and expectations that can significantly constrain their opportunities for self-expression, educational and occupational achievement, and rewarding interethnic relationships.

Identifying Others Based on Physical Appearance.
Along with the attributes of gender, age, and ethnicity, a person's overall physical appearance—including facial features, mannerisms, hygiene, hairstyle, height, weight, and body type—becomes relevant in virtually all of his or her interactions. These aspects of self give others cues about what to expect and serve as a basis for character judgments. In this sense, an individual's physical appearance serves as an important symbol. It represents "who the person is" and communicates this to others. Of course, the symbol provided by our appearance (or its specific components) must be interpreted by others. The meaning of our thinness, fatness, tallness, shortness, hair length, or earrings depends on our cultural, historical, and situational contexts.

Our awareness of how our physical appearance serves as a symbol to others is demonstrated in our careful preparations to present ourselves in public. Before going into many social situations, we spend a lot of time considering our physical readiness for it. Most of us, for instance, thoughtfully prepare for interactions with others by making sure our hair is combed, our face is clean, our clothes are appropriately casual or formal, our breath is fresh, our shirt or blouse is buttoned, and so on.[31] Of course, the degree to which we are concerned about these matters is a function of the specific situation in which we find ourselves.

In general, we regard physical appearances as valid bases for making inferences about the essential character traits and moral qualities of others. For better or worse, we examine physical attributes to discern whether others are friendly, serious, diligent, lazy, confident, nervous, intelligent, dull, good, evil, and so on.

In making "identifications" of others, we pay particular attention to their facial characteristics and expressions. As Georg Simmel observed, the face serves as a window to the self.[32] We see it as something that reveals people's inner nature and life experiences. In essence, we believe that people's experiences and ways of being become "crystallized into permanent features" on their faces. In addition, we regard others' faces as the most crucial medium through which to gauge their current feelings and attitudes. Through reading their facial expressions, we assess how they feel at the moment and how they are likely to act toward us. In turn, we identify them as happy, sad, angry, afraid, bored, kindhearted, and the like.

In this process of attributing traits and identities to others, we also use their faces, in combination with their bodies, as the basis for evaluating their physical attractiveness. If we deem them to be attractive, we assume that they possess a host of other desirable traits and qualities. For example, we tend to think they are more intelligent, personable, and likable than other people and that they have better sex lives, happier marriages, higher social status, and better mental health. In

Box 3-3 PERSON PERCEPTION ON THE STREETS: THE IMPACT OF AGE, RACE, AND GENDER

While conducting ethnographic research on the streets of Philadelphia, Elijah Anderson noticed that public perceptions of "strangers" varied quite dramatically. Some of the factors that shaped these perceptions included the people's clothing, jewelry, companions, demeanor, and physical movements. The most important factors, however, were the age, race, and gender of strangers, as Anderson highlights when describing who is most likely to be seen as threatening or dangerous on the streets:

> If a stranger cannot pass inspection and be assessed as "safe" (either by identity or by purpose), the image of predator may arise, and fellow pedestrians may try to maintain a distance consistent with that image.... In the street environment, it seems, children readily pass inspection, white women and white men do so more slowly, black women, black men, and black male teenagers most slowly of all. The master status assigned to black males undermines their ability to be taken for granted as law-abiding and civil participants in public places: Young black males, particularly those who don the urban uniform (sneakers, athletic suits, gold chains, "gangster caps," sunglasses, and [cell phones]), may be taken as the embodiment of the predator. In this uniform, which suggests to many the "dangerous underclass," these young men are presumed to be troublemakers or criminals. Thus, in the local milieu, the identity of predator is usually "given" to the young black male and made to stick until he demonstrates otherwise, something not easy to do in circumstances that work to cut off communication (p. 167).

Anderson points out that even when young black men act in ways that refute or disavow the image of predator, this does little to change public perceptions or public relationships between blacks and whites on the streets. "Common racist stereotypes persist, and black men who successfully make such disavowals are often seen not as the norm but as the exception—as 'different from the rest'—thereby confirming the status of the rest" (p. 168).

Source: Elijah Anderson, *Street Wise: Race, Class, and Change in an Urban Community* (Chicago: University of Chicago Press, 1991).

essence, we make inferences about their identities based on the notion that "what is beautiful is good." Social psychologists refer to this as the **halo effect**, or the tendency to believe attractive people have more socially desirable qualities than their less attractive counterparts do.

Finally, in evaluating the physical appearance of others, we make assessments based on the clothing that they wear. Their clothes operate as a kind of "social skin" that conveys important information about their statuses and characteristics. As Gregory Stone insightfully observed, we rely on people's clothing to discern many of their attributes, including their age, gender, ethnicity, social class, job, moods, feelings, attitudes, and political beliefs.[33] Clothes thus set the stage for us as we evaluate, identify, and interact with others. Through assessing their style of dress, we appraise their value, appreciate their moods, anticipate their attitudes (or behavioral tendencies), and assign them an identity. We thereby determine their meaning for us as we interact with them. Of course, those whose clothing is being assessed don't play a passive role in this process. They use their clothes as a prop to actively manipulate the impressions that we form of them and the identities that we attribute to them. We will discuss these dynamics further in Chapter Five, when we consider how people manage impressions and present selves to others.

Identifying Others Through Discourse. Although the appearance of others clearly affects how we think of them and, in many respects, shapes the nature of our interactions with them, it often fails to give us some of the details we want to uncover. For instance, we cannot gain full knowledge of important aspects of others' identities such as their occupation, social class, educational background, religious beliefs, political affiliations, or even ethnicity through observing their appearance alone.[34] We have to rely on their discourse, or verbal communications, to gather this information.

As Karp and Yoels[34] have pointed out, many of our everyday conversations with others are designed to elicit comments from them that will give us insight into their identities. As we interact with them, we ask questions and share remarks that reveal our interest in placing them as social objects. We might ask "What do you do?" to find out their occupation and education level. Or, we might ask "What does your spouse do?" to discover their marital status. Or, if we know them fairly well, we might ask "What's up?" to detect the identity they are putting forward in their current situation. If they say, "I'm going to start studying now," you think of them as a student. If, on the other hand, they say, "Hey, sit down and have a beer with me—I just bought a 12 pack and I'm going to get wasted," you regard them as a partier. In either case, you use their discourse to determine what identity to assign them and, correspondingly, what actions to adopt toward them.

As we respond to the discourse and implicit identity claims of others, we listen not only to the contents of their remarks but also to the tone, style, and patterns of their speech. In this process we make inferences about their social characteristics, along with their attitudes and moods, and consider whether these factors contradict the claims they make through their appearance. When contradictions or inconsistencies arise, we question the authenticity of the images the person is presenting.

Overall, then, we rely on the processes of both discourse and appearance as we form impressions and attribute identities to others. Each process informs and potentially contrasts with the other. Put simply, we compare what people say and how they say it to how they appear during their interactions with us. Doing so enables us to carefully evaluate the identity claims they are making and to decide whether to honor them.

Making Sense of Complex Configurations of Identity. As suggested in the preceding discussion, our interactions with others are often nuanced and complicated. In making sense of others, we rarely think of them in terms of one isolated characteristic, such as age. Instead, we see them in terms of a complex configuration of identities. For example, rather than categorizing people only in terms of their age, we identify them as young, rich, ambitious, African American, and female, or as old, middle-class, hardworking, Hispanic, and male, or as some other cluster of attributes. Thus, in making assessments of others, we consider the meaning and implications of the combination of attributes they possess. We do not respond to them one attribute at a time. Instead, we perceive and respond to them in terms of the impressions and interpretations activated by their particular combination of attributes.

Social psychologists have conducted much research on how we process and integrate the information we receive about the complex configuration of attributes that others present to us. In this research they have discovered that we use different **schemas** to interpret specific attributes, such as gender, when they are combined with certain other attributes. For instance, people tend to think differently about the attribute of male or female when it is connected with an ethnic status, such as white, African American, Latina, or Native American. They also think differently about a person's competence at performing various tasks based upon the combination of his or her gender and ethnicity.[35]

In addition to examining how gender and ethnicity become combined in the perceptual process, researchers have found that the schemas used to interpret these attributes are superseded at times by schemas that emphasize the linkages of occupation, role behaviors, physical characteristics, and character traits.

Overall, social psychological research indicates that we try to combine people's social, physical, and character attributes into a unified and coherent impression. We seek to organize them into a meaningful whole. We often do so by reevaluating and redefining attributes depending on whether we associate them (and their possessor) with a favorable or an unfavorable group. Thus, the long hours worked by a person associated with an ingroup illustrate his or her devotion, while the same number of hours worked by a person belonging to an outgroup reveals his or her compulsiveness and inability to relax.

The Peculiar Dynamics of Person Perception.

In discussing the process of person perception, we have highlighted how it is influenced by the linguistic categories we draw on as we come into contact with others. We have focused special attention on the schemas and stereotypes activated by "priority attributes" such as gender, age, and ethnicity. In so doing, we have drawn on a number of insights and concepts developed by cognitive social psychologists. These researchers recognize the importance of the social and symbolic aspects of human perception. Above all, they have highlighted how we perceive and act toward others on the basis of the impressions or images we form of them. These images are derived from stereotypes and schemas and thus are always somewhat incomplete and inaccurate. Yet they are all we have to guide us. We must act toward others based on our images of them and not in terms of who they might "really" be beyond these images. In this process we confer

attributes upon them that fit with our images of them and then respond to them as if they possess these attributes. Doing so enables us to engage in meaningful interaction with them.

In revealing these dynamics, cognitive social psychologists have helped us to see some of the central conceptual processes and social categories we bring to bear as we perceive others. Unfortunately, however, they have also overlooked some key factors, such as how people's perceptions of others are influenced by the nature and dynamics of their interactions with them. From a symbolic interactionist perspective, the analyses offered by cognitive social psychologists fall short in two important respects. First, they imply that the people (or groups) who are the targets of perception play a rather passive role in conveying information about themselves. Clearly this is not the case. Individuals (and groups) actively try to manipulate the information we receive about them. They conceal certain facts about themselves while advertising others in their efforts to shape our appraisals and impressions of them. Moreover, when interacting with other people who have different relationships with them, they adjust their strategies of information control, hiding some details they previously emphasized and accentuating others that had been previously concealed. As a result, a particular individual is a somewhat different object (with different meanings) to different observers. These observers' interpretations of the person are relative to the relationship they take part in with him or her. What is "true" about the individual from the perspective of a person in one relationship with him or her may be highly inaccurate from the perspective of another person in a quite different relationship with him or her.[36] Pragmatically speaking, then, the "reality" of the individual is not inherent to his or her characteristics and behaviors, but rather emerges out of the nature of his or her interactions with others. (We address these themes in further detail in Chapters Five and Seven.)

A second and related shortcoming of the analyses provided by cognitive social psychologists is their neglect of how particular types of social interactions and situations influence people's interpretations of the information presented by others. Within a given interaction, individuals direct their attention to selective features of others' appearances and actions based on how they define the specific situation. They consequently gather different information about a person and interpret that information differently depending on whether they define the situation as a party, a funeral, a job interview, a date, a business deal, an experiment, or something else. In some of these situations, a person's priority attributes, such as gender or ethnicity, may have little if any bearing on how he or she is perceived, but in others they may have a central impact.

Language, Naming, and the Construction of "Inner" Reality: Emotional Experience

As symbol-reliant creatures, human beings interpret and define the "reality" not only of their natural and social worlds but also of their internal world. They have to make sense of what happens "inside" their bodies in the same way that they make sense of what happens "outside" of them—by translating the sensations they experience into linguistic categories, or names. Ironically, then, people do not even have a direct and unmediated experience of their "insides." Instead, they must rely on symbols and *social* processes, particularly the processes of interpretation and interaction, to understand and meaningfully respond to their internal experiences. To illustrate this, we focus on how people define and respond to their emotional experiences.

Most people think of emotions as instinctive or spontaneous reactions they experience as they go through life. In many respects they see emotions as being similar to reflexes such as sneezing; that is, emotions are "naturally" triggered by certain stimuli and have to be released in specific behaviors. For instance, when you get cut off in

traffic, you "naturally" feel angry and curse the inconsiderate driver. Or, when you get a thoughtful gift from a family member, you "naturally" feel grateful and express this through a kiss or a hug. According to this commonsense view, emotions are internal, irrational, and almost automatic bodily reactions that lead individuals to act in particular ways. Because these reactions are not rational, people presumably have little ability to control or manage them.

For years many students of human emotion adopted a similar view. In turn, they focused their research on discovering the biological bases of emotion and on detecting how particular emotions served as the underlying sources of specific behaviors. This research gave little consideration to the social dimensions of emotions. In recent decades, sociologists, led largely by the analyses of symbolic interactionists, began to challenge this approach. They emphasized how emotions, like other meaningful human experiences, are profoundly social in their origins, nature, and expression. Through their analyses these sociologists illustrated how emotions cannot be understood simply as individual physiological reactions to specific stimuli. Instead, they must be seen as embedded in and arising out of social behavior, processes, and relationships.[37]

In analyzing emotion, symbolic interactionists emphasize how it is a nuanced *form of action* that involves a complex combination of experiences and processes that operate at various levels.[38] On one level, emotion involves biological processes; it includes physiological sensations and bodily experiences. We feel things "in our gut or heart" as we respond to specific situations. In some circumstances, we literally quake with fear, shake with rage, or feel overwhelmed by grief or excitement. Even when we feel less intense emotions, we often experience noticeable bodily changes, including an accelerated heartbeat, increased blood pressure and perspiration, and a rush of blood to the face. Yet, although our emotions have these biological aspects and implications, it is important to emphasize that they are ultimately grounded in and mediated through social rather than physiological realities.

According to symbolic interactionists, emotions arise and are expressed through an interactive process characterized by three phases.[39] In the first phase, a specific stimulus or situation is interpreted or defined. As we have stressed repeatedly in this chapter, people do not simply react to stimuli; they interpret them in light of their situation and then formulate a response, which often includes an emotion. Consider a scenario that unfolds in the hallway outside one of your classrooms. One young man, Dave, greets another man, Marcus, and then punches him sharply on the upper arm, inducing a sensation of pain. What does this mean? It depends on how Marcus defines the situation and the meaning of the punch. If Marcus sees Dave as a rival who is trying to initiate a fight, he will likely define the punch as an act of hostility. On the other hand, if Marcus sees Dave as a friend who is playfully jousting with him, he may define the punch as an act of affection.

As Marcus defines the "stimulus" of the punch, he moves into the second phase of the interactional process surrounding emotional experience. During this phase, he experiences an internal response to the defined situation. This response includes both physiological and symbolic processes. Physiologically, Marcus may be experiencing a fairly unpleasant sensation of pain, along with an increase in his heart rate and blood pressure. But, if he defines Dave's punch as an act of friendship, he will respond to these bodily sensations very differently than if he defines it as an act of hostility. This is where the symbolic processes fit. Through his social experiences, Marcus has learned how to name (or define) and appropriately respond to particular bodily sensations in the context of given situations. In this case, let's assume that Marcus is part of a friendship group that practices a greeting consisting of a sharp punch to the shoulder. Through his interactions with others in the group, Marcus has learned to define the pain that he currently experiences in

his shoulder as a sign of the caring and camaraderie that members of the group feel for one another.

During the third and final phase of the social process involved in emotional experience, Marcus communicates his emotional response to Dave's punch by drawing on conventionalized symbols, including words, gestures, and facial expressions. Assuming that he defines it as an act of friendship, he might convey that he feels caring and connection toward Dave by laughing loudly about the punch and then returning the gesture. In doing so, Marcus has used his thoughts, or cognitions, to suppress and transform the pain he initially felt into an expression that communicates the emotion of caring. He is thereby engaging in a nuanced process of emotion management that may or may not entail a genuine expression of his feelings about Dave or his punch. Marcus may choose to act "as if" he defines the punch as an act of friendship and "as if" he cares about Dave when he actually feels annoyed by both the punch and Dave. In this event, Marcus mimics the feeling expected of him without truly feeling it. On the other hand, he may choose to suppress his feelings of pain and to consciously call forth feelings of caring toward Dave, which he then expresses in laughter and the return of the ritual punch. When making this choice, he actually works on his feelings to evoke an emotional response that fits the expectations of the situation.

In presenting this scenario, we have tried to highlight how emotions are generated, defined, and expressed through a social process. Implicitly, we have also touched on some major assumptions of a symbolic interactionist approach to emotion. For the sake of clarity, let us briefly state these five assumptions:

First, emotions originate in and arise out of our participation in social life.[40] Our experience of feelings such as anger, joy, frustration, and satisfaction is tied to our social behavior, positions, and interactions. When we engage in behavior and interactions that allow us to successfully realize our goals in a situation, such as making connection with a friend or earning a good grade in a course, we are likely to feel happiness or satisfaction. On the other hand, when we engage in behavior and interactions that block our attainment of desired goals, we are likely to feel anger or frustration.

Second, the emotions we feel as a consequence of our action and interaction are embodied—that is, they are connected to physiological processes and reactions that take place in our bodies. However, these processes and reactions must be interpreted in terms of symbols and social categories. In other words, they must be named. Feelings such as "joy" and "anger" are not only experienced as bodily sensations, but are also named and thus socially defined, both by those experiencing them and those who observe this experience. In fact, while we can have the physiological sensations linked to a particular emotion, such as anger, we will not experience these sensations as the feeling of anger until we name them as such.[41] The process of naming allows us to organize and give the meaning of anger to particular sensations, such as an increased heartbeat and adrenaline flow. It also allows us to see ourselves as "angry" and to act upon ourselves in light of that definition, reflecting on and deciding how or whether to express that feeling in a given situation.

Third, as implied above, our emotions are *self-feelings*; they are experiences that refer to and have implications for self.[42] We link emotions to the self, saying "I am mad," "I am happy," "I am sad," "I am nervous," "I am in love," or "I am bored." As Norman Denzin has suggested, our emotions arise out of and reflect our self-interactions as well as our interactions with others.[43] In the process of experiencing emotion, we engage in acts and judgments directed toward the self. Doing so involves imagining ourselves in the eyes of others and responding to the self as a social object. Through this reflexive process we define ourselves as feeling a certain way—whether angry, sad, joyous, or passionate.

Fourth, while emotions involve the self, they are identified, shaped, and expressed in accord with the social definitions and expectations provided by the groups to which we belong. As a result, *emotions are social objects* that we manipulate and act toward much like other social objects. We can manage, express, and use emotions in various ways to realize our goals for self and to negotiate meaningful interactions with others. In this process, we are often guided by the "feeling rules" that predominate in our social groups.[44] Through our interactions with others in these groups, we learn an unwritten set of expectations about what emotions are appropriate to feel in given situations and how we ought to express or display them. For instance, we learn that we are supposed to feel happy at weddings and that we should express this feeling by smiling during the ceremony and by engaging in rowdier behavior afterward, such as throwing rice at the bride and groom and "celebrating" at the reception. We also learn to suppress or hide less positive feelings that might arise during the wedding, such as jealousy, anger, sadness, or worries about the likely success of the marriage.

Fifth, and perhaps most important, as we learn how to manage various emotions in light of feeling rules, we develop the ability proactively to shape and control our bodily sensations and emotional experiences. We do not simply react to situations based on physiological processes that take place within us. Instead, we learn how to interpret these processes and translate them into emotional experiences and actions that fit with the demands of specific situations. We also learn to formulate emotional acts in ways that involve both suppressing and calling forth various feelings. In turn, we use our emotions not merely to shape our actions to meet the expectations of others, but also to influence and direct the responses of others. For instance, we express sympathy toward a classmate who has done poorly on an exam not only because doing so is expected of us, but because we want to encourage him or her to see us as a "nice" person and to treat us thoughtfully. Emotions, then, become a crucial part of the processes of communication, role taking, and self-presentation. They serve as a vital channel of communication through which we convey how we are defining others, ourselves, and our situation and also how we try to shape others' responses to us, themselves, and this situation. Thus, the process of constructing and negotiating meaning is not simply cognitive; it is also emotional. We define reality through the processes of both thinking and feeling. Our cognitions do not simply shape our emotional responses; rather, our thoughts and emotions work hand in hand, mutually influencing each other.

SUMMARY

- What makes us distinctive as human beings is our ability to use and create symbols. This capacity enables us to transcend the bonds of our immediate environment. Unlike other animals, we do not simply respond to our experiences in the here and now. Instead, we build up our actions in terms of our images of the past, present, and future as well as our images of what is good, right, or important. In essence, we act and live in a world of our own creation—a world that is inherently abstract rather than concrete, a world of symbols that, in some senses, is imaginary.
- In addition to enabling us to transcend and transform our environment, symbols allow us to think, fantasize, remember, make plans, and create and pass along culture. Perhaps most important, symbols enable us to "name" the objects, events, and people we encounter in our world and, in so doing, to transform them into *social objects*. Through the naming process, then, we define the "reality" of the objects of our daily experience and know how to act toward them. In defining the "reality" of others, we engage in the same types of processes we use to define the reality of other social objects. We gather information through our senses, we sort and organize this information into categories or names, and we utilize these categories to interpret each other's meaning. In this process of person perception, we often rely on categories known as stereotypes. Stereotypes are mental images that attribute a common set of characteristics to members of a particular group or social category. They enable us to simplify the reality of others and to make fast decisions about them based on a small amount of information. Through drawing on stereotypes, we can assess others quickly, assign them social identities, anticipate their actions, and plan our own responses to these actions. Of course, stereotypes also have notable drawbacks, and we often pay a price for the efficiency and direction we derive from using them. They can lead us to distort, exaggerate, or overlook important information about others and, correspondingly, to respond to them on the basis of misleading or faulty assumptions. Stereotypes can also prompt us to "see" or call forth attributes and actions in others that fit our preconceived expectations.
- In general, we rarely define another person only in terms of a specific, isolated attribute. Instead, we respond to that individual in terms of his or her complex configuration of identities. Typically, we seek to organize this configuration into a coherent and meaningful whole—we form an overall impression of the person. We often do so by reevaluating and redefining his or her attributes depending on whether we associate him or her with a favorable group or an unfavorable group.
- We make sense of our "inner worlds" through the same processes of "naming" and symbolic interaction that we use to give meaning to the natural and social worlds. This phenomenon is revealed in how we define and respond to our emotional experiences. We identify and express our emotions through a three-phase interactional process that involves us in (1) interpreting a specific stimulus or situation in a particular way; (2) experiencing an internal response to that interpreted stimulus or situation; and (3) formulating and conveying

an emotional response by means of conventionalized symbols, including words, gestures, and facial expressions.

• While our emotions have a physiological component and seem to originate inside our bodies, they are rooted in our social acts and interactions. They are also shaped by the social definitions and feeling norms provided by the groups to which we belong. Our emotions, then, are social objects and socially constructed actions rather than biological states or reactions. In light of this, we manipulate and shape their meanings in the same manner in which we manipulate and shape the meanings of other social objects and acts. Most important, we actively manage and control our emotions as we engage in social acts and interactions. We also use them to communicate meanings to others, thereby influencing or directing how they respond to us.

GLOSSARY OF KEY TERMS

Central Organizing Trait
A character trait that has the greatest impact on the overall impression we form of another individual. According to research on the person perception process, the perceived "warmth" of another is a central organizing trait.

Culture
The ways of thinking, feeling, and acting that characterize a society or group. These ways of thinking, feeling, and acting are learned, transmitted, sustained, and transformed through our interaction and communication with one another.

Halo Effect
The tendency to believe that people with one positive trait are likely to have other positive traits.

Idioculture
A system of shared knowledge, beliefs, feelings, and behaviors that serves as a frame of reference and basis of interaction for members of a particular group.

Schema
A set of beliefs or preconceptions that organizes the information we gather about a specific object, person, or concept. Schemas allow us to simplify reality by interpreting specific instances in light of general categories.

Sign
An object or event to which a fixed or unchanging response is made. Its meaning is associated or identified with its physical form.

Social Cognition
Sorting and organizing data by naming or applying social categories to them, thereby giving them meaning.

Social Identity
A mental category that locates us in relation to others, highlighting how we are similar to and different from these others. A social identity can consist of a single characteristic, or it can consist of a cluster of traits and statuses.

Social Object
An object that we give meaning to through our interactions with one another. An object becomes a social object when we name it and act toward it in terms of that name.

Symbol
An object, gesture, or word that we use to represent, or

	take the place of, something else.
Stereotype	A mental image that attributes a common set of characteristics to members of a particular group.

QUESTIONS FOR REFLECTION OR ASSIGNMENT

1. Form two or more groups in class, each having an equal number of members. Next, have the groups compete with one another in doing the following task without *speaking a single word*. The task: group members should inform one another of the month and date they were born and then arrange themselves in chronological order—that is, from the earliest birthday in January to the last birthday in December. The first team to do so successfully "wins" the contest. After participating in the contest, analyze what happened. How did people in your group communicate what they needed to with one another? Did they use symbols? If so, what kinds of symbols did they use? What characteristics do these symbols have? Do they have the same characteristics and consequences as verbal symbols? What are the key consequences of symbols?

2. Go on a fifteen- to thirty-minute walk in a "nature center" or a wooded area. Try to see and hear as much as you can as you proceed on your walk. Stop and carefully examine the plants, trees, birds, animals, and insects that are in your vicinity. How many can you name? How many do you not have names for? Which are you more likely to notice? Would you agree with the statement: "People see things that they have words for"? Why or why not?

3. Do the names we give to certain people or situations make a difference? For instance, does it matter whether we call a person "crippled," "handicapped," or "disabled"? Does it matter if

we call someone an "AIDS victim," an "AIDS patient," or "a person living with AIDS"? Or does it matter if we call an adult female a "girl," a "lady," or a "woman"? Explain and offer support for your answer.

4. Analyze the speech of a local or national politician. What kind of language and symbols does he or she use when speaking? What does this language emphasize? What does it conceal? How does it frame the "issues" that the speaker addresses? Is language an important aspect of exercising power? How and why?

5. Interview someone with a chronic pain condition and ask the person to talk about the pain that he or she feels. What words does the person use to describe the pain? Does the person have difficulty putting the pain into words? If so, why would this be the case? Overall, what meanings does the pain have for him or her? What emotions does it evoke? How are these meanings and emotions influenced by the person's social interactions and social statuses, such as his or her gender, ethnicity, or class?

6. Think back to a group that you belonged to in the past, especially in your childhood. What unique terms or "special language" did this group use? Did members of the group call one another by nicknames? If so, what were some of these nicknames? What purposes did they serve for the group and its members?

SUGGESTED READINGS FOR FURTHER STUDY

Burke, Kenneth. *On Symbols and Society* (Chicago: University of Chicago Press, 1989).

Chayko, Mary. "From Cave Paintings to Chat Rooms: The Sociomental Foundation of Connectedness," in *Connecting* (Albany, NY: SUNY Press, 2002), pp. 7–37.

Hochschild, Arlie. *The Commercialization of Intimate Life: Notes from Home and Work*

(Berkeley, CA: University of California Press, 2003).

Sacks, Oliver. *Seeing Voices* (Berkeley, CA: University of California Press, 1989).

Waskul, Dennis and Philip Vannini. *Body/ Embodiment: Symbolic Interaction and the Sociology of the Body* (Ashgate Publishing, 2006).

Zerubavel, Eviatar. *Social Mindscapes: An Invitation to Cognitive Sociology* (Cambridge, MA: Harvard University Press, 1997).

ENDNOTES

[1] This quote is taken from an interview conducted by the first author, Kent Sandstrom, when studying the lived experience of men with HIV/AIDS. For further discussion of the themes highlighted in this interview, see Kent L. Sandstrom, "Preserving a Vital and Valued Self in the Face of AIDS," *Sociological Inquiry* 68(3), 1998, pp. 354–371.

[2] Suzanne Langer, *Philosophy in a New Key* (New York: Mentor Books, 1948).

[3] Ibid., p. 46.

[4] For a related and more detailed discussion, see Anselm Strauss, *Continual Permutations of Action* (New York: Aldine de Gruyter, 1993), pp. 140–160.

[5] James W. Vander Zanden, *Social Psychology*, 3rd ed. (New York: Random House, 1984), p. 36.

[6] Ibid.

[7] Ibid., p. 38.

[8] Alfred R. Lindesmith, Anselm L. Strauss, and Norman K. Denzin, *Social Psychology*, 7th ed. (Englewood Cliffs, NJ: Prentice-Hall, 1993), p. 55.

[9] In making these points we do not want to leave the impression that perception is only a matter of interpretations shaped by language and culture. Following the insights of John Dewey and George Herbert Mead, interactionists stress that perceptions emerge out of the transactions of people (as organisms with senses) and the environment. Thus, human perceptions arise out of what we bring to the environment in terms of sensory abilities, such as receptors in our eyes that translate different wavelengths and frequencies on the electromagnetic spectrum into the sensations we experience as color, and what the environment offers in terms of stimuli that can be successfully translated, such as particular electromagnetic wavelengths and frequencies. For a pertinent and more detailed discussion, see David Franks, "Mutual Interests, Different Lenses: Current Neuroscience and Symbolic Interaction," *Symbolic Interaction* 26 (4), 2003, pp. 613–630.

[10] John P. Hewitt, *Self and Society*, 6th ed. (Boston: Allyn and Bacon, 1994), p. 35.

[11] Jodi O'Brien and Peter Kollock, *The Production of Reality*, 2nd ed. (Thousand Oaks, CA: Pine Forge Press, 1997), p. 55.

[12] Tamotsu Shibutani, "Reference Groups as Perspectives," *American Journal of Sociology* 60, 1955, pp. 962–965.

[13] Gary Alan Fine, *With the Boys: Little League Baseball and Preadolescent Culture* (Chicago: University of Chicago Press, 1987), p. 125.

[14] Anselm L. Strauss, *Mirrors and Masks* (San Francisco: Sociology Press, 1959).

[15] Joel Charon, *Symbolic Interactionism: An Introduction, an Interpretation, an Integration,* 4th ed. (Englewood Cliffs, NJ: Prentice-Hall, 1992), p. 46.

[16] Susan Curtiss, *Genie: A Psycholinguistic Study of a Modern-Day "Wild Child"* (New York: Academic Press, 1977). See also Kingsley Davis's classic article, "Final Note on a Case of Extreme Isolation," *American Journal of Sociology* 52 (5), 1947, pp. 432–437.

[17] Oliver Sacks, *Seeing Voices: A Journey into the World of the Deaf.* (Berkeley: University of California Press, 1989).

[18] Helen Keller, *The Story of My Life* (New York: Doubleday, 1917).

[19] James W. Vander Zanden, *Social Psychology*, 2nd ed. (New York: Random House), p. 43.

[20] Walter Lippman, *Public Opinion* (New York: Harcourt, 1922), p. 16.

[21] Mark Snyder, "When Beliefs Create Reality: The Self-Fulfilling Impact of First Impressions on

Social Interaction," in A. Pines and C. Maslach, eds., *Experiencing Social Psychology* (New York: Alfred Knopf, 1977), pp. 189–192.

22 Solomon Asch, "Forming Impressions of Personality," *Journal of Abnormal and Social Psychology* 41, 1946, pp. 258–290; Solomon Asch, *Social Psychology* (Englewood Cliffs, NJ: Prentice-Hall, 1952).

23 Ibid.

24 J. Wishner, "Reanalysis of 'Impressions of Personality,'" *Psychological Review* 67, 1960, pp. 96–112.

25 See Deborah Prentice and Erica Carranza, "What Women and Men Should Be, Shouldn't Be, Are Allowed to Be, and Don't Have to Be: The Contents of Prescriptive Gender Stereotypes," *Psychology of Women Quarterly* 26 (4), 2002, pp. 269–281; Sandra L. Bem, *The Lenses of Gender* (New Haven, CT: Yale University Press, 1993); B. J. Skrypnek and Mark Snyder, "On the Self-Perpetuating Nature of Stereotypes about Men and Women," *Journal of Experimental Social Psychology* 18, 1992, pp. 247–305; Cecilia Ridgeway and S.J. Correll, "Unpacking the Gender System: A Theoretical Perspective on Gender Beliefs and Social Relations," Gender & Society 18, 2004, pp. 510–531.

26 James Wiggins, Beverly Wiggins, and James Vander Zanden, *Social Psychology*, 5th ed. (New York: McGraw Hill, 1995), p. 183.

27 See Lincoln Quillian, "Does Unconscious Racism Exist," *Social Psychology Quarterly* 71(1), 2008, pp. 6–11; Lincoln Quillian, "New Approaches to Understanding Racial Prejudice and Discrimination." *Annual Review of Sociology* 32, 2006, pp. 299–328; R.H. Fazio and B.C. Dutton, "Categorization by Race: The Impact of Automatic and Controlled Components of Racial Prejudice," *Journal of Experimental Social Psychology* 33, 1997, pp. 451–470; Lincoln Quillian and Devah Pager, "Black Neighbors, Higher Crime? The Role of Racial Stereotypes in Evaluations of Neighborhood Crime," *American Journal of Sociology* 107: 717–767. For a contrasting view, see Philip Tetlock and Gregory Mitchell, "Calibrating Prejudice in Milliseconds," *Social Psychology Quarterly* 71, 1, 2008, pp. 12–16.

28 M. B. Brewer and R. M. Kramer, "The Psychology of Intergroup Attitudes and Behavior," *Annual Review of Psychology* 37, 1984, pp. 515–521.

29 J.R. Kluegel and E. R. Smith, *Beliefs About Inequality: American's Views of What Is and What Ought to Be* (New York: Aldine de Gruyter, 1986). For a more recent measure of implicit racial prejudice, see Project Implicit. Demonstration Web Site. Available at http://www.implicit.harvard.edu. Accessed August 16, 2008.

30 Lincoln Quillian, "Does Unconscious Racism Exist," (Note 27); see also Judith A. Howard, *Gendered Selves, Gendered Situations* (Thousand Oaks, CA: Sage, 1997), p. 78.

31 David Karp and William Yoels, *Sociology and Everyday Life* (Itasca, IL: F. E. Peacock, 1986).

32 Georg Simmel, "Sociology of the Senses: Visual Interaction," in Robert E. Park and Ernest W. Burgess, eds., *Introduction to the Science of Society* (Chicago: University of Chicago Press, 1924).

33 Gregory P. Stone, "Appearance and the Self: A Slightly Revised Version," in Dennis Brissett and Charles Edgley, eds., *Life as Theater: A Dramaturgical Sourcebook,* 2nd ed. (Chicago: Aldine Press, 1990), pp. 141–162.

34 David Karp and William Yoels, *Sociology and Everyday Life* (Note 31), p. 78.

35 Rose Weitz and Leonard Gordon, "Images of Black Women Among Anglo College Students," *Sex Roles* 28, 1993, pp. 19–34; Martha Foschi and Shari Buchan, "Ethnicity, Gender, and Perceptions of Task Competence," *Canadian Journal of Sociology* 15 (1), 1990, pp. 1–18.

36 George McCall and J. L. Simmons, *Identities and Interactions* (New York: The Free Press, 1966), pp. 119–120.

37 See Arlie R. Hochschild, *The Commercialization of Intimate Life: Notes from Home and Work* (Berkeley, CA: University of California Press, 2003); Arlie R. Hochschild, "Emotion Work, Feeling Rules, and Social Structure," *American Journal of Sociology* 87, 1979, pp. 551–575; Steven L. Gordon, "The Sociology of Sentiments and Emotion," in Morris Rosenberg and Ralph Turner, eds., *Social Psychology: Sociological Perspectives* (New York:

Basic Books, 1981), pp. 562–592; Trudy Mills and Sherryl Kleinman, "Emotions, Reflexivity, and Action: An Interactionist Analysis," *Social Forces* 66, 1988, pp. 1009–1027; Susan Shott, "Emotion and Social Life: A Symbolic Interactionist Analysis," *American Journal of Sociology* 84, 1979, pp. 1317–1334.

[38] Alfred R. Lindesmith, Anselm L. Strauss, and Norman K. Denzin, *Social Psychology* (Note 8), p. 98.

[39] Ibid., p. 100.

[40] John P. Hewitt, *Self and Society*, 7th ed. (Boston: Allyn and Bacon, 1997).

[41] Ibid.

[42] Norman K. Denzin, *On Understanding Emotion* (San Francisco: Jossey-Bass, 1983).

[43] Norman K. Denzin, "A Note on Emotionality, Self, and Interaction," *American Journal of Sociology* 89(2), 1983, pp. 402–409.

[44] Arlie R. Hochschild, "Emotion Work, Feeling Rules, and Social Structure," (Note 37).

CHAPTER FOUR

~

SOCIALIZATION: THE CREATION
OF MEANING AND IDENTITY

What if you had been born into a different society? How would your life have been different? Imagine, for instance, that you had been born as an Akaraman child in the jungles of Peru. Your parents and elders would welcome you into a culture that has no concept of "freedom," "self-sufficiency," or "the individual."[1] You would do nothing independently of a small group of same-sexed intimates; you would work, play, hunt, and eat with others in this group. You would even sleep together as a group, piling yourselves into a bundle of bodies every night for warmth and comfort. You would also learn that it is appropriate to engage in communal acts of cannibalism and homosexuality with your fellow group members.

Imagine, by contrast, that you had been born as a Mundugumor child in New Guinea. Your parents would raise you in a culture that emphasizes the virtues of self-reliance and aggression.[2] Both your mother and father would see childrearing as burdensome and would display little if any tenderness toward you, even as an infant. In fact, whenever you were not nursing, your mother would put you in a harsh, scratchy basket—at least until you learned to kick your way out of it. Once you made your way out of this basket, you would have to cling tenaciously to your mother's hair and cry loudly to gain any attention from her.

In general, your parents and other adults would treat you with neglect and hostility. Through doing so, they would teach you to fend for yourself and compete aggressively with others to get what you want in life. Your fellow Mundugumor would thus encourage you to embrace beliefs and practices that would differ dramatically from those embraced by the Akarama.

How can we account for the remarkably diverse beliefs and practices that people learn to adopt as Akaramans, Mundugumor, or members of other societies? In addressing this question, symbolic interactionists, like other sociologists, rely heavily on the concept of socialization. That is, we stress that human beings acquire beliefs and preferences by means of the process of **socialization**—an ongoing, interactive process through which individuals develop identities and learn the ways of thinking, feeling, and acting that characterize their society. Thus, in explaining why Akaramans prefer to bundle up at night with a group of same-sexed others, symbolic interactionists, along with most sociologists, emphasize that this behavior results from the Akaramans' socialization.

Unlike some sociologists, however, symbolic interactionists do not see socialization as a fully predictable process that compels people to think, feel, and act in accord with the dictates of their society. Nor do interactionists believe that socialization simply promotes cultural uniformity and the smooth reproduction of social order. Instead, we stress the dynamic, reciprocal, and somewhat unpredictable nature of socialization. We view people as active agents who significantly influence the contents and outcomes of their own socialization. We also believe that as people participate in the socialization process they acquire resources and skills that enhance their creativity and autonomy.[3] For instance, through socialization young children learn how to think, talk, understand, play roles, and fashion selves. In developing these capacities, they influence and often resist the goals, hopes, and actions of adults. Children do not passively conform to the values and wishes of adults. All too often (at least from parents' perspectives) children rebel against these values and wishes, teaching adults what they should "really" expect from them. In doing so they act as agents of socialization as well as targets of this process.

Most important, from the interactionist perspective the socialization process is reciprocal. People are simultaneously "socializees" and "socializers." Consider your experience as a student in this course. Beginning with the first class session, your professor has taught you, directly or indirectly, what he or she expects of a good student. If he or she lectures every class period, you may have learned that you ought to remain relatively quiet, taking notes and talking only when you have a relevant question or comment. If, by contrast, your professor uses a cooperative learning approach, you may have discovered that you ought to talk frequently and participate actively in group discussions. Regardless of which style your professor has used, you have simultaneously taught him or her how you view the roles of student and instructor. For example, if you have resisted attempts to involve you in cooperative learning exercises, you have demonstrated your feelings about the "appropriate" relationship between student and professor. You may have nonverbally conveyed your preference for listening to lectures. If your classmates similarly convey

this view, you may jointly teach the professor that cooperative learning won't work in this class. As a result, your instructor may choose to lecture more often. If so, you will have influenced the outlooks and actions of someone who supposedly controls you.

Of course, few situations are this simple. The flow of socialization frequently changes, without clearly meeting the goals or interests of any parties involved. Socialization, then, is not simply a one-dimensional process through which some people impose their attitudes, values, and beliefs on others. Nor is it a process that merely prepares people to play out predefined roles. Instead, as symbolic interactionists emphasize, socialization has multiple purposes and outcomes. Its most important outcome is the production of individuals who can adjust themselves and their behavior to the situations they face. The successfully socialized person is someone who can skillfully meet the challenges of different situations, coordinating his or her actions with others to solve problems, achieve desired goals, and create meaningful identities. Thus, according to interactionists, socialization is effective when it produces resourceful actors who can think, act, interact, and pursue their interests within the broad guidelines provided by their culture.

In addition to emphasizing how socialization creates resourceful individuals, symbolic interactionists stress that socialization is tied to immediate circumstances. People's thoughts, feelings, and actions may be affected as much by their current surroundings as by their past experiences, including those they had as young children.

While stressing the continuing impact of socialization, interactionists distinguish between primary and secondary socialization. Primary socialization refers to the process by which children learn to become mature, responsible members of their society. This learning occurs through our core social institutions, particularly the family. Secondary socialization, by contrast, refers to the more specific formal training that individuals experience throughout their life, such as learning how to drive, learning how to parent, or learning an occupation.

The primary socialization process shapes the development of children. Within this process, children learn two fundamental things that allow them to become fully human. First, they learn the *culture*—or ways of thinking, feeling, and acting—of their society. Second, children learn who they are—they develop a sense of *self*. This self makes them feel special, different from everyone else, unique within their group. At the same time, the self emerges, develops, and is sustained through processes of *social* interaction. The self therefore has a paradoxical nature: It is both personal and social in character. Symbolic interactionists focus on how we develop this paradoxical sense of self and how it influences our behavior. In the following section we describe the interactionist theory of self-development, highlighting the insights of two founders of this theory, Charles Horton Cooley and George Herbert Mead.

SELF-DEVELOPMENT AND THE STAGES OF SOCIALIZATION

Symbolic interactionists stress that an individual's self is responsive to and shaped by social forces. While recognizing that children are born with different temperaments and potentials, we contend that children are not born with a sense of self. Nor do children acquire this sense as a natural consequence of their biological development. They must learn who they are through their interactions with others. It is through these interactions that children come to believe that they have distinct selves and that these selves are meaningful. Put another way, the self of a child is not an internal feature but rather reflects and develops out of social relationships.

In championing this view of the self, interactionists are guided by the insights of early twentieth-century sociologist Charles Horton Cooley.[4] After carefully observing the development of his daughter, Cooley concluded that children acquire a sense of who they are through their interactions with others: they develop a **looking-glass self**. By this term Cooley meant simply that a child, such as his daughter, learns to see herself in terms of the "reflection" provided by others. This learning occurs through a three-step process. First, the child imagines how she appears to others around her, especially to important others such as her parents and family members. She tries to see herself through their eyes. Second, and simultaneously, the child imagines how others *judge* her. Based on their actions and expressions, she gauges whether they see her as "good" or "bad" or as lovable or bothersome. Third, guided by her interpretations of others' reactions and judgments, the child develops a self-feeling. If she sees her parents responding to her as a good or lovable child, she will internalize their responses and feel gratified. In contrast, if she sees her parents reacting to her as a "bad" or bothersome child, she will judge herself unfavorably and feel ashamed.

In revealing the dynamics of the looking-glass self, Cooley stressed the importance of the interpretation process engaged in by the child. The child cannot directly see herself in the way others view her. She must interpret their responses and imagine how others look at and feel about her. This means she may misjudge others' perceptions of her. For better or worse, her sense of self develops based on how she *thinks* others see her, not on their actual appraisals. Thus, the child's looking-glass self is not a direct reflection of others' views and judgments, but rather an imagined reflection.

As Cooley noted, the process by which a "looking-glass self" is formed does not end with early childhood. A person's self-image continues to be influenced by the responses of others throughout his or her life. Consider your own self-concept. Your current image of self as, for example, smart or not so smart is influenced by the appraisals of friends, family members, and professors. Although there are objective measures you can use to gauge your intelligence, such as your grade point average or test scores, the

Box 4-1 BE CAREFUL WHAT YOU WISH FOR: THE "GLORIED SELF" AND ITS COSTS

In a fascinating ethnographic study, Patricia and Peter Adler examined how the sudden attainment of celebrity transformed the self-images of members of a highly successful college basketball team. In the excerpt that follows, the Adlers illustrate how the "looking-glass selves" of these players were influenced by the hero worship and adulation directed toward them by fans and the media. They also demonstrate how the players were active rather than passive participants in the construction of their "gloried selves," selecting particular social appraisals as the basis of their self-images and self-presentations. Initially, the players tried to resist the influence of the images of glory reflected toward them. As time passed, however, they found these images too intoxicating and seductive to refuse. They subsequently embraced and enacted the "gloried self" that others—particularly the media—attributed to them. Unfortunately, they discovered that this self became a kind of trap. The more they used it to guide their self-presentations, even in a playful or detached way, the more they incorporated it into their self-conceptions. The attainment of a "gloried self," then, is not without its costs. Indeed, the Adlers' findings suggest that if you aspire to become a celebrity, you may want to rethink your ambitions. The price of celebrity is often the loss of a personal and authentic sense of self.

The Adlers describe the development and consequences of the "gloried self" as follows:

... The forging and modification of reflected selves began as team members perceived how people treated them; subsequently, they formed reactions to that treatment. One of the first things they all noticed was that they were sought intensely by strangers. Large numbers of people, individually and in groups, wanted to be near them, to get their autographs, to touch them, and to talk to them. People treated them with awe and respect. One day, for example, the head coach walked out of his office and found a woman waiting for him. As he turned towards her, she threw herself in front of him and began to kiss his feet, all the while telling him what a great man he was....

Players also found themselves highly prized in interacting with boosters (financial supporters of the team). Boosters showered all players with invitations to their houses for team meetings or dinner. They fought jealously to have players seen with them or gossiped about as having been in their houses. It soon became apparent to players that boosters derived social status from associating with them.

...This situation caused players to recognize that they were "glory bearers," so filled with glory that they could confer it on anyone by their mere presence. They experienced a sense of the "Midas touch": They had an attribute (fame) that everybody wanted and which could be transmitted. Their ability to cast glory onto others and their desirability to others because of this ability became an important dimension of their new, reflected self-identity.

The Media Self

A second dimension of the self created from the glory experience was influenced largely by media portrayals....Most of the athletes who came to the University had received some media publicity in high school (68 percent); but the national level of the print and video coverage they received after arriving, coupled with the intensity of the constant focus, caused them to develop more compelling and more salient media selves than they had possessed previously.

Radio, television, and newspaper reporters covering the team often sought out athletes for "human interest" stories. These features presented media-framed angles that cast athletes into particular roles and tended to create new dimensions of their selves. Images were created from a combination of individuals' actual behavior and reporters' ideas of what made good copy. Thus, through media coverage, athletes were cast into molds that frequently were distorted or exaggerated reflections of their behavior and self-conceptions. Team members, for whom the media had created roles, felt as if they had to live up to these portrayals. For instance, two players were depicted as "good students"—shy, quiet, religious, and diligent. Special news features emphasized their outstanding traits, illustrating how they went regularly to class, were humanitarian, and cared about graduating. Yet one of them lamented:

"Other kids our age, they go to the fair and they walk around with a beer in their hand, or a cigarette; but if me and Dan were to do that, then people would talk about that. We can't go over to the clubs, or hang around, without it relaying back to Coach. We can't even do things around our teammates, because they expect us to be a certain way. The media has created this image of us as the 'good boys,' and now we have to live up to it."

Other players (about 20 percent) were embraced for their charismatic qualities; they had naturally outgoing personalities and the ability to excite a crowd. These players capitalized on the media coverage, exaggerating their antics to gain attention and fame. Yet the more they followed the media portrayal, the more likely it was to turn into a caricature of their selves. One player described how he felt when trapped by his braggart media self:

"I used to like getting in the paper. When reporters came around, I would make those Mohammed Ali type outbursts—I'm gonna do this, I'm gonna do that. And they come around again, stick a microphone in your face, 'cause they figure somewhere Washington will have another outburst. But playing that role died out in me. I think sometimes the paper pulled out a little too much from me that wasn't me. But people seen me as what the paper said, and I had to play that role."

Particular roles notwithstanding, all the players shared the media-conferred sense of self as celebrity. Raised to the status of stars, larger than life, they regularly read their names and statements in the newspaper, saw their faces on television, or heard themselves whispered about on campus. One team member described the consequences of this celebrity:

"We didn't always necessarily agree with the way they wrote about us in the paper, but people who saw us expected us to be like what they read there. A lot of times it made us feel uncomfortable, acting like that, but we had to act like they expected us to, for the team's sake. We had to act like this was what we was really like."

Ironically, however, the more they interacted with people through their [media-induced] selves, the more many of the team members felt familiar and comfortable with those selves ("We know what to do, we don't have to think about it no more"). The media presented the selves and the public believed in them, so the athletes continued to portray them. Even though they attempted to moderate these selves, part of them pressed for legitimacy and acceptance. Over time, the athletes believed these portrayals increasingly [and became]...more engrossed or more deeply involved in their media selves. The recurrent social situations of their everyday lives served as the foils against which both their public and their private selves developed. The net effect of having these selves placed upon them and of interacting through them with others was that athletes eventually incorporated them into their core self....

Source: Patricia Adler and Peter Adler, "The Gloried Self," *Social Psychology Quarterly* 52, 1989, pp. 299–310. Reprinted by permission of the American Sociological Association.

assessments of others are equally important. If others keep telling you what a great student you are and treat you like a genius, you are likely to accept their judgments and see yourself as intelligent. A similar process applies for traits like attractiveness or celebrity. If others continually define you as a "fox" or a "hunk," you are likely to incorporate these views—and the behaviors they imply—into your self-concept.[5]

Through the concept of the looking-glass self, Cooley highlighted how people come to know themselves through the responses of others. However, as we alluded above, Cooley did not have a one-sided or overly socialized view of self-development. He did not presume that our sense of self simply or directly reflects the appraisals we receive from others. Instead, he noted that we selectively interpret and respond to the feedback of others. (We will discuss this point at more length in Chapter Five.) In fact, Cooley emphasized that "the self-respecting [person]... discriminates and selects, considers all suggestions with a view to his [or her] character, and will not submit to influences not in line of his [or her] development."[6] Cooley also stressed that we develop and express a feeling of selfhood through active appropriation, or behaviors in which we lay claim to, or strive to possess, things as our own.[7] Cooley saw this behavior reflected in the assertive and sometimes aggressive acts of young children who exclaim "'*my*,' '*mine*,' 'give it to *me*,' '*I* want it,' and the like," often in opposition or resistance to others.[8] In a related vein, Cooley recognized that even as adults, our feelings of "me," "mine," and "I" are "applied with a strong sense of their meaning only to things distinguished as peculiar to us by some sort of opposition or contrast" to others.[9] Thus, Cooley did not regard the self as something we passively acquire and sustain through our interactions with others.

While Cooley offered a groundbreaking view of how we form a self through both reflected appraisals and appropriative activity, his theory of self-development had a notable shortcoming; that is, it did not explain how we develop the ability to know others or take their perspective. Fortunately, one of Cooley's colleagues, George Herbert Mead, took up this task and presented a profound account of how individuals learn to take the perspective of others.[10] Mead proposed that children acquire the capacity for **role taking** through their primary socialization. They acquire this ability gradually, through three sequential phases or stages:[11] the preparatory stage, the play stage, and the game stage.

The Preparatory Stage

Mead suggested that early in life the child lacks a developed sense of self and has difficulty distinguishing his or her own roles from the roles of others. At this point the child imitates parents or immediate others, but only occasionally. Imagine yourself as a toddler. When you feel like it, you mimic your parents or siblings. When your mom or dad reads a book, you turn the pages in your own book. When your older brother sweeps the floor, you get out your play broom and sweep, too. When your older sister dances, you dance along with her. You even attempt to imitate your parents when they say "Mom" and "Dad" by responding "ma" and "da." Imitation is a key part of your activity and development, but it does not, in itself, amount to role taking. You are merely mimicking others' behavior without fully understanding what it means. In this process, however, you learn that your actions evoke responses in others. Perhaps you learn that crying leads to being held and comforted. Thus, you develop a mental image of cause and effect between sounds and acts. Through repeated experiences and the images of cause and effect they produce, you learn the meaning of various objects and words.[12] An especially important learning experience occurs when you recognize that you have a "name," such as Kate or Carlos, that identifies *you* and distinguishes you from others. After you learn your name, your capacity for self-reflection emerges. That is, you start to think about and act toward yourself as a social object—as a self that others respond to. Up to this time you are in the preparatory stage, engaging in behavior that you do not associate with words or symbols.

The Play Stage

As you grow older, you acquire language and develop the ability to label objects and people with words that have shared meaning—words like *mom, dad, baby, cat,* and *car.* You learn to use significant symbols. You also learn to play at the roles made apparent by important people around you, such as your family members. Based on your observations of these others, you incorporate their words and deeds into your play. You emulate others through two types of play. First, you play at roles performed by *significant others,* such as your parents. In modeling your parents' actions, you may have pretended to shave, vacuum, cook, or tend to your baby brother. By placing yourself in the role of parent, you treat yourself, for the moment at least, as being like your mother or father. In doing so you also prepare yourself for eventually becoming a parent in the future and for communicating with others who play this role. Sociologists refer to this form of play as anticipatory socialization.

At the same time, you engage in other forms of play that do not directly prepare you for future roles. Perhaps you play the role of fantasy others,[13] such as pirates, Ninja warriors, or intergalactic heroes. Through this play you practice creating, assuming, and performing influential roles. For instance, in assuming the part of an intergalactic hero, you act as if you can fly a spacecraft, dodge enemy attacks, face down a gruesome creature, and blast it with a ray gun. As a result, you see yourself as powerful and competent. Or, to put this in Mead's terms, you respond to yourself in terms of the role that you are playing.

In describing the nature and outcomes of role taking in the play stage, Mead stressed that as a young child you can assume only one role at a time and you often move quickly from playing at one role to playing at another. Overall, your role-taking activities are inconsistent and unorganized. Further, you do not yet possess a crystallized or unified image of self.[14] As Mead remarked when describing a child's qualities in the play stage:

> The child is one thing at one time and another at another, and what he is at one time does not determine what he is at another. That is both the charm of childhood as well as its inadequacy. You cannot count on the child; you cannot assume that all the things he does are going to determine what he will do at any moment. He is not organized into a whole. The child has no definite character, no definite personality.[15]

Yet, while Mead pointed out the inconsistent nature of a child's activities and character during this phase of socialization, he also highlighted how the child's involvement in role playing permits the acquisition of a more developed sense of self. Through playing at the role of significant others, real or imaginary, you (as a child) learn to respond to yourself in the same way as these others respond. At this point, you may not understand how the roles you play, and the selves implied by them, fit into a larger role system. Slowly you become more socially astute and self-reflexive. As you engage in more complex activities, evaluating yourself from multiple perspectives, your sense of self develops.

The Game Stage

After you become skillful in taking the role of specific others, you are faced with a growing number of situations where you must respond to the expectations and perspectives of several people simultaneously. According to Mead, you develop the capacity to do so through participating in games. Games differ from play because they have an organized body of rules, or regulated procedures, toward which individuals must orient their actions and interactions. In contrast to play, games require you to respond to yourself in terms of the interrelated roles assumed by other participants. To participate in a game, one must take the perspective of all the other players.

Through interacting with peers in the games, you develop skill at taking a variety of perspectives and formulating your actions in relation to these perspectives. You begin to look at yourself not only through the eyes of a specific other, but through the eyes of a group or "team." To illustrate this process, Mead used the example of baseball. When playing baseball, you have to see your position in relation to the other players. If you are playing left field and a ground ball is hit toward you, you need to take a number of perspectives to make the best play. If there are base runners, you need to see the play as they would to assess where to throw the ball. At the same time, you must imagine what your coaches and teammates expect. After fielding the ball, you will need to gauge the actions of the infielders. Your eventual choice of where to throw the ball will be based on your understanding of the actions of the runners and infielders. This understanding will derive from your ability to take their roles and see yourself in terms of these roles.

Mead recognized that children gradually develop this advanced role-taking capacity as they participate in games like baseball. Their role taking becomes more sophisticated as they gain more experience in games. We can observe this when watching children of different ages playing baseball. In many communities in the United States, young boys and girls play tee-ball, hitting a cushioned ball off of a batting tee. As they grow older, these boys and girls move on to the more challenging games of baseball and softball. In all of these games, players are expected to hit a ball, run around bases, and get opponents out by fielding the ball and throwing it to the correct bases. Tee-ball games, however, have a much more disorganized flavor than the baseball or softball games. Although fun to watch, tee-ball players often have little awareness of what is happening around them. When the ball is hit toward them, they might run toward it or away from it. At times nearly all of the fielders will run toward the batted ball, abandoning their positions. (One of the authors remembers how during his son's first tee-ball game, every player on the field tried to retrieve a ball hit to deep center field, much to the delight of the batter, who trotted around the uncovered bases.) Frequently tee-ball players are not very clear about what to do, even if they pick up the ball when it is hit to them. Coaches and parents may yell "Throw it to first!" or "Tag the runner!" but the players often ignore these instructions, instead choosing to chase the runner and throw the ball at him or her. While amusing, this behavior clearly shows that the players do not have the ability to take the role of several others or to coordinate their actions with them. By contrast, older players are much more aware of the expectations of other players. When the ball is hit to them, they anticipate the actions of their opponents and teammates. They know where the ball should be thrown and who will be there to catch it. This knowledge allows them to make complex plays that involve the exchange of several throws.

In Mead's view, these older players have acquired the crucial capacity to take the role of several others and to combine these roles into a consistent symbolic perspective. They can take the role of the **generalized other**. The generalized other refers to the perspectives and expectations of a network of others, or of the community as a whole. When assuming this perspective, we respond in terms of the organized roles of others and their shared standards. We see ourselves from the vantage point of the community (e.g., the team) and embrace their rules, expectations, and perspectives. Their standards and outlooks become our own.

Through internalizing the standards and outlooks of the generalized other, we acquire a more consistent and unified self. We no longer change our images of self dramatically as we interact with specific others, as we did during the play stage. Instead, we combine others into an integrated and consistent whole—"society." Our image of self thus develops and becomes more unified as our understanding of society develops and becomes more unified. In essence, as our social experiences become more varied and complex, we acquire a more stable self, or what Mead called "a self in the fullest sense."[16]

In highlighting the stages through which we develop our capacities for role taking, Mead offered a profound sociological insight. He argued that the self is fundamentally *social* in its origins and development. The self emerges and becomes established through our relationships and interactions with others. Through these interactions, we learn to take the role of others and see ourselves as social objects. This capacity is the essence of selfhood.

Yet Mead did not propose a socially deterministic conception of selfhood and human nature. While emphasizing the social roots and nature of the self, Mead did not suggest that we merely internalize and conform to the expectations and appraisals of those with whom we interact. He believed that we have the power to shape ourselves, others, and the larger society. In fact, Mead stressed that we are not simply constrained by society or the community as a result of our socialization. Discussing the relationship between the individual and community, he made the following remarks:

> We can reform the order of things....We are not simply bound by the community. We are engaged in a conversation [i.e., symbolic interaction] in which what we say is listened to by the community and its response is affected by what we have to say....The process of communication is one in which the individual not only has the right but the duty of talking to the community of which [s]he is a part, and bringing about those changes which take place through the interaction of individuals.[17]

Mead believed that the basis of the individual's ability to "talk back to" and influence the community was, ironically, the social self, or the capacity to act toward the self as an object. This capacity gives us the ability to communicate with ourselves as we do with others. We can criticize ourselves, argue with ourselves, take pride in ourselves, build up our courage, or tell ourselves how to act. Above all, we can think, plan, anticipate the consequences of engaging in different behaviors and adjust and direct our actions accordingly. These abilities allow us to construct lines of behavior actively and creatively rather than simply react to the expectations of others.

Through his insightful analyses, Mead revealed the importance of the socialization process in shaping the contents and expressions of our sense of self. He demonstrated how the self can be seen as a social product, emerging through our interactions with others and developing in accord with our increasingly sophisticated abilities to internalize the attitudes of others and view the self as a social object. As a result of these social processes, we acquire a self that is a "society in miniature"—that is, a self consisting of a dialogue among many internalized roles and perspectives. This profoundly social self is a means through which we regulate our behavior, adjust it to others' expectations, and construct meaningful acts.

Refinements of Mead's Theory of Socialization and Self-Development

While inspired by Mead's contributions, interactionist scholars have subsequently critiqued and clarified his ideas, elaborating on the processes and activities through which people engage in socialization and acquire selves. For example, Cathryn Johnson has identified several stages of emotional development which are interdependent with the preparatory, play, and game stages discussed by Mead. In doing so Johnson extends Mead's model, particularly by portraying how people develop the capacity for emotionality. Johnson describes seven developmental stages through which we "learn to share emotions with others, and learn to identify and interpret our own and others' emotional selves."[18] Most importantly, she demonstrates the intricate interconnections between self-development and emotional development.

Other analysts have offered more specific refinements of Mead's model of socialization and self-development. For instance, drawing on his studies of young children, Gregory Stone revised and extended Mead's ideas about the play stage of socialization.[19] Stone offered three general criticisms of Mead's analyses of children's behavior in this stage. First, he suggested that the activities Mead described as children "playing at roles" is more accurately conceptualized as childhood *drama*. Stone contended that defining this behavior as drama enables us to better distinguish it from other play forms, such as tests of poise, which become important in socialization and self-development. Second, Stone critiqued Mead for failing to make a conceptual distinction between the visible and immediate roles that children play at and the less visible and mythical roles they enact in their play. According to Stone, these two types of play should be categorized separately as anticipatory drama and fantastic drama. In the former, the child adopts perspectives and identities that she is likely to assume in later years; in the latter, the child assumes perspectives and identities she is not likely to enact or encounter in the future. Finally, Stone argued that Mead erred when assuming that children are openly aware of the roles they perform in their dramatic play. This often does not hold true. Children are frequently ignorant or unaware of some contents of the roles they play, such as the details of what a parent actually does when working or cooking. Children may also be unaware of the nuances of a role, such as how a parent deals with money problems or handles tensions with in-laws.

Following the lead of Stone, William Corsaro has closely examined the activities of younger children and expanded Mead's ideas about play and self-development.[20] Corsaro illustrates how one important form of play engaged in by young children, "spontaneous fantasy," has implications for self-development and communication skills. In their spontaneous fantasies with friends, children imaginatively take on the qualities of all kinds of creatures. As they engage in this play,

children create new and ever-evolving worlds of imagination and innovation.[21] Most important, spontaneous fantasy serves as a means by which children learn valuable lessons and skills for adult life and interactions. For instance, through jointly fighting monsters, aliens, lions, or other imagined dangers, young children develop their skills at coping with dilemmas, threats, and uncertainties that arise in everyday life. They also acquire communication strategies and turn-taking abilities that help them coordinate their actions with others, establish group cohesion, and build a peer culture. In addition, children's collaborative fantasies teach them how to make plans, exercise leadership, interpret other's signals, deal with unexpected events, and quickly redirect their actions. All these skills prepare children to navigate their way through the complex social worlds they will enter as they grow older.

Through his insightful research on fantasy play, Corsaro has illustrated how young children hone their skills at communication, interpretation, and imaginative role taking. He demonstrates that these children participate as active agents in their socialization and self-development. Corsaro extends Mead's theoretical analyses, especially by revealing how spontaneous fantasy enables children to enhance their interaction skills, build and share a peer culture, and fashion meaningful selves.[22]

Along with Stone and Corsaro, other symbolic interactionists have tried to clarify Mead's notions about socialization and the genesis of the self. In the 1970s Norman Denzin, examining childhood socialization, argued that by the age of three, most children can systematically take one another's roles, present selves, construct intricate games, and influence adults. Denzin challenged those who claimed that children automatically pass through the play and game stages of socialization as they age. Based on his ethnographic study of preschool children, Denzin argued that the "movement from one stage to another is contingent on the development of sufficient language skills and on the presence of interactive experiences."[23] He emphasized that Mead nowhere specified the age sequence of the play and game stages and implied that "some persons may never progress to the generalized other phase of taking the other's attitude."[24] Denzin concluded that the course of children's self-development is shaped by their context, with the most important factor being the patterns of interaction to which they are exposed. Overall, Denzin pointed out that children's self-development is not tied directly to their chronological age but, instead, is linked to their *interactional* age and experience. In Denzin's view, if children experience exceptional and enriching interactions, their capacity for self-reflexivity arises more rapidly and progresses more fully. Thus, parents who are actively involved in their children's upbringing should have positive effects on their reflective and social skills.

Another interactionist, Tamotsu Shibutani, refined Mead's theory of self-development in a somewhat different way. Shibutani elaborated on Mead's ideas about the evolution of the "generalized other." Mead implied that what starts as one generalized other develops into many as an individual's role-taking abilities and social worlds expand. Shibutani extended this argument by suggesting that individuals learn to adopt a number of general, orienting perspectives, especially within complex industrial societies.[25]

In modern life, people interact with various groups, become involved in these groups, and come to share a "reference perspective" with other members. This perspective guides their actions in a specific social world, such as a classroom, and shapes their views of themselves in this context. To understand this idea, think of the perspective you adopt as a student. Whose outlooks and standards do you take into account in deciding how to act? Are you guided primarily by what you believe your classmates think and expect? By what your friends think and expect? By what your professors think and expect? Would you adopt the same reference perspective when attending a party? According to Shibutani, the group whose perspective you use to organize your thoughts, actions, and self-images in

a given social world is your **reference group**. It serves as a generalized other for you. As you participate in a number of different contexts, you adopt the perspectives of many reference groups. You do not simply take the role of one generalized other to define and direct your "self"; you assume the role of several generalized others. While Mead vaguely alluded to this idea in his theory of self-development, Shibutani made the claim more explicit. Shibutani also pointed out how the adoption of many reference perspectives is a byproduct of our involvement in increasingly complex, diverse, and differentiated social worlds. In recent years other interactionists have accentuated this point, highlighting how the fragmentation in our "postmodern" society is reflected in our outlooks and self-images.

Finally, in recent years interactionists such as Leslie Irvine have suggested that Mead's language-driven model of self-development needs to be significantly revised and extended. Based on her studies of people and their companion animals, Irvine argues that animals such as dogs and cats have the capacity for selfhood and, thus, may not be as different from humans as Mead proposed and as people commonly think. More specifically, Irvine contends that "factors beyond spoken language matter for the creation of the self" and that cats and dogs possess several dimensions of subjectivity that constitute a "core" self.[26] These dimensions include (1) a sense of agency, (2) a sense of bodily coherence, (3) a sense of emotion, and (4) a sense of self-history. Irvine also asserts that animals have the capacity to role take and, correspondingly, to share thoughts, feelings, and intentions with their human companions. She points out that

> [t]he selves of animals, evinced through agency, affectivity, coherence, and history, acquire another dimension through interaction that reveals their capacity to share thoughts and feelings. Although we humans can put our accounts of this experience into words, the capacity for intersubjectivity does not depend on language.[27]

In sum, Irvine's research poses significant challenges to Mead's model by suggesting that it needs to move past the limits of spoken language in conceptualizing the stages of socialization and the development and experience of selfhood. In the future, interactionist researchers are likely to take up this challenge by extending their studies of animal selfhood and selfhood among "alingual" persons, such as individuals living with advanced Alzheimer's disease or severe mental disabilities.[28]

SOCIALIZATION AND THE CREATION OF GENDER IDENTITY

Symbolic interactionists emphasize that as we become socialized, we not only define ourselves as members of a society, but recognize that we are members of a gender. We learn to identify ourselves as male or female and to think, feel, and act according to gender expectations. In other words, we develop a **gender identity,** a deeply held image of self as masculine or feminine.[29]

Many people find it difficult to accept that gender identity is socially acquired. For them, being male or female is a matter of nature rather than socialization. They point to the physical and hormonal differences between boys and girls and contend that they inevitably result in social, emotional, and behavioral differences. To some extent this is true, but in response symbolic interactionists emphasize how boys' and girls' feelings, actions, and identities are also shaped by their relationships with others. While acknowledging that children are born with the biological features of one sex or another, interactionists note that children are assigned to a gender category at birth and then learn what this category means in their society. Children do not inherit a "natural" understanding of how to act "masculine" or "feminine" or how to classify themselves in terms of these categories. They acquire this understanding through their interactions.

In examining how children learn the meanings of masculinity and femininity, interactionists and other sociologists have highlighted the influence exerted by *agents of socialization*, including parents, siblings, teachers, peers, churches, the mass media, and even language. From birth, parents socialize boys and girls into separate gender roles through differences in touch, talk, emotional response, play activities, and toy and book choices.[30] In addition, teachers promote gender differences by segregating boys and girls in classroom seating arrangements, assigning boys and girls to sex-stereotyped classroom chores, organizing contests between boys' and girls' teams, interacting more often with boys than girls, and subjecting boys to harsher punishments for misbehavior.[31] Nevertheless, while parents and teachers influence children's gender development, children are not completely passive or powerless in this process. Children actively participate in their own gender socialization and in the shaping of their gender identities. In doing so, they do not always mirror or reproduce the gender ideals of the adult world.

Creating Gender Identity in Early Childhood

One of the interactionists who has illustrated the active part that children play in acquiring and creating gender identities is Spencer Cahill.[32] Cahill notes that children are born into a social world divided by gender. In looking to their social surroundings, they discover that clothing and hair length are used as criteria for categorizing people into different genders. A child growing up in the United States learns that men usually have shorter hair than women, typically wear shirts and pants, and do not wear dresses. These cultural cues provide the child with standards for gender classification and give him or her a framework for making sense of physical differences between people. In this respect, the child relies on the same cultural cues that adults routinely use when judging gender.

Drawing on these cultural cues, the young child also learns how to display his or her own gender appropriately. As the child grows out of infancy, he or she learns how to dress, look, and act in order to be recognized as a boy or girl. In this sense, being a boy or girl is not something that a child is but something that he or she *does*. In developing the capacity for self-reflection, the child also learns to define himself or herself as a boy or girl. The child is guided in this process by the gender labels applied to him or her by parents and other caregivers. When these adults call the child a "big boy" or "big girl," the child tends to define himself or herself in these terms.

A second important component of becoming a boy or girl is gender display. Because a child strongly values his or her gender identity, he or she seeks to confirm it through gender displays that evoke positive responses. In fashioning these displays, the child models behavior after the actions and appearances of same-sex others seen at home or in books, movies, and TV shows. The child does not simply imitate these others, but actively constructs a gender appearance and identity drawing on their behavior.[33]

As Cahill points out, young children test the appropriateness of gender displays in their interactions with others. When they do so they learn that their displays may be rejected. Consequently, young children's gendered behavior and self-images are influenced by the responses of others, especially significant others like parents. But young children also discover that they can influence the gender-related responses and actions of others. For instance, they learn that by labeling activities as "boys only" or "girls only," they can effectively exclude others.

As children enter the period of preadolescence, they interact more frequently in same-sex peer groups and perform more gender displays that are designed to elicit approval from peers rather than parents or other adults. Children become oriented toward their peers and the construction of a **peer culture**—a culture that both reflects and resists the values and practices of mainstream adult culture. This peer culture is characterized by its own strategies of gender socialization and identity development. In the following section we examine and highlight these gendered dynamics.

Re-creating Gender Identity: Preadolescent Culture and Play

Guided by a desire to understand the development of small group cultures, Gary Alan Fine engaged in a three-year study of the interactions of nine- to twelve-year-old boys who played Little League baseball.[34] By observing these boys in games and practices, as well as by hanging out with them when they were "doing nothing," Fine learned how they created a common peer culture and socialized each other into its moral code—a code that shaped their images and performances of masculinity. This moral code had four key elements, each of which involved the display of gender-appropriate feelings and behaviors.

The first element of the code was *toughness*. The boys actively emphasized and displayed toughness through aggressive remarks that indicated that they would "pay their dues" for the sake of the team and "take out" (or injure) opponents when expected to do so. The boys also conveyed toughness by continuing to play when they got hurt and by repressing their fears when feeling intimidated, such as when facing a pitcher who had a "wicked fastball." Players who failed to display these behaviors often became the targets of their teammates' sarcasm and disapproval.

The second important element in the moral code was *emotional self-control*. The boys believed that it was essential to control their feelings and show stoic acceptance of the world, something that was more challenging for some boys than others. For example, a few of the boys cried or moped when things didn't go their way, others expressed anger frequently or loudly, and some showed high sensitivity to pain. When these boys didn't successfully keep their anger, tears, or complaints under control, their teammates communicated that this behavior was wrong and ought to be kept in check, even if they felt some sympathy.

In addition to emphasizing toughness and self-control, the boys in Little League expected each other to be competitive and to have a strong *desire to win*. They resented or criticized teammates who were not seen as contributing to the goal of victory. Winning was a primary value for these boys, especially if they were members of strong teams. They even saw winning through forfeit as preferable to losing. Along with the value they placed on winning, the boys stressed the virtue of looking like a "winner," particularly through emulating the appearance of major league ballplayers. Those boys who showed up for games in dirty uniforms or mismatched socks became the objects of sarcastic teasing. Their clothing didn't appear "professional" and thus didn't communicate the appropriate message about who they should be on the diamond.

Finally, the boys in Little League championed the virtue of *in-group unity and loyalty*. They demonstrated this loyalty through cheering for teammates, refusing to "rat" on one another, and accepting the moral evaluations of the team and coaches. They also exhibited group loyalty and unity through observing the unstated moral rule that no player should make himself out to be better than his peers. Players who broke this rule were stigmatized for acting too "hot" or "cool" and, when making excessive claims for themselves, got labeled as "hot dogs," "prima donnas," or "braggarts." While others could talk up a boy's abilities, the boy himself could not. Most important, all of the boys learned their place in the peer hierarchy and took steps to enforce this hierarchy when others stepped out of place. Their status and behavioral displays as players became profoundly moral in character.

The values of toughness, emotional control, winning, and loyalty stressed in the peer culture of Little Leaguers parallel the stereotypical masculine ideals embraced by many adults in the United States. The moral code of these boys in many ways reflects the code of masculinity that exists in the larger society. As Fine has illustrated, however, because preadolescent boys don't have the cognitive abilities and social experience of older males, they often display and talk about masculine behavior in an exaggerated manner. They do so through participating in "dirty play."[35]

The dirty play of preadolescent boys takes place primarily within their friendship groups and revolves around two themes: sex and aggression. As Fine points out, preadolescent boys devote considerable time to talk about sexuality. They quickly recognize that an ability to talk about sex brings them credit and bolsters their status in the eyes of peers. They also learn that sexual talk serves as a means to convince others that they are sexually mature, active, and knowledgeable. Through this talk, preadolescent boys demonstrate their manhood to their same-sex peers. They also align themselves to the values of their peer culture.

Fine discovered that the sexual talk and activity of preadolescent boys took on a variety of forms. (See Box 4-2 for a more detailed illustration and discussion of some of these forms.) For instance, they teased one another about crushes on girlfriends, thereby ensuring that they remained loyal to each other and pursued only "suitable" female partners. The boys also talked at length about their sexual exploits and tried to impress each other with their knowledge of erotic activities such as "French kissing." In addition, they often exaggerated their contact with girls, claiming that they had girlfriends when they actually interacted with the girls most frequently in groups or through intermediaries. Often the boys attempted to define their sexualized selves by talking about that aspect of sexuality they viewed as the opposite of sexual maturity: homosexuality. Although they knew little about homosexuality, they used the label of "gay" (as well as other homophobic terms) to stigmatize others as immature or insufficiently masculine. At the same time, they implicitly claimed that they were "mature" and appropriately masculine.

Closely related to the sexual talk and activity of preadolescent boys was their need to show that they were masculine by being daring and bold. They did this by aiming insults at each other, often in a sexual way, and by directing aggressive pranks toward strangers. These pranks varied in different communities but included activities such as "egging" houses, "mooning" traffic, making prank phone calls, and playing "Ding Dong Ditch" (ringing doorbells and running away). Typically the boys took part in this ritualized dirty play with a good friend and then described the details of their adventure to other peers or friends in order to exhibit their bravery and masculinity.

In analyzing these pranks, Fine observed that although adults may see them as "deviant" or "awful," they are best understood as social actions that preadolescents use to shape their public identities. Through these acts, which are viewed as heroic by peers, preadolescent boys claim and shape identities in arenas dominated by people of higher age and status. They engage in pranks as a way to display positive qualities of self, such as daring and emotional control, and to gain renown in their peer group.

Overall, Fine emphasized that the pranks and other dirty play of preadolescent boys serve important purposes in their moral and gender socialization. First, these actions enable them to define themselves in opposition to other groups who share some of their characteristics, such as preadolescent girls. Through teasing or tormenting girls, preadolescent boys erect a barrier. In this process they gain a distinctive sense of who they are and experience a strong measure of communal feeling. Second, the dirty play of preadolescent boys socializes them to society's expectations. This play "is a transformation of things boys see enacted by older boys or by adults, or learn about through the media."[36] It reflects and emerges from the unofficial morality that gets transmitted in the socialization process, such as aggression,

sexism, and racism. While adults often wish that children did not get exposed to this seamier side of public morality, children pick it up through various sources and occasionally express and reinforce it in their play. But these expressions of unsavory play are best understood as the attempts of preadolescent boys to act "mature" and live up to adult standards. That is, in an effort to validate their maturity, these boys talk and act in ways that address issues from which they had previously been excluded.

In evaluating the dirty play of preadolescent boys, we must remember that this play frequently occurs within friendship groups. These groups serve as staging areas for socialization and self-development.[37] Within them, preadolescent boys find a supportive environment for performing activities considered improper elsewhere. This environment allows them to test their poise and display their daring without having to face major threats to self. Friendship groups also give preadolescents a forum for acquiring knowledge and learning behaviors, such as sexual techniques, without embarrassment. Moreover, these groups offer preadolescents a relatively safe atmosphere for presenting different identities and for discovering the appropriate self they should project in various situations. Through interacting with their friends, preadolescents learn what actions and identities are "cool," "lame," or "dorky."

Fine's analyses of the talk, play, and friendships of Little Leaguers reveal how boys powerfully influence each other's gender socialization and self-development. Through their interactions with peers, boys in Little League learn those values that define masculinity within their peer culture and, to a large extent, reflect the images of masculinity that prevail in the broader culture. Most crucially, through taking the role of their peers (as a "generalized other"), these boys learn how they are supposed to channel their behavior, suppress their tears or complaints, control their bodies, and manage their appearance. In essence, they learn what it means to be masculine and how to act like men.

Box 4–2 SEXUAL THEMES IN MALE PREADOLESCENCE

One of the authors of this book, Gary Alan Fine, conducted an ethnographic study of Little League baseball, titled *With the Boys*. While "hanging around" with the preadolescent boys who played in Little League, Fine noticed that they spent a great deal of time talking about sex and members of the opposite sex. In the following excerpt he describes how and why they engage in this form of talk.

Males maturing in our sexualized society quickly recognize that sexual prowess is a mark of maturity. One must convince others that one is sexually mature, active, and knowledgeable. Boys must try to be men. Although the techniques change, males throughout the life course are subject to the same demanding requirements.

Often evaluations occur while teasing a boy about his taste in members of the opposite sex. When boys see another's girlfriend, they often playfully remark how unattractive she is: Frank is joking about Stew's girlfriend in Stew's presence: "She's about this tall [he extends his arm far over his head to indicate her height] and weighs ten pounds." Part of the humor is that Stew is short and somewhat stocky. Stew admits that he knows this girl but claims he doesn't like her (although from his tone I gather he does) (field notes, Sanford Heights).

Justin, Whitney, Harry, and Ray are talking about girls:

Justin: (talking about Kip Taviss' girlfriend): I think Nancy's a jerk.

Ray: Tell Taviss that.

Justin (laughing): I will.

Harry: If anyone acts doofy, Laurel acts doofy. [Laurel is Whitney's girlfriend.] (field notes, Hopewell)

Rich Toland has a crush on his new girlfriend, Erica. He tells his friends: "I've got the best girlfriend I've ever had. She's the cutest girl my age [12] I've ever seen. We made out today." Because Erica lives on the other side of town, none of Rich's friends know her. Rich proudly invites Tom Jordan to come with him the next time he visits Erica. When Tom returns, he satirizes Erica's looks: "She was the ugliest girl I've ever seen. She has no teeth." (Tom then describes her teeth—he says "she has several very short teeth and one really long one, and a big nose.") Tom adds: "She isn't really, really bad, but she isn't great. She's the ugliest I've ever seen that anyone liked." After this Rich stops talking about Erica and soon stops seeing her (field notes, Sanford Heights).

Only the very few high-status preadolescents of the world, such as Justin or Tom, can get away with having a girlfriend without being ridiculed by their peers. Few could say what Tom told his friend Rich: "I love Sharon so god darn much....I'd make out every night with her if I could" (tape transcript, Sanford Heights). In one discussion of girls who attended the Hiawatha school, the consensus of the boys present was that Tom's girlfriend Sharon was the prettiest girl in school. While some objective standards of evaluation may be involved—even at this age some girls are considered more attractive than others, despite their beaus—these evaluations serve social control functions within the male group. First, they indicate that a "just world" is operating in terms of heterosexual relationships. A boy should not have a girlfriend of more status than he, even if his girlfriend has to be insulted. Further, these evaluations are a means by which the preadolescent leaders can underline their positions as opinion leaders by establishing the "correct" evaluation of girlfriends, as apparently happened in Tom's comments about Erica. Finally, this system warns males of the danger of becoming too affectionate toward females, as "objective" ratings are subject to change. Although boys desire to have girlfriends who are "cute" or "sexy," comments about a girl's charms are social constructions designed to typify her swain and prevent too much psychological intimacy....

Talk about sexual behaviors. Despite what boys (and journalists) sometimes claim, not much sexual behavior actually occurs—at least it did not in these suburban communities....Getting beyond "second base" is rare. Preadolescents may not be able to display their sexual sophistication by describing their own actions; however, they shape the perceptions that others have of them through their talk. Boys sometimes adopt a sexually swaggering stance in their conversations, as in this account of how to "French kiss":

Tom: First of all, you gotta make sure you don't get no more "Ahhhk!" burps in your mouth (Hardy and Frank both laugh). It would be very crude to burp.

Frank: And one thing, don't spit while frenching.

Tom: And make sure you don't breathe out of your mouth (all laugh) unless you're doing mouth-to-mouth resuscitation. After all that frenching, you just gotta do mouth-to-mouth to keep your air up. OK, now you take a squirt of your favorite after shave. You rub it on your hair, and you rub it all around you. And you (Tom giggles hysterically), and you rub it all around. It sure feels good (more giggling). Well, anyway, I get to my second lesson. First, you walk in, you see a sexy girl in the telephone booth. You don't know who she is, just see the back of her. Gotta make sure she doesn't have a big butt, you know. You just walk into the telephone booth, put your arm around her and say "Hi." And she goes "Uhhh! Ohhh, hi" [tone sounds surprised at first, then "feminine" and "willing"]. With her tongue around, wrapped around, wrapped around the microphone, her teeth, her teeth are chattering from so much shock. You just take your pants...no...well.

Hardy: You take her pants.

Tom: Well, you just stick out your tongue, and you say [Tom sings in a mock romantic fashion], "Want to, oh baby, you mean it, you get me under your skin." (taped transcript, Sanford Heights)

This conversation is not much different from those of other "precocious" preadolescents. Through the content of these conversations, boys learn what is expected of them by their peers. The significance of this talk does not derive from the acquisition of sophisticated techniques of French kissing (although some content learning does occur); rather, boys are presenting themselves to male peers as "males." This conversation fantasy dramatically suggests that males expect each other to be sexually aggressive and that females await their attempts with undisguised arousal. This short dialogue offers a world view that is consistent with male domination and female submission. By this talk, preadolescents acquire verbal skills that allow them to handle themselves within the context of similar lines of talk and prepare them to act like "males."

Source: Gary Alan Fine, *With the Boys: Little League Baseball and Preadolescent Culture* (Chicago: Universit\y of Chicago Press, 1987). Reprinted with permission of the University of Chicago Press. All rights reserved.

Like preadolescent boys, preadolescent girls also socialize one another into gender roles through their friendship groups and peer culture. In contrast to boys, however, girls are not as likely to gather in hierarchical cliques that enforce and enact a dominant set of gender expectations, or a hegemonic code of "femininity." Instead, girls "gather in different groups, or cliques, reflective of various ways to define femininity."[38] In other words, they join with other girls who define girlhood in the same way they do. Girls also form cliques "characterized by greater emotional intimacy, self-disclosure, and supportiveness" than those formed by boys.[39] In general, during their interactions with each other, preadolescent girls are far more likely to monitor each other's emotions and engage in gestures of intimacy (e.g., combing each other's hair and commenting on each other's appearance) than their male counterparts. In addition, they are more likely to focus on romance when talking about sexuality, to bond through sharing secrets, and to place a premium on being "nice" rather than "mean."[40] Moreover, while different cliques of girls define "niceness" in diverse ways, they usually equate this term with sharing, refraining from physical and direct aggression, and avoiding selfish behavior.[41] Girls, then, have a different experience of gender socialization within their peer culture than boys do. Through this experience they learn a different moral code—a code that places more emphasis on the values of niceness, emotional intimacy, romance, and concern for others than on toughness, emotional control, sexual conquest, and competition. Of course, not all girls stress "niceness" or cooperation in their interactions with each other. According to some researchers, girls who are poor, working class, or socially marginalized are more likely to value toughness, exchange insults, and play in hierarchical games than more privileged or popular girls.[42] Moreover, most girls act in a "mean" or hostile way toward others at times. For instance, McGuffey and Rich found that most girls are just as aggressive as boys when they become involved in personal conflicts. The only difference is that they display their aggression in different ways as they deal with these conflicts; that is, girls rely more on group exclusion and social manipulation (e.g., gossip and friendship bartering) than on physical violence.[43]

Boys and Girls Together: Learning and Maintaining Gender Boundaries

The analyses we highlighted in the previous section, such as those developed by Gary Alan Fine, illustrate how children socialize one another into gender identities through their same-sex interactions. These analyses, however, do not address another important question: How do children take part in gender socialization through their cross-sex interactions? Fortunately, a number of studies have examined this issue. These studies consider how boys and girls interact with one another in schools and how these interactions influence their constructions of gender and gender identities.[44]

Based on ethnographic studies of children in elementary schools, Barrie Thorne demonstrated that the daily worlds of preadolescent boys and girls are characterized by patterns of gender separation. Although parents, teachers, and other school officials often encourage this separation, boys and girls themselves also contribute to it. They do so by defining particular activities, spaces, and objects as exclusively "for boys" or "for girls." For example, on school playgrounds boys and girls recognize skateboard areas and large sports fields as boys' space, while they view hopscotch squares and jungle gym areas as girls' space. This demarcation of play areas clearly creates and reinforces gender separation.[45] These boundaries encourage boys and girls to interact primarily with members of their own gender and, correspondingly, to acquire different standards for evaluating their talk, actions, and identities.

Because they learn and abide by different standards, boys and girls often view themselves and their actions differently. They discover that they cannot present themselves in a way that consistently pleases all of their peers. They must orient their talk, actions, and selves to one of two gender audiences. Yet by doing so, boys and girls re-create the gender boundaries that promote the continued separation of their activities and identities.[46]

Thorne documents that the gender boundaries that are re-created and reaffirmed in children's interactions should not be viewed as impermeable. Nor should they be overstated. Preadolescent boys and girls regularly cross the gender divide and engage in some group activities, such as kickball and dodgeball, which have a balanced mix. The contacts between the genders, however, have a "with-then-apart" quality, and the "with" phase is as essential to the maintenance of gender boundaries as the "apart" phase. During their interactions together, boys and girls often emphasize and display their alleged differences, thereby placing themselves on "opposite sides" and heightening gender boundaries.

In explaining this phenomenon, Thorne developed the concept of **borderwork**. Borderwork refers to interaction that goes across gender boundaries but, rather than challenging or transcending these boundaries, reflects and even strengthens them.[47] This form of interaction occurs in the chase games that boys and girls regularly play together, such as "catch and kiss," "girls chase the boys," and "kiss and kill." These games are characterized by a gender structure and struggle. Within them, gender identities rather than individual identities rise to the forefront. This is reflected in frequently heard expressions such as "Help, a girl's chasing me!" or "C'mon, let's get that boy!"[48] The boys and girls taking part in these games define themselves and their interactions in gendered terms. They sort themselves into separate and opposing teams. In some cases the chasing contests become entangled with rituals of pollution, as in "cootie tag," where particular individuals or groups are labeled as contaminating. As Thorne reveals, a pattern of gender bias and inequality emerges as preadolescent boys and girls identify and transmit "cooties" in their chase games. Girls as a group become defined as

the ultimate source of contamination, while boys *as* boys do not become defined in this way.[49]

Although these definitions emerge in the context of play, they become important aspects of the borderwork that informs the gender identities of boys and girls. Thorne argues that chase games and other forms of borderwork activate and reinforce the dominant gender ideology in the United States. This gender ideology has two key features. First, it presents gender as a dualistic phenomenon—that is, it portrays boys and girls, or men and women, as not only different but as rivals who have a cautious, socially distant, and antagonistic relationship. In a related vein, this ideology presumes that males have and deserve more power than their female counterparts. The second key feature of the dominant gender ideology is its exaggeration of differences between the genders and its disregard for variations within each gender. According to Thorne, borderwork serves as a mechanism through which boys and girls call forth dominant gender beliefs and define themselves as separate and fundamentally different from one another. For instance, boys think of themselves as different from and better than girls, whom they associate with contamination. Girls, on the other hand, think of themselves as unlike and preferable to boys, whom they associate with aggression and trouble. Yet, while seeing themselves as preferable to boys, girls recognize that boys have distinct social advantages, such as the opportunity to enjoy more freedom, space, and power. This recognition, in turn, alters how girls see themselves, particularly by the time they reach junior high school—they learn that their status as a girl depends heavily on their ability to secure the approval of boys.[50]

In summarizing, the cross-gender borderwork of preadolescent boys and girls serves as a means through which they socialize one another into gender identities. As Thorne proposes, borderwork is a ritual form that expresses the realities of gender in our society and encourages children to accept these realities. But, as boys and girls engage in the rites of

Box 4-3 PLAYING IN THE GENDER TRANSGRESSION ZONE

In the following excerpt, Shawn McGuffey and Lindsay Rich highlight how boys and girls actively police the boundaries of acceptable gendered behavior, particularly as they play in the "gender transgression zone," or GTZ. In the process, McGuffey and Rich reveal how and why children negotiate gender boundaries as they interact in the GTZ. They also illustrate how and why high-status boys have more power than others to negotiate and challenge gender boundaries in this contested area.

Since boys and girls tend to organize themselves into gender-homogeneous [or same-sex] groups, they are generally aware that their sphere of gender-appropriate activities has boundaries. When they transgress these bounds, they enter a contested area that we refer to as the "gender transgression zone."[1] Since gender identity is a continual process whereby meanings are attributed by and to individuals through social interaction this contentious area is extremely consequential in the development of children. In the GTZ, gender boundaries are constantly being negotiated. Therefore, it is in the GTZ that we should expect to find continuities, as well as changes, in the construction of "gendered" activities and thus the definition of what is hegemonically [or dominantly] masculine and what is "other," typically defined as "effeminate."

Considering the importance of the GTZ as the social location where hegemonic notions of gender are challenged and defended, who ultimately decides the rules of negotiation in the GTZ and how? The evidence from this study suggests that high-status boys control the rules of the game in the GTZ....

High-status boys have the unique power of negotiating gender boundaries by accepting, denying, or altering gender codes. The power of high-status boys to alter boundaries was strikingly borne out by a series of events that, for weeks, redefined a feminine gender-stereotyped activity, hand-clapping games, into a hegemonically masculine one. This example of the defeminization (and thus, from the hegemonic standpoint, destigmatization of girls' behavior) illustrates the ruling dynamic of gender relations in the GTZ. In this camp, boys who even entertained the notion of playing hand-clapping games were confronted, ridiculed, and/or excluded by proponents of hegemonic masculinity.

Here is how the defeminization occurred. One day, right before the closing of the camp, Adam—the highest-ranked boy—was the only boy left waiting for his mother to pick him up. Four girls remained as well and were performing the Rockin' Robin hand-clapping routine. When one of the girls left, one of the three remaining girls asked Adam if he would like to learn the routine. He angrily replied, "No, that's girly stuff." Having been a camp counselor for three years, the first author knows every clapping routine from Bo Bo See Aut In Totin to Miss Susie's Steamboat. He, therefore, volunteered. The girls were amazed that he knew so many of what they referred to as "their" games. After a while, only two girls remained and Rockin' Robin requires four participants. Surprisingly, Adam asked to learn. Before he left, Adam had learned the sequence and was having a good time.

We believe that Adam transgressed for three reasons. One, all the other boys were gone, so there were no relevant or important (to him) witnesses to his transgression. Thorne repeatedly states that witnesses hinder gender deviance: "Teasing makes cross-gender interaction risky, increases social distance between girls and boys, and has the effect of making and policing gender boundaries."[2] Second, Adam saw the first author [Shawn McGuffey] participate freely in an activity that was previously reserved for girls. Third, as the highest-ranked boy, Adam has a certain degree of freedom that allows him to transgress with little stigmatization. Thorne asserts that the highest status boy in a hierarchy has "extensive social leeway" since his masculinity is rarely questioned. The next day, Adam was seen perfecting the routine he learned the day before. Many of the boys looked curiously and questioned why Adam was partaking in such an activity. Soon after, other boys started playing, and boys and girls were interacting heterosocially in what was formerly defined as a "girls-only" activity. Cross-gendered hand-clapping games continued for the rest of the summer and remained an area in which both girls and boys could come together. Defeminization occurred because Adam—the highest-status boy—set the standard and affirmed this type of entertainment as acceptable for boys. This incident supports our view that high-status boys control gender negotiations by showing that gender boundaries can be modified if someone of high status changes the standard of hegemonic masculinity.

To make hand-clapping more masculine, nonetheless, the first author documented boys changing the verses of the most popular hand-clapping game, Rockin' Robin, to further defeminize the activity. One of the original verses is, "All the little birdies on J-Bird Street like to hear the robin go tweet, tweet, tweet." The boys changed this to "All the little birdies on J-Bird Street like to hear robin say eat my meat!" About a month later, the first author discovered another altered verse from the boys. They changed "Brother's in jail waiting for bail" to "Brother's in jail raising hell!" Since these verses were not condoned at the camp—though we are sure the children used them out of the hearing distance of counselors—girls cleverly modified one of the profane verses by singing, "Brother's in jail raising H-E-double hockey sticks." This, too, the boys picked up and started applying as their own. Hand-clapping games moved from the girls' sphere to the GTZ. Defeminization of hand-clapping exposes the constant fluctuation and restructuring of gender norms in childhood play....[It also illustrates how children actively participate in defining and transforming what is considered acceptable behavior for their gender.]

1. Sharon Bird, "Welcome to the Men's Club: Homosociality and the Maintenance of Hegemonic Masculinity," *Gender and Society*, 10, 1996, pp. 120–132.
2. Barrie Thorne, *Gender Play: Girls and Boys in School* (New Brunswick, NJ: Rutgers University Press, 1993), p. 54.

Source: C. Shawn McGuffey and B. Lindsay Rich, "Playing in the Gender Transgression Zone," *Gender and Society* 13(5), 1999, pp. 608–627. Reprinted by permission of Sage Publications, Inc.

borderwork, they gain perspective into dominant gender patterns and find room to critique and resist, as well as reinforce, these patterns. As a result, the cross-gender rituals of preadolescents do not simply compel them to accept and reaffirm prevailing gender expectations; instead, these rituals serve as avenues through which preadolescents actively participate in the re-creation of gender norms and relations within the larger culture.

In analyzing the gender relationships of preadolescent children, Barrie Thorne, like Gary Alan Fine, illustrates how the peer culture and interactions of children function as mechanisms that allow them to make sense of adult culture and its values. Children often fail to understand adult messages fully, and, within their peer culture, they work out their confusion or uncertainty. By interacting with peers, children interpret, clarify, and test the values and scripts of the adult world. They also "fill in the gaps" of their socialization by adults. For example, through their peer culture they learn more details about what it means to be a male or female and how to display one's gender appropriately. This helps them to acquire the knowledge and skills necessary to participate in adult life. However, children's peer culture does not merely reflect or reestablish adult values and roles. In producing this culture, children build a social world that also questions adult authority, resists adult expectations, and influences adult culture. As the studies of Thorne and Fine suggest, the peer culture of children often challenges and criticizes adult authority and, at times, provokes change in the adult social order.

SOCIALIZATION AS AN ONGOING PROCESS: TURNING POINTS IN IDENTITY

In the preceding sections we have focused on the socialization of children. Now we turn our attention to the socialization of youth and adults. As individuals pass through childhood into adolescence and the various phases of adulthood, they go through many **status passages**, or "movements in and out of social statuses."[51] These passages differ greatly in their content, structure, and consequences for self. Some passages (graduations, weddings, religious confirmations) are guided by rules and rituals that specify when and how they can occur, who can be involved, what steps must be followed, and when new statuses are achieved. Other passages are far less structured and standardized. In most cases, status passages permit a wide range of choices and behavior among the individuals involved, even in deciding the details of how and when to enter a new status.

The specific nature of a passage depends to a large extent on such factors as whether it is voluntary or involuntary, desirable or undesirable, important or insignificant, sudden or gradual, planned or unexpected, reversible or irreversible, and individual or collective. Taken together, these factors influence how participants act during a status passage and, correspondingly, how they experience it and evaluate its implications for self. Consider a woman becoming a "mother." Her transition into this status will be quite different if she is thirty-two years old, deeply wants to have a baby, and has the strong support of a loving partner than it will be if she is sixteen years old, doesn't want the baby, and has little or no support from her boyfriend or parents. Obviously the latter case will be a more challenging passage into motherhood.

Regardless of the specific properties and dynamics of a passage, the person undergoing it participates in a process of socialization, learning what it means to occupy the new status, whether it is the status of mother, student, or corporate executive. In turn, the person depends on interactions with others to become educated about the rights and obligations that go along with this status. Sometimes this task is relatively easy. The individual has others around him or her eager to provide information and directives about what it means to enter a status, such as parent, and how the role should be performed. In other cases, though, statuses are not as significant or clearly defined (e.g., the status of a person with arthritis), and an individual's immediate others will not be able to offer much information or guidance.

Passage into Adulthood

As anthropologists and sociologists have documented, life in human societies is characterized by several major passages, including birth, childhood to adulthood, marriage (in many cases), divorce (in some cases), midlife, aging, and death. These transitions are sometimes marked by **rites of passage**, or rituals and ceremonies that accompany and help us to handle the changes in status we experience over the course of our lives. These rituals or ceremonies provide public acknowledgment of our entrance into a new status and also serve as community events that allow others to offer us gifts, advice, and emotional support.[52]

In tribal cultures, an individual's passage from childhood to adulthood is clearly marked by rites of passage.[53] For example, in the Cheyenne culture of the nineteenth century, a boy could only become a man through undergoing an elaborate ritual called a vision quest. From early boyhood he was instructed in how to prepare for and endure the tests involved in this ritual, which required him to live alone on a sacred mountain for four days and nights without food or water. During this time, the boy had to face the trials of loneliness, boredom, fear, hunger, and thirst, all the while seeking a vision for himself and the members of his tribe. After enduring these trials and seeing a vision, he returned to meet with the council of elders and tell them the story of his quest. They subsequently interpreted the boy's vision, gave him a new name based on it, and granted him acceptance into manhood. In turn, he was expected to ride and hunt with the other men in his tribe and to leave his childhood home. He also became eligible for marriage.

In a similar vein, a girl growing up in the Washoe nation could only enter womanhood after going through a ritual that required her to fast in a dark, sacred lodge for four days and three nights. Like the Cheyenne boy, she learned about the nature and importance of this rite of passage from the time she was a young child. In accord with tribal expectations, she was expected to go to the sacred lodge, which symbolized "Grandmother Earth," at the sign of her first period. Near the end of the fourth day, the tribe's "medicine grandmother" called her out of the lodge. After leaving the lodge, the girl had to run to the top of a nearby mountain carrying a basket of hot coals. When she reached the top of the mountain, she had to locate four piles of kindling, symbolizing the four dimensions of herself, and a brightly painted stick, representing her heart path. She then had to start the kindling on fire with the coals, praying for guidance and courage. When the smoke went up from the kindling, she could pick up the painted stick and race down the mountain to the village, where the entire tribe waited to celebrate her entrance into womanhood through an all-night Woman Dance. Her passage into womanhood was culminated the next morning when she went to a local stream and washed herself.

Obviously, the passage from childhood to adulthood is characterized by very different kinds of rituals and ceremonies in Western societies. It is also marked by a lengthy, transitional phase called adolescence—a phase in which an individual is "betwixt and between" the status of child and adult. Yet even during adolescence people go through rites of passage that indicate they are assuming some of the roles and responsibilities of adulthood. These include religious graduations, such as confirmation, bar-mitzvah, or batz-mitzvah. They also include benchmark events such as obtaining a driver's license, getting hired for a job, graduating from high school, going to college, turning eighteen (and losing one's legal status as a "minor"), and, in the United States, turning twenty-one and acquiring the legal right to drink alcohol.[54]

For many youth in the West, one of the notable markers of entrance into adulthood is leaving home to go to college. Like other major status passages, the transition from high school to college student is marked by three phases: separation, liminality, and incorporation.[55] Think about your own experiences during your senior year of high school. During this time, if not before, you began the process of separating from your status as a high school student. If you took the "traditional" path to college, you also started to prepare more seriously for your future life as a college student, looking at information about different institutions and thinking about what and where you wanted to study. You then decided which schools to visit, considered what majors to pursue, and made plans regarding roommates and places to live. So, in many senses, you began distancing yourself from the status of high school student long before you graduated. Of course, your official separation from that status took place at your high school commencement ceremony. This change in status was even marked by the rituals that characterized this ceremony, such as walking on the stage to receive your diploma and switching your tassel when the music sounded and signaled the end of the event. Most crucially, once the commencement was finished, you were no longer a high school student, even if you wanted to be. There was no turning back; you had officially become a high school graduate.

During the summer after your graduation, you entered the liminal phase of your passage into the status of college student. That is, you found yourself between your old and new student statuses. In this phase you most likely engaged in a careful assessment of which of your identities mattered most to you and reflected your sense of who you really wanted to be in the future.[56] You may have also started to worry more about what it actually meant to be a college student. Fortunately, the college or university you chose to attend probably invited you to an orientation session, both to ease your anxiety and to prepare you for your new status. When attending this session, you learned

about some of the details of college life, such as how and where to get a student i.d., how to set up your university email account, how to pick up your financial aid, how to register for classes, how to plan your academic program, how to get involved in campus activities or organizations, and how you could and couldn't act in the residence halls. You also had an opportunity to meet older students, academic advisors, faculty members, and other new students who shared their perspectives about what it meant to be a college student and what challenges you would encounter as you tried to balance the demands of studying, working, and spending time with friends.

After attending the orientation, you may also have talked with friends, siblings, or parents about their experiences in college, seeking their insights into "what you really need to know and do" to succeed as a college student. Most important, through going to the orientation and talking with a variety of others, you learned more about the new status you would occupy in the fall, reduced your uncertainty about it, and began to move into the incorporation phase of your status passage.

As you moved into your dorm room or apartment and/or started classes, you clearly stepped across the threshold into your new status as a college student and, in many respects, into the status of adult. These statuses became affirmed and incorporated into your sense of self by the changes in the institutional rituals and practices that occurred around you. For example, you no longer had to worry about getting tardy slips for being late to class or about getting a hall pass to leave a class early. Moreover, unlike high school, the start and end of your classes were not signaled by bells or buzzers and you didn't have to worry about having your attendance checked, at least in many of your classes. Instead, your instructors gave you much more responsibility for controlling your own schedule and behavior.

Your movement into and embracement of the status of college student was also facilitated by the new relationships you developed at your campus, the new activities you engaged in, the new study skills and habits you formed, the new knowledge you acquired, and the new ways you presented yourself to others and interacted with them. Additionally, your passage into your new status became more firmly cemented as you met the academic standards of college, such as passing exams, turning in quality papers, and receiving good (or at least acceptable) grades. Finally, if all went well, your transition and incorporation into the status as a college student was reinforced by the ways that significant others, such as your parents and friends, responded to you. For instance, they may have shown you new respect for the increased maturity you had shown since starting college or for the new knowledge or experiences you had acquired as a college student.

Most important, your interactions with others served as the means by which you became socialized into your status as a college student and learned what it meant for your sense of self, your everyday activities, and your future. In this respect, the process of becoming a college student shares a key property of other status passages—it is shaped by relationships and interactions.

Turning Points and Epiphanies: The Case of HIV/AIDS

Although a number of status passages are relatively routine, some become powerfully transforming events in a person's life. Symbolic interactionists refer to these events as "turning point moments" or **epiphanies**—moments of crisis or revelation that disrupt and alter a person's fundamental understandings, outlooks, and self-images.[57] These moments typically arise when a person is rapidly propelled from one status to another, either willingly or unwillingly. At times, these turning points occur after a period of training and preparation, as in the case of some religious baptisms and conversions.[58] Frequently, however,

they emerge when a person suddenly enters an unanticipated status.

Most people who contract a serious illness, such as terminal cancer or a major heart disease, experience an epiphany when they learn of their condition. After getting diagnosed, they become redefined socially. Their diagnosis casts them into a new and problematic health status—a status that disrupts and even shatters their previously cherished beliefs, routines, and self-images. This produces a crisis and initiates processes of identity transformation and resocialization. That is, individuals who are diagnosed with a serious illness are prompted to "make sense" of the meaning of their newly acquired health status and to feel its implications for their images and enactments of self. In doing so, they are guided by their social interactions and relationships.

To illustrate these processes, we will describe how individuals become "persons with HIV/AIDS."[59] Before doing so, we want to note that the Centers for Disease Control and Prevention (CDC) recently released a report indicating that rates of new HIV infection in the U.S. are substantially higher than previously reported. In fact, rates of HIV infection are 40 percent higher per year than the CDC had estimated.[60] Moreover, HIV rates have increased most significantly among three groups: Americans 13–29 years of age, African American men and women, and gay and bisexual men. HIV/AIDS also continues to be the leading cause of death for black women between the ages of 25 and 34 and the second leading cause of death among black men in that same age group.[61] Currently, the CDC estimates that more than 1.6 million people in the United States are living with HIV/AIDS.

So, what happens after an individual learns that he or she has an HIV infection? How does he or she become a "person living with HIV/AIDS"? An individual does not obtain this status simply by contracting a biological disorder known as HIV (human immunodeficiency virus); he or she must also go through a series of interpretive and interactive processes. Most often, individuals take the first steps toward becoming persons with HIV/AIDS by assessing their risk for the disease and deciding to have a diagnostic test. Of course, they are influenced in this process by information and concerns shared with them by others, including lovers, spouses, friends, or HIV/AIDS educators. When others evaluate these individuals as "at risk" for HIV and as needing to get tested, they are more likely to assess themselves in the same way. If they decide to get tested and HIV antibodies are found in their blood, they will receive a sero-positive diagnosis from a physician or medical specialist. At this point, they officially learn that they have HIV disease.

This discovery, however, marks a beginning rather than ending in the process of becoming a person with HIV/AIDS. An HIV diagnosis does not speak for itself. Those individuals who are diagnosed with HIV disease must figure out what this means for their lives. They determine the meaning of their health status in the same way that they determine other meanings—through interactions and relationships with others. They gauge how others define and respond to their HIV status and tend to define and respond to themselves similarly.

Let us illustrate this point by comparing the experiences of persons diagnosed with HIV/AIDS in the 1980s to those diagnosed more recently. During the early years of the AIDS epidemic, those diagnosed with HIV faced a hostile and fearful social environment and often were targets of discrimination, particularly if they were gay men. At that time, some conservative activists and religious leaders, such as Jerry Falwell and Pat Robertson, argued that AIDS revealed the "immoral" and "unnatural" nature of homosexuality and served as God's punishment. Moreover, medical researchers and the mass media described AIDS as a "homosexual cancer" or "gay plague." As a result, individuals diagnosed with HIV/AIDS encountered stigma and rejection in many of their social relationships, including relationships with co-workers, friends, family members, and lovers.

In addition to encountering these challenges to self, people with HIV/AIDS had difficulty finding physicians who could or would treat them during the early years of the epidemic. Many doctors knew little about HIV disease at that time, and some felt afraid to treat anyone infected. When persons with HIV sought treatment from these physicians, they often faced stigma and discrimination. Moreover, even when they found physicians who had some knowledge of HIV and who offered support, these individuals had no hope of receiving effective medications or treatments to delay the progression of their illness. They discovered that they were incurably and terminally ill.

As a result, people diagnosed with HIV in the early to mid-1980s reacted with profound shock, dismay, and despair. They saw themselves as modern-day "lepers" who were doomed to a rapid and unpleasant death. These definitions of self reflected the messages they received and the interactions they experienced. In many contexts, individuals with HIV/AIDS were encouraged to view themselves as tainted, threatening, and blameworthy, particularly if they were gay men. They had difficulty disregarding or countering these messages because they lacked access to resources that would allow them to define themselves and their illness more positively—resources such as effective medical treatments, nonstigmatizing definitions of HIV/AIDS, and supportive HIV-related networks.

During the past two decades, people living with HIV disease have gained greater access to effective medications, destigmatizing images of their illness, and HIV-related support systems. They have also received more understanding and assistance within workplaces, medical settings, friendship networks, and families. In turn, they have found it easier to define HIV disease in more positive ways (e.g., as a chronic and treatable condition) and to assert more favorable identities as persons "living with" this disease.

In spite of these improved circumstances, individuals diagnosed with HIV/AIDS in recent years must still grapple with disruption and challenges to self. After being diagnosed, they face the prospect of stigmatization, especially if they have engaged in injection drug use or nonnormative sexual activity. They also wrestle with the threat of major losses, including disruptions in their bodies, relationships, and futures. In making sense of their illness and its implications, these individuals are guided by the responses of their intimate others. If their lovers, friends, or family members react to them as if they are contaminated, disabled, or dying, they are likely to feel stigmatized. By contrast, if their intimate others continue to treat them "normally" and support them, persons with HIV are less likely to feel devalued and restricted by their illness, especially if they have access to antiretroviral medications that allow them to remain asymptomatic. The meanings they attach to their health status (and selves) arise from their ongoing interactions with intimate others.[62] These interactions are important arenas through which they become socialized into their HIV status.

In making this point, we also want to stress that people living with HIV disease play an active role in shaping the dynamics of their intimate interactions and the meanings that arise out of them. In many cases, these individuals teach their intimate others that HIV disease need not significantly change the relationships and interactions they share together, at least for many years. Furthermore, they often act to build or renegotiate intimate relationships that allow them to offset the stigmatizing or troublesome features of their illness and to realize valued selves. For instance, a number of persons with HIV/AIDS reach out to others living with the illness and develop formal or informal support networks. Within these peer networks, they share information about HIV symptoms and treatments, provide one another with emotional support, and acquire resources and strategies that help them to address the reactions they encounter in other settings or relationships. They also find ways to sustain a sense of purpose, vitality, and self-worth in the face of their illness.[63]

Through peer networks and interactions, people living with HIV/AIDS adjust to their health status and its effects on who they are. They also acquire resources that help them challenge and redefine the negative meanings of their health status. Of course, the relationships these individuals form with their peers do not have only positive consequences for their conceptions of HIV disease and self. As they see peers struggle with unpleasant medication-related side effects, troublesome symptoms, or diminished physical capacities, persons with HIV disease become increasingly aware of how the illness may eventually lead to unwelcome changes in their own bodies, selves, and relationships. They learn firsthand that HIV disease can result in suffering, disability, disruption, and, in some cases, death.

We have described the experiences of individuals diagnosed with HIV to illustrate how acquiring the status of "person with HIV disease" is as much a matter of socialization as biology. A person must learn what this status means and how it will affect him or her. An individual acquires this knowledge through his or her ongoing interactions with others. These interactions are influenced by (and in turn influence) the broader cultural meanings associated with HIV disease in our society. Most crucially, as in the case of other status passages, these interactions serve as a means by which a person with HIV becomes socialized into his or her status and, at the same time, socializes others about its meanings and implications.

SUMMARY

- This chapter outlines the symbolic interactionist approach to socialization, the process through which people acquire culture and learn social meanings. Unlike other sociologists, interactionists do not conceive of socialization as a process by which some people impose their values and beliefs on others and compel them to fit into predefined roles. Instead, interactionists emphasize that socialization flows in many directions and has multiple purposes and outcomes. Its most important outcome is the production of self-conscious social actors who think and act resourcefully in a variety of situations.

- Through the primary socialization process individuals acquire the human capacity for selfhood—the ability to define themselves as social objects. This capacity develops as they participate in increasingly sophisticated stages of role taking. As infants, individuals do not engage in role taking; they can only mimic the words and actions of those with whom they interact. But as they age and participate in play and games, they gradually improve the ability to take the perspective of others and to respond to themselves in terms of these perspectives. Eventually, when they develop their role-taking abilities to the fullest sense, people learn to evaluate themselves and their actions from the perspective of the "generalized other," or the community as a whole.

- In developing their capacities for role taking, individuals internalize the attitudes of others and become self-reflexive. This enables them to adjust their actions to the expectations of others. However, people do not necessarily act in ways that conform to others' expectations. They have the ability to act creatively, spontaneously, and unpredictably. This is rooted in the dialectical nature of their selves. People possess selves that consist of two elements: the "I," or initiating subject, and the "me," or self as social object. These two components of self are intimately connected. Their dialogue provides individuals with the basis for creating and regulating their conduct. Individuals experience impulses to act and then imagine how others might respond. In turn, they consider alternative actions and eventually choose to engage in behavior that resolves the tension between their impulses and internalized social standards. In some cases, this behavior is conventional, but in others it is creative or unexpected.

- In focusing on the self that individuals develop, interactionists also highlight its gendered dimensions. They recognize that in acquiring a self, people develop a gender identity, or a conception of self as male or female. This identity originally forms in early childhood as individuals interact with their significant others and learn to define and respond to themselves as boys or girls. This process of self-labeling, however, is only one component of children's early gender development. The other component is gender display. Because children learn to value their gender identities, they seek to confirm them though gender displays that elicit validating responses from significant others. In fashioning these displays, children actively draw on the actions and appearances modeled by same-sex others in their social environment.

- As children age, becoming preadolescents, they interact more regularly in peer groups and engage more frequently in gender displays designed to gain peer approval. They also participate in the construction of peer culture—a culture that both reflects and resists the values and practices of mainstream adult culture. Within this culture, children fill the gaps of the gender socialization they receive from adults. They teach one another what it means to be male or female, including important details about how to display their own gender and how to observe and reinforce gender boundaries in their social interactions. In doing so, children prepare to play adult gender scripts and roles. But, at the same time, they create a shared culture that allows them to question adult authority, challenge adult expectations, and influence adult social worlds.

- As individuals move from childhood into adulthood, they enter a wider array of social worlds and experience a number of status passages. These passages vary significantly in their consequences for self. Some of these passages are regularized and fairly predictable, such as the passage from high school to college student. Other passages, however, become profoundly transforming events, or epiphanies. Epiphanies are moments of crisis that disrupt and alter a person's basic understandings, outlooks, and self-images. Individuals often experience epiphanies when they are diagnosed with serious illnesses, such as cancer or HIV disease.

- Finally, and perhaps most important, symbolic interactionists stress that human beings are active rather than passive participants in the socialization process. People eagerly fill themselves with the "stuff of culture" and fashion rich social meanings—selves, genders, statuses, and identities—that provide them with the essence of their humanity.

GLOSSARY OF KEY TERMS

Borderwork   Interaction that goes across gender boundaries but, rather than challenging or transcending these boundaries, reflects and even strengthens them.

Epiphany   Moments of crisis or revelation that disrupt and alter one's fundamental understandings, outlooks, and self-images.

Game Stage   The phase of socialization in which we learn to take the role of a network of others, or the "generalized other." In so doing, we learn to look at ourselves and our behavior from the standpoint of a number of other perspectives or roles. We thereby acquire a sense of society and its moral standards.

Gender Identity   A strongly held image of self as male or female.

Gender Socialization   The process by which we learn the ways of thinking, feeling, and acting that our group defines as appropriate for males and females.

Generalized Other   The perspective and expectations of a network of others or of the community as a whole. The generalized other is reflected in the social standards we internalize and subsequently use to evaluate our own behavior. For some symbolic interactionists, the generalized other can also refer to the set of persons whose perspectives and expectations are considered by us as we construct our behavior. Other interactionists propose that this set of persons would be more aptly described as a "reference group."

Looking-Glass Self   The notion that the self reflects the responses of others. More specifically, the self develops through a three-step process: (1) imagining one's appearance in the eyes of others, (2) imagining their judgment of that appearance, and (3) internalizing their perspectives and developing a corresponding self-image and self-feeling. This term was originally coined by Charles Horton Cooley.

Peer Culture   A culture created by children that both reflects and resists the values and practices of mainstream adult culture. This culture is characterized by its own strategies of gender socialization and identity development.

Play Stage   The phase of socialization in which we learn to take the role of specific others, such as

	parents, teachers, or superheroes, by playing at these roles.
Preparatory Stage	The phase of socialization in which we lack a developed sense of self and have difficulty distinguishing our roles from the roles of others.
Reference Group	A group whose perspective serves as our frame of reference in organizing our thoughts, actions, and self-images in a given context.
Role Taking	The process of assuming the perspective of others, or putting ourselves in their position.
Rites of Passage	Rituals and ceremonies that accompany and help us to handle the changes in status we experience over the course of our lives.
Socialization	An ongoing process of interaction through which we develop identities and acquire culture. Primary socialization refers to the process by which we learn to become mature, responsible members of their society. This learning takes place through the core social institutions, most particularly the family. Secondary socialization refers to the more specific, formal training that we experience throughout the course of our lives, such as learning an occupation. Through this training we become inducted into specific social groups or worlds and acquire selves within them.
Status Passage	The movement of individuals in and out of particular statuses.

QUESTIONS FOR REFLECTION OR ASSIGNMENT

1. What is involved in becoming a "human being"? For instance, what qualities and skills do we need to acquire in order to become fully human? Where do these qualities and skills come from? Are they primarily inherited or learned?

2. Who were the most important agents of socialization in your childhood? What were the key messages and values they tried to give you? What kind of "looking glass" did they serve as for you? That is, how did they see and respond to you? How did this behavior influence your self-image and self-esteem?

3. How did you socialize your parents or caretakers? For example, how did you teach them what it meant to be a parent to you? What influence did you have on their values, outlooks, and actions? Did your parents change in any way in response to your temperament, attitudes, or behavior? (You might want to ask them this question.) Did you have more power when interacting with your parents as an adolescent than as a younger child? Do you have even more power when interacting with them now? If so, what gives you this power?

4. What were some of your favorite games as a young child? What roles and rules did you learn through these games? What identities did they give you? How did they help you understand the standards of your group or community? What standards (or rules) were most emphasized? Why?

5. Who was your "generalized other" as a child? How did this change as you entered elementary school? How did this change as you entered middle school or junior high school? Did you develop more than one "generalized other"? If so, what does this experience suggest about Mead's theory?

6. What was life like as a boy or girl in your elementary school? Whom did you play with most

often? Why? What was their gender? How did you interact with members of the other gender, especially on the playground? What contests or games did you engage in with them? Who typically won? How and why did they win? What did this teach you about what it meant to be male or female?

7. How do adolescents socialize each other into gender roles and identities? How do they announce their gender through their appearance? Through their talk? Through their interactions with members of the other gender? How do they "police" gender boundaries?

8. Interview your parents and ask them how life changed when they got married or began working full-time. What did they learn early in that marriage or job? What impact did it have on their previous relationships, such as their friendships or family relationships? How did it affect their sense of who they were? How did they change as a result of the marriage or job? What did they learn about themselves (or others) that they did not expect to learn?

9. Interview or read a story about a person who has a serious illness. How did he or she initially react when diagnosed with this illness? Who did the person turn to in order to learn more about the illness and its implications? Did the person talk with others diagnosed with this illness? What impact has the illness had on the person's social relationships? For example, how has it changed his or her friendships, marriage, or social life? Also, how has it changed the person's self-conception and self-esteem?

SUGGESTED READINGS FOR FURTHER STUDY

Adler, Peter, and Patricia Alder. *Peer Power: Preadolescent Culture and Identity* (New Brunswick, NJ: Rutgers University Press, 1997).

Becker, Ernest. *The Birth and Death of Meaning*, 2nd ed. (New York: Free Press, 1971).

Cahill, Spencer. "Fashioning Males and Females: Appearance Management and the Social Reproduction of Gender," *Symbolic Interaction* 12, 1989, pp. 281–298.

Fields, Jessica. *Risky Lessons: Sex Education and Social Inequality* (Rutgers, NJ: Rutgers University Press, 2008).

Irvine, Leslie. "A Model of Animal Selfhood: Expanding Interactionist Possibilities," *Symbolic Interaction*, 27, 2004, pp. 3–21.

Thorne, Barrie, *Gender Play: Girls and Boys in School* (New Brunswick, NJ: Rutgers University Press, 1993).

ENDNOTES

[1] Tobias Scheenbaum, *Keep the River on Your Right* (New York: Grove, 1969).

[2] Martha C. Ward, *A World Full of Women* (Boston: Allyn and Bacon, 1996), p. 40. See also Margaret Mead, *Sex and Temperament in Three Primitive Societies* (New York: William Morrow Co., 1963).

[3] See Dennis Brissett and Charles Edgley, eds., *Life as Theater: A Dramaturgical Sourcebook*, 2nd ed. (Chicago: Aldine Press, 1990).

[4] Charles Horton Cooley, *Human Nature and the Social Order* (New York: Charles Scribner and Sons, 1902).

[5] In making this point, we do not mean to suggest that your self-concept is a direct reflection of the conceptions of others. Instead, as we implied in the preceding discussion, your self-concept is a reflection of how you *think* others see you. We will discuss the relationship between the self-concept and the reflected appraisals of others at greater length in Chapter Four.

[6] Charles Horton Cooley, *Human Nature and the Social Order,* (Note 4), p. 236.

[7] David D. Franks and Viktor Gecas, "Autonomy and Conformity in Cooley's Self-Theory: The Looking-Glass Self and Beyond," *Symbolic Interaction* 15(1), 1992, pp. 49–68.

8 Charles Horton Cooley, "Self as Sentiment and Reflection," in Gregory P. Stone and Harvey Farberman, eds., *SocialPsychology Through Symbolic Interaction* (Waltham, MA: Glinn-Blaisdell, 1970), p. 381.

9 Ibid.

10 See George Herbert Mead, *Mind, Self, and Society* (Chicago: University of Chicago Press, 1934).

11 Interactionists disagree about whether Mead's theory of self-development should include the preparatory (or preplay) stage as well as the play and game stages. While we acknowledge that Mead never clearly identified the preparatory stage, we agree with those interactionist scholars who claim that he implied this stage in his writings. See Bernard Meltzer, *The Social Psychology of George Herbert Mead* (Kalamazoo, MI: Center for Sociological Research). Also see Gregory P. Stone, "The Play of Little Children," in Stone and Farberman, eds., *Social Psychology Through Symbolic Interaction*, 2nd ed. (New York: Wiley and Sons, 1981), pp. 249–256.

12 James Wiggins, Beverly Wiggins, and James Vander Zanden, *Social Psychology*, 5th ed. (New York: McGraw-Hill, 1995), p. 57.

13 Gregory P. Stone, "The Play of Little Children," (Note 11), pp. 249–256. Although Mead did not discuss imaginary or fantasy play in much detail, he did allude to its role in self-development. For example, see Mead, *Mind, Self, and Society*, (Note 10), p. 150.

14 See David A. Karp and William C. Yoels, *Sociology and Everyday Life* (Itasca, IL: F.E. Peacock Publishers, 1986), p. 47.

15 George H. Mead, *Mind, Self, and Society*, (Note 11), p. 159.

16 Ibid., p. 154.

17 Ibid., p. 168.

18 Cathryn Johnson, "The Emergence of the Emotional Self: A Developmental Theory," *Symbolic Interaction* 15(2), 1992, p. 183.

19 Gregory P. Stone, "The Play of Little Children" (Note 11), pp. 249–256.

20 William Corsaro, *Friendship and Peer Culture in the Early Years* (Norword, NJ: Ablex Publishing Company, 1985).

21 Gil Richard Musoff, "Interactionism and the Child: Cahill, Corsaro, and Denzin on Childhood Socialization," *Symbolic Interaction* 19(4), 1996, pp. 303–321. Musoff's article inspires and informs much of our following discussion of Corsaro's and Denzin's contributions to Mead's theory.

22 See William Corsaro, "Discourse Processes Within Peer Culture: From a Constructivist to an Interpretive Approach to Childhood Socialization," in Peter and Patricia Adler, eds., *Sociological Studies of Child Development*, Vol. I (Greenwich, CT: JAI Press, 1986), pp. 81–101.

23 Norman K. Denzin, *Childhood Socialization* (San Francisco, CA: Jossey-Bass, 1977).

24 Ibid., p. 81.

25 Tamotsu Shibutani, "Reference Groups as Perspectives," *American Journal of Sociology* 60, 1955, pp. 962–965. See also Joel Charon, *Symbolic Interaction: An Introduction, an Interpretation, an Integration*, 4th ed. (Englewood Cliffs, NJ: Prentice-Hall, 1992), p. 74, for an elaboration of points similar to those we offer in our discussion of Shibutani's analyses. Charon proposes that interactionists should add a fourth stage, the "reference group stage," to Mead's stages of self-development. We do not think this is necessary, but we do believe that interactionists should focus more attention on how people develop the ability to adopt many different general perspectives as well as the perspective of a more encompassing "generalized other."

26 Leslie Irvine, "A Model of Animal Selfhood: Expanding Interactionist Possibilities," *Symbolic Interaction*, 27(1), 2004, p. 9.

27 Ibid., p. 17.

28 See Clinton Sanders and Arnold Arluke, "If Lions Could Speak: Investigating the Animal-Human Relationship and the Perspectives of Nonhuman Others," *Sociological Quarterly* 34, 1993, pp. 377–390; Clinton Sanders. *Understanding Dogs: Living and Working with Canine Companions.* (Philadelphia: Temple University Press, 1999); Arnold Arluke and Clinton Sanders, *Regarding Animals* (Philadelphia: Temple University Press, 1996); Jaber Gubrium, "The Social Preservation of Mind: The Alzheimer's

Disease Experience," *Symbolic Interaction* 6, 1986, pp. 37–51; Robert Bogdan and Steven Taylor, "Relationships with Severely Disabled People: The Social Construction of Humanness," *Social Problems* 36, 1989, pp. 135–148.

29 In some cultures, male and female are not the only gender categories assigned or observed. For example, among the traditional Navajo, individuals could be classified into a third gender, referred to as *nadle*. The nadle status was ascribed to anyone whose sex was ambiguous at birth, but people could also choose to become nadle. Nadle performed the tasks and duties of both women and men.

30 See Ann Oakley, *Sex, Gender and Society* (New York: Harper & Row, 1985); Claire Renzetti and Daniel Curran, *Women, Men, and Society*, 3rd ed. (New York: Allyn and Bacon, 1995).

31 See C. S. Dweck, W. Davidson, S. Nelson, and B. Enna, "Sex Differences in Learned Helplessness," *Developmental Psychology* 14, 1978, pp. 268–276; L. A. Serbin, D. K. O'Leary, R. M. Kent, and I. J. Tonick, "A Comparison of Teacher Response to the Preacademic and Problem Behavior of Boys and Girls," *Child Development* 44, 1973, pp. 776–784; Myra and David Sadker, *Failing at Fairness* (New York: Charles Scribner's Sons, 1994); American Association of University Women, *How Schools Shortchange Girls* (Washington, DC: AAUW Educational Foundation and the National Education Association, 1992).

32 Spencer Cahill, "And a Child Shall Lead Us? Children, Gender and Perspectives by Incongruity," in Nancy Hermann and Larry Reynolds, eds., *Symbolic Interaction: An Introduction to Social Psychology* (Latham, MD: Altamira Press, 1994), pp. 459–469.

33 See Spencer Cahill, "Language Practices and Self-Definition: The Case of Gender Identity Acquisition," *The Sociological Quarterly* 27, 1986, pp. 295–311; "Reexamining the Acquisition of Sex Roles: A Social Interactionist Approach," *Sex Roles* 9, 1983, pp. 1–15.

34 Gary Alan Fine, *With the Boys: Little League Baseball and Preadolescent Culture* (Chicago: University of Chicago Press, 1987).

35 Gary Alan Fine, "The Dirty Play of Little Boys," *Society* 24, 1986, pp. 63–67.

36 Ibid., p. 66.

37 Gary Alan Fine, *With the Boys*, (Note 34), p. 104; see also Gary Alan Fine, "Friends, Impression Management, and Preadolescent Behavior," in Stone and Farberman, eds., *Social Psychology Through Symbolic Interaction*, (Note 11), pp. 258–272.

38 C. Shawn McGuffey and B. Lindsay Rich, "Playing in the Gender Transgression Zone," *Gender and Society* 13(5), October 1999, pp. 608–627.

39 Ann M. Beutel and Margaret M. Marini, "Gender and Values," *American Sociological Review* 60(3), 1995, pp. 436–438.

40 Barrie Thorne and Zella Luria, "Sexuality and Gender in Children's Daily Worlds," *Social Problems*, 33(3), 1986, pp. 176–190.

41 C. Shawn McGuffey and B. Lindsay Rich, "Playing in the Gender Transgression Zone," (Note 38).

42 See Barrie Thorne, *Gender Play: Girls and Boys in School* (New Brunswick, NJ: Rutgers University Press, 1993) and C. Shawn McGuffey and B. Lindsay Rich, "Playing in the Gender Transgression Zone," (Note 38).

43 C. Shawn McGuffey and B. Lindsay Rich, "Playing in the Gender Transgression Zone," (Note 38).

44 Barrie Thorne, *Gender Play: Girls and Boys in School* (New Brunswick, NJ: Rutgers University Press, 1993); Patricia and Peter Adler, *Peer Power: Preadolescent Culture and Identity* (New Brunswick, NJ: Rutgers University Press, 1998); Donna Eder (with Catherine Evans and Stephen Parker), *School Talk: Gender and Adolescent Culture* (New Brunswick, NJ: Rutgers University Press, 1995).

45 Barrie Thorne, *Gender Play*, (Note 42).

46 Spencer Cahill, "And a Child Shall Lead Us?" (Note 32), p. 465.

47 Barrie Thorne, *Gender Play*, (Note 42), p. 64.

48 Ibid., p. 69.

49 Ibid., p. 74.

50 This point was highlighted by Martha Copp in a personal communication sent to the first author.

51 Alfred Lindesmith, Anselm Strauss, and Norman Denzin, *Social Psychology*, 7th ed. (Englewood Cliffs, NJ: Prentice-Hall, 1991), p. 235.

52 Jean Stockard, *Sociology: Discovering Society*, 2nd ed. (Belmont, CA: Wadsworth, 2000).

53 The following discussion draws on information provided by Steven Foster and Meredith Little in "The Vision Quest: Passing from Childhood to Adulthood," in Louise Carus Mahdi, Steven Foster, and Merideth Little, eds., *Betwixt and Between: Patterns of Masculine and Feminine Interaction* (Lasalle, IL: Open Court Press, 1987), pp. 79–110.

54 Ibid., p. 82.

55 See Arnold Van Gennep. *The Rites of Passage* (Chicago: University of Chicago Press) and Victor Turner, *The Ritual Process: Structure and Anti-Structure* (Ithaca, NY: Cornell University Press, 1969).

56 For a detailed discussion of the issues and feelings students grapple with as they prepare to go to college and the strategies they use to solidify their new identities, see David A. Karp, Linda Lytle Holmstrom, and Paul S. Gray, "Leaving Home for College: Expectations for Selective Reconstruction of Self," *Symbolic Interaction* 21 (3), pp. 253–276.

57 Norman K. Denzin, *Interpretive Interactionism* (Beverly Hills, CA: Sage, 1989).

58 For an incisive analysis of turning points and the dynamics of religious conversion, see David Snow and Cynthia L. Phillips, "The Lofland-Stark Conversion Model: A Critical Reassessment," *Social Problems*, 27(4), 1980, pp. 430–447. Snow and Phillips point out that objective changes in one's life situation, such as loss of a job, divorce, failure in school, or even diagnosis with an illness, do not necessarily translate into "turning point moments" for one's identity. Whether a specific event represents a turning point is not objectively given, but rather is a matter of subjective interpretation and attitude. As Snow and Phillips observe: "There are few, if any, consistently reliable benchmarks for ascertaining when or whether one is at a turning point in one's life. As a consequence, just about any moment can be defined as a turning point" (p. 439). Moreover, with respect to religious conversion, turning points are more likely to be an outcome of the conversion process than a "cause" or precipitating condition for that process. In fact, a turning point "may symbolize conversion itself, for converts are gripped by the realization that they are not the same as they were a few moments ago and that their life situation and view of the world have changed, and for the better" (p. 440).

59 The following discussion is based on the ethnographic research of one of the coauthors, Kent Sandstrom. See Kent L. Sandstrom, "Confronting Deadly Disease: The Drama of Identity Construction Among Gay Men with AIDS" *Journal of Contemporary Ethnography* 19, October 1990, pp. 271–294; Kent L. Sandstrom, "Renegotiating Sex and Intimacy: The Sexual Self-Images, Outlooks, and Relationships of Gay Men with HIV/AIDS," *Symbolic Interaction* 19(3), Fall 1996, pp. 241–262; Kent L. Sandstrom, "Preserving a Vital and Valued Self in the Face of AIDS," *Sociological Inquiry* 68(3), 1998, pp. 354–371.

60 "HIV Incidence." Department of Health and Human Services, Centers for Disease Control and Prevention. Accessed August 16, 2008 at http://www.cdc.gov/hiv/topics/surveillance/incidence.htm.

61 "HIV/AIDS in the United States." Department of Health and Human Services, Centers for Disease Control and Prevention. Accessed August 16, 2008 at http://www.cdc.gov/hiv/resources/factsheets/us.htm.

62 Kent L. Sandstrom, "HIV/AIDS and Emotion Work: Negotiating and Managing Support." Paper presented at the Annual Meetings of the American Sociological Association, New York, August 16–20, 1996.

63 See Kent L. Sandstrom, "Searching for Information, Understanding, and Self-Value: The Utilization of Peer Support Groups by Gay Men Living With HIV/AIDS," *Social Work in Health Care* 23(2), 1996, pp. 51–74.

CHAPTER FIVE

~

THE NATURE AND SIGNIFICANCE OF THE SELF

For if I try to seize this self of which I feel sure, if I try to define and summarize it, it is nothing but water slipping through my fingers. I can sketch one by one all the aspects it can assume, all those things that have likewise been attributed to it…but aspects cannot be added up….Between the certainty I have of my existence and the content I try to give that assurance, the gap will never be filled.

—Albert Camus, *The Myth of Sisyphus*

Imagine it's your last semester in college. Graduation is rapidly approaching and you're feeling increasingly anxious about what you're going to do after you get your degree. You even wonder if you should change majors and continue going to college. One day, though, you listen to your voicemail messages as you walk across campus and you get a pleasant surprise: there's a message from a prominent company that is interviewing college seniors for jobs. The message says that representatives from this company have looked over your résumé and decided to interview you for a job—and it's not just any job, it's an interesting and high-paying one! In fact, it's the kind of position you've always dreamed of and you're excited to even be interviewing for it. A few minutes later, however, you start to feel more mixed about this opportunity. You feel butterflies welling up in your stomach and you begin to worry about the details of your prospective interview. You ask yourself: What are the interviewers going

to be looking for? What will they expect me to wear? What will they expect me to say? What can I do to convince them that I'm the person they should hire? How can I make a good impression and get the job?

After wrestling with these questions, you decide to call your best friend and ask for advice. She congratulates you on getting the interview and assures you that you're an intelligent and interesting person who is sure to impress the interviewers. She also stresses that the interview will go well if you just remember to "be yourself." You thank her for this advice, noting that she has helped you to feel more relaxed about the interview. Unfortunately, this feeling doesn't last long. Shortly after you're done talking with her, you start to worry again and you question the wisdom of her advice. You ask what it actually means to "be yourself." You wonder if that means being who you are when you're around your friends, or around your family, or around your classmates, or on your own. As you think about this question, you realize that "being yourself" means different things in different situations. This revelation makes you feel even more perplexed about your prospective interview. You wonder which of the many ways of "being yourself" you should emphasize as you talk with the interviewers. You also wonder which of the many aspects of your self they would see as desirable, particularly for the job the company wants to fill.

As this scenario implies, people's images and presentations of self are fluid and variable. Although we are not always aware of it, we tend to see and express ourselves differently at different times and in different situations. To get a better sense of this, imagine how you would present yourself to a job interviewer as opposed to your friends. If you are like most people, you would try to look your best when meeting a job interviewer, and you would tell him or her that you are a hard worker who has the knowledge, skills, and ambition necessary to be a good employee. If you are doing well in college, you might also point to your high GPA and stress how it demonstrates your sense of dedication and responsibility. Overall, you would try to convey that you are the kind of person the interviewer would want to hire. Now, keeping that in mind, imagine presenting yourself to a group of friends in exactly the same way, saying "I'm a hard worker who has the knowledge, skills, and motivation necessary to be a great friend to you. I'm just the kind of person you'd like to have around when you need to get something done!" How would your friends react? How long would it take them to make fun of you for acting so strangely? How would their reactions make you feel about yourself? Would these reactions motivate you to change your self-presentation so that it fit more closely with their expectations? In other words, would your friends' reactions make you want to act like the person you normally are with them?

In posing these questions, we encourage you to consider how your sense of self is bound up with particular contexts and interactions. By imagining what would happen if you interacted with your friends in the same way as you did a job interviewer, you can see how your sense of who you are—as well as your sense of what you should convey to others about yourself—varies from situation to situation. You can also recognize how your images and expressions of self depend to a great extent on the context.

Of course, in highlighting this point we recognize that we have not told the whole story of how you see and think about yourself. Like most people, you probably have an underlying sense of who you "really" are—a sense that does not change dramatically from one situation to the next. Your understandings of this real or essential self are grounded in and confirmed by your social experiences, such as the experiences you have with others who allow you to express yourself in a comfortable and seemingly natural way. At the same time, however, your understandings of your real self are shaped by those social experiences that do not make you feel comfortable or genuine. For instance, if you find yourself in a situation where you have to be nice to someone you do not like, where you have to act interested in a subject you do not care about, or where you have to talk in a stilted or artificial way, you are likely to feel "phony" and to lament the fact that you can't just "be yourself." Ironically, then, your sense of who you really are derives from experiences that leave you feeling insincere and constrained as well as from those that leave you feeling genuine and free to act as you wish.[1]

We hope this discussion has prompted you to think more deeply about your "self" and its nature. If you feel a little confused, we encourage you to take heart. The self is a complex and paradoxical phenomenon, and even social psychologists have difficulty making sense of it, as illustrated by their debates about various dimensions of the self, such as where it comes from, what it consists of, why it is important, how it is organized, how it is presented, and whether it is singular or plural in character. In the following sections of this chapter we will address many of these concerns, and, in the process, we will try to enhance your understanding of the nature and significance of the self. In doing so we will delineate the key features of a symbolic interactionist approach to the self.

WHAT IS THE SELF?

As we mentioned above, social psychologists often debate about what the self is and how it should be defined. Those who adopt a more psychological orientation tend to see the self as a *private* possession rooted in and reflective of an individual's personality, which includes his or her enduring values, beliefs, motives, traits, and dispositions. According to these analysts, the self is a relatively stable structure that exists inside of the individual, shaping his or her behavior across various situations. By contrast, sociologically oriented social psychologists see the self as fundamentally *social* in nature. They emphasize how a person's self is acquired and realized through social relationships. They also stress that this self is a fluid process that changes over time and across situations. Some sociologically oriented social psychologists even argue that a person does not carry a self from situation to situation.[2] Instead, they contend that

an individual must fashion a self anew in every social interaction, relying on others to collaborate in this process. The self that a person establishes, then, is not something he or she owns; rather, it is something that others temporarily lend to him or her.[3]

While most symbolic interactionists embrace a sociological orientation to the self, they disagree about the extent to which the self transcends a given situation, directs an individual's behavior, and with gets reflected in, as well as established by, his or her ongoing interactions.[4] Fortunately, despite these areas of disagreement, interactionists share several basic assumptions about the self. One of their core assumptions is that the self is a process of reflexive and communicative activity. According to interactionists, the **self** refers to a reflexive process that includes a person's *subjective stream of consciousness* (perceptions, thoughts, feelings, plans, and choices) as well as his or her *concept of self* as a physical, social, and moral being.[5] Interactionists also emphasize that this reflexive self is shaped by an individual's relationships with others. As we noted in the previous chapter, interactionists contend that individuals develop the capacity for reflexive selfhood through interacting with others. It is through interaction that

---

Box 5-1 THE BOUNDLESS AND MALLEABLE SELF: THE INSIGHTS OF WILLIAM JAMES

One of the first thinkers to analyze and specify the "contents" of the self was William James, a prominent philosopher and psychologist. In his classic book *Psychology*, James proposed that the self has a dual nature and exists simultaneously as an "I" and a "me." According to James, the I refers to the self as subject, or "knower," which actively experiences, feels, perceives, imagines, decides, remembers, or plans. The me, on the other hand, refers to the self as an object of experience that becomes "known" to the conscious I. Most crucially, James observed that the me, or self-as-known, extends far beyond the boundaries of our skin and includes a broad range of contents. Indeed, in discussing the nature and components of the me, James made the following remarks[1]:

> Between what a man calls me and what he calls mine the line is difficult to draw. We feel and act about certain things that are ours very much as we feel and act toward ourselves. Our fame, our children, the work of our hands, may be as dear to us as our bodies are,

and arouse the same feelings and the same acts of reprisal if attacked. And our bodies themselves, are they simply ours, or are they us? Certainly, men have been ready to disown their very bodies and to regard them as mere vestures, or even as prisons of clay from which they should some day be glad to escape.

We see then that we are dealing with a fluctuating material: the same object being sometimes treated as a part of me, at other times as simply mine, and then again as if it had nothing to do with us at all. In its widest possible sense, however, a man's Me is the sum total of all that he CAN call his, not only his body and psychic powers, but his clothes and house, his spouse and children, his ancestors and friends, his reputation and works, his house and yard, and even his yacht and bank account. All these things give him the same emotions. If they grow and prosper, he feels triumphant; if they dwindle and die away, he feels cast down—not necessarily in the same degree for each thing, but in much the same way for all.

In making these observations, James emphasized two key points. First, our sense of self cannot be clearly or sharply distinguished from our bodies and other material objects. In fact, it is often strongly associated with material items, such as our clothing, cars, houses, relatives, land, or creative works. As James suggested, we can attach our sense of self, as well as our self-esteem, to an almost unlimited number of material objects—including things like shoes, jackets, hairstyles, tattoos, rings, cars, CDs, and pieces of furniture. In this sense, our self becomes virtually boundless in nature. Second, our sense of self fluctuates and becomes invested differently in the same objects in different situations. For example, a baseball cap may be an essential aspect of who we are as we watch a game played by our favorite team. When we return home, however, the cap may have little if any significance for our image of self.

In related writings, James pointed out that another fluctuating aspect of the me is the "social me," which consists of the recognition and respect we get from others. James noted that this "social me" is formed and transformed as we interact with others. Indeed, he asserted that we have "as many social selves as there are individuals who recognize [us] and carry an image of [us] in their minds," and we generally show "a different side" of ourselves to different groups of people. James thus saw the "social me" as multifaceted and flexible, changing in response to the expectations and reactions of our changing audiences.

As you will see when reading this chapter, James's ideas have had a significant influence on interactionist thinkers. George Herbert Mead adopted and refined James's notions of the I and the me when describing the dynamics of the self-process. Louis Zurcher also drew upon James's discussion of the material, social, and spiritual components of the me when identifying the four key components of self-conception. In addition to this, Erving Goffman borrowed insights from James in describing how we manage and alter our presentations of self in different situations.

1. When James wrote these thoughts, it was conventional to use man, he, and his as generic terms that referred to both males and females. In recent years, we have become more aware of the negative consequences of these linguistic practices.

Source: William James, *Psychology* (New York: Holt, 1892), p. 18.

individuals learn to take the role of others and see themselves as social objects, much like other social objects. Moreover, it is through interaction that individuals experience, sustain, and transform their sense of who they truly are. Their sense of selfhood, then, is inextricably linked to their relationships with others. It is both a social product and a social process.

In highlighting the social nature and dimensions of the self, symbolic interactionists focus their attention on (1) the self as a social process, (2) the self as a social structure, and (3) the self as a staged production or dramatic effect. Some interactionists also focus on how and why the nature of the self is changing in contemporary or "postmodern" societies. In our discussion we offer an overview of what interactionists highlight in addressing each of these themes.

THE SELF AS SOCIAL PROCESS

What am I? A thing which thinks. What is a thing which thinks? It is a thing which doubts, understands, affirms, denies, wills, refuses, which also imagines and feels.

—Renee Descartes, *Meditations*

As we noted in earlier chapters, symbolic interactionists draw heavily on the ideas of George Herbert Mead, particularly when discussing the self and its dynamics. In analyzing the self Mead focused not only on its social nature, origins, and contents (the "me" dimensions), but also on the part it plays in perceiving, defining, and acting in the world (the "I" aspects). Mead proposed that the key feature of the self-process is communication, particularly language and symbols.[6] For Mead, the self is anchored in language and operates as a communicative process, particularly as it reflects on itself during the course of thought or interaction.[7]

Following Mead, interactionists stress that the self operates as a communicative process in two fundamental ways. First, the self is characterized by a continuous process of inner conversation—a conversation between the "I," or initiating subject, and the "me," or self as social object. As Mead highlighted, these two aspects of the self are intimately connected and can be understood only in terms of one another.[8] The **"I"** refers to the spontaneous, impulsive, and initiating tendencies of the individual. The **"me,"** on the other hand, refers to the internalized attitudes of others through which one views oneself and one's actions. This aspect of the self develops through the processes of socialization and role taking.

For Mead, the "I," or self as subject, can be understood as the initiator and formulator of action. It refers to a person's response to the expectations or stimuli that arise in the present situation. To illustrate this, imagine that your professor announces a pop quiz on today's readings. Your "I" would quickly respond to this announcement. Its reaction might be "*I* think this stinks! *I'm* not going to take a stupid quiz, *I'm* leaving!" But, before you bolt from the class and abide by the impulses of your "I," an informal conversation begins within you. You reflect on your impulse to leave and, in this process, your "me" emerges. The "me" reacts to the "I" by saying, "What would happen to *me* if I left? What would the professor or my classmates think of *me*? They might see *me* as a slacker." In response, you might grit your teeth and take the pop quiz. If so, your "me" (or internalized role of responsible student) will have redirected the response of your "I." Of course, you might choose to ignore the "me" and leave, thinking "To hell with responsibility. I'm out of here!"

Mead stressed that the "I" and "me" engage in an ongoing, rapid-fire dialogue. He also noted that they influence and evolve into one another continually. To illustrate this dialogue, let's reflect on the pop quiz. If you stay in class and take the quiz, you act in accord with your "me"—at least for the moment. When the professor asks the quiz questions, your "I" emerges again. As you respond to each question you are engaging in the "I" phase of conduct. When this response (or quiz answer) subsequently becomes a part of your memory, it becomes an object of reflection and you react to it in the "me" phase. In this later phase you might think, "This answer isn't too bad. The professor will probably give me credit for it." Your "I" phase will then respond to this "me" phase, which itself was a response to an "I" phase just a moment earlier.

The crucial point is that the ongoing internal conversation between the "I" and "me," or self as subject and object, provides you with the basis for organizing and controlling your behavior, not only in the classroom but in all arenas of your life. As you enter various situations, you experience impulses to act, imagine how you and others would respond to acting on these impulses, conceive of alternative actions, and eventually resolve the internal dialogue of the "I" and "me" into some line of action. For instance, if you are attending a party and see an attractive person across the room, you decide whether or not to introduce yourself. While the decision you make will be influenced by the responses of your "me," which may be saying "Wait a minute, you're already involved with someone," your final decision will not necessarily conform to the voice of the "me," or the internalized social standards it reflects. As Mead highlighted, you are not simply conformist; you can engage in novel, impulsive, idiosyncratic, or unexpectedly selfish or generous acts. These acts arise out of conflicts and discrepancies that occur between the "I" and the "me" phases of your self.[9]

Most crucially, as we formulate lines of action based on the internal conversation of the "I" and the "me," we engage in the process of **self-indication**, or thinking. This process serves as the means by which we define and make sense of things in the world around and inside us. Anything we become conscious of is something we indicate to ourselves, such as the rays of sun streaming through a window, the music coming from a CD player, the smell of cookies baking in the oven, or the rumblings of an empty stomach. As Herbert Blumer pointed out, when we engage in self-indication, we internally note things, evaluate them, grant them meaning, and consider how to act based on that meaning.[10] Through this process we transform the external world of "things" into an internal world of meaningful social objects and thus build a bridge between our individual perceptions and the larger social world.[11]

While our capacity for self-indication links us to the larger social world, it also gives us a substantial element of freedom in formulating our behavior. It frees us from responding in a predetermined way to the stimuli (including objects, people, and events) in our environment. Because we are thinking or self-indicating creatures, we have the capacity to act toward stimuli creatively, accepting them, rejecting them, or transforming them based on how we define them. Consider how you might react if one of your friends leaned over and kissed you softly on the cheek at the end of a long conversation. Depending on the context, you could interpret this act in a variety of ways. For instance, you could interpret your friend's kiss as merely an expression of kindness or affection, downplaying the possibility that it has any sexual or romantic overtones. Or, by contrast, you could define the kiss as an exciting erotic overture that prompts you to reevaluate your friend as someone who could become your lover. Or, you could define your friend's kiss as an unwelcome and unpleasant sexual advance that threatens the future of your relationship. Or, of course, you could give other meanings to the kiss, depending on the nature of the preceding conversation and the history of your interactions with this friend. Most important, you do not simply react to your friend's kiss, you *choose* how to respond to it based on how you define it.

As we make sense of stimuli and engage in the process of self-indication, we evaluate and define the situation in which we act. We communicate information *to* ourselves about the objects, people, and events that we see and experience. We also communicate information *about* ourselves to the particular self (e.g., employee or student) we are enacting in this context. Indeed, symbolic interactionists stress that the process of selfhood means that we have the ability to see ourselves in context, and we respond to a given context in terms of how we think of ourselves in it.[12] Put simply, we see and act toward a situation—including the objects, people, and events in it—in relation to our image of self in that situation. To illustrate, let's consider the example of the friend's kiss again. Interactionists contend that we will see and respond to this kiss based on how we define ourselves in relation to the friend in the situation at hand. If we define ourselves as "just a friend" in that context, we will tend to respond to the kiss in a way that confirms that image of self. On the other hand, if we define ourselves as "someone who could become more than a friend," especially as the situation unfolds, we will be inclined to respond to the kiss in a manner that validates a different image of self and leads to a different course of interaction. Our decision about how to respond to our friend's act, then, will be greatly influenced by how we see ourselves, particularly in relation to him or her, in that context.

In emphasizing how our images and expressions of self are linked to situations, interactionists highlight a second fundamental way the self operates as a process; that is, it changes in character and expression as we enter different contexts and interact with different people. According to interactionists, we have a highly mutable and flexible sense of self, and the specific self we perform depends on the context we are in. As Mead observed:

> We carry on a whole series of different relationships to different people. We are one thing to one [person] and another thing to another....We divide ourselves up in all sorts of different selves with reference to our acquaintances. We discuss politics with one and religion with another. There are all sorts of different selves answering to all sorts of different social reactions.[13]

Mead even proposed that a "multiple personality" is in some senses a normal and necessary condition of modern life, although he recognized that a fully developed self had to have some sense of unity. In highlighting the multiple and shifting character of the self, Mead drew on the related observations of William James, the pragmatist philosopher who observed that, practically speaking, a person "has as many different social selves as there are distinct groups of persons about whose opinion he [or she] cares."[14] James pointed out that we show a different side of ourselves to the different groups we care about, as illustrated by the fact that we express ourselves differently to friends than to parents, to classmates than to professors, and to co-workers than to bosses. According to James, this tendency to be a different person in different groups means that in practical terms we divide the self into several different social selves, regardless of whether we think of it as singular in nature.

Later in this chapter we will explore the changeable character of the self in more detail, particularly as we examine how the self is presented and enacted in everyday interaction. Before doing so, however, we will consider how and why interactionists regard the self as a *social structure* as well as a social process.

THE SELF AS SOCIAL STRUCTURE

While emphasizing the processual nature of the self, interactionists embrace George Herbert Mead's claim that "the self, as that which can be an object to itself, is essentially a social structure."[15] Mead proposed that language plays a crucial role in the development of the self as a social structure. Once we acquire language we develop an increasingly sophisticated ability to assume the perspective of others and respond to ourselves in terms of this perspective. As young children, we acquire this ability through playing at specific roles, such as superhero, parent, or teacher (see Chapter Four). In doing so, we respond to ourselves in terms of the role of *significant others* and adjust our actions accordingly. At this point, however, we only develop separate images of self that correspond to each of the distinctive roles that we play. As time passes and we take part in more complex interactions, we learn to see ourselves in terms of an organized community of roles, or the generalized other. Through responding to ourselves in terms of this generalized and integrated perspective, we acquire a more unified conception of self. For instance, when you become a college student, you learn to see yourself as a "student" not only in terms of the perspectives of your fellow students, but also in terms of the perspectives of advisers, professors, administrators, and support staff. To the extent that these perspectives are similar, you will have a unified view of yourself as a student. The unity and structure of your "student self" will reflect the unity and structure of the broader community to which you belong.[16]

Drawing on Mead's insights, interactionists emphasize how the structure and contents of our self-conceptions get built into us from the outside in. Through taking the role of others, we learn to define and respond to ourselves in terms of social outlooks and standards. Our self-concepts, then, are fundamentally social products, consisting of the roles, perspectives, and identities we internalize through our social experiences and interactions. While we like to think of ourselves as uniquely individual, the contents of our self-images contradict this belief. Our notions of who we are and what we can become are profoundly social; they are anchored in the roles and identities we acquire through our relationships.

The Self-Concept: Its Structure and Contents

While generally agreeing on how the self emerges and develops, interactionists part company in terms of the relative weight they accord to the structure of the self, on the one hand, and the processes through which the self is created and enacted, on the other. Those analysts who place greater emphasis on the structure of the self are sometimes referred to as "structural interactionists." They focus on the nature and relevance of the **self-concept**, or the overarching view that a person has of himself or herself as a physical, social, moral, or spiritual being.[17] In analyzing the self-concept, structural interactionists consider not only how we define ourselves, but also how these definitions affect our behavior. Typically, their analyses are grounded in conventional social scientific methods, such as open-ended questionnaires and survey research. Some also use an instrument called the Twenty Statements Test, or TST, which was created in 1950 by Manford Kuhn, the founder of the Iowa School of Interactionism (see Box 5-2).[18]

In developing the TST Kuhn contended that it was an ideal way to assess and measure the contents and structure of the self. Kuhn proposed that the self consists primarily of an organized set of "self-attitudes" (or "me's") and the TST offered individuals an easy and straightforward way to express these attitudes. Moreover, it provided researchers with a handy method for identifying and measuring these central components of a person's self-concept.

Self-Attitudes and the Key Components of the Self-Concept. The attitudes we have in regard to ourselves are typically the characteristics we mention when asked to describe ourselves; they are the kinds of responses we would list on a measure of our self-concept such as the Twenty Statements Test. As Kuhn noted, *self-attitudes* can be expressed in the form "I am _____." For instance, statements like "I am tall," "I am fun-loving," "I am a dog lover," "I am a human rights activist," or "I am a member of the Reform Party" are expressions of self-attitudes. As illustrated in these statements, self-attitudes are beliefs we have about ourselves that associate us with certain physical attributes, character traits, personal interests, social roles, or group memberships.

The self-attitudes we express on the TST can be classified into four general modes of response that reflect and reveal the central features of our self-concepts. According to Louis Zurcher,[19] these modes include the following:

Box 5-2 ON KNOWING THYSELF: THE "WHO AM I?" TEST

To measure people's self-concepts, symbolic interactionists often rely on an instrument called the Twenty Statements Test, developed by Manford Kuhn. It's an easy test to take and it's designed to reveal the "self-attitudes" that are important to you. We'd like you to try it. To do so, take out a piece of lined paper and number from 1 to 20. Then, on each line, write a different answer to the question "Who am I?" As you write these answers, respond as if you are giving these answers to yourself and not to somebody else. Also, write your responses quickly and in the order they occur to you. Don't worry about the logic, sequence, or importance of your answers. When you have completed the 20 lines, you have finished taking the TST.

So, what do your answers reveal about you? According to the analysts who use the TST, your answers illustrate several important things about who you are. They indicate the social groups and statuses with which you identify. They also reveal your likes and dislikes, goals and ambitions, interests, ideological beliefs, and self-evaluations (e.g., your evaluations of your mental and physical abilities). Moreover, your answers to the TST show how important particular identities are to you. In most cases, you will list your most salient identities in the first five sentences of the TST. In addition, your answers to the TST reveal the various types of identities that constitute your self and the evaluations you make of these identities. For instance, your responses may show that you see yourself as a good student, a hard worker, and an effective writer, thereby illustrating that you have a high sense of self-esteem and self-efficacy. Finally, your answers to the TST reveal the types of self-attitudes—physical, social, reflective, or oceanic—in which you anchor your self-concept.

To demonstrate how the TST reveals the anchorage of your self-concept, we are going to ask you to code your responses based on the scoring protocol developed by Thomas McPartland and his associates.[1] Place the code of A next to the responses on your TST that identify you as a physical being (e.g., your height, weight, name, hair color). Place the code of B next to the responses that identify you in terms of social roles, statuses, or groups (e.g., student, employee, church member). Place a C by those responses that identify you in terms of characteristic styles of action, habit, or mood (e.g., funny, kind, active, hot-headed). Place a D by the responses that do not seem relevant to social action or contexts (e.g., "I am a living person"). After completing this process, count the number of responses you coded with each letter and write down your results (e.g., 3 A's, 9 B's, 6 C's, and 2 D's). The letter with the highest number is your primary mode of self-anchorage.

Your mode of self-anchorage is important because it shapes both your behavior and the nature of your self-concept. According to Louis Zurcher,[2] if you are anchored in the A mode (i.e., you coded a large majority of your TST responses with an A), your behavior tends to meet only minimal adult expectations. You also tend to be a narcissistic person who is absorbed with buying things and looking good. The news gets better if, like most people, your TST responses are predominantly B's or C's. If you are anchored in the B mode, you tend to act in socially effective and responsible ways, fulfilling the requirements of your roles. Unfortunately, you may also be somewhat rigid and fearful of personal change. By contrast, if you are anchored in the C mode, you tend to be more reflective and flexible in your actions than A- or B-mode people. You are also likely to be introspective and to strive for personal and social change. The downside of these tendencies is that they can provoke feelings of marginality or confusion and lead you to agonize over identity questions. On the other hand, if you are anchored in the D mode, you tend to be much "freer" in your actions than those anchored in A, B, or C mode. In fact, you may be so "free" and variable in your behavior that you commonly violate situational norms and act in bizarre or extravagant ways. You may also tend toward escapism and detachment from social commitments or relationships. If you are not escapist, though, you can offer insightful and creative perspectives to others and attain deeper levels of spiritual awareness.

Before you get too concerned about your self-anchorages and their implications, we want to stress that the "negative" characteristics we described above are typically associated with people compulsively locked into a specific mode, not with individuals whose sense of self is anchored in several modes. Thus, if the results of your TST show that you had nine B-mode, six C-mode, four A-mode, and two D-mode responses, this does not mean that you are a rigid or inflexible person who is afraid of change. As Zurcher emphasized, most of us develop self-concepts that are characterized by a variety of modes. This gives us the capacity to draw flexibly on various aspects of our selves as we interact with different people and meet the demands of diverse situations.

1. Thomas S. McPartland, *Manual for the Twenty Statements Problem*, rev. ed. (Kansas City: Greater Kansas City Mental Health Foundation, 1959).
2. Louis Zurcher, *The Mutable Self* (Beverly Hills: Sage, 1977).

The A mode, which reveals the physical self.
The B mode, which reveals the social self.
The C mode, which reveals the reflective self.
The D mode, which reveals the oceanic self.

The A mode, or physical self, is reflected in self-identifying responses that refer to our actual physical characteristics (e.g., height, weight, or hair color) as well as other information (e.g., name and address) typically found on our driver's license or identity card. The B mode, or social self, is revealed in responses that link us to social roles (father, daughter, employee, basketball player), social statuses (gender, social class, ethnicity, sexual orientation), or group memberships (family, church, school, sorority). Examples of responses that reflect the social self include "I am a student," "I am a criminology major," "I am a beer drinker," or "I am a sister." The C mode, or reflective self, is revealed in abstract statements that transcend specific social roles or situations. These responses include the feelings, character traits (e.g., curious,

cautious, shy, extroverted) and behavioral tendencies (e.g., liberal, spiritual, supporter of human rights causes) we attribute to ourselves. Examples include such statements as "I am a thoughtful person," "I am a jazz lover," or "I am a party hound." The D mode, or oceanic self, is reflected in statements that are "so vague that they lead us to no reliable expectations about behavior."[20] Statements such as "I am one with the universe" or "I am someone who loves humankind" would be indicative of the oceanic self.

Based on frequent and repeated samplings of responses to the TST, Zurcher observed that most people can manifest all four types of self-concept. However, as a result of their socialization experiences, a majority of individuals come to prefer one mode over the others, thus manifesting a fairly consistent dominant mode. During the 1950s and 1960s, most Americans who took the TST revealed that they anchored their self-concept primarily in the B mode, or the social self. However, this trend shifted in the

1970s and 1980s. As David Snow and Cynthia Phillips found in a TST-based study of 1,125 American college students, 68 percent anchored their self-concept in the C mode, or reflective self, while only 16 percent anchored it in the B mode.[21]

Zurcher theorized that this transition from the B mode to the C mode reflected the emergence of what he called the **mutable self**—a self-concept that is highly adaptive to rapid social and cultural change.[22] According to Zurcher, the mutable self integrates all four modes of self-conception: physical, social, reflective, and oceanic. It also enables its possessor to avoid fixating on any one of these modes to the exclusion of others, thereby allowing him or her to draw flexibly on the different modes to adjust to the various people and situations he or she encounters in everyday life. In essence, by developing a mutable self, an individual becomes well suited for living in our rapidly changing society because this self allows him or her to alternate easily between A, B, C, and D modes in addressing the demands that arise in different situations. As Zurcher suggested, the person with a mutable self has a process orientation and thus does not become traumatized or immobilized by rapid social and personal change. Instead, he or she has the ability to tolerate, evaluate, and cope effectively with the transitions and uncertainties provoked by this type of change.

Identities and Their Salience. As revealed by Zurcher's research, all of us have multiple modes of self-conception. Each of these modes is associated with particular kinds of identities. For example, the B mode is associated with role identities while the C mode is associated with dispositional identities. Although our self-concepts are made up of many types of identities, we do not give all of them equal weight—some of our identities are more important to us than others. As Sheldon Stryker observed, our identities are organized hierarchically based on the salience they have for our self-concepts and the degree to which we are committed to them. The rank of a specific identity in our "hierarchy of salience" depends largely on its likelihood of coming into play in a given situation or across different situations.[23]

Our hierarchy of **identity salience** has several important implications for our outlooks and actions. First, the higher the rank or salience of a specific identity, the more often we will try to draw on that identity as we assess and define a situation and coordinate our behavior with others in that situation. For example, if you rank the identity of "party animal" as highly salient, you will be more likely to define a given context as an opportunity to act in terms of that identity. You will seek to play the role of party animal as often as possible, perhaps even resenting those times when you cannot perform this role. Second, when you define a given identity as highly important, you will be more inclined to develop the skills, qualities, and relationships that are relevant to it, thereby reinforcing your commitment to it. If you are a talented musician, you are likely to "jam" regularly with other musicians, thus cultivating skills and friendships that lead you to invest more deeply in that identity. This investment may in turn prompt you to neglect other skills or relationships that you could have developed. Third, our commitment to and enactment of highly salient identities can diffuse or carry over to other statuses. This pattern is illustrated by the person with the prominent identity of police officer who carries her job demeanor and air of authority into her interactions with relatives, neighbors, or friends. To a considerable degree, this person becomes the professional role she plays at work. This effect is known as a role-person merger.[24]

In general, structural interactionists contend that the greater our commitment to an identity, the greater its influence on our behavior and self-concepts. Summed over time and across situations, those identities to which we are most committed shape our self-definitions and direct our ongoing behavior, promoting continuities in that behavior. Thus, when we lose a central identity, such as the identity of lover, spouse, or parent, we are likely to experience a significant sense of discontinuity and a loss of self. At the very least, we will struggle with feelings of uncertainty about who or what we are in the face of this loss. On the other hand, when we lose a more peripheral identity, such as the identity of beginning golfer or part-time dishwasher, we are likely to feel few if any negative implications for self.

Self-Esteem and Its Sources: Beyond the Looking-Glass Self

Most social psychologists regard self-esteem as a key dimension of self-conception. Indeed, much of the research on self-conception focuses on this dimension, and some studies even equate the notions of self-esteem and self-concept.[25] Symbolic interactionists distinguish between these two notions, using the concept of **self-esteem** to refer to the positive or negative feelings we attach to our selves and the judgments we make of our own worth (e.g., our appraisals of self as good or bad, better or worse, respectable or unrespectable). In analyzing the dynamics of self-esteem, interactionists contend that it is grounded in and shaped by (1) the reflected appraisals of others, (2) social comparisons, and (3) experiences of self-efficacy.

Reflected Appraisals. The idea that our self-evaluations reflect the responses and reflected appraisals of others is a core assumption of interactionist sociology, as we noted in Chapter Four when discussing Charles Horton Cooley's theory of the looking-glass self. As Cooley proposed, we develop a sense of self, as well as feelings about this self, by looking at ourselves through the eyes of others. If we believe that others evaluate us favorably, we feel "gratified" and develop high self-esteem. On the other hand, if we believe others view us negatively, we feel "mortified" and develop low self-esteem. In essence, the imagined appraisals of others serve as a mirror to us, shaping our self-evaluations and self-feelings.

Cooley's simple but elegant theory of the looking-glass self is commonly taught in introductory sociology and social psychology courses. Unfortunately, instructors often teach this theory in a misleading way, suggesting that our self-esteem simply reflects the evaluations of others. As we noted in the previous chapter, Cooley had a much more nuanced view of self-formation. He emphasized that we are active rather than passive participants in the process of developing and sustaining a self. Our self-appraisals are based on our selective *interpretations* of others' views and judgments. Thus, in using the metaphor of the looking-glass self, Cooley did not mean to suggest that we develop self-evaluations that directly correspond to the actual appraisals of others. In fact, he stressed that this situation rarely occurs. Cooley recognized that we often misinterpret the appraisals of others and, correspondingly, develop self-evaluations based on distorted reflections.[26]

In recent years interactionist scholars have clarified and extended Cooley's ideas about reflected appraisals and their impact on self-esteem. In the process these analysts have provided empirical support for Cooley's thesis that our self-esteem substantially reflects our *perceptions* of others' appraisals of us[27]; that is, our feelings about ourselves largely reflect how we think others feel about us. Ironically, our self-esteem is *not* strongly associated with the actual appraisals of others. This weak association results from several factors. One is that social life is characterized by deception, making it difficult for us to get honest and direct feedback from others, particularly if the feedback is unfavorable. The norms of interaction in our society constrain others from giving us honest appraisals, encouraging them to substitute tact or diplomacy for unvarnished truthfulness. As a consequence, we are often unaware of how others truly feel about us.[28]

Another reason for the disparity between our self-esteem and the appraisals of others is that not all others have the same significance to us. We give greater weight to the assessments of our significant others, such as our close friends or family members, when we evaluate ourselves. We also see their reflected appraisals as more credible or valid than others. In essence, then, we commonly choose whose appraisals will matter to us and whose will not. We also make choices about the circumstances under which the appraisals of specific others will matter.[29] If we think that someone does not have an important or credible appraisal to offer regarding our current situation or behavior, we are likely to disregard his or her evaluation and its implications for self. For example, if you are a fan of rap music, you are likely to ignore your parents' appraisals of whether you are dressed appropriately to go to a Dr. Dre concert. By contrast, you will pay much closer attention to the appraisals of your friends who are avid Dr. Dre fans.

As Viktor Gecas noted, perhaps the most significant reason for the low correlation between our self-evaluations and the actual appraisals of others is "the active distorting influence of the self-concept."[30] We are predisposed to see others' appraisals in a positive light. Because of the *self-enhancement motive,* or our motivation to feel good about ourselves, we tend to have a biased interpretation of others' evaluations of us, distorting or reframing their evaluations so that they reflect favorably on our self.[31] For instance, we tend to notice and recall friends' appraisals that focus on our positive characteristics or accomplishments, thereby supporting rather than threatening our self-evaluations. We also tend to deflect or downplay the negative appraisals of rivals and, in some cases, protect our self-esteem by claiming that their unfavorable judgments reflect their prejudice or character flaws. Overall, we are clearly less inclined to pay attention to, or be influenced by, any social appraisals that conflict with or jeopardize our existing self-evaluations.[32] Thus, when we imagine how others view us, we often see an image that reflects how we want them to view us rather than how they actually see us.

To summarize, symbolic interactionists emphasize that our self-evaluations do not simply mirror the reflected appraisals of others.

Rather, our self-judgments emerge out of a complex, interpretive process—a process in which we actively and selectively perceive others' appraisals, filtering and distorting their evaluations and choosing particular evaluations as the basis of our self-esteem. This process is revealed in our tendency to hear a comment such as "You wrote a very good paper but it could have been organized more clearly" as "You wrote a very good paper."

Social Comparison. When assessing ourselves and our relative merits, we invariably use reference points as a basis of comparison. When asking "How good, competent, or worthy am I?" we answer in terms of our response to the question "Compared to whom or what?" Our self-esteem relies heavily on processes of social comparison.

Structural interactionists such as Morris Rosenberg and Howard Kaplan have proposed that our self-esteem depends on three key comparison levels.[33] The first level of comparison is the past self. When evaluating ourselves, we consider whether we are as virtuous or competent as we used to be and whether we are developing into a better person. We may ask whether we are doing as well in our classes or job or are experiencing as much personal "growth" and success as we did in the past. If we do not "measure up" when making these assessments, we are likely to experience diminished self-esteem.

A second level of comparison consists of our personal goals or aspirations. We evaluate our successes and worth not only in terms of what we accomplish, but also in terms of our potential, or what we believe we can accomplish.[34] This tendency explains why some students feel ashamed or disheartened after getting an A– on an exam. Since they believe that they should have gotten an A, anything less seems like a failure.

The third and most influential level of comparison is our comparisons to others. Social psychologists have found that we carefully select which individuals or groups will serve as the bases for our comparisons. When we select specific individuals or groups, we are often trying to preserve or enhance our self-esteem. One way we do so is by comparing ourselves to others who are "worse off" while avoiding comparisons with those who are "better off." For example, the student who gets a C on his biology exam can preserve his self-esteem by comparing himself to the students who received failing grades, not to those who earned A's. Similarly, the professor who teaches at a lower-ranking state university can salvage her self-esteem by comparing herself to professors who teach at community colleges, not to those who teach at Ivy League schools.

In many cases, however, we choose to assess our virtues and accomplishments by comparing ourselves to others we define as similar. Indeed, our comparisons to these similar others have the greatest relevance for our self-esteem.[35] We experience a bigger increase in our self-esteem from doing well in comparison to those we see as being like us, even if they are members of a relatively unsuccessful group, than we do from performing equally well in a larger and more accomplished group. This tendency supports the wisdom of the old cliche that "it is better to be a big fish in a little pond than to be a little fish in a big pond."

In general, we exercise a measure of control over the comparisons we make by selectively associating with other people. When we want to protect our sense of self-esteem, we associate with similar others who will validate or reinforce our positive self-attitudes. This behavior is especially likely if we are members of a stigmatized or oppressed group. Rather than accepting negative appraisals as an accurate assessment of our self-worth, we may choose to identify with those who are like us (in terms of ethnicity, social class, sexual orientation, political beliefs, or whatever) and feel proud about belonging to this group. By making this choice, we are more likely to preserve or bolster our sense of self-worth, especially in comparison to similar others who lack such a group identification.

Self-Efficacy. While recognizing the impact of reflected appraisals and social comparisons on our self-esteem, interactionist scholars also highlight the importance of self-efficacy as a basis of positive self-feeling. **Self-efficacy** refers to a person's sense of being competent and "in control" as he or she acts in the world and interacts with others. In discussing self-efficacy, interactionists draw again on the ideas of Charles Horton Cooley, who contended that effective action is a crucial and somewhat independent dimension of self-formation. Cooley claimed that we build a sense of self through vigorous and purposeful activity that allows us to *do something* to our environment, thereby asserting ourselves in it and producing effects upon it. According to Cooley, this behavior is rewarding in its own right and provides us with a basis of positive self-feeling that transcends the appraisals of others.[36]

In developing Cooley's arguments, contemporary interactionists have pointed out that this "intrinsic" or efficacy-based dimension of self-feeling may be more relevant for our self-esteem than the "extrinsic" dimension that relies on others' assessments. Efficacy-based self-esteem is defined as intrinsic because it refers to an experience of self-worth that is uniquely our own as individuals. This sense of self-worth essentially describes the feeling of self we experience when we are on top of things, navigating life's challenges successfully and demonstrating that we are masters of our own actions.[37] We experience this form of self-worth in a variety of ways, such as when we "ace" a difficult exam, deliver an inspiring speech, paint a beautiful picture, negotiate a great deal, or win a video game.[38]

Of course, we often try to reap the benefits of both intrinsic and extrinsic self-esteem; that is, we try to act in ways that allow us to feel on top of things while also getting us positive appraisals from others. For instance, if we are playing in an athletic event, such as a volleyball game, we try to do well not only because it gives us a sense of efficacy, but also because it leads teammates to see us as a valuable player.

The Impact of the Self-Concept

As we have illustrated, the self-concept is more than just a collection of attitudes, identities, and evaluations; it has an organizing structure. This structure is reflected in the rankings we give to various identities and in our preferred bases of self-esteem. The specific structure of our self-concept is important because it influences our perceptions and behaviors across a variety of social interactions and settings.

According to structural interactionists, our self-concept has a number of important consequences for our outlooks and actions. First, it provides us with a source of stability and continuity as we interact with others and formulate lines of action. When we enter various social situations, we use our self-concept as a frame of reference in deciding how to act. While we take the demands of each situation into account, we have a tendency to act in ways that fit with our fundamental notions of who we are—notions that may or may not mesh with the expectations or reflected appraisals of others in that context. Second, depending on its makeup, our self-concept provides us with a basis for personal satisfaction or dissatisfaction. As various scholars have observed, a healthy self-concept is crucial to our mental and emotional well-being. Research on mental health demonstrates "clear and consistent relationships of low self-esteem to psychological depression, anxiety, somatic symptoms, impulse to aggression, vulnerability, negative emotional states, and other neurotic symptoms."[39] Third, in addition to shaping our outlooks and actions on a personal level, our self-concept has a significant impact on how we think and act in various institutional arenas of social life, such as schools, workplaces, and political settings. In fact, a number of studies reveal that our self-concept influences our academic performances, our occupational values and choices, our political attitudes and behaviors, and even our likelihood of engaging in deviance.[40] Based on these findings, structural interactionists propose that the self-concept should be regarded as a social force in its own right, shaping larger institutions as well as being shaped by them.

THE SELF AS DRAMATIC EFFECT

The self, as a performed character, is not an organic thing that has a specific location, whose fundamental fate is to be born, to mature, and to die; it is a dramatic effect arising diffusely from a scene that is presented, and the characteristic issue, the crucial concern, is whether it will be credited or discredited.

—Erving Goffman, *The Presentation of Self in Everyday Life*

While acknowledging that we have overarching images of self that we carry from situation to situation, some social psychologists contend that these images do not shape our behavior nearly as much as the structural interactionists suggest—or as much as we commonly think. Following the lead of Erving Goffman, the founder of dramaturgical theory, these social psychologists propose that our actions are far more influenced by the nature and demands of the situations in which we interact. They also claim that our conceptions of self, whatever they may be, are only important insofar as they get expressed and realized through our interactions with others. "Who we are," according to these theorists, is rooted most fundamentally in how we act and in how others respond to those actions, particularly as we present ourselves to them in the dramas of everyday life. In turn, a comprehensive understanding of "who we are" requires a consideration of the intricate rituals and performances that characterize our daily presentations of self.

Staging the Self in Everyday Life

As we noted in Box 5-1, the idea that people "stage" themselves differently in different situations could be found more than a century ago in the work of William James. This idea can also be found in the writings of George Herbert Mead and Kenneth Burke, who were inspired by James and the early pragmatists. Yet it was Erving

Goffman, drawing on the insights of James, Mead, and Burke, who most profoundly revealed and portrayed the dramaturgical nature of human selfhood.

Goffman's basic ideas are fairly simple. He proposed that social life mirrors the theater. When interacting with others, we are much like actors on a stage. We have to translate our desires, feelings, beliefs, and self-images into communicable form, drawing on words, gestures, scripts, props, scenery, and various features of our appearance. In doing so, we engage in role "performances" which communicate our intentions and identities to the "audience" (i.e., others) in a given situation. When taking part in these performances, we have many reasons for trying to control the impressions that others form about us and the situation at hand.[41] Often we want others to think favorably of us, so we try to act in ways that make this more likely. Having others think well of us means that they will respond to us positively, defining us as worthwhile, appropriate, and desirable social actors. It also means that they will be more likely to accept our projected definition of the situation and to support our involvement in a variety of desired activities, thus enhancing our social power and personal freedom.

In our efforts to realize these goals, we commonly engage in the arts of **impression management**; that is, we try to talk and act in certain ways, or to avoid talking and acting in certain ways, so that others will form desired impressions of us and our current situation. As Goffman highlighted, the arts of impression management are essential to the process of self-presentation. Whenever we interact with others, we emphasize some of our social and personal characteristics while downplaying or concealing others. In doing so we may display, exaggerate, or make up positive attributes while disguising less appealing personal qualities or identities. This does not necessarily mean that when we manage others' impressions we are being "phony" or deceptive. In many situations we have to resort to impression management to convey our true attributes, such

as honesty, kindness, or intelligence, because these attributes are not immediately apparent to others or our actions can be misunderstood. Unless we carefully say or do things that reveal these attributes to others, they are not likely to recognize or confirm that we possess them. In turn, they will not grant us a desired self. In essence, then, if we do not learn to become "good actors," skilled in the arts of impression management, we are not likely to have our preferred images of self validated by others.

Since other people cannot directly perceive or evaluate our thoughts, feelings, motives, and character, they must depend on signs and symbols to assess the "reality" of who we are. Above all, they must rely on the information that we communicate to them about ourselves, particularly through our presentations of a **personal front**. Our personal front consists of the expressive resources we consciously or unconsciously draw on in our everyday interactions and performances.[42] In presenting a personal front we rely on three key types of expressive resources: the setting, our appearance, and our manner. The **setting** refers to the physical place or "scene" where interaction takes place and our performances unfold. It is where the curtain goes up on our everyday enactments of self, and we find ourselves playing roles, projecting identities, and delivering lines. Some typical examples of settings include offices, classrooms, churches, bars, clubs, and dorm rooms. When we interact in these settings, we manipulate various aspects of the "scenery," such as props, furnishings, and lighting, to stage our performances successfully. For example, in the classroom a professor may use items such as chalk, lecture notes, computers, videos, and desks to facilitate an engaging class and show that he or she is an excellent teacher.

The second expressive resource, **appearance**, refers to "the personal items that identify us as individuals," including our clothing, hairstyle, facial expressions, hygiene, and titles.[43] These personal items convey information about the social statuses that we occupy. Examples of such items include the uniform worn by a nurse, the dreadlocks worn by a reggae musician, the scowl worn by a drill sergeant, or the title of "Doctor" used by a physician or professor. We all rely on accessories like clothing, hairstyles, facial expressions, and titles to communicate information about ourselves to others. Goffman proposed that these aspects of our appearance facilitate our everyday interactions, providing others with useful cues about who we are, what role we are likely to play in the situation at hand, and how they should define and respond to us.

The third expressive resource, **manner**, refers to the mood, disposition, or style of behavior we display as a performer. We convey our manner to others when we address them rudely, politely, meekly, aggressively, or in some other way. Through our manner we tell others what kind of temperament and behavior they can expect from us as we interact with them. For instance, when we greet others with a warm hello, we inform them that we are ready to engage in a friendly interaction and that we have polite or civil intentions.

Paramount to the presentation of our personal front—and the management of others' impressions—is the process of **dramatic realization**.[44] We engage in dramatic realization when we emphasize important facts about ourselves that might go unnoticed, making them "real" or significant to others through our skillful performances. Examples include alluding to your excellent grade point average when discussing a paper with a professor or highlighting your accident-free driving record when asking your parents to borrow their new car. We also take part in dramatic realization when we subtly or consciously show others how much skill or effort it takes to pull off a performance, as some students do when letting professors know how tired they are from "studying all night" for a big exam. Most important, through the process of dramatic realization we make certain that others know that we "have what it takes" to engage in a particular performance, that we are appropriate for the part, and that we are aware of the social expectations attached to that part.

Elijah Anderson has insightfully illustrated how inner-city youth engage in impression management in his studies of interaction on the streets of Philadelphia. Anderson notes that interaction in this setting is informed by "the code of the street," which consists of informal rules that "prescribe both proper comportment [on the streets] and the proper way to respond if challenged....At the heart of the code is the issue of respect—loosely defined as being treated 'right' or being granted one's 'props' (or proper due) or the deference one deserves."[45]

To get treated with respect on the streets, a young man must present a personal front that demonstrates that he is "not someone to be 'messed with' or dissed."[46] Anderson chronicles how the proper management of appearance is crucial to sustaining one's honor and status on the streets, noting that

> Jackets, sneakers, gold jewelry, even expensive firearms, reflect not just taste...but also a willingness to possess things that may require defending. A boy wearing a fashionable, expensive jacket, for example, is vulnerable to attack by another who covets the jacket and either can't afford to buy one or wants the added satisfaction of depriving someone else. However, if a boy forgoes the desirable jacket and wears one that isn't hip, he runs the risk of being teased or even assaulted as an unworthy person.[47]

In a related vein, Anderson illustrates how the presentation of one's manner, particularly by showing toughness or "nerve," is vital to earning respect and protecting oneself on the streets. As he observes:

> ...one of the most effective ways of gaining respect is to manifest nerve. A man shows nerve by taking another person's possessions, messing with someone's woman, throwing the first punch, "getting in someone's face," or pulling a trigger. Its proper display helps check others who would violate one's person, and it also helps build a reputation that works to prevent further challenges.[48]

More generally, Anderson discovered that even civil and law-abiding youths have an interest in "going for bad" on the streets, "for it is a way to keep others at bay. The right look, moves, and overall behavior ensure safe passage...."[49] Through going for bad, inner city youths warn predatory peers from bothering them. They also convey that they are ready to defend themselves and their bodies from potential harm. As one young man revealed when describing the manner he displayed when negotiating the streets:

> When I walk the streets, I put this expression on my face that tells the next person I'm not to be messed with. That "You messing with the wrong fellow. You just try it, try it." And I know when cats are behind me. I be just lookin' in the air, letting them know I'm checkin' them out. Then I'll put my hand in my pocket, even if I ain't got no gun. Nobody wants to get shot, that shit burns, man. That shit hurt. Some guys go to singing. They try to let people know they crazy. 'Cause if you crazy [capable of anything], they'll leave you alone. And I have looked right in they face [muggers] and said, "Yo, I'm not the one." Give 'em that crazy look, then walk away. 'Cause I know what they into. They catch your drift quick.

Thus, when interacting on the streets, inner-city youth carefully manage their presentations of self, seeking to display a personal front that not only allows them to earn respect, but also to avoid victimization and potentially serious harm.

Regions of Self-Presentation

In formulating his dramaturgical theory of social life, Erving Goffman stressed that an important structural element of self-presentation is the manipulation of regions, or places that separate our "front stage" conduct from our "backstage" behavior. Some of our behavior takes place *front stage* before an audience, in a setting where we try to maintain an appropriate appearance for the part we are playing. Other behavior occurs *backstage*, in a region where we may knowingly violate or contradict the front stage performances we are giving.

To illustrate the differences between front stage and backstage areas, let us use the example of a restaurant where you are hypothetically working as a server. The front stage area of the restaurant would be its dining room, where the customers (or "audience") are eating and drinking. In this area, you and the other staff are expected to present yourselves as contented, efficient, and courteous. On the other hand, the backstage area would be the kitchen, where you and your co-workers tend to act very differently than you do in the dining room. For instance, upon entering the kitchen you may abandon your previously polite front and begin arguing with the cooks, cursing the dishwashers, and complaining about the demanding "jerks" at your tables.

As Goffman observed, the barriers between front and backstage regions are often crucial for successful impression management because they prevent members of the audience from seeing conduct that would undermine or discredit a public performance. They also allow "performers" (e.g., servers) to release some of the stress that has built up during their front stage activities. In many senses, backstage regions—such as bathrooms, kitchens, dens, and locker rooms—are analogous to dressing rooms in the theater. They give us a space where we can relax, let our hair down, and "get ourselves together" before we have to perform in a front stage region again. When backstage, we can "be ourselves," or at least we can be different selves than we are in public, without risking the loss of our public image.

In highlighting the differences between our front stage and backstage behaviors, Goffman revealed that we do not always feel "on" or dramaturgical. Nor do we always intend to be dramaturgical, managing others' impressions of us and the situation. Sometimes we care a great deal about how we come across to others; sometimes we care very little. As Brissett and Edgley point out, in any particular interaction our dramaturgical awareness

> depends on both the significance and tolerance of the other. For whatever reason, some others are just more important to [us]. At the same time, some audiences are very enabling, while others are very critical and challenging.[51]

In turn, the degree to which we feel "on" when interacting with others is determined, in large measure, by our level of involvement with them and by their responses to us.

As Goffman recognized, we become so used to performing roles in our everyday lives that we tend to think of ourselves as just doing things, not as being "actors" who carefully manage our performances for others. Yet Goffman demonstrated that even when we engage in many routine activities, such as sitting in a chair or wearing a uniform to work, we are involved in **dramaturgy**, communicating information about ourselves to others and managing their impressions of us—regardless of whether or not we intend to be dramaturgical. In highlighting this fact, Goffman illustrated that whether we like it or not, or plan it or not, our behavior is expressive: It announces and establishes who we are in a given situation.

The Self as Situated Identity

Before we can interact successfully with others, we must agree with them about what kind of situation we are in and how we are related to one another in that situation. In other words, we must figure out what identities each of us will occupy in relation to one another. For instance, we must determine whether we are interacting as customer to clerk, employee to employer, husband to wife, friend to friend, or competitor to competitor. In doing so we engage in the process of **identity negotiation**—a process through which we locate ourselves and others as social objects in a given situation, thereby establishing how we should act toward one another. Fortunately, in our everyday interactions we often negotiate and establish

identities without much difficulty. In fact, we ordinarily don't have to think much about doing so. When we enter a grocery store, for example, we can easily identify the cashiers and other staff. They wear name tags or shirts with the store logo, dress in a way that seems appropriate for their job, and occupy themselves with such tasks as stocking shelves, waiting on customers, and ringing up groceries. They also act like we expect grocery store employees to act, greeting us with a smile and asking us if we need any assistance. The same is true for a variety of other social situations—classrooms, concerts, hospitals, churches, libraries, restaurants, and family gatherings. We identify people with relative ease and place them in relation to us.

What characterizes all of these situations is a familiar but almost invisible process of identity negotiation in which people announce their own **situated identities** (e.g., customer) and place others in their situated identities (e.g., cashier). As Goffman emphasized, we implicitly and explicitly announce our identities in a situation through our expressive behavior. When we present a front effectively, and our role performances sustain the identity we project through this front, others feel compelled to honor this identity. In essence, when we present ourselves skillfully as a certain kind of person (e.g., as a customer, a student, or a professor), we exert moral pressure on others to respond toward us as if we were that kind of person and, thus, to support our performance and identity claims. If nothing about our talk or performance puts our identity claims into dispute, we have a *right* to expect others to honor them, at least until they can provide compelling reasons not to do so.

This right, however, is only one of the two key moral principles that guide our **presentations of self**. Along with this right, we have an *obligation* to act in a manner that is consistent with the self that we are presenting. For instance, if we are presenting ourselves as a parent, we not only have the right to be treated with respect and deference by our children, but also have the obligation to treat them respectfully, to offer them appropriate guidance, and to ensure that they are properly supervised.

When performing a particular role and presenting a related self, we are expected to maintain a minimal level of coherence among our setting, appearance, and manner. As long as we do so, the audience to our role performance is likely to see it as sincere or acceptable. At times, though, we slip up in our performances, saying or doing the wrong things and misreading the expectations of others. This leads to discomfort and embarrassment for everyone involved. To avoid or alleviate these feelings, we often rely on face-saving behaviors, such as audience expressions of "tact" or personal displays of "remedial work" designed to repair disrupted interactions.[52] Other people show us tact whenever they overlook flaws or gaffes in our role performances and offer continued support for our projected selves. Imagine, for example, that you are giving a presentation in one of your classes and, just as you make a key point, a large droplet of saliva sprays from your lips and lands near someone sitting in the front row. Although several of your classmates cannot help but notice it, none of them are likely to shout out, "Hey, you just about spit on someone in the first row!" Instead, they will probably show tact and act as if nothing unusual or embarrassing took place. Of course, we cannot always rely on others to be so considerate in regard to our gaffes or miscues. Sometimes they will see these acts as a reason to call our performances and projected identities into question. To address such challenges and avoid embarrassing "scenes," we have to engage in appropriate forms of remedial work, such as offering others acceptable apologies or accounts for our problematic behavior (see Chapter Six). The goal of interaction is to assure that events proceed smoothly.

In closing this section, we want to highlight some of the more significant insights that dramaturgical theorists have offered in regard to the self and social interaction. Above all, these analysts have revealed how interaction is a fluid and intricately coordinated process—a dance of give and take—that requires all of us to engage in expressive performances. Through these performances, we announce and negotiate selves (in the form of situated identities) that establish who we are in relation to others in a given context. Like other social meanings, these selves are situationally relative; that is, they are sustained for a while but then may become irrelevant in the face of new possibilities. When we enter new situations, we often have to create and enact new selves. As noted by Brissett and Edgley, "Moments are full of created selves, rising and falling, building and tearing down in a never-ending creation of new realities which constitute the drama of life."[53]

For dramaturgical theorists, then, it is absurd to ask the question: "Who am I?"—at least in a general way. This question can only be answered situationally. The self is not a private possession or abstract entity that we can separate from our behavior and relationships. Instead, the self is an outcome of our situated actions and interactions. We establish a self anew in every situation, relying on the help and collaboration of others as we manage their impressions and negotiate identities with them. Through these interactive processes others grant us a self—but it is a self that lasts only until we become involved in a new situation.

In highlighting the situational character of the self, dramaturgical theorists stress that "who we are" changes as we move around through the drama of everyday life. When we interact with diverse people, we express and realize different selves. In light of this, it is hopeless to search for a "true" and abiding self. According to dramaturgical theorists, the self is inevitably fleeting in nature: We can only realize who we are in relation to our situation and audience at a particular moment. In making these arguments, dramaturgical theorists echo the sentiments expressed by Albert Camus at the beginning of this chapter; that is, if we try to seize the self of which we feel sure, if we try to define and summarize it, we discover that it "is nothing but water slipping through our fingers."

Box 5-3 DRAMATURGY ON-LINE: THE PRESENTATION OF SELVES AND BODIES IN "CYBERSEX"

Some analysts hail the growth of the Internet, emphasizing how it is a vast, transnational "free market" of ideas that is opening up new and more liberating possibilities for human beings, not only as a source of information, but also as a space where people can "connect with" others and explore a seemingly endless array of communities and identities. Clearly the Internet is gaining in popularity and many individuals see it as a venue where they can try out new and different types of connections, interactions, and identities. Some people even use the Internet to find "electronic communities" where they can change or "play with" identities such as their race, gender, sexual orientation, or marital status. In turn, they see the Net as a space where they can present and realize selves that do not have the same characteristics and limitations as the ones they present in their everyday, face-to-face interactions. Because of this, they may experience more freedom, pleasure, and self-realization when interacting on the Net than they do in other social realms.

Many people experience "cyberspace" as a unique and appealing social world because it offers them a great deal of flexibility in their presentations of self, particularly since they can keep their actual bodies invisible (at least in most electronic venues). Because their bodies are "behind the scenes," on-line interactants can more easily distort and manipulate the appearances they present to others. In many respects, the bodies and selves they construct during on-line interactions are limited only by the reach of their imaginations. Of course, as we have highlighted throughout this text, the contents of their imaginations are profoundly influenced by their interactions, relationships, and culture.

In the following excerpt, Dennis Waskul, Mark Douglass, and Charles Edgley reveal how people present bodies and selves while engaging in cybersex, or what they call "outercourse." In the process, these analysts describe the dramaturgical displays (and deceptions) that individuals engage in while constructing themselves as sexual beings on-line. They also illustrate how people negotiate what would seem like a highly embodied activity—sex—in a disembodied environment, thereby transforming their bodies into a virtual and dramaturgical performance. Finally, Waskul, Douglass, and Edgley insightfully reveal how people are not nearly as "free" in their cybersexual negotiations as they might think or claim; that is, their presentations of sexual selves and bodies clearly reflect cultural beliefs about what a "sexy" person should look like. Thus, while individuals may be separated from their "real" bodies when engaging in cybersex, they are not freed from the confines of their culture. Even in the disembodied context of cyberspace, they fashion selves and body performances in terms of the images, meanings, and dramaturgical resources provided by their culture.

In cybersex, as long as relationships remain on-line, participants never so much as see each other, regardless of how many words they exchange. The self, the body, and the whole scene of interaction amount to a shared consensual hallucination substantiated and validated in textual dramaturgies that involve other disembodied participants.[1] Each participant contributes to the performance of the other in a negotiated agreement that determines the desires, expectations, and requirements of the situation. Or, as one respondent succinctly stated, "Looks and communication all tie together." Thus, the disembodied context enables participants to sidestep cultural specifications of beauty, glamour, and success, but it does not subvert these concepts.[2] The fluidity of both body and self-presentation does not free participants from the shackles of the beauty myth but only allows them to redefine themselves in accord with that myth...

Because participants [in cybersex] can present a virtual body that supports a cyber-self enactment and because these enactments contain culturally prescribed standards of beauty and sexiness, it should not be surprising to observe a conspicuous absence of fat, ugly persons with pimples, small breasts, or tiny penises. Consider, for example, these typical descriptions of self and body that participants on a commercial on-line system anonymously report:

I have brown hair, blue eyes, average height, average build, bigger-than-average [penis].

I'm 22, 6'0" tall, about 176 pounds, long brown hair (mid back)....Good shape, and love to have a good time. I'm not stuck up, but I am very attractive...

The above are typical descriptions. However, participants do not have to claim either actual or typical appearances. When on-line, persons can present a virtual body that is strikingly attractive, has hyberbolic sexual organs, and absolute specialties in sexual techniques. Take, for example, the following:

My hobbies include...selectively meeting attractive Women and sexing them with my 13" penis.

I'm a 21 year old single female 5'7" with bluegray eyes. 124 lbs. 44DD-28-30.

I am 5/'2, 110, blnde/brn waist length hair, green eyes, 48DD.

Some participants (perhaps a majority) likely embody the sexual performance of a virtual body with exaggerated physical appearances, abilities, and dimensions of sexual organs. Furthermore, these embodiments probably will adhere to (if not extend) social and cultural standards of beauty and sexiness. This is certainly the case when one considers commonly reported breast sizes. One large on-line commercial service allows users to create a "profile"—a brief summary of simple demographic and biographical information. The users of the system create all profiles, and persons can include anything they wish to tell other electronic participants about themselves. Although there is no category for reporting the dimensions of one's virtual body, nonetheless some people do....

Sex is an act that requires, or is at least dependent on, physical bodies. One's body in relation to the bodies of others forms the essence of a sexual encounter. Yet in cyberspace there can be no body, or fixed physical entity of the person. Nonetheless, cybersex does not escape claims of the flesh. Indeed, it fundamentally depends on them, extends them, and latently supports cultural and social standards for interpreting them. In text-based on-line leisure environments, participants transform their bodies into symbol alone—representations, descriptive codes, and words that embody expectations, appearances, and actions. Thus, they transform their bodies into a dramaturgical performance. What participants send to and from computer terminals are not merely words and self-enactments but body performances.

In concluding their analyses of cybersex, Waskul, Douglass, and Edgley point out that while participants in this activity typically view it as a playful form of interaction, or "self-game," it is a sign of more serious social trends. It reveals "much broader shifts in sociocultural beliefs, practices, and technologies. 'These include repeated transgressions of the traditional concept of the body's physical envelope and the locus of human agency.'"[3] According to Waskul, Douglass, and Edgley, cybersex and similar Net-based forms of leisure interaction

...extend and normalize the potential not only for multiple self-enactments but also for the malleability of body presentations in a manner that parallels the fluidity of contemporary selfhood. Although Goffman claims that the body is little more than the "peg" on which we hang a person's self, only in everyday, rarely is face-to-face reality is the body so inert. New communications environments challenge traditional assumptions about the interplay among body, self, and social world. Traditional sociological definitions of self as that which the body contains or holds are increasingly questionable assertions—especially with regard to the experiences of virtuality...

The body is more than a prop that is used in a variety of ways to support a multiplicity of self-enactments. Increasingly, the meanings of the actions taken by human agencies define both bodies and selves. As this study suggests, the most stable personal characteristic—our sense of who we are and where we are in space—is now open to redefinition. Given the possibilities of selfhood made manifest in the emerging datasphere as a new arena for human experience, and the relationship of these experiences to the bodies that may or may not be grounded in this matrix of virtual experience, new questions arise about what constitutes a person.

1. William Gibson. *Neuroromance*. New York: ACE, 1984.
2. Elizabeth Reid, *Cultural Formations in Text-based Virtual Realities*. M.A. thesis, University of Melbourne, 1994.
3. Dennis Waskul, Mark Douglass, and Charles Edgeley, "Cybersex: Outercourse and the Enselfment of the Body," *Symbolic Interaction* 23 (4), 2000, p. 394.

Source: Dennis Waskul, Mark Douglass, and Charles Edgeley, "Cybersex: Outercourse and the Enselfment of the Body," *Symbolic Interaction* 23 (4): 375–395, 2000.

Beyond Goffman: The Drama of Self Versus the Experience of Self

While appreciating the insights that dramaturgical theory offers, interactionists criticize this theory for failing to see how and why people construct and experience selves that extend beyond situated identities. Drawing on other theoretical perspectives, such as structural interactionism, many interactionists contend that each of us brings a relatively stable and enduring self to our social situations. This enduring or "biographical" self has links to our self-concept and to the past, present, and future. It also influences our everyday presentations of self. For instance, when we act toward ourselves and others in a given situation, we are affected by our memories of the past, including our memories of the roles we have performed, the statuses we have achieved, the relationships we have negotiated, and the successes and failures we have experienced. We are also influenced by our thoughts of the future, including our thoughts of who we might become in the next situation or even several years from now. When we fashion acts and identities in a particular situation, then, we do so as people who have lives that extend beyond that situation—lives that include pasts and futures, as well as goals and responsibilities other than those we are currently enacting.[54] This means that we often link our present behavior to our past and future selves. It also means that when we interact with immediate others, we may focus on aspects of our lives and selves that have nothing to do with our current situation. When talking with our co-workers, for example, we may discuss matters totally unrelated to our jobs, such as what we did with our friends over the weekend or where we are planning to travel on our vacation next month.

As Robert Zussman has highlighted, we can see the biographical self being formed and expressed in "autobiographical occasions."[55] These are occasions when people construct stories of their lives. One example of such an occasion is a family reunion. When gathering with other relatives at a reunion, people tell stories and disclose details about their lives, including details about their past, present, and future selves. People engage in similar kinds of storytelling when they go on a date, appear for a job interview, or go through life transitions such as graduations, weddings, career changes, or retirements. In responding to these occasions and formulating stories about themselves, individuals construct, sustain, and sometimes transform biographical selves.

Most important, through focusing attention on how people construct and enact biographical selves, interactionist scholars have revealed why a comprehensive analysis of the self must go beyond consideration of how people present and realize situated identities. To provide a more complete understanding of the dynamics of selfhood, social psychologists must also consider the *experience of self,* particularly the experience of a biographical self that gives elements of coherence and continuity to a person's everyday presentations of self.

THE EXPERIENCE OF SELF IN POSTMODERN SOCIETY

In an emerging postmodern world the construction and maintenance of an integrated self becomes deeply problematic because the social structures necessary to anchor the self have themselves become unstable and ephemeral.

—David Karp, *Speaking of Sadness*

Just how coherent is the self in the complex and heterogeneous societies that characterize the modern world? If, as interactionists suggest, we develop integrated and unified selves by adopting the perspective of an organized community or generalized other, what kind of selves do we form in societies characterized by diverse and rapidly changing communities? Can we even hope to construct and sustain coherent selves in such social contexts?

In addressing these questions, interactionists draw on analyses developed by postmodern social theorists. Writing within disciplines ranging from literature to philosophy to sociology, postmodern theorists contend that a profound cultural transformation is underway in societies such as the United States—a transformation that has far-reaching implications for the nature and experience of the self. Indeed, postmodern theorists suggest that this transformation has produced shifts in the character of the self that are at least as significant as the changes provoked by the Industrial Revolution of the nineteenth century.

A key claim of postmodern analysts is that the self is "under siege" in advanced industrial societies, largely due to the impact of broader technological and cultural changes. At the heart of these changes is the explosive growth of communication technologies, including e-mail, the Internet, cell phones, translation phones, answering machines, fax machines, conference phones, satellites, televisions, and movies. These technologies allow us to maintain relationships across great distances and to belong to groups and communities that span the globe. They also expose us to a wide variety of people who embrace diverse beliefs, perspectives, and lifestyles. This exposure, in turn, leads to what one postmodern theorist, Kenneth Gergen, calls the *social saturation* of the self.[56]

According to Gergen, communication technologies, along with technologies such as airplanes and automobiles, have led to a steady increase in the number and variety of relationships in which we are engaged. In contrast to a century ago, when social relationships were largely confined to the distance of an easy walk, we now casually form and maintain relationships with people who live hundreds or even thousands of miles away. We also have detailed knowledge of the lives and experiences of countless others who reside in communities very different from our own. This results in what Gergen calls the *populating of the self*, or the internalization of the voices and perspectives of myriad others. Through this process of social saturation we acquire many identities and ways of being. We also develop new patterns of relationship. Among these is the "microwave relationship"—a relationship in which we establish and maintain intimacy through brief periods of intensity (e.g., "quality time") rather than the extensive daily contact that, historically, was the foundation of close relationships and stable identities.[57] In place of these everyday, enduring relationships, postmodern life is characterized by multiple roles and selves and limited involvements with a large number of others, including many people who have little in common with us. (Think of your own daily interactions. How many people do you interact with in your classes, dorms, and dining centers, or in stores, businesses, and e-mail conversations, who have very different backgrounds from your own?)

Gergen proposes that these features of postmodern life lead us to adopt multiple perspectives on ourselves, making it difficult for us to form a unified self, or core identity. As we take part in a variety of "incoherent and disconnected relationships" and perform a number of unrelated roles, we acquire a new pattern of self-consciousness,

which Gergen calls "multiphrenia," or many-mindedness.[58] In essence, we interpret our experiences and ourselves in many different and contradictory ways and evaluate ourselves according to many different and contradictory standards. This is why we often feel unsure, inadequate, and fragmented. "Neither our hearts nor our minds speak with a single voice or a unified self."[59]

Gergen contends that as we grapple with this postmodern condition, we become less committed to traditional notions of the self as an enduring and deeply personal phenomenon. Instead, we replace these notions with an understanding of the self as relational—as something we create and re-create through our connections and interactions with others. According to Gergen, this understanding leads us to "realize increasingly that who and what we are is not so much the result of our 'personal essence' (real feelings, deep beliefs, and the like) but of how we are constructed in various groups."[60] Guided by this realization, we are no longer inclined to ask ourselves, "Who am I?" Rather, we ask others, "Who can I be with you in this situation?"

For Gergen, then, the postmodern self bears a close resemblance to the dramaturgical self described by Goffman. It is profoundly fluid and social, enacted and established in situated performances. Gergen, however, emphasizes that this self has emerged as a byproduct of rapid technological and cultural change. He also notes that it has two distinct advantages over the traditional self it is replacing. First, the postmodern self is highly adaptive to change, giving individuals the flexibility to cope effectively with the shifting situational demands they face as they perform diverse social roles. Second, it has liberating possibilities. That is, because it is unencumbered by needs for consistency, unity, and unvarying authenticity, the postmodern self can be free to play with different identities, relationships, and commitments, knowing that each is valid in different contexts and from certain standpoints. For instance, a student can opt to be a "geek" in the afternoon and a "party girl" in the evening, trading in a bookish self in the classroom for a boisterous self in the bar, without feeling as though these two identities are at odds.

Gergen's observations parallel those shared by interactionist analysts, such as Louis Zurcher and John Hewitt, who have written about the significant changes taking place in the character of the self in recent decades. In *The Mutable Self*, Zurcher proposes that the accelerating pace of social change has placed demands on us to develop a new orientation toward the self, one that sees it as more important to have a changing and flexible self than a stable self. This orientation, also known as the mutable self, is characterized by tolerance, openness to a variety of experiences, and adaptability in the face of change.[61] Through adopting such an orientation, we can tolerate, assess, and respond more effectively to the disruptions and uncertainties provoked by rapid processes of social change.

In a related vein, John Hewitt observes that in contemporary society our sense of self is much more likely to be rooted in "a more or less self-conscious selection of a community as its main support."[62] This self-selected community, or community of choice, serves many of the same functions as the traditional communities of the past. It provides us with a network of similar others who support our conceptions of self. Moreover, even when this community is geographically dispersed and based on a narrow set of criteria of similarity, such as a shared interest in camping or biking, it provides a sense of continuity and integration, allowing us to experience a somewhat enduring and coherent self.

Hewitt recognizes, however, that many of us have a rather tenuous relationship to the community or communities with which we identify. While we may identify strongly with one community—such as a profession, a religious organization, or a leisure group—we do not link all of our activities or identities exclusively to this community. Instead, most of us identify rather mildly with several communities, including work groups, campus groups, church groups, athletic teams, and other leisure organizations. Typically we also shift our allegiances and involvements from one community to another, identifying with a number of communities over the course of our lives. In addition, we sometimes find ourselves on the margins of two or more communities, unable to identify with or ignore any of them.

Most crucially, Hewitt proposes that because our identification with a community is less than total in today's society, we are in many respects more self-conscious than the members of more traditional communities. Rather than experiencing the self as the creation of a stable, enduring community that surrounds us from birth and clearly tells us who we are, we are increasingly likely to experience the self as something that we must discover or create, particularly through forming connections with a supportive or like-minded community of others. In making this point, Hewitt echoes one of Gergen's key insights; that is, we have become increasingly aware that *it is our connections with others that make us who and what we are*. Yet Hewitt parts company with Gergen in regard to the disappearance of the "personal self," or the experience of self as a personal essence. Rather than seeing this experience of self diminishing or disappearing, Hewitt suggests that it is being realized in new forms of self-selected community.

More recently, Jaber Gubrium and James Holstein have also challenged the claim that the personal self is disappearing, proposing instead that "the personal self continues to take shape as the central narrative theme," or key organizing idea, around which we express identity.[63] Gubrium and Holstein assert that contemporary times are trying for the self not because the personal self has disappeared from the social landscape, but rather because it is being produced in a rapidly growing, widely varying, and increasingly competitive set of institutions. Self-construction has become a big business, characterized by the proliferation of institutions that make it their stock-in-trade to design, discern, and produce identities for us.

According to Gubrium and Holstein, the stories we formulate about our personal selves are increasingly anchored in institutionally produced narratives, or "discursive environments." Discursive environments refer to "institutional domains characterized by distinctive ways of interpreting and representing everyday realities."[64] Some examples of discursive environments include schools, health clubs, counseling centers, support groups, self-improvement programs, recreational organizations, correctional facilities, and on-line forums.[65] These environments establish the general parameters for the construction of recognizable and accountable personal selves. For instance, counseling centers and support groups produce selves in terms of "too much" or "too little" of virtually every combination of thought, feeling, and action.[66] This can range from too much anxiety, guilt, and concern for approval, which are among the criteria for "co-dependency," to too little passion about life or regard for oneself, which are central features of depression.

Of course, many discursive environments promote mainly positive images of self, seeking to enhance or bolster the self rather than create troubled identities. Recreational and leisure organizations, for example, provide activities, resources, and connections that foster opportunities for building and realizing valued personal selves. Campers, gardeners, and golfers, along with bird watchers, softball players, and many others, find that the social contexts of their hobbies offer not only recreation but also diverse ways of defining and conveying identities. This is clearly revealed in the growing number of people participating in motorcycle clubs. They express and realize the identity of "biker" not only through riding motorcycles but also through wearing biker clothing, reading and writing biker magazines, participating in road rallies, and going on organized trips.

In highlighting how the relationship between the self and society has shifted in our postmodern times, Gubrium and Holstein point out that "personal selves" are being produced in more social settings than ever before. A thriving and growing number of institutions are serving up countless possibilities for self, providing individuals with a diverse range of options for discerning and constructing their core identities.

In assessing the implications of this situation for the future of the self, Gubrium and Holstein offer some optimistic appraisals that counter the gloomy conclusions of many postmodern theorists. They point out that our ability to choose among options in fashioning a self—"indeed, to use some options in order to resist others, or to construct new ones—can be as liberating as it is overwhelming and debilitating."[67] They also suggest that the self is remarkably resilient, which means that ultimately it is likely to adapt positively to the challenges it faces in today's society. Patricia Adler and Peter Adler offer support for this view in their intriguing study of the lives and selves of transient resort workers. Although these workers had a highly mobile lifestyle with rapidly shifting social networks, they did not experience the loss of a core self. Instead, their selves adapted and thrived in response to their transient life situation, "emerging with renewed self-orientation and a stronger driving center," as well as a higher level of flexibility.[68]

SUMMARY

- The self is a complex phenomenon. Even social psychologists struggle to comprehend its nature and significance, as revealed in the debates they have about its origins, contents, structure, dynamics, and ramifications. Like other social psychologists, symbolic interactionists debate about various features of the self, such as the degree to which it is situational and the extent to which it shapes a person's ongoing behavior. Interactionists largely agree, however, that the self refers to a process of reflexive and communicative activity—a process that includes a person's subjective stream of consciousness as well as his or her concept of self as a physical, social, and moral being. Interactionists also agree that the self emerges out of, and is sustained by or transformed through, an individual's relationships with others.

- Following George Herbert Mead, interactionists regard the self as both a social structure and a social process. Yet they disagree about the relative weight that should be accorded to the structure of the self as opposed to the processes through which it is constructed and realized. Those interactionists who stress the structure of the self tend to focus on the nature and implications of the self-concept and self-esteem. In doing so, they highlight not only how we define and feel about ourselves, but also how these definitions and feelings shape our actions, interactions, and larger institutional contexts. By contrast, dramaturgical theorists contend that our self-conceptions and self-feelings change in accord with the demands of the situations within which we interact. They stress that the self is an adjustive process, shifting in character and expression as we enter different contexts and interact with different people. Inspired by Erving Goffman, these analysts focus on the intricate rituals and dramas through which we present and realize selves in various situations. They reveal that the self is fundamentally expressive; that is, we can only establish "who we are" in a given interaction through engaging in the arts of impression management.

- In highlighting the expressive character of the self, dramaturgical theorists tend to overlook the enduring, "biographical self" that we bring to our social situations. We define and respond to ourselves as persons who have lives that extend beyond our immediate situations—as persons who have pasts and futures as well as goals and responsibilities other than those we are currently enacting. This means that we often link our current actions, including our identity announcements and negotiations, to our past and future selves.

Our presentations of self, then, are not only shaped by the demands of our given situation, they are also informed by our enduring conceptions and experiences of self.

- In today's society, it has become increasingly difficult to sustain a coherent and unified sense of self. The growth of communication technologies and the accelerating pace of social change has placed the self "under siege," exposing it to the diverse and often contradictory perspectives of countless others. According to postmodern scholars, the result is that we feel uncertain and fragmented, making us less committed to the notion that we possess a unified and deeply personal self. Instead, we are more likely to see and experience the self as socially constructed—as something we create and re-create through our relations with others.

- While appreciating many of the insights that postmodern theorists offer regarding the changing experience of self, interactionists dispute their claims that the personal self is vanishing. Indeed, interactionists such as John Hewitt, Jaber Gubrium, and James Holstein contend that nothing could be further from the truth. The personal self continues to be the central narrative theme through which we express our identity—it is the self we live by. However, the personal self has very different social foundations than it did in the past. Increasingly, it is anchored in institutions and communities that specialize in the business of self-construction. These institutions and communities present us with both challenges and opportunities as we try to discern "who we really are" in a rapidly changing social world.

GLOSSARY OF KEY TERMS

Appearance   The personal items that identify us as individuals, such as our clothing, hairstyle, grooming, and titles (Goffman). Our appearance informs others of our social status and our temporary state, such as whether we are working or relaxing.

Dramatic Realization

A process by which we emphasize important facts about ourselves that might go unnoticed, making them "real" or significant to others through our skillful performances.

Dramaturgy

Behavior through which we communicate information about ourselves to others, thereby managing their impressions of us.

The "I"

the aspect of the self that is the source of our spontaneous, impulsive, and initiating tendencies. According to Mead, the "I," or self as subject, can be understood as the initiator and formulator of action. It engages in ongoing dialogue with the "me," or internalized attitudes and expectations of others.

Identity Negotiation

The process through which we locate ourselves and others as social objects in a given situation, thereby establishing how we should act toward one another. This process relies on the coordination and alignment of identity announcements and placements.

Identity Salience

The rank or prominence of a specific identity in your personal hierarchy of identities. The more prominent or important a given identity, the more often we will draw on it as we interact with others and coordinate our actions with them.

Impression Management

Our efforts to talk and act in certain ways, or to avoid talking and acting in certain ways, so that others will form desired views of us and our situation.

Manner

Those expressions that reveal our style of behavior, mood, and disposition as a performer; the manner we convey sets the tone for ensuing interactions.

The "me"

The internalized attitudes of others through which we view ourselves and our actions. This aspect of the self develops through the processes of socialization and role taking. It responds to the impulsive and initiating tendencies of the "I."

Mutable Self

A self-concept that is highly adaptive to rapid social and cultural change. According to Zurcher, the mutable self integrates all four modes of self-conception—physical, social, reflective, and oceanic.

Personal Front

According to Goffman, the expressive equipment we consciously or unconsciously use as we present our selves to others. Our personal "front" includes our appearance, manner, and setting.

Presentation of Self

The ways we present ourselves to others in order to elicit favorable impressions and to control their definitions of the situation.

Self

A process of reflexive activity that includes our subjective stream of consciousness (perceptions, thoughts, feelings, plans, and choices) as well as our conception of self as a physical, social, and moral being. In essence, the self is a reflexive process that enables us to formulate, monitor, control, and react to our own behavior.

Self-Concept The overarching image that one has of oneself as a physical, social, spiritual, or moral being.

Self-Efficacy Our sense of being competent or "in control" as we act in the environment and interact with others.

Self-Esteem The positive or negative feelings we attach to our selves and the judgments we make of our own worth. We typically judge ourselves as good or bad, better or worse, respectable or unrespectable.

Self-Indication The process through which we define and make sense of things in the world around and inside us. The process of thinking is based on self-indication.

Setting The spatial and physical items in a situation (e.g., props and furnishings) that we use in staging our performance.

Situated Identity The self that we direct outward and have confirmed by others in a given situation, based largely on the social characteristics we present to them. When granted a situated identity, we are placed or located as a social object in a given situation. This allows us to know how to act toward ourselves and others in that situation.

QUESTIONS FOR REFLECTION OR ASSIGNMENT

1. After analyzing people for many years, Harry Stack Sullivan, a famous philosopher and psychiatrist, concluded that "individuality is an illusion." Do you agree or disagree with Dr. Sullivan's conclusion? If so, why is individuality an illusion? If not, what is there about you that is uniquely individual and why is it important? (In your answer be sure to state how you define "individuality.")

2. Complete the Twenty Statements Test (TST) and respond to the following questions regarding the various identities you listed:
   a. Which of these identities are most fundamental to your sense of self? (To help you answer this question, try crossing out the statements you wrote down until there are only a few left.) Which identities are most salient in your everyday life? Why? To which of these identities are you most strongly committed? Why?
   b. How did you acquire or develop these identities? What other people were (or are) important in this process? That is, what others were (or are) your "significant others" or key reference groups? How were (or are) they important in validating and sustaining these aspects of your "self"?
   c. How has your image of self changed since you were in high school (or during the past five years)? How would you account for or explain this change in terms of an interactionist perspective?

3. Pretend that you have to describe your "self" to an actor who will perform your character in a play. What kinds of moods, gestures, expressions, postures, and habits would be reflective of who you "really" are? If this actor tried to imitate you, by way of parody, what would she or he emphasize? If your friends or family members had to describe you as a person, what would they say? Would you describe yourself in a similar way? Why or why not?

4. Imagine you're going out on a date with someone you really like. What kind of "self" will you present to this person on your first date? How will you manage your appearance and

manner to influence your date's impressions of you? How will you use props and equipment as the date unfolds? What kind of information will you share about yourself? What kind of information will you hide? How can you apply Goffman's dramaturgical concepts (such as impression management and self-presentation) to describe what happens on your date?

5. Do you see your gender as an essential aspect of your "self"? Why or why not? Do you see your race as a core aspect of your self? Why or why not? How are your gendered and racial images of self influenced by your interactions with others?

6. Imagine that you won several million dollars in a state lottery. Do you think this would change your self-concept? Why or why not? How would others (e.g., friends, family, co-workers, the media) be likely to define and react to you after you became a millionaire? What impact would this have on your sense of self? Do you think that you would acquire a "gloried self" in any way? Would you want to acquire such a self? Why or why not?

7. Do you see yourself as having a changeable or mutable self? Do you think you will have a different image of self in the future? For example, who do you think you will be in five to ten years? Who would you "really" like to become? How likely are you to become this person? What other people will be important in this process? How and why will they be important in helping you realize your future goals for and images of self?

8. Do you think that you have a "saturated" or "postmodern" self? Why or why not? How optimistic are you about your ability to adapt to our rapidly changing society? How do you think your self-concept will change in responding to larger social and economic changes? Do you think your self will become more or less fragmented in the future? Why?

SUGGESTED READINGS FOR FURTHER STUDY

Athens, Lonnie. "The Self as a Soliloquy," *The Sociological Quarterly* 35(3), 2005, pp. 521–532.

Charmaz, Kathy. *Good Days, Bad Days: The Self in Chronic Illness and Time* (Piscataway, NJ: Rutgers University Press, 1991).

Irvine, Leslie. *Codependent Forevermore: The Invention of Self in a 12 Step Group* (Chicago: University of Chicago Press, 2008).

Karp, David. *Speaking of Sadness: Depression, Disconnection, and the Meanings of Illness* (New York: Oxford University Press, 1993).

Perinbanayagam, Robert. *Games and Sport in Everyday Life: Dialogues and Narratives of the Self* Boulder, CO: Paradigm Publishers, 2007).

Williams, J. Patrick and Heith Copes. "How Edge Are You? Constructing Authentic Identities and Subcultural Boundaries in a Straightedge Internet Forum," *Symbolic Interaction* 28(1), 2007, pp. 67–90.

ENDNOTES

1. Robert C. Solomon, *The Big Questions*, 2nd ed. (New York: Harcourt Brace Jovanovich, 1986).

2. Erving Goffman, *The Presentation of Self in Everyday Life* (New York: Doubleday, 1959). For a similar view of the self, see Dennis Brissett and Charles Edgley, eds., *Life as Theater: A Dramaturgical Sourcebook*, 2nd ed. (New York: Aldine Press, 1990).

3. Spencer Cahill, "Erving Goffman," in Joel Charon, ed., *Symbolic Interaction: An Introduction, an Interpretation, an Integration*, 4th ed. (Englewood Cliffs, NJ: Prentice-Hall, 1992), pp. 185–200.

4. Morris Rosenberg, "The Self-Concept: Social Product and Social Force," in Morris

Rosenberg and Ralph H. Turner, eds., *Social Psychology: Sociological Perspectives* (New York: Basic Books, 1981), pp. 593–624.

5 This definition is derived from Chad Gordon, "Self-Conceptions: Configurations of Content," in Chad Gordon and Kenneth J. Gergen, eds., *The Self in Social Interaction* (New York: John Wiley & Sons, 1968), pp. 115–136; and from Viktor Gecas, "The Self-Concept," *Annual Review of Sociology* 8, 1982, pp. 1–33.

6 George Herbert Mead, *Mind, Self, and Society* (Chicago: University of Chicago Press, 1934).

7 James Holstein and Jaber F. Gubrium, *The Self We Live By: Narrative Identity in a Postmodern World* (New York: Oxford University Press, 2000), p. 29.

8 George Herbert Mead, *Mind, Self, and Society*, (Note 6), pp. 173–176.

9 Ibid., p. 178.

10 Herbert Blumer, *Symbolic Interactionism: Perspective and Method* (Englewood Cliffs, NJ: Prentice-Hall, 1969).

11 James W. Vander Zanden, *Social Psychology*, 4th ed. (New York: Random House, 1987), p. 150.

12 Herbert Blumer, *Symbolic Interactionism: Perspective and Method*, (Note 10).

13 George Herbert Mead, *Mind, Self, and Society*, (Note 6), p. 142.

14 William James, *Psychology* (New York: Holt, 1892), pp. 189–226.

15 George Herbert Mead, *Mind, Self, and Society*, (Note 6), p. 140.

16 Ibid., p. 196.

17 Viktor Gecas, "The Self-Concept," (Note 5), pp. 1–33.

18 The structural approach to the self emerged out of the early TST-based studies that Kuhn and his students conducted in their efforts to measure the contents of the self. Kuhn developed the TST because he wanted to test and refine the ideas of George Herbert Mead and other founders of interactionism, such as John Dewey and Charles Horton Cooley. Although Kuhn respected the work of these scholars, he saw their ideas as largely "conjectural orientations" that needed to be tested by research and developed into a more rigorous set of theoretical generalizations. Kuhn felt particularly concerned about Mead's ideas regarding the "I," or the spontaneous and unpredictable phase of the self. According to Kuhn, Mead's descriptions of the "I" were not only ambiguous and confusing but also resistant to concrete definition and testing. In turn, Kuhn chose to drop this notion out of his analysis, instead focusing his research on the "me," or the self as object, which was much easier to define and test. For related discussion, see Manford Kuhn, "Major Trends in Symbolic Interaction Theory in the Past Twenty-Five Years," *Sociological Quarterly* 5, 1964, p. 70.

19 Louis Zurcher, *The Mutable Self* (Beverly Hills, CA: Sage, 1977).

20 Ibid., p. 46.

21 David A. Snow and Cynthia L. Phillips, "The Changing Self-Orientations of College Students: From Institution to Impulse," *Social Science Quarterly* 63(3), 1982, pp. 462–476.

22 Louis Zurcher, *The Mutable Self*, (Note 19). In a separate but related analysis, Ralph Turner proposed that a growing number of Americans had experienced a change in the locus of self, a change from conceptualizing their "real" self in terms of roles and statuses to conceptualizing it in terms of impulses, feelings, and styles of behavior. See Ralph H. Turner, "The Real Self: From Institution to Impulse," *American Journal of Sociology* 81, 1976, pp. 989–1016.

23 Sheldon Stryker, "Identity Theory: Developments and Extensions," in K. Yardley and T. Holmes, eds., *Self and Identity: Psychosocial Perspectives* (New York: Wiley, 1987), pp. 89–104. See also Sheldon Stryker, *Symbolic Interactionism: A Social Structural Version* (Reading, MA: Cummings, 1980).

24 Ralph H. Turner, "The Role and the Person," *American Journal of Sociology* 84, 1978, pp. 87–110.

25 Viktor Gecas, "The Self-Concept," (Note 5).

26 Charles Horton Cooley, *Human Nature and the Social Order* (New York: Charles Scribner and Sons, [1902] 1964).

27 David C. Lundgrean, "Social Feedback and Self-Appraisals: Current Status of the Mead-Cooley Hypothesis," *Symbolic Interaction* 27(2), 2004, pp. 267–286; Alicia D. Cast, Jan E. Stets, and Peter J. Burke, "Does the Self Conform to the Views of Others?" *Social Psychology Quarterly* 62, 1999, pp. 68–82; Richard B. Felson, "The (Somewhat) Social Self: How Others Affect Self-Appraisals," in J. Suls, ed., *The Self in Social Perspective*. Vol. 4 (Hillsdale, NJ: Erlbaum, 1993), pp. 1–26; J. S. Schrauger and T. J. Shoeneman, "Symbolic Interactionist View of Self-Concept: Through the Looking Glass Darkly," *Psychological Bulletin* 86, 1979, pp. 549–573; Morris Rosenberg, "Which Significant Others?" *American Behavioral Scientist* 16, 1973, pp. 829–860.

28 Viktor Gecas, "The Self-Concept," (Note 5), p. 6.

29 David D. Franks and Viktor Gecas. "Autonomy and Conformity in Cooley's Self-Theory: The Looking-Glass Self and Beyond," *Symbolic Interaction* 15 (1), 1992, pp. 49–68.

30 Vicktor Gecas, "The Self-Concept," (Note 5), p. 7.

31 An exception to this tendency is provided by depressed persons. Rather than seeing others' appraisals in a positive light, a depressed individual may interpret them negatively. See David Karp, *Speaking of Sadness: Depression, Disconnection, and the Meanings of Illness* (New York: Oxford University Press, 1993).

32 For an intriguing illustration of how individuals disregard social appraisals that conflict with their self-evaluations, see Susan Haworth-Hoeppner and David Maines, "A Sociological Account of the Persistence of Invalidated Anorexic Identities," *Symbolic Interaction* 28(1), 2005, pp. 1–23.

33 Morris Rosenberg and Howard A. Kaplan, *Social Psychology of the Self-Concept* (Arlington Heights, IL: Harlan Davidson, 1982).

34 This level of social comparison is perhaps best expressed in William James's famous formula: self-esteem = success/pretensions. In explaining this formula, James noted that our self-esteem is determined by the ratio of our actual successes or accomplishments to our presumed potential, which results in a fraction where "our pretensions are the denominator and the numerator our successes." See William James, *Psychology* (New York: Holt, 1892), p. 189.

35 Viktor Gecas and Michael L. Schwalbe, "Beyond the Looking-Glass Self: Social Structure and Efficacy-Based Self-Esteem," *Social Psychology Quarterly* 46, 1983, pp. 77–88.

36 Charles Horton Cooley, *Human Nature and the Social Order*, (Note 26).

37 Dennis D. Brissett, "Towards a Clarification of Self-Esteem," *Psychiatry* 35, 1972, pp. 255–263.

38 While accentuating the importance of self-efficacy as an "intrinsic" dimension of self-esteem, interactionists are also careful to note that it has social foundations. We can only become aware of ourselves as efficacious through drawing on language, a socially shared system of symbols that, of course, we acquire through social interaction. Moreover, as Dennis Brissett observed (see Note 37), even though we experience self-efficacy on an internal and emotional level, it does not inhere in our individual psyches. Rather, it is built up in and realized through our social experiences and relationships. Brissett also emphasized that the efficacy-based dimension of our self-esteem offers us a source of autonomy as we formulate our actions, enabling us to choose lines of behavior independent of, or even opposed to, the evaluations and reactions of immediate others. In many situations, we may choose to engage in activities or role performances that will provide us with a sense of self-efficacy rather than positive social appraisal. When doing this, we show that we are more concerned with experiencing a sense of competence and control than we are with gaining the approval of others.

39 Morris Rosenberg, "The Self-Concept: Social Product and Social Force," in Morris Rosenberg and Ralph H. Turner, eds., *Social Psychology: Sociological Perspectives* (New York: Basic Books, 1981), p. 614.

40 Ibid.

41 Erving Goffman, *The Presentation of Self in Everyday Life* (New York: Doubleday, 1959), p. 151.

42 Ibid.

43 Gregory P. Stone, "Appearance and the Self: A Slightly Revised Version," in Gregory P. Stone and Harvey Farberman, eds., *Social Psychology Through Symbolic Interaction* (New York: Macmillan, 1981), pp. 187–202.

44 Erving Goffman, *The Presentation of Self in Everyday Life*, (Note 1).

45 Elijah Anderson, *Code of the Street: Decency, Violence, and the Moral Life of the Inner City* (New York: Norton, 1999), p. 33.

46 Ibid., p. 73.

47 Ibid., pp. 73–74.

48 Ibid., p. 92.

49 Elijah Anderson, *Streetwise: Race, Class, and Change in an Urban Community* (Chicago: University of Chicago Press, 1991), p. 177.

50 Ibid.

51 Dennis Brissett and Charles Edgley, eds., *Life as Theater: A Dramaturgical Source Book*, (Note 2), p. 6.

52 Erving Goffman, *The Presentation of Self in Everyday Life*, (Note 1).

53 Dennis Brissett and Charles Edgley, eds., *Life as Theater: A Dramaturgical Source Book*, 2nd ed., (Note 2), p. 18.

54 John Hewitt, *Self and Society*, 8th ed. (New York: Allyn and Bacon, 2000), p. 125.

55 Robert Zussman, "Autobiographical Occasions," *Contemporary Sociology* 25, 1996, pp. 143–148.

56 Kenneth Gergen, *The Saturated Self: Dilemmas of Identity in Contemporary Life* (New York: Basic Books, 1991).

57 Ibid.

58 Ibid.

59 Spencer Cahill, ed. *Inside Social Life: Readings in Sociological Psychology and Microsociology*, 3rd ed. (Los Angeles: Roxbury Publishing, 2001), p. 290.

60 Kenneth Gergen, *The Saturated Self*, (Note 56), p. 170.

61 Louis Zurcher, *The Mutable Self*, (Note 19).

62 John Hewitt, *Self and Society*, (Note 54), pp. 123–124.

63 Jaber Gubrium and James A. Holstein, "The Self in a World of Going Concerns," *Symbolic Interaction* 23(2), 2000, p. 96. For related discussion, see also James A. Holstein and Jaber Gubrium, *The Self We Live By: Narrative Identity in a Postmodern World*, (Note 7).

64 Ibid., p. 103.

65 For detailed illustrations of Internet-based "discursive environments" that produce and sustain selves, see J. Patrick Williams and Heith Copes, "How Edge are You? Constructing Authentic Identities and Subcultural Boundaries in a Straightedge Internet Forum," *Symbolic Interaction* 28(1), 2007, pp. 67–90; Kerry O. Ferris, "Transmitting Ideals: Constructing Self and Moral Discourse on *Loveline*," *Symbolic Interaction* 27(2), 2004, pp 247–266; Patricia and Peter Adler, "The Cyber Worlds of Self-Injurers: Deviant Communities, Relationships, and Selves," *Symbolic Interaction* 31(1), 2008, pp. 33–56.

66 Ibid., p. 104.

67 Ibid., p. 112.

68 Patricia Adler and Peter Adler, "Transience and the Postmodern Self: The Geographic Mobility of Resort Workers," *The Sociological Quarterly* 40, 1999, p. 53. For a more extensive discussion of how transient resort workers construct and sustain selves as they move about and adapt to their changing circumstances, see Patricia Adler and Peter Adler, *Paradise Laborers: Hotel Work in the Global Economy* (Ithaca, NY: Cornell University Press, 2004).

CHAPTER SIX

~

ROLE TAKING, ROLE MAKING, AND THE COORDINATION OF ACTION

Life, identity, and meaning are all understood as consisting of nothing more than…exercises in role-playing. Social reality is experienced through the performance of life, the performance of the everyday.

—Daniel Mackay

As members of a society, we share common beliefs or perspectives with others, and based on these beliefs we arrive at agreements about "what is going on" in a given situation. These agreements, or **definitions of the situation**, allow us to coordinate our actions with others and realize desired goals, such as driving our cars safely, performing our jobs effectively, attending interesting classes, or going out on fun dates. To do any of these things, we must fit our actions together with the actions of other people (even if they are not present), and we can do so only through sharing a common definition of the situation with them.

DEFINING SITUATIONS AND THEIR REALITY

Fortunately, in many situations we do not have much difficulty agreeing with others about what is going on. As a result, we find it fairly easy to predict and understand their perspectives and to coordinate our behavior with theirs. Think, for example, of what happens when we take part in

a routine activity such as buying a candy bar at the store. Once our role as "customer" is established, we can easily coordinate our actions with the "clerk," performing the cultural scripts that go along with these roles. Even in less routine situations, such as dances or sporting events, we can readily adjust our behavior to the actions of others around us, knowing what our partners, teammates, or opponents are likely to do at a particular moment. Similar phenomena are evident in politics, medicine, education, and assembly line work, where the performance of a job depends on a shared set of expectations. It is through observing and enacting these shared expectations that definitions of a situation become "real" and individual behaviors become organized into social acts.

Although we often experience little trouble in establishing a common definition of a situation, this is not always the case. Indeed, a number of the situations we encounter are somewhat ambiguous or unstructured; that is, they are not clearly defined in our eyes or in the eyes of our fellow interactants.[1] This ambiguity is a result of the uncertainties we have about what specific roles will emerge in a situation, how these roles will be enacted, and what meanings they will take on for ourselves and others.

Typically the problem that arises in an unstructured situation is that two or more definitions can be given to it, each of which has different and potentially conflicting implications for the individuals involved. If these alternative definitions are embraced by different people interacting in the situation, negotiation is needed. Consider, for example, the act of attending a party. The rules and expectations of going to a party can differ widely among different groups. Think of the parties that your grandparents throw, those your parents give, and those you attend with your friends. Even among people of the same age, parties can be quite distinct in terms of their expectations. Some teenagers like to attend "raves," and anyone attending them should not be shocked by extensive drug use, blatant displays of sexuality, or loud music. Other teenagers throw more restrained and sedate parties, where drinking, drug use, or sexual activity is frowned upon. When you feel uncomfortable at a party, you can decide to leave quickly or you can try to figure out the proper rules of behavior.

If you attend a college or university that has a Greek system, consider the first time you attended a fraternity party. How did you know what behavior was proper? Either through your observations or the suggestions of friends, you learned how such parties proceed. Perhaps you felt comfortable at such events and continued to attend, or perhaps you decided this was not how you wanted to spend your Friday nights. In some instances, as when you are partying with roommates, a process of negotiation may be involved—you might have to make adjustments in your preferred style of partying to get along with your roommates and coordinate your actions effectively with theirs.

Generally speaking, when we see that our definition of a situation does not match with the definitions of others, we proceed in one of the following ways: we let the disagreement pass and try to go on; we end the interaction; we accept the definitions of others; or we try to impose our own definitions. If the situation is important, we often negotiate a compromise among competing definitions of the situation. This compromise, or "working consensus," allows us to continue interacting with others despite some disagreements about what exactly is going on.

Competing definitions of a situation are not always easily resolved, however. At times it is difficult to negotiate a widely shared definition of a situation. The definition proposed by one person or group may be directly challenged by other definitions, resulting in serious interpretive and interpersonal conflict. As an example, consider the conflict that arose in defining the following situation:

> A Cincinnati police officer shot and killed an unarmed 19-year-old man Saturday morning in Over-the-Rhine [a local neighborhood], drawing sharp criticism from residents who allege city police are using excessive force against African Americans. Authorities said Timothy Thomas was shot in the chest shortly after 2 a.m. by Officer Stephen Roach, a four-year veteran. Mr. Thomas is an African American; Officer Roach is white. According to police, Officer Roach had been helping two off-duty officers who had spotted Mr. Thomas in the 1300 block of Vine Street. Mr. Thomas was wanted by police for 14 failures to appear in court on various misdemeanors and traffic charges. The two officers broadcast Mr. Thomas' description over police radios. Officer Roach responded to the call and chased Mr. Thomas for five minutes. Late Saturday night, police officials would not elaborate on what happened when Officer Roach caught Mr. Thomas near the intersection of Thirteenth and Republic streets. "Mr. Thomas was shot once and died at University Hospital at 3:02 a.m.," said Hamilton County Coroner Carl Parrott, Jr. "Investigators did not find a weapon at the scene," said Lt. Ray Ruberg, police spokesman. "Officers are trained to fire their guns only if they fear for their lives, leaving investigators to determine what kind of

threat was present," Lt. Ruberg said. Officer Roach has been placed on paid administrative leave.[2]

Initially, the Cincinnati Police Department (CPD) accepted the definition of the situation proposed by Officer Roach, who claimed that he shot Mr. Thomas only after seeing him draw a gun from his waistband. This definition, however, was not supported by the available evidence—the police did not find a gun at the scene of the shooting. The CPD then constructed a new explanation of what happened; they proposed that Office Roach complied with official police procedure, even though he misperceived Mr. Thomas's actions. According to police spokespersons, the definition of "imminent danger" that guided Roach's actions was one any police officer would have adopted; therefore, Roach was not guilty of any crime in the shooting.

This definition of the situation was immediately contested by members of the African-American community, who saw the shooting as yet another example of the racism practiced by the Cincinnati police. Their claims were bolstered by a local newspaper account that pointed out that fifteen young black males had been shot and killed by Cincinnati police officers since 1995, and, only five months before, another African American had "died of manual asphyxiation soon after being taken into Cincinnati police custody."[3] Fueled in part by this information, the leaders of a local civil rights group, the Black United Front, along with Mr. Thomas's family and friends, directly disputed the CPD's definition of the shooting. They alleged that the incident had stemmed from racial profiling and police brutality. In an effort to reveal and challenge those practices, they filed a lawsuit accusing the CPD of thirty years of illegally targeting and harassing blacks on the basis of race.[4]

A new and competing definition of the situation—one that attributed Officer Roach's actions to racist police practices and beliefs—was subsequently adopted by black political groups in the

city and provoked protest actions that led to skirmishes between police and blacks, resulting in the arrest of sixty-three people, the imposition of a citywide curfew, and the threat of intervention by the Ohio National Guard.

As this example illustrates, people can find it difficult to arrive at a shared agreement about what has happened, or what is happening, in a given situation. But why is this the case? According to symbolic interactionists, individuals construct definitions of situations as they try to organize interactions and events in a way that makes sense. Because people live in different social conditions and have different personal histories, not all definitions seem equally plausible to them. For instance, Officer Roach's definition of the shooting incident was more likely to seem plausible to fellow officers who face danger and uncertainty on the beat than to African-American families whose children have been killed by the police. The fact that various groups across Cincinnati competed in defining the "reality" of a police shooting reveals that this reality was not merely an objective fact but rather was experienced differently by different members of the community, who drew on alternative and conflicting sets of meanings based on their social experiences.

In explaining how and why people experience the same situation and events in different ways, interactionists emphasize that our social experiences act as a lens through which we interpret situations and give them meaning. They also point out that our social experiences—and our definitions of situations—are shaped by (1) the beliefs and categories (e.g., stereotypes) that we have acquired from the groups to which we belong and (2) the rules and role performances that we draw on and enact in a given context. In light of this viewpoint, interactionists would expect that the shooting of an African-American youth would not be defined and experienced as the same reality by the police as it would be for the local African-American community. The police would be likely to embrace definitions of the shooting as a "legitimate" action, taking place within officially recognized procedures. By contrast, members of the African-American community, who have been disproportionately affected by police shootings, would be likely to accept definitions of the shooting as yet another example of police-related racism.

Because interactionists have focused on how definitions of the situation are established in the course of interaction between individuals and groups, they have emphasized how role performances serve as a key vehicle through which these definitions are socially constructed. To learn and perform roles successfully, we must be able to reflect on and evaluate our actions from the standpoint of others. We must also learn cultural definitions of situations; that is, we must learn when, where, why, and how to engage in specific role performances, such as daughter, sister, student, or employee. In fact, much of our socialization consists of learning the common definitions of our society, as well as the roles we are expected to play in different situations. In the following section we examine social roles and role performances. We also consider the dynamics of role taking and role making, highlighting how and why these dynamics are integral to the construction of social order.

ROLES, ROLE TAKING, AND ROLE MAKING

As we interact with other people, we try to place them in social categories: teacher, mother, teenager, liberal, Protestant, salesperson, cousin, customer, roommate, artist, sports fan, partner, and so on. We classify people, lumping them together in terms of their common attributes and actions (see Chapter Three). As we engage in this activity, we set out to define the situation in which we find ourselves. For example, we have to assess whether someone talking to us on the phone is a scientific pollster or a telemarketer, whether someone standing next to us at the grocery store is an employee or a fellow customer, or whether someone looking over our apartment is a landlord or a housing inspector. We can make these assessments fairly quickly and accurately because of our knowledge of roles. **Roles** tell us what obligations and expectations apply to our behavior when we occupy a particular social status in a particular situation. Roles thus carry a normative force; we feel obligated to do what our roles demand of us and ashamed if we fall short.

Roles are important because they enable us to "formulate our behavior mentally so that we can fit our action to that of others."[5] Through roles we can combine a range of activities into manageable chunks or units, making it easier for us to predict and respond to others' behavior. In many respects, roles allow us to treat others who occupy the same social positions in nearly identical ways. Being aware of roles, we can disregard many of the personal traits or differences of others as we interact with them, since we can expect them to act in some standardized ways as occupants of a given status. For example, we "know" and thus expect that every restaurant server is someone who takes orders and delivers food to customers. This knowledge makes it easy for us, as customers at a restaurant, to coordinate our actions with those of the server and get the meals that we want.

As many social psychologists have emphasized, roles are always related to and intermeshed with other roles. Without patients, there are no doctors; without students, no professors; without parishioners, no ministers; without criminals, no police; without players, no coaches. And, of course, vice versa: Without doctors, there would be no patients, and so on down the list.

Every role that we play is reciprocally linked to at least one other role, establishing an interrelated set of obligations and expectations. The obligations of one role, such as parishioner, are the expectations of its reciprocal role: pastor. At the same time, the expectations of the parishioner role are the obligations of the pastor role. These interlocking sets of obligations and expectations, which we sustain through our ongoing interactions with one another, serve as the basis of society. As James Vander Zanden proposed, we are tied to one another through our reciprocal role relationships, and we "experience these definable relationships as social order or social structure."[6]

Role Taking

To coordinate our actions with the actions of those who are linked with us in a reciprocal network of roles, we must engage in role taking; that is, we must look at ourselves and our actions from their standpoint. This imaginative process arises and unfolds as we decide how to act in a particular situation. Through role taking, we anticipate the consequences of our prospective lines of behavior and then either pursue them or change their course. We also rely on role taking as we define the situation we find ourselves in, *assuming the perspectives of others* to detect the role they are projecting, to coordinate our proposed lines of action with theirs, and to negotiate the meaning of our interactions with them.

As we engage in role taking, we try to determine how others define and experience a given situation. We assess the meaning of their actions, trying to figure out what their plans and intentions are in this situation and what implications their conduct has for our own proposed role performances. We then decide on a course of action based on our interpretation of their intentions and unfolding behavior. After initiating this course of action and seeing the responses of others, we may discontinue it, modify it, postpone it, redirect it, or pursue it more vigorously. Rarely can we play out our proposed roles in precisely the way we wish. Instead, we have to make ongoing adjustments in our role performances as we try to coordinate them with the performances and reactions of others.

To illustrate how the process of role taking shapes behavior and interaction, let us consider the case of Reverend Damon Lynch, one of the African-American pastors who became involved in organizing protests against the Cincinnati

police.[7] After the shooting of Timothy Thomas, Reverend Lynch anticipated that many black youths might choose to engage in violent behavior, such as rioting. As a pastor, Reverent Lynch wanted to discourage such behavior, so he decided to take to the streets. Initially, he thought about adopting a "preacher role" and lecturing the youths he encountered on the evils of violence. But, after reflecting on how they would respond to this role, Reverend Lynch realized they would probably view him as naive, irrelevant, or misguided. As a result, he changed his proposed course of action, choosing instead to play the role of a "community leader" who asked the youth on the streets to join him in a nonviolent demonstration. Through formulating and enacting this role, Reverend Lynch persuaded the angry youth to see him as a political ally rather than as a naive or misguided adversary. He also convinced many of them to alter the violent course of action they had originally planned to pursue. Through the process of role taking, Reverend Lynch fit together his lines of behavior with the youth in a way that enabled him to play the role of leader while also redefining the shooting incident as a cause for a demonstration rather than a riot. Of course, after some of the youth took part in rioting, Reverend Lynch had to again make adjustments in his role performance, shifting his attention toward discouraging further violence.

Generally speaking, all of us have a fair amount of role-taking ability, based on our internalization of a repertoire of many roles and perspectives. This repertoire, along with our ability to use analogies, allows us to adopt the perspectives of a wide range of people. Our role-taking efforts, however, always involve some guesswork and are never completely accurate. Our skills and accuracy in role taking are shaped by three factors.[8] The first factor is the extent of our social experiences. We acquire skill and knowledge in role taking not only from our own direct experiences in playing various roles, but also from our indirect observation of the roles others perform, especially in relation to us. The second factor is "the conventionality of the identities and performances involved" in a given interaction.[9] Role taking is typically a selective process that focuses on the more apparent, superficial, and conventional characteristics of another person. In concentrating on these characteristics, we can identify a person as a "social type," such as a professor or student, but we do so at a price. That is, when taking the other's perspective in this generalized way, we are likely to be somewhat inaccurate because we are guided by a partial, limited, or distorted idea of who he or she is. The third factor that influences our role-taking abilities is our degree of familiarity with another individual. We may acquire this familiarity directly, through a long-term relationship with the person, or indirectly, through interactions with other similar persons. We are most likely to take the role of another person accurately when we know him or her well or have a low degree of social distance from him or her—that is, when we share similar social statuses and backgrounds with the person.[10] By contrast, we will have more difficulty taking the role of others accurately when they differ significantly from us, particularly when these differences tend to constrain us from interacting with them regularly.

Role Making

As illustrated by the example of Reverend Lynch, our enactment of roles involves not only role taking but also innovation and adjustment. We must continuously create and modify elements of our role performances as we try to coordinate them with the actions of others. Our performances, then, are not predetermined or rigidly scripted; instead, they are subject to ongoing modification and innovation. As we play roles, we take part in **role making**; that is, we improvise some features of our behavior in order to construct a role performance that fits with the performances of others while also remaining attuned to our personal goals and inclinations.

Of course, we are not completely free to improvise as we devise a role performance. Our

involvements in role making are constrained to some extent by role-related expectations. For instance, when playing the role of student you are expected to attend class, take notes, participate in discussion, read books and articles, and complete your assignments on time. These expectations, however, do not dictate how you perform all aspects of the student role; they only provide you with broad guidelines or a "rough draft" for action. You must improvise to some degree as you play out the role of student in various contexts.

To understand the complexities involved in role making, consider again the actions of Reverend Damon Lynch. Following the unrest that emerged in his neighborhood, Reverend Lynch decided that as a minister he should play the role of community leader. Yet in formulating this role he was constrained by a web of competing and contradictory role expectations attached to his status as minister. For example, some of the members of his congregation wanted him to stay out of politics and concentrate on his duties as preacher and pastor, which included delivering sermons, counseling church members, and paying visits to the sick and elderly. Others wanted him to serve as neighborhood "peacekeeper," focusing his attention on preventing the spread of violence. Still others wanted him to play the part of political agitator, organizing local citizens to take action to address the injustices engaged in by the Cincinnati police. In the face of these clashing expectations, Reverend Lynch had to engage in a juggling act, negotiating and balancing the demands of different groups and formulating a role as neighborhood leader that blended with the other duties he had as a minister.

People engage in role making not only to resolve conflicting role expectations but also to avoid or counteract negative role expectations. One of the ways we "role make" to deflect unfavorable expectations is by displaying symbols or gestures suggesting that these expectations should not apply to us. For instance, homeless youth and young black men try to address the fear or hostility that others direct toward them by engaging in "disidentifying" gestures. Some do so by using public spaces in a way that puts anxious or fearful others at ease, giving them extra room when standing next to them on an elevator or a subway platform. Some also convey a high degree of politeness, friendly humor, or helpfulness when interacting with fearful others, going out of their way to show that they are respectful and considerate. In addition to these gestures, they may act in ways that communicate their conventionality and civility, such as stressing their belief in mainstream values or wearing fashionable clothing. Through these gestures, homeless youth and young black men convey that others should not see them as dangerous or anticipate that they will engage in harmful behavior.

In discussing the process of role making, interactionists highlight two themes. First, roles do not dictate how we act. Rather, they provide us with a set of guidelines and an organizing framework to draw on as we *create* a performance that addresses the specific demands of a situation. Role performances almost always require some elements of improvisation because they have to be tailored and adjusted to meet the conditions that arise in a given situation. While roles have certain expectations attached to them, these expectations do not provide us with all of the directions we need to formulate a line of action in a situation. A great deal of spontaneous decision making occurs in everyday life. Second, the process of role making relies on self-consciousness and, thus, role taking. We must be aware of our "own role performance in the making so that it can be adjusted to suit personal goals, the demands of the situation, and the expectations of others."[12] To have this kind of self-awareness about our role performance, we must adopt the perspective of others, or engage in role taking. For example, to know how to conduct a class discussion so that it will be engaging to students, a professor must know what students find interesting and how they expect a "good" class discussion to be organized and facilitated. If the professor fails to grasp the students' expectations, the class discussion is likely to be boring or disappointing. The professor tries to discern the students' perspective by looking at the discussion from their vantage point. Thus, upon seeing a number of students expressing their views in response to one of the topics of the discussion, the professor can assume that this topic is interesting to them and worthy of further exploration. On the other hand, when noticing some students yawning or looking out the window when another topic emerges, the professor can assume that they find this topic boring and that the focus of the discussion should be changed. The professor uses his or her grasp of the students' perspectives to direct and adjust his or her performance in facilitating the discussion.

Role Making in Role Exits. People engage in role making not only when constructing their role performances, but also when exiting from important roles, such as spouse, custodial parent, doctor, teacher, or worker. As Helen Rose Ebaugh has observed, when individuals disengage from significant roles, they typically become involved in the process of "becoming an ex."[13] This process begins as they experience growing doubts about their ability or willingness to continue performing a specific role. As people consider the costs and benefits of the role and weigh alternatives, they reach a turning point that leads them to give up the role and pursue a new direction. They often discover, however, that they cannot simply walk away from this role. Instead, they must go through a complex process of adjustment and adaptation—a process in which they try to disengage from the expectations and self-perceptions associated with the role while also creating and adapting to a new "ex-role."

According to Ebaugh, one of the first steps individuals take in creating and adjusting to an ex-role is to emit cues, such as changes in their style of dress or behavior, that tell others they have changed their status and expect to be treated differently than in the past. For example, many divorced people buy new wardrobes, lose weight, remove their wedding rings, and otherwise alter their appearance to signal that they are available for dating. Of course, as Ebaugh points out, it can be challenging for "exes" to figure out how to present their changed role and status to others. They often have much to learn about what it means to be an "ex," whether they are an ex-spouse, an ex-doctor, an ex-alcoholic, or an ex-convict.

Perhaps the biggest challenge that exes face is how to address the reactions of others who are used to dealing with them in terms of their former role. This task is particularly difficult for individuals disengaging from roles with a high degree of **role residual**, or identity hangover. As Ebaugh notes, "Role residual is the continued identification an individual maintains with a prior role such that the individual experiences certain aspects of the role after he or she has in fact exited from it."[14] An example is provided by the high school athletic star who gets injured when playing in college and has to withdraw from competitive sports. When returning home for visits, he or she may discover that the local community still responds to him or her in the role of star athlete, even though he or she no longer participates in athletics. This treatment makes it challenging for him or her to exit the role, even if he or she wants to. As this example illustrates, it is difficult for individuals to leave a role unless others around them cooperate (or they elect to abandon their relationships with these others). In most cases, people can only successfully "become an ex" through coordinating their actions with others and engaging in a mutual process of adjustment and adaptation—a process that involves both their decreased involvement with the group connected with their former role and the group's decreased involvement with them, especially in terms of that role. Thus, even the process of role exit depends on the negotiation and coordination of social behavior.

THE COORDINATION OF SOCIAL BEHAVIOR: ALIGNING ACTIONS

The idea that people work together and adjust their behaviors to allow interaction to flow smoothly is critical to symbolic interactionist analysis. The phrase "fitting together lines of action," first used by Herbert Blumer, means that in order to cooperate, we take into account others' actions and adjust our behavior to theirs to make joint action possible. This cooperation is particularly important on occasions when large numbers of people must react for a situation to flow smoothly, as when crowds exit from a stadium after a football game or a rock concert.

What features of behavior are necessary for a cooperative act to unfold? To explain social order, we need to address the question of how that order develops, or how people achieve so much cooperation despite their different outlooks, interests, and goals. Carl Couch, a prominent symbolic interactionist, proposed that several features are crucial for the construction of order in interaction.[15] First, the involved individuals must recognize that others are present and that these others represent an audience for their actions. Second, during their interaction these individuals must construct a set of compatible and interrelated roles that indicate they are a part of the same social situation. Finally, they must also create a shared focus and establish a joint goal. In establishing a social relationship, people build a shared past and a projected future. Consider the example of a recreational softball team. The players must recognize that they are a team, determine each person's position on the team, and create a team culture and set of shared goals. This culture refers to the shared understandings that come to characterize the group.

If you reflect on your relationships with family or friends, you will recognize shared jokes, nicknames, holiday traditions, or stories that define you and are unknown to those outside your group. Perhaps your family has traditions for celebrating Christmas, Chanukah, Kwanza, or Ramadan, or perhaps you and your friends call each other by private nicknames. The existence of shared pasts allows people to adjust their responses to each other rapidly and without self-consciousness, responding to one another's words and actions almost instantaneously.

Aligning Actions and Motive Talk

An important way we coordinate our behavior with others is through what interactionists call "aligning actions."[16] Aligning actions highlight the importance of role taking. We often experience role taking as a simple matter. For instance, we walk along campus sidewalks without worrying much about bumping into other people. But how is this possible when so many people are walking on the sidewalk simultaneously? We engage in what amounts to a pedestrian ballet. We implicitly understand how and where we should walk to avoid others. We are also sent implicit cues as to what others are likely to do next, and we can respond accordingly, just as they receive cues from us. We anticipate and understand other people's conduct while recognizing their expectations of us. As a result, social order is possible.

In speaking of aligning actions, interactionists usually refer to verbal communications, such as accounts or disclaimers, which produce a shared reality. In our everyday interactions we often find that we must explain our intentions, either directly or indirectly. In describing our motives and presenting them to others, we generate social consensus, fit our actions together with theirs, and sustain a sense of social order.

Symbolic interactionists distinguish between motives and motivations. *Motives* are the public explanation that we give for our behavior, whereas *motivations* refer to internal drives. As C. Wright Mills noted, motives are "terms which persons typically use in their interpersonal relations."[17] In essence, motives are rhetorics, or persuasive forms of talk, that people draw on to deal with the unanticipated consequences of conduct. When we do something that is unexpected or questionable, we engage in *motive talk*, offering a public explanation to excuse ourselves and facilitate smooth interaction. Sometimes the calls for motive talk can be explicit, but frequently they occur because we recognize that others will question us in their minds, just as we would question them if the situation were reversed.

Whenever we make a public error, we seek to repair the breaches it causes in social interaction. We need to make sure that the interaction order flows smoothly. We also try to ensure that others regard us as morally legitimate and competent social actors. Think about those times when you mistakenly say the wrong thing, or forget someone's name. You probably react immediately with a comment or nonverbal expression which reveals that you, like your audience, recognize that you have "screwed up." On other occasions, someone may question your actions directly, as in a situation where you interrupt a friend when she is telling you a story. Offering the explanation that you need to leave because you have an important meeting will typically suffice. By contrast, if you tell your friend that you just don't feel like listening to her, you will be seen as rude and may lead her to gossip about your "mood." Not answering at all may lead her to think you are impolite or arrogant. Responding appropriately bolsters your public identity and demonstrates that you appreciate and accept the rules of your community, even if you don't always follow them.

C. Wright Mills coined the term **vocabularies of motive** to refer to the words, phrases, or rhetorics that people use to provide "legitimate" explanations for their actions.[18] These vocabularies are situationally specific; that is, they can be used effectively only in particular situations or classes of situations. They also differ in various groups and are accorded more or less legitimacy within these groups. For example, members of Alcoholics Anonymous (AA) learn and use a vocabulary of motives that emphasizes that alcoholic behavior is a consequence of an "illness beyond their willpower to control" rather than a "moral weakness."[19] When interacting with each other, AA members draw on this vocabulary to understand and account for many of the problematic behaviors they have engaged in over time. In the process, they acknowledge the harmfulness of their alcohol-related actions but also release themselves from assuming full moral responsibility for these actions.[20] They explain that their problematic behavior resulted from an illness over which they had no control. Of course, in circles outside of AA, such as a fraternity that regularly hosts "keg" parties, this disease-based explanation of alcohol consumption is not likely to be seen as credible or legitimate.

Vocabularies of motive provide us with accounts that we can draw on to remedy our mistakes, repair disrupted interactions, and restore relationships. **Accounts** are statements we make to explain unanticipated, inappropriate, or questionable acts. After making a mistake or acting in an unexpected way, we typically use one of two types of accounts: excuses or justifications. We offer an *excuse* when we admit our behavior is wrong but deny responsibility for it. If you are late to class, you may provide the excuse that your car battery died or that a power failure prevented your alarm clock from ringing. When offering an excuse, you show that you recognize the validity of social expectations and emphasize that your error or noncompliance is not due to a rejection of these rules. By contrast, when providing a *justification* for an inappropriate action, you accept responsibility for it but suggest that it should not be seen as improper. If someone condemns you for smoking, you may justify your behavior by asserting that you think smoking is a legitimate and pleasurable behavior that helps you to stay thin. In turn, you claim that the moral judgment made against you is unfair. (For further discussion of how we use justifications to neutralize or counteract negative attributions, see Chapter Seven.)

Whereas we provide accounts *after* engaging in questionable conduct, we present **disclaimers** *before* taking part in such behavior. When using disclaimers, we recognize that our future actions will be seen as improper and set the scene so that we are not tarred by others' judgments. For instance, when we share an "off-color" joke, we begin by making a disclaimer that serves not only to warn our audience but also to show them that we recognize our comments might not be approved by everyone. When people engage in behavior that is capable of being interpreted as biased, prejudiced, or inappropriately sexual, they may provide a disclaimer to suggest that such an interpretation is inaccurate. Through role taking, we understand how others might respond and we deal with their objections before they occur. Examples of disclaimers abound in everyday life, as reflected in statements such as "I don't believe in gossiping, but this sounded important..."; "I'm not prejudiced, some of my best friends are..."; or, "You might get mad about this, but I think you need to know that...." In each of these examples, people use a disclaimer to ward off the unfavorable or discrediting implications of their prospective line of action. They also try to manage the flow of interpretation, sustain smooth interaction, and negotiate a social order in which people "treat one another's acts with discretion, with good judgment, and with deserved good will."[21]

EMOTIONS AND THE COORDINATION OF BEHAVIOR

Although our discussion thus far has stressed the cognitive aspects of interaction and definitions of a situation, the emotional aspects of these processes are equally significant. Every definition of a situation includes emotional expectations and ideas that set the tone for interaction. At weddings, for instance, we are expected to feel happy rather than sad, even if we secretly harbor concerns about the future success of the marriage. We are also expected to abide by certain rituals and guidelines when conveying our happiness. For example, we are encouraged to express our joy at a wedding by congratulating the newlywed couple, giving them a gift, attending the reception and dance, and clinking our waterglasses so that they will kiss. Now, if we decided to express our happiness by shouting "Way to go!" in the middle of the wedding ceremony or by trying to have the first dance with the bride or groom, we would be violating the emotional norms that apply in this situation. Our emotional expressions would be seen as out of line with the definition of the situation, and they would provoke negative reactions from others.

A wedding offers only one example of how a definition of a situation is characterized by a set of emotional expectations, or **feeling rules**.[22] Feeling rules offer guidelines for interaction and consist of understandings about what kinds of emotions are acceptable or desirable, who is entitled to feel and express them, and what forms of expression and display are permissible. In general, feeling rules tell us both how we can *expect to feel* in a given situation and how we *ought to feel* in that situation.[23]

According to Arlie Hochschild, we align our behavior with the feeling rules that characterize a situation through engaging in **emotion work**, or the process of evoking, suppressing, and otherwise managing our feelings.[24] Hochschild proposes that as we perform roles in our everyday lives we engage in two key forms of emotion work: surface acting and deep acting. When we take part in surface acting, we try to "act the part" that is expected of us in a specific situation, even if that part does not match our underlying mood. If we are at a funeral, we wear dark colors, speak in hushed or subdued tones, and express our regrets and sympathy to grieving survivors. This conduct is a form of surface acting because it does not necessarily reflect our "real" or inner feelings. In truth, we may feel some relief that a particular person has died, especially if he or she had treated us badly. We realize, however, that it would be inappropriate for us to express such sentiments at the funeral. In turn, we choose to act "as if" we are feeling sad, displaying an emotion that fits with the prevailing definition of the situation.

In contrast to surface acting, deep acting consists of the efforts we engage in to suppress or evoke certain feelings. Through deep acting, we self-consciously strive to call forth a set of inner feelings that match the expressions we are conveying to others. That is, we try to conform inwardly as well as outwardly to the feeling rules that govern a situation. For instance, when we are at a funeral, we try to feel genuinely sad and not merely to wear a sad face. We do so by thinking sad thoughts, reflecting on the sad or unpleasant consequences of the death, restricting our bodily movements, and sighing. All these activities evoke or reproduce the genuine feelings of grief called for in the situation. Thus, when we engage in deep acting at occasions such as a funeral, we are much like a stage actor who tries to conjure up the feelings called for in a script: we strive to ground our outward expressions of emotion in genuine inner feelings.

In her analyses of surface acting and deep acting, Hochschild reveals how emotion management is an integral feature of our social interactions, emerging not only on special occasions such as weddings and funerals but also in everyday settings such as workplaces, schools, and homes. Whatever our situation, we coordinate our actions with others based on feeling rules, and we typically experience, display, and manage our emotions in accordance with these rules. Doing so enables us to take the role of others effectively, to formulate appropriate lines of action, and to engage in relatively smooth or predictable interactions, thereby meeting the demands of the situation and sustaining social order.

Emotions and Role Attachments: Role Embracement Versus Role Distance

In discussing the notions of surface acting and deep acting, Arlie Hochschild draws on the insights of Erving Goffman, the founder of dramaturgical theory, who wrote at length on the nature and dynamics of role performances. Goffman pointed out that while we play a variety of roles in life, we often choose to enact these roles with differing levels of conviction or self-involvement. In some cases, we heartily embrace and identify with a role, allowing it to shape how we think, feel, act, and interact with others.[25] This process of **role embracement** can be seen almost daily in people performing certain occupations, such as traffic officers at intersections during rush hour. While this type of role embracement is often rewarding or benign, it occasionally has hazardous consequences, as Gary Marx revealed when studying FBI agents doing undercover investigations.[26] Marx observed that when agents go deeply undercover, they must engulf themselves in playing the role of a career criminal and embrace the interests, tastes, hobbies, and relationships that accompany this role. Through observing and interacting with other criminals, undercover agents gain acceptance and learn outlooks and behaviors that allow them to play the role of criminal convincingly. At the same time, however, they learn the normalcy of such outlooks and behaviors in this social world and feel pressures to abandon their role as an FBI agent and become a career criminal.

Role embracement also takes place commonly among individuals playing leisure roles. For example, interactionists such as Gary Alan Fine, Matt Lust, and Dennis Waskul have found that people who play fantasy games, such as Dungeons and Dragons, often struggle to separate themselves from the roles and characters they play. Indeed, some players embrace their game-related roles so strongly that these roles define their identities outside of the game situation.[27] According to Fine, these players become "so thoroughly engrossed that they have difficulty retreating back into everyday life and conventional morality."[28] While this occurs only temporarily, some of the players come to recognize the profound power of the fantasy. Moreover, most of the players come to understand that the boundaries between person, player, and fantasy persona are often blurred and that their fantasy role performances are a blend of the persons they believe themselves to be in everyday life and the fantasy personas they enact.

Based on his observation of a variety of role performances, Goffman noted that in addition to embracing certain roles, we can choose to detach or dissociate ourselves from some role performances. When engaging in this behavior, which Goffman described as **role distance**, we "play at" a role in a detached or insincere way.[29] We also reveal, directly or indirectly, that we are choosing not to embrace

this role and thus should not be identified with it. In his ethnographic study of a mental hospital, Erving Goffman observed that patients regularly engaged in role distance as a way to counteract the stigmatizing consequences of institutional labels and practices.[30] Goffman noted that the patients displayed their detachment from the undesirable role attributed to them through the use of "secondary adjustments." Within the mental hospital, these adjustments consisted of the unauthorized practices that patients engaged in to get around organizational expectations without directly challenging those in power.[31]

Of course, we can find secondary adjustments in a variety of settings, such as schools, workplaces, and prisons, where the open expression of feelings and the performance of desired roles is curbed by the threat of punishment or retaliation. In these settings, people find ways to communicate their feelings covertly (e.g., cursing under their breath or secretly mimicking the actions and expressions of their "oppressors"). Through such secondary adjustments, people distance themselves from the stigmatized role they are playing and maintain a sense of autonomy and self-value without jeopardizing the existing social order.

POWER, CONSTRAINT, AND THE COORDINATION OF BEHAVIOR

Symbolic interactionists, like most other social psychologists, recognize that a key feature of interaction and the coordination of behavior is *constraint*. Interactionists have often been criticized for unduly stressing "agency," or the freedom that people have to resist, evade, or overcome social constraints. Critics contend that because interactionists emphasize how we make roles, define situations, and negotiate identities, they overlook or downplay the many ways in which individual behavior is constrained by social structure.

Interactionists counter this criticism by stressing that both freedom and constraint characterize human behavior. They also point out that

Box 6-1 ROLE DISTANCE AND SECONDARY ADJUSTMENTS: THE CASE OF FEMALE PRISON GUARDS

When studying female guards working in male prisons, Lyn Zimmer discovered that they distanced themselves from certain aspects of the guard role as performed by men. Although the female guards emulated their male counterparts in many respects, they relied more heavily on their relational skills when interacting with inmates. As a result, they generally avoided using the coercive strategies employed by the male guards. Instead, the female guards engaged in secondary adjustments in an effort to humanize the guard role, transforming some of their contacts with prisoners into helpful exchanges, such as providing assistance with letter writing or offering informal counseling. While the women were sanctioned by male guards and superiors for making these role adjustments, they received a powerful payoff: The prisoners were more compliant in their interactions with them.

As Zimmer's study illustrated, the extent to which people engage in role distance varies and depends in part on their assessment of the objective features of their context, or the features they cannot control. Female prison guards resisted some aspects of the traditional guard role and tried to adjust and humanize it, but their resistance was limited by the sanctions that male guards directed toward them, such as making it apparent that they would not help them in dangerous situations. When distancing oneself from a role leads to dire consequences or painful outcomes, it is more likely to be done covertly. People are likely to turn to secondary adjustments when they sense that they are stuck in a role and that the opportunity for role making is small. On the other hand, when people sense that they have a fair amount of freedom and control in their role performance, they are more likely to improvise, transforming the role in ways that make it more personally rewarding and meaningful. In the process they find ways "to be" the role they are playing rather than focusing on ways "not to be" this role.

Source: Lyn Zimmer, "How Women Shape the Prison Guard Role," *Gender & Society* 1, 1987, pp. 415–431. ©1994 by The Society for the Study of Social Problems.

analysis of the link between individual agency and social structure has a long history in interactionist thought and was implicitly addressed in the writings of Mead, Cooley, Blumer, and Goffman. Following the lead of these founders, interactionists ask: To what extent do we have freedom in choosing our courses of action, and to what extent do social structures shape our choices and actions?

Interactionists recognize that constraint is present everywhere in social life and that much of the social world is not of an individual's making, such as systems of patriarchy, power, and class. Thus, interactionists clearly recognize

that people's capacities to fashion roles, negotiate identities, and define situations are far from unlimited. In the next section of this chapter we consider how people's actions and interactions are constrained, particularly within unequal relationships.

Relationships, Power, and Constraint[32]

The more frequent, extensive, intimate, and enduring our interactions are with others, the more likely it is that they will become patterned by relatively stable expectations. As we engage in ongoing exchanges with other people, we establish shared ideas about the identities we will occupy, the goals we will pursue, and the roles we will perform. We also build a shared future. This allows for mutual commitment, planning, and coordination. It also enables us to establish a **relationship**, or an association with others that consists of shared expectations about identities, values and meanings, goals, roles, and a future.

Relationships, of course, are not static. They change over time and go through various phases or stages, particularly as the individuals involved in them adopt different roles, perform different types of work, and exchange different resources. Some relationships last for decades and adapt fairly easily to a number of transitions and challenges. Many, however, have a short career and break down quickly in the face of change or conflict. Sometimes these relationships end by mutual agreement of the participants, but in other cases they end because of the dissatisfaction of only one participant.

Relationships differ not only in longevity but also in symmetry. In some relationships, we interact with others as peers and have about the same amount of power they do. More commonly, though, we interact with others on an unequal basis: we possess either more or less power than they do because of the statuses we occupy. As David Karp and William Yoels note, interactions between men and women, bosses and workers, "and even parents and children are inextricably bound up with the issue of power."[33] The interactions that take place between people who are members of different social classes, genders, races, or age groups are characterized by unequal power relations and can only be understood by analyzing the characteristics of asymmetrical relationships.

The Characteristics of Asymmetrical Relationships

A relationship is asymmetrical when one of its participants establishes control or dominance, disproportionately imposing his or her will on the other participants and setting conditions, making decisions, and engaging in actions that determine the form and course of the relationship. We include the term "disproportionately" in our definition because we recognize that subordinates, or less powerful people, are not without power or resources; indeed, they often have ways to initiate action and evade the control of superordinates, or more powerful people. Nonetheless, subordinates have disproportionately less power than their superordinates.

Sources of Power. **Power** is the capacity to get other people to think, feel, or act the way you want them to even if they do not want to think, feel, or act this way. As French and Raven have pointed out, power takes on many forms.[34] It can be expressed through coercion, or forcing others to do something against their will, such as when bank robbers force tellers to give them money by pointing a gun at them. Power can also be rooted in rewards, or the ability to give others the resources, benefits, or information they need or want. Moreover, power can be derived from expertise, especially when one possesses unique knowledge or skills required by others, or it can be anchored in one's organizational position, such as the position of CEO. Finally, power can be based on one's ability to attract others and to gain their respect, admiration, or loyalty. National celebrities and well-respected community leaders provide examples of this form of influence, which is known as referent power.

People exercise various forms of power through diverse means, such as creating symbols, managing impressions, dispensing rewards, controlling information, or using force.[35] But how do people get away with imposing their will on others? And why do some people stay in relationships where they feel constrained and unsatisfied? According to Richard Emerson, power results from unequal dependency.[36] For example, one person, Tyra, has something that another person, Denard, needs or values more than she does. Denard consequently becomes more dependent on Tyra and is subject to her control. In turn, Tyra is able to extract a greater proportion of rewards or benefits from their relationship.

Dependency is a key factor in many relationships, including employer–employee relationships. In general, as individual workers we need our employers more than they need us, usually because there are more workers available than there are jobs. On the other hand, if we are a highly skilled or talented person, we might find employers competing for our services. Typically, however, the unequal relationship between employers and employees allows companies to hire and pay people at a level sufficient to maintain their profitability.

While dependency is an important dimension of asymmetrical relationships, it is not sufficient to account for dominance in a relationship. Dominance is established through having the means to sanction behavior, distribute rewards, and overcome resistance. Dominance thus involves the use of resources, which consist of anything used to control the behavior of others.[37] Resources provide the basis of a person's (or group's) power over others. The most commonly accepted categories of resources are constraints, inducements, and persuasion. *Constraints* add disadvantages to a situation and include punishments, coercion, and withholding privileges. *Inducements* add advantages to a situation and include rewards such as increases in money, goods, services, status, or freedom. *Persuasion* involves changing the minds of others without adding anything to the situation, leading them to act voluntarily in accord with one's wishes. As William Gamson observed, through the use of information, wisdom, manipulation, personal appeal, or control of communication, subordinates come to prefer what their superordinates want.[38]

Individuals involved in asymmetrical relationships may have differing levels of various resources. For instance, your boss may be stronger than you but you may be more creative. Certain resources, however, cannot be utilized in a given situation because they are defined as inappropriate. The fact that your boss is physically strong does not give him or her the right to beat you up for non-compliance. Moreover, when your boss decides to commit resources to a particular plan of action, he or she does not automatically ensure your agreement or compliance with that plan. Bosses can misuse resources, overestimating the value of specific constraints, inducements, or persuasions in eliciting our cooperation. Bosses can also underestimate us as subordinates, failing to recognize how we can resist and redirect their plans.

Overall, our dependency on superordinates is reduced by the opportunities we have to choose alternative actions or relationships offering greater rewards. Often we do not challenge the domination of more powerful people because we do not see ourselves as having any alternatives. Our ability to imagine and pursue viable alternatives enhances our bargaining position, increases our range of possibilities, and provides us with a resource to be used. For instance, if we see ourselves as having another job possibility, we are less likely to submit to the unreasonable demands of our boss.

Ways of Exercising Power. The processes of interpretation and role taking are crucial to understanding power. In many cases our bosses expect our compliance and do not engage in much role taking or assessment. Like other superordinates, or powerful people, they tend to become insensitive to the powerless because they do not anticipate resistance. By contrast, those people with less power tend to role take more extensively and thus develop greater role-taking skills.[39] As Karp and Yoels reveal, a variety of social psychological studies have found that less powerful people, such as women and African Americans, have better role-taking abilities than more powerful others, such as men and whites.[40] This finding suggests that role taking is a function of social position and that role-taking skill can be a compensatory strategy that enables the less powerful to anticipate the actions of the powerful, to manipulate or influence some of their actions, and to avoid threatening situations.

In general, power is established and maintained in a relationship through the effective use of resources. Constraints, inducements, and persuasion are used in different circumstances with varying consequences. Constraints differ depending on whether they are shown, threatened, or actually used. When the powerful engage in a show of constraint, they display their potential strength, as when they flex their muscles or display their guns. These actions are designed to intimidate. When the powerful threaten to use constraints, they suggest that they will apply them in the future if subordinates fail to comply with their wishes. When the powerful actually use constraints, they try to restrict the actions of subordinates through coercion, punishment, and the withdrawal of privileges. While such an exercise of power can be very effective, it tends to be used as a last resort. The continuous use of constraints reveals instability in a relationship and tends to increase feelings of alienation and resistance among subordinates, provoking them to organize and fight back.

When the powerful use inducements in a relationship, they indicate that they will reward a specific behavior if it is forthcoming. These rewards vary from expressions of approval to increases in money to giving us more control over our time. In work settings, our bosses often use inducements, such as promotions or increases in pay and power, to secure our goodwill and continued compliance. They use these rewards to prevent resistance and to encourage us to act in accord with their wishes.

In addition to using constraints and inducements, the powerful shape the thoughts, feelings, and actions of subordinates through various means of persuasion. The powerful are more likely to rely on persuasion when subordinates tend to be supportive. As Peter Hall proposed, persuasion includes **symbolic mobilization,** or the use of verbal and nonverbal symbols to create, maintain, and strengthen one's position, and **information control**, or the strategic management of information, the maintenance of secrecy, and the development of intelligence.[41]

Hall points out that superordinates, such as executives, administrators, or political leaders, use symbolic mobilization in three ways.

First, they create the proper image of themselves in the eyes of subordinates. For example, they convey the image that they are leaders who are decisive, responsible, and in control. In doing so, they strive to remain "in character" and to avoid defensiveness. Second, the powerful also manipulate the less powerful by appealing to their commitment or loyalty to a larger group, such as their family, company, or country. Finally, when faced with potential or real resistance, the powerful frequently attempt to simulate conditions of authority, suggesting that they represent a group or organization and have the right to exercise power over all of its members. In asserting their authority, they make claims such as "I am acting in your interests and know what is best for you, so trust me" or "If we just sit down and talk, you will be able to see that I am acting correctly."[42]

In addition to relying on symbolic mobilization, superordinates often exercise power through controlling information and thereby managing the emotions of the less powerful. When anticipating resistance, superordinates try to gather information and develop intelligence about subordinates. Bosses, for instance, may talk with select workers to find out whether the "rank and file" are in the mood to form a union. The powerful also make decisions about whether to disclose important information, when to disclose it, and what to disclose. Employers planning major changes in their company try to find the proper way and time to share this news. Sometimes they want to surprise employees and keep them off balance. At other times, they want subordinates to know their plans in advance so they can prepare to make necessary adjustments. In addition to selectively disclosing information, superordinates exercise power by concealing information that would discredit them, such as mistakes, self-serving motives, and indiscreet or illegal activities. Perhaps most crucially, superordinates also control less powerful others by regulating their discourse, imposing rules about what they can say, how they can say it, and with whom they can share information (see Box 6-2).

Box 6–2 DISCOURSE, EMOTION MANAGEMENT, AND
THE REPRODUCTION OF INEQUALITY

Sociologists have focused a great deal of research on the kinds of social inequalities that exist, how sizable they are, and how they affect people's life chances and experiences. Unfortunately, sociologists have conducted relatively little research on the processes that produce and perpetuate inequalities. In recent years, interactionist scholars have tried to address this oversight, directing attention toward the everyday processes and interactions through which inequalities based on gender, ethnicity, class, and sexuality are created and reproduced.

The following excerpt is taken from an article in which Michael Schwalbe and his colleagues describe the generic social processes through which various inequalities are created, enacted, and reproduced. These processes include boundary maintenance, othering, emotion management, and subordinate adaptation.

The excerpt highlights how elites regulate discourse in ways that allow them to shape perceptions of "reality," manage the emotions of subordinates, and maintain positions of power and privilege.

*   *   *

Sustaining a system of inequality, one that generates destabilizing feelings of anger, resentment, sympathy, and despair, requires that emotions be managed. [and one of the notable ways that elites manage emotions is by] regulating discourse....

Discourse is more than talk and writing; it is a way of talking and writing. To regulate discourse is to impose a set of formal or informal rules about what can be said, how it can be said, and who can say what to whom.[1] A courtroom is at one extreme in regard to degree of formal regulation; a barroom at the other. Inasmuch as language is the principal means by which we express, manage, and conjure emotions, to regulate discourse is to regulate emotion. The ultimate consequence is a regulation of action.

Cohn's study of the "techno strategic" language of defense intellectuals provides an example of how a form of discourse can mute potentially inhibiting emotions.[2] Cohn reports that technostrategic discourse strictly avoids reference to human pain and suffering, and instead uses the abstract and dispassionate language of strikes, counter-strikes, megatonnage, and megadeaths. Given the rules of this discourse, to speak of pain and suffering is to discredit one's self as a "soft-headed activist instead of an expert."[3] We see here a form of discourse being used as an emotional anesthetic that allows technical experts to more efficiently serve the interests of political and military elites.

Corporate managers, as Jackall shows,[4] use a similar rationalist discourse when making decisions that will hurt people. This discourse helps corporate managers stay focused on profits, even taking pride in their ability to make tough decisions that are "best for the company." In this case, corporate elites use a form of discourse—a language of efficiencies, returns, and fiduciary responsibilities—that keeps compassion at bay and facilitates the pursuit of narrow economic interests. As in the world of defense intellectuals, the privileged discourse of corporate managers can also be used to exclude or discredit those who are unable or unwilling to engage in it.

Discourse can be regulated to simultaneously quell some emotions and evoke others. This is most apparent in wartime, when political and military elites try to regulate the national discourse in ways that arouse and sustain enthusiasm for mass violence, while provoking hatred for enemy leaders and decreased sympathy for civilians on the other side. In the case of war, discourse must be regulated institutionally, via the mass media. This is accomplished by describing events, if they are described at all, in the frames preferred by elites,[5] and by excluding dissident voices that might, by using alternative language and frames, evoke resistant emotions in the citizenry.

When a form of discourse is established as standard practice, it becomes a powerful tool for reproducing inequality, because it can serve not only to regulate thought and emotion, but also to identify Others and thus to maintain boundaries as well. Those who wish to belong to the dominant group, or who simply want to be heard) may feel compelled to use the master's linguistic tools. Hegemonic discourses are not, however, eternal. As Wasielewski[6] suggests, discourses that deny expression to the pain and anger of the oppressed create a powerful emotional tension) which in turn fosters the emergence of charismatic leaders. Such leaders catalyze change by articulating what is repressed and linking the resolution of repressed feelings to dissident action. All hegemonic discourses may thus carry within them the seeds of their own destruction.

1. J. Potter and M. Wetherell, *Discourse and Social Psychology* (Thousand Oaks, CA: Sage, 1987).
2. Carol Cohn, "Sex and Death in the Rational World of Defense Intellectuals, Signs 12, 1987, pp. 687–718.
3. Ibid, p. 708.
4. Robert Jackall, Moral Mazes: *The World of Corporate Managers* (London: Oxford University Press, 1988).
5. William Gamson and Andre Modigliani, "Media Discourse and Public Opinion on Nuclear Power: A Constructionist Approach." *American Journal of Sociology* 95 (1), 1989, pp. 1–37.
6. Patricia Wasielewski, "The Emotional Basis of Charisma," *Symbolic Interaction* 8, 1985, pp. 202–222.

Source: Michael Schwalbe, Sandra Godwin, Daphen Holden, Douglas Schrock, Shealy Thompson, and Michele Wolkomir, "Generic Processes in the Reproduction of Inequality: An Interactionist Analysis," *Social Forces* 79(2), 2000, pp. 419–452.

Finally, along with the strategies of symbolic mobilization, information control, and emotion management, superordinates control interaction through gestures of dominance such as staring, frowning, pointing, looking stern, invading others' space, making others wait, initiating touch, interrupting others, changing the topic of conversations, restricting others' access to conversation, requiring others to do undesirable or unrecognized work, and limiting others' opportunities to make important decisions or even to "tell their own stories."[43] Superordinates also constrain interaction through the process of **altercasting,** or casting others in roles or identities they prefer them to occupy. A clear example is provided by upper middle-class white women who define the women of color they employ to do housework as irresponsible, childlike, and happy to serve.[44]

Social Life as a Negotiated Order

Symbolic interactionists recognize that social order is a negotiated process and not something that simply or automatically happens. Social order must be worked at and constructed through our ongoing interactions. As we fit our lines of action together, we "arrive at mutually shared agree-ments, tacit understandings, binding contracts, unhappy compromises, and coerced accommo-dations."[45] And we do so through processes of constraint, inducement, persuasion, manipula-tion, and bargaining. Thus, order often does not emerge in a smooth or unconflictual way. Instead, it is negotiated out of conflicts of interest, goals, and emotions in the process of interaction.

The notion that social order is a negotiated process was first proposed by Anselm Strauss and his colleagues. In the early 1960s they examined psychiatric hospitals and found that these institu-tions could be understood through the negotia-tions of the individuals and groups within them.[46] Strauss and his colleagues discovered that each professional group in the hospital had received different forms of training, which led to differ-ences in their outlooks and actions. Patients were defined and treated differently by the nurses, social workers, occupational therapists, psycholo-gists, psychiatrists, and psychiatric residents. Each group had a different ranking in the hier-archy of the psychiatric hospital, and the differ-ences in their training and rank led them to have conflicting definitions of the hospital situation. This conflict was aggravated by the clashing ide-ologies embraced by the psychiatrists. Some had a psychoanalytic orientation and recommended talk-based therapy, while others had extensive neurological training and were more likely to rec-ommend the use of drug-based therapies or elec-troshock therapy.

Within this context of competing interests, outlooks, and emotions, negotiation among the staff provided the means for putting together a working consensus that allowed coordinated action to occur. Through their ongoing nego-tiations, psychiatrists, nurses, patients, and other staff struck bargains, adopted rules, and arrived at understandings that enabled them to address the conflicts and problems that arose in the hospital. Yet these bargains, rules, and understandings were fleeting. Strauss and his colleagues found that the continual turnover in staff led to a situation where rules and agreements were regularly for-gotten, revised, or cast aside, even as new ones were being created or re-created. The rules and agreements accepted at a particular moment were often different from those that had been in effect in the past and those likely to be established in the future.

Based on their observations of interactions in the psychiatric hospital, Strauss and his col-leagues reached the following conclusion:

> [N]o one knows what the hospital "is" on any given day unless he has a comprehensive grasp of the combination of rules, policies, agree-ments, understandings, pacts, contracts, and other working arrangements that currently obtain. In a pragmatic sense, that combina-tion "is" the hospital at the moment, its social order....It is necessary continually to recon-stitute the bases of concerted action, of social order....[47]

Strauss went on to conduct further research on hospitals and, based on his investigations, argued that all social order is ultimately negoti-ated order. According to Strauss, organization is not possible without some form of negotiation. The nature of specific negotiations depends on the structural conditions of the organization. Negotiations, for Strauss, follow lines of com-munication. That is, they are patterned, not ran-dom. Negotiations also are limited in time and are renewed, revised, and reconstituted again and again. Moreover, structural changes in the organization require a revision of the negotiated order. When we look at any organization or large social system, we find negotiations at work. These negotiations are informed and influenced by the *negotiation context*, or the set of structural con-ditions and past negotiations that surround and directly affect their content, process, and conse-quences. As Martha Copp has pointed out, "Past negotiations may shape future courses of action, modify structural conditions, or undergo a pro-cess of *sedimentation*, in which they join the set of standard operating procedures and become part of the social structure."[48]

The important point that Strauss and other interactionists make is that larger structures are ultimately built on the negotiation that occurs in smaller structures. This observation allows interactionists to understand structural realities, such as inequality, in terms of the collection of individual interactions and negotiations. A social system depends on individuals acting toward other individuals in particular ways. However, it is not simply the behaviors themselves that create the social structure, but rather their sedimentation into a system that individuals understand as normatively appropriate. This is very important in understanding phenomena such as social inequality, in which it is not simply individual behaviors that lead to broader systems of economic or political inequity; instead, it is the social assumption that these forms of power relationship are legitimate. Inequalities are grounded in part in shared beliefs about the rules or expectations of justice systems. For example, most Americans believe that it is right and proper for doctors to make more money than nurses and for nurses to make more money than hospital orderlies. This belief allows doctors to have large salaries and orderlies to barely get by. Even though no hospital could exist without either doctors or orderlies, the rewards given to the two sets of workers are dramatically different. Different, too, is the power involved. To be sure, doctors have more training than orderlies, and fewer individuals might be able to have the educational abilities that would permit them to be doctors; however, there is a greater potential supply of people who would like to be doctors than those who would like to be orderlies. This disjuncture between these two types of occupations, and the subsequent negotiation that occurs between them in terms of their rights and responsibilities constitutes part of how symbolic interactionists see the construction of social order and the reproduction of unequal relationships.

SUMMARY

- Interactionists stress that we, as members of society, share common beliefs and, based on these beliefs, arrive at agreements about "what is going on" in various settings. These agreements, or definitions of the situation, inform and shape our actions. They tell us what roles we should adopt in a given interaction and what roles others are expected to adopt, thereby allowing us to coordinate our behavior with theirs and realize desired goals.

- In defining situations, we rely on the process of role taking. Through this process, we anticipate how others are likely to respond to our proposed role performance in the situation at hand. We assess the meaning of their behavior, trying to figure out their plans and intentions, and the implications their actions will have for our own prospective course of behavior. We then decide what role to adopt—and how to enact it—based on our interpretation of their intentions and unfolding behavior. After initiating a particular role performance (e.g., "class clown" or "diligent student") and seeing how others respond to it, we may discontinue it, modify it, redirect it, or pursue it more vigorously. Rarely can we play out our proposed roles in precisely the way we wish. Instead, we have to adjust and change our performances as we try to coordinate them with the performances and reactions of others. Thus, our role performances require innovation and adjustment, or what interactionists call "role making." We must improvise some features of our behavior in order to construct a role performance that fits with others' performances in a given situation.

- A key task we face as we define situations and fashion role performances is to coordinate our actions effectively with others. This task is particularly challenging when we act in surprising ways, violate social norms, or otherwise disrupt the smooth flow of interaction. When this happens, we often rely on "motive talk" to put others at ease and align our actions with theirs. Motive talk includes the use of verbal strategies, such as accounts and disclaimers, that offer explanations of surprising, questionable, or inappropriate behavior. By using these strategies we demonstrate that we appreciate and accept social rules. We also preserve definitions of situations, repair the breaches that emerge in the negotiation of social order, and realign our actions with the actions of others.

- The process of social coordination is grounded not only in cognitive activities, but also in emotional expectations and responses. Every definition of a situation is characterized by feeling rules that offer guidelines for interaction and tell us what emotions are acceptable or desirable, who is entitled to feel and express them, and what forms of expression are permissible. These feeling rules shape our experience and display of emotions as we interact with others. In essence, as we coordinate our actions with others in a given situation, such as a funeral, we are expected to manage our emotions so that they fit with the feeling rules that govern that situation. We do so by engaging in two forms of emotion work: surface acting and deep acting. With surface acting, we try to "act the part" that is expected of us, even if that part does not match our underlying mood. With deep acting, we try to evoke a set of inner feelings that match the expressions we are conveying to others. That is, we try to conform inwardly as well as outwardly to the feeling rules that apply in the situation.

- As we coordinate our actions with others, we must also deal with social constraints and the power differences that often characterize our interactions—differences rooted in imbalances in dependency, resources, and alternatives. Superordinates, or the more powerful participants in interactions, establish and maintain control through the effective use of resources. They rely on constraint when other means have failed or are regarded as inapplicable. They use inducements to overcome indifference and ensure the continued compliance of subordinates. They tend to use persuasion, which includes both symbolic mobilization and information control, when others tend to be supportive. Finally, superordinates also rely on techniques such as altercasting to cast subordinates into roles that they prefer them to occupy, thereby constraining their ability to negotiate identities and improvise role performances.

- While recognizing the impact of social constraints, interactionists argue that social order is always a negotiated process. Order emerges out of, and becomes transformed or sustained through, our ongoing negotiations with others. When we look at any organization or larger social structure, we find that it consists of competing interests, outlooks, and sentiments that must be worked out through a mass of negotiated agreements. We also find that these agreements are limited in time; they must be renewed, revised, and reconstituted through ongoing negotiations.

GLOSSARY OF KEY TERMS

Account A statement we make to explain unexpected, inappropriate, or questionable acts. These statements may be excuses or justifications. When we offer an *excuse*, we admit that our conduct is wrong but deny that we are responsible for it. When we provide a *justification*, we accept responsibility for engaging in an inappropriate act but suggest that it should not be seen as improper.

Altercasting Casting or placing another into a role that we prefer him or her to occupy.

Definition of a Situation An agreement that we reach with others about "what is going on" in a given situation. This agreement allows us to coordinate our actions with others and to realize desired goals.

Disclaimer A rationale we offer prior to taking part in questionable behavior. When using disclaimers we recognize that our future behavior will be seen as improper and try to set the scene so that we are not tarred by others' judgments.

Emotion Work The process of evoking, suppressing, and otherwise managing feelings. As we perform roles in our daily lives, we engage in emotion work through surface acting and deep acting. When we surface act, we try to "act the part" that is expected of us in a specific situation, even if that part does not match our underlying mood. When we deep act, we self-consciously try to suppress or evoke certain feelings, particularly by calling forth inner feelings that match with the expressions we are conveying to others.

Feeling Rules Guidelines for interaction that consist of understandings about what kinds of emotions are acceptable or desirable, who is entitled to feel and express them, and what forms of expression and display are permissible. Feeling rules tell us both how we can expect to feel in a given situation and

how we ought to feel in that situation.

Negotiated Order The notion that social order emerges out of, and becomes established or reproduced through, processes of negotiation.

Power The capacity to get others to think, feel, or act the way we want them to, even if they don't want to think, feel, or act this way.

Relationship An association with others that consists of shared expectations about identities, values and meanings, goals, roles, and a future.

Role The obligations and expectations that apply to our behavior when occupying a particular social status in a particular situation.

Role Distance Performing a role in a detached or insincere way, thereby displaying that our sense of self is not invested in the role.

Role Embracement Identifying strongly with a role and allowing it to shape how we think, feel, act, and interact with others.

Role Making A process in which we improvise some features of our behavior to construct a role performance that fits with the performances of others while also remaining attuned to our personal goals and inclinations.

Role Residual According to Ebaugh, the continued identification we maintain with a prior role such that we experience certain aspects

Vocabulary of Motive
of the role after we have in fact exited it.

A set of words, phrases, or rhetorics that we use to provide "legitimate" explanations for our actions.

QUESTIONS FOR REFLECTION OR ASSIGNMENT

1. What are the most important role performances that you might give in your life? When you think about these performances, what difference would it make if others did not take them seriously? What problems would this pose for you? How would you go about drumming up the emotion that might be necessary for the performance to be believable? If you could not "feel the part" that you were playing, what would you do?

2. What occupational roles would promote the highest degrees of role distance for you? Why? What occupational roles would promote the highest degrees of role embracement for you? Why?

3. Identify a role in which gender is never relevant. Can you do it? What is the role, and what features of the context or interaction make gender less important? Why? What do you consider to be one essential characteristic of masculinity and femininity as they are culturally prescribed in the United States today?

4. What are the most common accounts given by college students when they (a) turn down a "date," (b) get drunk, and (c) skip classes or turn in papers late? Which type of account (e.g., excuses or justifications) are they most likely to rely on when engaging in each of these behaviors? Why is this the case?

5. What are the most commonly accepted role expectations for women and men when arranging a "first date"? How do they learn and internalize these expectations? How did you learn about dating roles and norms? Have you ever challenged or violated the norms for arranging a first date? If so, how? If not, why not?

6. Analyze a relationship in which you have less power than the other person involved. What gives the other person more power than you? How does he or she exercise this power (e.g., does he or she rely on constraints, inducement, or persuasion)? How do you exercise power in this relationship? Do you think you know more about the powerful person than he or she knows about you? Why or why not?

SUGGESTED READINGS FOR FURTHER STUDY

Altheide, David. "Identity and the Definition of the Situation in a Mass-Mediated Context," *Symbolic Interaction,* 23 (1), 2000, pp. 1–27.

Anderson, Leon, and David A. Snow. "Inequality and the Self: Exploring Connections from an Interactionist Perspective," *Symbolic Interaction* 24(4), 2001, pp. 395–406.

Chang, Johannes Han Yin. "Symbolic Interaction and Transformation of Class Structure: The Case of China," *Symbolic Interaction* 23 (3), 2000, pp. 223–251.

Schwalbe, Michael, Sandra Godwin, Daphne Holden, Douglas Schrock, Shealy Thompson, and Michele Wolkomir. "Generic Processes in the Reproduction of Inequality: an Interactionist Analysis," *Social Forces* 79, 2000, pp. 419–452.

Silva, Eric. "Public Accounts: Defending Contested Practices," *Symbolic Interaction* 30(2), 2007, pp. 245–266.

Waskul, Dennis and Matt Lust. "Role-Playing and Playing Roles: The Person, Player, and Person in Fantasy Role Playing," *Symbolic Interaction* 27(3), 2004, pp. 333–356.

ENDNOTES

[1] George McCall and J. L. Simmons, *Identities and Interactions* (New York: The Free Press, 1966). Our discussion of the problems that arise in defining unstructured situations draws heavily on insights offered by McCall and Simmons.

[2] "Officer Shoots, Kills Suspect: Man Was Unarmed, Wanted on Misdemeanor," *Cincinnati Enquirer*, April 8, 2001, p. A1.

[3] Ibid.

[4] Ibid.

[5] James Vander Zanden, *Social Psychology*, 4th ed. (New York: Random House, 1987), p. 238.

[6] Ibid., p. 239.

[7] Howard Wilkinson and Marie McCain, "Officer Indicted in Death; Feds Launch Police Review," *Cincinnati Enquirer*, May 8, 2001, p. A1.

[8] George McCall and J. L. Simmons, *Identities and Interactions*, (Note 1), p. 135.

[9] Ibid.

[10] Gregory P. Stone. "Appearance and the Self: A Slightly Revised Version," in Gregory P. Stone and Harvey A. Faberman, eds., *Social Psychology Through Symbolic Interaction* (New York: Macmillan, 1980), pp. 101–113.

[11] Elijah Anderson, *Code of the Street: Decency, Violence, and the Moral of the Inner City* (New York: Norton, 1999); Anne Roschelle and Peter Kauffman, "Fitting In and Fighting Back: Stigma Management Strategies Among Homeless Kids," *Symbolic Interaction* 27 (1), 2004, pp. 23–46.

[12] John Hewitt, *Self and Society*, 8th ed. (Boston: Allyn and Bacon, 2000), p. 64.

[13] Helen Rose Ebaugh, *Becoming an Ex: The Process of Role Exit* (Chicago: University of Chicago Press, 1988).

[14] Ibid., p. 173.

[15] Carl Couch, "Symbolic Interaction and Generic Sociological Principles," *Symbolic Interaction* 8, 1984, pp. 1–13.

[16] John P. Hewitt and Randall Stokes, "Disclaimers," in Gregory P. Stone and Harvey A. Faberman, eds., *Social Psychology Through Symbolic Interaction* (New York: Macmillan), 1986, pp. 363–374.

[17] Hans Gerth and C. Wright Mills, *Character and Social Structure: The Psychology of Social Institutions* (New York: Harcourt, Brace and World, 1953), p. 114.

[18] C. Wright Mills, "Situated Actions and Vocabularies of Motive," *American Sociological Review* 5, 1940, pp. 904–913.

[19] David R. Rudy, *Becoming Alcoholic: Alcoholics Anonymous and the Reality of Alcoholism* (Carbondale: Southern Illinois University Press, 1986).

[20] Ibid., p. 47.

[21] John P. Hewitt and Randall Stokes, "Disclaimers," (Note 16), p. 366.

[22] Arlie Hochschild, "Emotion Work, Feeling Rules, and Social Structure," *American Journal of Sociology* 85, 1979, pp. 551–575.

[23] Ibid.

[24] Ibid.

[25] The concept of role embracement is developed by Goffman in his essay, "Role Distance." See Erving Goffman, *Encounters: Two Studies in the Sociology of Interaction* (Indianapolis: Bobbs-Merrill, 1961), pp. 106–107.

[26] Gary T. Marx, "Unintended Consequences of Undercover Work," in James M. Henslin, ed., *Down to Earth Sociology*, 6th ed. (New York: The Free Press, 1991), pp. 279–286.

[27] Gary Alan Fine, *Shared Fantasy: Role-Playing Games as Social Worlds* (Chicago: The University of Chicago Press, 1983); Dennis Waskul and Matt Lust, "Role-Playing and Playing Roles: The Person, Player, and Person in Fantasy Role Playing," *Symbolic Interaction* 27(3), 2004, pp. 333–356.

[28] Daniel Martin and Gary Alan Fine, "Satanic Cults, Satanic Play: Is 'Dungeons and Dragons' a Breeding Ground for the Devil?" in James T. Richardson, Joel Best, and David G. Bromley, eds., *The Satanism Scare* (New York: Aldine De Gruyter, 1991), p. 112.

[29] Erving Goffman, *Encounters*, (Note 25).

[30] Erving Goffman, *Asylums* (Garden City, NY: Anchor Books, 1961).

[31] Ibid., p. 189.

32 This section of the chapter draws heavily on ideas that Peter Hall shared with us in personal conversations and in an unpublished manuscript titled "Micro Social Organization: Interaction, Relationships, and Small Groups."

33 David Karp and William Yoels, *Sociology and Everyday Life* (Itasca, IL: F. E. Peacock Publishers, 1986), p. 104.

34 J. French and B. Raven, "Bases of Social Power,' in Dorwin Cartwright, ed., *Studies in Social Power* (Ann Arbor: University of Michigan, 1959), pp. 150–167.

35 Walter Buckley, *Sociology and Modern Systems Theory* (Englewood Cliffs, NJ: Prentice-Hall, 1967).

36 Richard M. Emerson, "Power-Dependence Relations," *American Sociological Review* 27, 1962, pp. 31–41.

37 Robert Dahl, "The Concept of Power," *Behavioral Science* 2, 1957, pp. 201–218.

38 William Gamson, *Power and Discontent* (Homewood, IL: Dorsey, 1968).

39 Darwin Thomas, David Franks, and James Calonico, "Role Taking and Power in Social Psychology," *American Sociological Review* 37, 1972, pp. 605–614.

40 David Karp and William Yoels, *Sociology and Everyday Life*, (Note 33).

41 Peter M. Hall and John P. Hewitt, "The Quasi-Theory of Communication and the Making of Dissent," Social Problems 18, 1970, pp. 17–27.

42 Ibid., p. 20.

43 Leon Anderson and David A. Snow, "Inequality and the Self: Exploring Connections from an Interactionist Perspective," *Symbolic Interaction* 24(4), 2001, pp. 395–406.

44 Mary Romero, *Maid in the U.S.A.* (New York: Routledge Press, 1992).

45 James Vander Zanden, *Social Psychology*, (Note 5), p. 216.

46 Anselm Strauss, Leonard Schatzman, Rue Bucher, D. Erlich, and M. Sabshin, *Psychiatric Ideologies and Institutions* (Glencoe, IL: Free Press, 1964).

47 Ibid., p. 218.

48 Martha Copp, "Negotiated Order," in George Ritzer. ed., *Encyclopedia of Social Theory.* Vol. II (Thousand Oaks, CA: Sage Publications), p. 526.

CHAPTER SEVEN

~

THE POLITICS OF SOCIAL REALITY: CONSTRUCTING AND NEGOTIATING DEVIANCE

In recent years school officials have encountered a new type of problem student: the computer prankster. As students have gained increased access to computers at home and school, they have figured out how to use them to break rules and challenge school authorities. At a number of schools, students have smuggled in home-made software programs to change their grades, sabotage school records, and disable the school's computer system. In addition, students have used their computer savvy to engage in other "devious" activities, such as altering school web pages, installing forbidden video games, sending threatening e-mail messages, and designing websites that ridicule teachers or administrators.

Given the fact that many of these computer pranks violate school rules and break laws, why are school officials agonizing about how to deal with the students involved? Why don't they treat these students like others who violate significant school rules? The key problem, it seems, is that many of the computer pranksters are among the best and brightest pupils. They are the "saintly" students: they attend school regularly, have excellent grade point averages, and rarely cause problems in the classroom. They also aspire to attend top-ranking colleges and often come from affluent families. School officials therefore feel reluctant to suspend or expel these students, or even to suspend their computer privileges. They know that such

sanctions may harm the students' grades, prevent them from taking desired college-preparatory courses, and hurt their chances for getting admitted into elite colleges. They also know that the students' affluent and powerful parents may see these punishments as unduly harsh, leading to complaints and conflicts, including potential legal battles.

To address this situation, a number of schools have started to implement a new form of punishment—sometimes called "nerd discipline"—to deal with computer pranksters.[1] In most cases, this punishment consists of putting the offending pranksters on monitored probation, meaning they can use school computers only in closely scrutinized settings. By adopting this approach, school authorities can avoid the dilemmas involved in suspending top students or restricting their access to important computer-based classes. At the same time, they can argue that they have effectively punished the pranksters, thereby reducing the threat of their deviance and upholding school rules.

What do you think of this approach? Do you see the computer pranksters as "deviants" who need to be punished? Do you believe school officials are acting fairly or wisely in putting the students on monitored probation? If not, how do you think they should respond? As you consider these questions, think about how this situation (and the reactions of school officials) would differ if the pranksters had different social characteristics and backgrounds. What if these students were from poor families, had low grade point averages, skipped school regularly, and had no plans to attend college? How do you suppose officials would treat them if they had used computers to threaten their classmates, trash their teachers, change their grades, and sabotage school records? Would officials be likely to adopt a special form of discipline that would allow these students to remain in school and continue using school computers? Or would they be more inclined to punish these students harshly, using school policies as a basis for suspending or expelling them?

In posing these questions, we're asking you to think about some of the social factors that influence people's definitions of and reactions to rule-breaking behavior such as computer pranks. On a broader level, we're also encouraging you to recognize how deviance, like other human realities, is a socially constructed phenomenon. In the next section of this chapter we help you better understand the social creation and shaping of deviance. In doing so, we highlight the key premises of the labeling theory of deviance, which derives from the symbolic interactionist perspective. We also address several questions that are central to social psychological discussions of deviance and the negotiation of identity. These questions include: What is deviance? How do people become recognized and defined as deviant? What implications do deviant labels have for their self-images and social relationships? How do they cope with and counteract these implications?

WHAT IS DEVIANCE?

Sociologists generally use the term **deviance** to describe acts or attributes that depart in an undesirable way from a group's norms and evoke negative social reactions. These acts or attributes can range from studying too much to being overweight, cheating on an exam, dyeing one's hair

purple, driving while intoxicated, or belonging to a terrorist group. Almost all of us engage in some acts or possess some attributes that others see as deviant. If you doubt this fact, think about whether you ever drive over the speed limit, lie about your age, skip classes, fudge on your taxes, drink alcohol illegally, or engage in nonmarital sex. If you don't do any of these things, consider whether you have any attributes that others would view as deviant, such as being too thin, too fat, too dark-skinned, too light-skinned, too liberal, too conservative, too uptight, or even too virtuous. Although nearly all of us can be seen as deviant in some way, most of us do not actually get defined as deviant. Why not? The sociological answer is that deviant identities do not simply flow out of deviant behavior or attributes. It is more complicated for someone or something to become recognized as deviant than we commonly believe. As we go through our daily lives, most of us presume that a high degree of consensus exists about who and what is deviant. For instance, we assume that everyone in our community would agree that it is bad to poison the water we drink and that anyone who does so should be punished. However, if we explored the level of agreement that existed regarding exactly what constitutes poisoning of the water supply—at least a *deviant* form of poisoning—we would probably find a notable amount of dissent and conflict. What some citizens would see as an irresponsible or criminal poisoning of the water, others would view as "a safe and allowable disposal of industrial waste" or as "a harmless runoff" of fertilizer or pesticides.

To make the matter of deviance even more complex, some sociologists point out that norm violations are not necessarily detrimental for society. In fact, they argue that these violations serve beneficial purposes, such as clarifying moral boundaries, promoting social unity, and encouraging societies to change so that they can address newly emerging problems. Thus, while norm violations are often regarded as annoying or troublesome acts that threaten social order, it is important to remember that, on a deeper level, they can also contribute to the (stability, continuity, and smooth functioning of a group or society.)

Before examining the nature and ramifications of deviance in greater depth, especially from a symbolic interactionist perspective, let us look at the two approaches commonly adopted in defining deviance: absolutism and relativism.

The Absolutist View

According to the absolutist view, deviance is a quality that inheres in the very nature of an act or attribute; that is, deviance is intrinsic to particular acts or attributes. Absolutists would argue that certain behaviors and qualities are inherently good, right, and proper, whereas others are clearly bad, immoral, or inappropriate. The deviance of an act or attribute, then, is not determined by the standards or judgments of a specific social group. Rather, right and wrong exist prior to and independent of humanly created rules, customs, or judgments. Moreover, these "objective" standards of right and wrong apply to all times, contexts, and cultures. In turn, an act or attribute either *is* or *isn't* deviant, regardless of who is involved, whether it is observed, why it occurs, or what circumstances lead to it. Guided by these assumptions, absolutists see deviance as something inherently abnormal, immoral, and threatening that should be corrected, eliminated, or at least carefully controlled.[3]

This view of deviance as an objective phenomenon, or as a property intrinsic to certain acts or attributes, is linked to two other assumptions, both of which are deeply rooted in commonsense understandings of deviance.[4] The first of these assumptions is that people who commit a deviant act or possess a deviant attribute are qualitatively different—morally, psychologically, and even physically—from normal, conforming individuals. The second assumption is that social control efforts, including the monitoring, labeling, legal processing, and formal sanctioning of deviance, are simply reactions to norm-violating acts or attributes and not causes of them.

In line with the assumption that deviants are fundamentally different from other people, absolutists suggest that those who engage in deviant behavior have qualities or dispositions unlike those possessed by more conventional folks. According to the logic of absolutism, deviants are distinctively "warped," "weird," "perverted," "maladjusted" or "evil" persons. For example, the absolutist presumes that if a person engages in a deviant act such as using heroin, it is because she is essentially different from people who do not use heroin. Since she is breaking the law, her moral, psychological, or biological makeup must differ from the makeup of her law-abiding counterparts.

Guided by this assumption, absolutists believe that it is the deviant's aberrant actions or characteristics that lead to social control efforts, rather than vice versa. Thus, absolutists view formal mechanisms of social control, such as the criminal justice system, as well as informal mechanisms, such as gossip and ridicule, as important and necessary means for regulating deviance. Absolutists believe that these control mechanisms are designed above all to curtail the prevalence and severity of deviance in a community. That is, they exist primarily to deter deviants from continuing down their wayward path. This deterrence in turn benefits not only those engaging in deviance, but also the "normal" members of the larger community.

The Relativist View

In contrast to the absolutist view, the relativist view of deviance (which is embraced by more social psychologists) emphasizes that standards of morality and normalcy do not exist independently of socially created rules, customs, and judgments. Instead, definitions of right and wrong, as well as normalcy and abnormalcy, differ widely in various settings, cultures, and periods of history. For the relativist, deviance cannot be understood in terms of absolute notions of right and wrong. What one group in a specific place and time sees as immoral behavior may be completely acceptable or even normative to a different group in another place and time. Consider the example of a young man who feels attracted to a young woman in his neighborhood and decides that he wants to marry her. Rather than dating this woman, he takes her to his house, locks her in a room, and refuses to release her until she agrees to be his bride. In our culture this young man's actions would meet with strong disapproval. In fact, he would probably be arrested for kidnapping. In Hmong culture, however, this man's actions would be accepted and perhaps even encouraged. He would be viewed as someone engaging in *zij poj niam* (or marriage capture), a traditional practice for selecting a wife among Hmong tribesmen from the hills of Laos.[5] Let's consider another example: a thirteen-year-old girl becomes involved in sexual liaisons with some of the neighborhood boys she knows. Most Americans would disapprove of this behavior and stigmatize the girl involved, referring to her as promiscuous (or, less politely, as a "slut"). By contrast, members of the Ila culture in Africa would see the girl's actions as perfectly normal. Indeed, during harvest time they would give her a house of her own where she could play at "being a wife" to boys of her choice, thereby encouraging her to become sexually involved with them.[6]

Pointing to many examples of this kind, relativists argue that deviance is not an objective or unchangeable phenomenon that transcends culture, history, and context. Instead, they contend that deviance, like beauty, is in the eyes of the beholder. Whether an act or attribute is deviant depends on the group perspective used to evaluate it. According to relativists, then, deviance is not a quality intrinsic to an act or attribute. Rather, it is a judgment that some individuals or groups make when responding to the behavior or characteristics of others.

In analyzing deviance, symbolic interactionists adopt a relativist rather than an absolutist point of view. They stress that deviance is a social constructed reality that can be understood only in terms of the values, perspectives, and reactions of a particular group or culture. In fact, interactionists emphasize that the deviance of an act or attribute is determined by the values, perspectives, and reactions of the members of a group or culture. Thus, when theorizing about deviance, interactionists focus above all on the *social audience* "since it is the audience which eventually determines whether or not any episode of behavior or any class of episodes is labeled deviant."[7]

LABELING THEORY AND THE SOCIAL CONSTRUCTION OF DEVIANCE

Unlike absolutists, symbolic interactionists do not regard deviant behavior as unusual. Nor do they believe that the actions, outlooks, or motivations of "deviants" differ fundamentally from those of conformists. As a result, they do not try to explain why certain people engage in deviance. Instead, interactionists focus on questions overlooked by most traditional sociological approaches to deviance, such as: How is deviance produced by the creation and application of rules? Who makes these rules? How, when, and why do they apply or enforce them? Why are some individuals more likely than others to be recognized and labeled as rule breakers? And, how are they affected by this labeling? That is, how do their actions, interactions, and self-concepts change after they become labeled as deviant?

Guided by these questions, symbolic interactionists concentrate on the social and political processes through which deviant identities are created and sustained. In doing so they are informed by the following assumptions articulated by Howard S. Becker:

> [S]ocial groups create deviance by making the rules whose infraction constitutes deviance and by applying those rules to particular people and labeling them as outsiders. From this point of view, deviance is not a quality of the act the person commits but rather a consequence of the application by others of rules and sanctions to an "offender." The deviant is one to whom

that label has been successfully applied: deviant behavior is behavior that people so label.[8]

Becker's ideas provide the foundation for an interactionist approach known as the **labeling theory of deviance**. In contrast to other sociological approaches, this theory highlights the importance of the labeling of acts or attributes that violate norms, rather than the nature of the acts or attributes themselves. It suggests that rule makers and enforcers are at least as involved in the creation of deviance as the alleged deviant. By passing powerful legislation (e.g., antidrug or anti-immigration laws) and then applying this legislation to targeted groups, rule makers and enforcers actively participate in the production of deviance. They also dramatize the evils associated with specific acts or attributes and make it more likely for certain people to become labeled as deviant.

Guided by these insights, labeling theorists stress that the creation of deviance is not a simple or straightforward matter. Indeed, for deviance to be constructed, a complex and interrelated series of social processes must take place. These processes include (1) banning, (2) detection, (3) attribution, and (4) reaction.

The Banning Process: Moral Entrepreneurs and the Making of Deviance

Deviance is manufactured through the labor of individuals and groups who draw on "the resources and power of organizations, institutions, agencies, symbols, ideas, communication, and audiences."[9] Those individuals and groups who work hardest at the business of "making deviance" are known as **moral entrepreneurs**. They shape the production of deviance through their participation in two key forms of moral enterprise: rule creation and rule enforcement.

Rule Creators. As Howard Becker has emphasized, rule creation is not an automatic process; someone has to take the initiative to have a rule formulated and adopted. Becker refers to the people who engage in this work as rule creators.[10] In many cases rule creators are crusading reformers, such as James Dobson or Ralph Nader, who want to bring about a change in the dominant rules of a society, especially through making new rules into law. These reformers are often guided by an absolutist ethic: They see certain acts or attributes as truly and totally wrong without qualification.[11] They also believe that almost any means are justified to eradicate such behavior. As Becker notes, crusading reformers are fervent and righteous, sometimes even self-righteous. Besides wanting to see to it that other people do what they think is moral, they presume that if people do so it will be good for them.

So how do crusading reformers and other rule creators succeed in getting their moral perspectives transformed into social rules or laws? They begin by stirring up social awareness, usually by claiming that a specific act or condition, such as the spread of "road rage," poses a threat to the present or future well-being of society. Since no rules exist to address this alleged threat, rule creators try to foster the impression that pertinent rules or laws need to be formulated. In support of their cause, they seek out and utilize the testimonials of relevant "experts," including scientists, physicians, psychiatrists, political officials, eyewitnesses, ex-participants, and others with special knowledge about the issue. They also rely on the news media to disseminate these testimonials to the public as "facts."[12]

After stirring up social awareness, reformers and rule creators must convince others of the merits of their views and generate a large-scale moral conversion. Having identified the nature of a threat and the rules needed to address it, they face the task of converting neutral parties and past opponents into supportive allies. In this process rule creators draw upon a variety of dramaturgical techniques and make use of elements of novelty, culture, rhetoric, and propaganda. For example, when presenting information about the threat they have discovered, they strategically manipulate statistics and use rumors and folklore to make it seem widespread.[13] They also try to secure the endorsements of prominent "opinion leaders," including actors, athletes, media personalities, politicians, and religious spokespersons.[14] These opinion leaders do not need to possess expert knowledge on a particular issue; they simply need to be admired and respected. Their celebrity gives them credibility in the eyes of the public and makes them influential in moral crusades. Most important, as reformers gain the support of opinion leaders and begin to convert others to their cause, they legitimize their own beliefs and their moral crusade gains greater social and political force.

Ultimately, if rule creators succeed in their efforts and convince a majority (or even an organized and powerful minority) of people to accept their definitions, they are likely to see these definitions get transformed into norms, elevated into laws, or encoded into both norms and laws. Regardless of which of these scenarios occurs, rule creators see their moral crusade as successful if it results in the **banning** of a problematic behavior or condition—that is, if it the public to define this behavior or condition as bad, wrong, or immoral and to label those associated with it as "deviants" who need to be punished, controlled, or corrected.[15]

While crusading reformers often play a central role in the banning process, legislators can also serve as key initiators or facilitators of this process, as illustrated by the activities of the Iowa Legislature.[16] Over the past decade, Iowa lawmakers have filed dozens of bills that sought to criminalize previously legal behavior. While the legislators often insist that these bills address pressing public safety issues, many have seemed more focused on making crimes out of minor annoyances or pet peeves. For instance, one of the first bills introduced in the Iowa Senate in 2000 sought to create the crime of "laser pointer harassment." This bill identified the prospective criminals as "those who aim pointers with mischievous intent." According to the backers of this bill, some teenagers had gotten involved in potentially dangerous pointer pranks around the state and this had elicited the concern of a few local police departments. In light of this concern, legislators thought that remedial action (i.e., an official ban) was needed.

Along with criminalizing laser pointer harassment, Iowa legislators have sought to reduce the "dangers to public safety" posed by people who put spinning hub caps on their cars, individuals who drive without turning on their headlights when it is raining, and people who use cell phones while driving in parking lots. In addition to creating legal bans for these behaviors, some Iowa legislators have tried to establish new "covenant marriage" licenses that would make it more difficult to get a divorce. These legislators contend that the new licenses are necessary because too many people aren't taking their marital vows seriously enough.

In fairness to the Iowa legislators, not all of them have supported bills designed to create new crimes and, thus, more criminals. Also, many have proposed bills that would criminalize certain behaviors because of pressures imposed on them by concerned constituents or powerful claimsmakers, such as police officers. Moreover, in some cases the legislators have responded to the demands or directives of the federal government. Through its funding mandates, the federal government frequently pushes state legislators to fashion new safety laws. For instance, the Iowa Legislature passed mandatory seat belt laws only after the federal government threatened to hold back highway funds if they failed to do so. Also, during the year 2000, the federal government extended incentives to Iowa (and other states) for passing legislation that would lower drunken-driving limits and prohibit passengers from riding in the back of pickup trucks. It was not surprising, then, that a pickup bill was one of the first items filed during the 2000 session of the Iowa House.

Rule Enforcers. Once rule creators succeed in banning an act or condition, **rule enforcers**

step into action, trying to ensure that the ban is observed. In the United States, as in most societies, police officers are the key enforcers of bans, and they tend to be highly selective in their enforcement efforts. Typically the police monitor and arrest individuals who have lesser amounts of social power, usually because of their racial, religious, economic, political, or gender statuses.[17] This is illustrated in the police practice of "racial profiling," or targeting non-white drivers when pulling over vehicles to search for illegal drugs.[18] What racial profiling dramatically reveals is that the application of rules, like the creation of rules, is frequently a *political* endeavor—an endeavor that legitimizes the moral views and aims of powerful groups at the expense of others. Those groups who are the targets of selective enforcement practices are likely to see the political elements involved and, because of this, may start up an oppositional moral crusade. When organizing such a crusade, they highlight the injustices they have suffered as a result of selective rule enforcement. They also try to change existing laws or enforcement practices so that these injustices are addressed.

The Detection Process: Seeing Deviance and Deviants

The process of banning only sets the foundation for the construction of deviance. To become defined as deviant, a person has to be detected and recognized as a rule violator. As we noted earlier, almost everyone engages in some kind of rule breaking. This usually takes the form of **primary deviance**—temporary, isolated, and often trivial rule violations that are fairly easy to conceal.[19] In most cases these violations are not observed by others and thus do not trigger their attention or concern.

Certain kinds of deviant acts or attributes, however, are likely to be detected. For instance, rule-breaking behavior that takes place in public is by definition more likely to be observed than that which occurs in private. Moreover, stigmatizing attributes such as large birthmarks that appear on highly visible regions of the human body, such as the face, are more easily detected than those that appear on private regions, such as the buttocks. Most crucially, the probability that specific acts or attributes will be recognized as "deviant" depends in large part on their visibility or their likelihood of being detected directly (through the observations of an onlooker) or indirectly (through the reports of others).

As Tiedeman and Hawkins have emphasized, several structural factors increase the visibility of deviance.[20] These factors include the following:

- *The physical design of a setting.* If a setting has open spaces, bright lighting, and unobstructed sight lines, then rule-breaking acts and attributes will be more easily observed.
- *The presence of electronic detection devices.* Devices such as surveillance cameras, closed-circuit monitors, metal detectors, and electronic alarms increase the chances of deviant behavior being detected. Many companies have resorted to installing hidden surveillance cameras to monitor their employees or customers and to spot any rule-breaking activity. This practice, of course, makes it more likely for company detectives or "loss prevention" specialists to see deviance occurring.
- *The placement of detecting personnel.* The placement of police officers and other rule enforcers (e.g., store detectives) clearly affects the extent of visibility of various rule-breaking actions. For instance, the patrolling patterns of police officers directly influence the nature and distribution of crime rates in a region. When the police focus their surveillance efforts on particular areas, they guarantee that more deviance will be detected in these areas, regardless of whether more rule breaking actually does take place there. Ironically, then, by concentrating their patrols on high crime areas, the police help ensure that rates of detected crime remain high in these areas.

- *The presence of deviance-detecting "experts" in gate-keeping positions.* The growing number of experts serving in various gate-keeping positions has translated into the increased "discovery" of deviance, or characteristics seen as symptomatic of deviance. For example, in public school systems highly trained psychologists and counselors "use more tests and rating scales on children today than ever before, therefore finding more problems in need of correction."[21] This trend is clearly illustrated in the diagnosis of hyperkinesis. In recent years hyperkinesis (or hyperactivity) has become a fairly common diagnosis among schoolchildren. In fact, rates of hyperactivity are as high as 35 to 40 percent in some urban school systems. However, these rates are at least partially attributable to the growing prevalence of experts trained to discover and diagnose hyperactivity.

- *Significant contact with social control bureaucracies.* The visibility of deviance is also affected by the amount of contact a person has with social control bureaucracies. Those individuals who have extensive contact with public agencies such as social services departments, public housing agencies, state employment services, or criminal justice organizations live a relatively public life: their actions are more open to scrutiny by agents of social control. Moreover, as they have greater contact with social control bureaucracies, their "secondary visibility" increases. That is, it becomes more likely for their rule-breaking conduct to be detected by one bureaucracy and reported to others, particularly those who have the expertise and authority to deal with this conduct. Interagency communication of this kind has become more convenient and widespread as increasingly sophisticated information technologies have become available. This development has in turn escalated the secondary visibility of those who come into contact with social control bureaucracies.

- *Limited access to private spaces.* Some people have to spend more time in public places because they lack access to private areas. As a result, their rule-breaking acts or characteristics are more likely to be monitored. This is particularly true for poor people in urban neighborhoods. Because of inadequate housing and overcrowded conditions, the urban poor have to interact more frequently in public spaces and are more visible to outsiders (e.g., the police) than those in other social classes. Overall, the urban poor are more likely to have their rule violations detected because they have to spend more of their daily lives in public space. This, of course, makes their "deviant" acts or characteristics more visible to witnesses. As Tiedeman and Hawkins stress, "the poor are less likely to enjoy mobility and access to private places such as country clubs, restaurants, and cocktail lounges and are simultaneously more closely watched" by the police and other social control agents.[22] Furthermore, because the poor have greater contact with social control bureaucracies than other social classes, they have a higher level of secondary visibility.

While all of these structural factors promote the visibility of rule violations, certain types of attributes also make it more likely for individuals to be recognized as deviant. One of these attributes is physical or mental impairment. As people go through their daily rounds, they assume that others will "appear to be normal"; that is, they will walk normally, talk coherently, see and hear adequately, have a standard level of physical stamina, and have the ability to participate in a normal conversation.[23] If someone does not have these attributes, people are inclined to see him or her as deviant. Those individuals who have particularly noticeable bodily aberrations, such as a physical deformity, debilitating illness, or senile mind, are especially likely to be regarded as deviant. Although they have not committed a deviant act, others view them as "tainted" social actors

Box 7-1 DEVIANCE AS UNTIMELY ACTION

William Reese and Michael Katovich have pointed out that a number of temporal (or time-related) factors also make us more or less likely to see acts as deviant. In general, deviant acts are "untimely" acts; that is, they are acts that fall outside of conventional temporal frames and expectations. According to Reese and Katovich, "when an act takes place adds as much to its meaning as any intrinsic aspect of the act. Sex on the first date means something altogether different than sex on the fifth or twelfth date." Similarly, "a phone call or ringing doorbell at 2 A.M. is an entirely different event than the same sounds at 2 P.M." (p. 163).

In the following excerpt, Reese and Katovich illustrate how temporal considerations are central to the process of defining deviance. More specifically, they highlight two of the temporal factors—timing and frequency—that become salient in defining drinking behavior as problematic or alcoholic.[1]

Timing

Diagnosticians regard drinking a single ounce of alcohol in the morning, especially on the way to regular work (or to church), as potentially problematic and eventually symptomatic. Referred to as an "eye-opener" or "bracer," the early morning drink is often a social cue to alcoholism and evidence that outside help may be required. It is doubtful that the imbibing of a single drink at any other time could invoke such firm or absolute typification. Indeed, many regard it as a sufficient condition of alcoholism—so much so that other criteria of deviance (e.g., location, quantity, or social repercussion) pale in comparison. When not accompanied by a special occasion, the morning drink is untimely and deviant. In contrast, heavy drinking throughout birthdays, anniversaries, and some holidays is timely and nondeviant.

Given the pervasiveness of this proscription, early drinkers establish temporal boundaries for themselves, such as, "I never drink before noon (or 5 P.M.)." Such self-imposed strictures often appear more as attempts at maintaining self-concept and as staged activity than as voluntary temperance. Moreover, social acceptance of champagne brunches and bloody-mary breakfasts indicates that "taboo time" can be manipulated by special occasions. Early-morning drinks on some fishing/hunting trips approach social drinking occasions in some circles. Nevertheless, drinkers who regularly seek out such "legitimating" contexts are not likely to remain above suspicion, for they come to be perceived as violating a second temporal norm—frequency.

Frequency

Not only when but how often an act takes place can locate it on the normal deviancy plane. Acts may become defined as deviant if they occur too often or if they are too rare. Diagnosticians commonly define alcoholism as drinking too often. The admonition of "everything in moderation, nothing to excess" tempers habits of ingestion in terms of frequency. This is especially true in regard to alcohol. Daily use is considered strong evidence of a problem, again beyond issues of quantity or social outcome. Drinking even once a week or ten times a year are sufficient criteria of alcoholism for less tolerant typifications. However, as the time frame expands from day to week to year (and thereby becomes more ambiguous), the finality of the judgment is informed and tempered by other aspects of the act (i.e., state of inebriation or family, occupational, or health consequences). Frequent drinkers who are sensitive to such attributions of deviance can manipulate appearances of frequency. In the tavern culture, for instance, some drinkers are "regulars" every Friday at a given bar and conceal being Thursday regulars at a second and Wednesday regulars at a third. Certain occupations, such as outside salesperson, can facilitate such distortion of the public self for extended periods of time until other temporal violations betray the problem. Corporate actors may drink frequently but only at "high-class" establishments symbolic of corporate success. Such manipulations of space, while highlighting the interrelatedness of space-time embedment for deviance documentation, open a potential for fertile insight: Space can be, and often is, used to recontextualize temporal transgressions.

1. In their insightful analysis Reese and Katovich identify nine temporal factors that are involved in the construction of alcoholism. These factors include duration, tempo, pacing, rhythm, sequencing, synchronicity, and chronicity, as well as timing and frequency.

Source: William Reese and Michael A. Katovich, "Untimely Acts: Extending the Interactionist Conception of Deviance," *Sociological Quarterly* 30(2), 1989, pp. 159-184. Reprinted by permission of the Midwest Sociological Society.

because their bodily appearance falls outside of the bounds of normalcy.

People are also more likely to be viewed as deviant if they display attributes—such as dishonesty, selfishness, or "unnatural" desires—which are seen as signs of a flawed or blemished character, especially when these attributes are linked to a known history of criminality, mental illness, alcoholism, drug addiction, child abuse, homosexuality, unemployment, or political extremism.[24]

Another attribute that makes people more likely to be recognized as deviant is membership in a discredited or oppressed group, such as an ethnic, racial, religious, or political group defined as undesirable by members of the larger society. This is clearly illustrated in the case of Jewish people, who have been persecuted and killed in various times and places simply because of their religious heritage. Of course, members of other groups, such as Gypsies, Kurds, blacks, Italians, Palestinians, and the Irish, have also been defined and persecuted as deviant in various times and contexts. Whether a group is targeted as deviant depends in large part on the amount of power they possess within a society or region. If they have relatively little power, they are more apt to

have discrediting moral definitions imposed on them by dominant groups—and these definitions are more likely to stick.

As Erving Goffman has observed, attributes like those listed above are sources of **stigma**, or social devaluation.[25] If we display such attributes, we possess a "mark of social disgrace" that is likely to become the focus of others' attention and concern, making it difficult for us to engage in smooth or pleasant interactions with them. As bearers of a stigmatizing trait, we violate others' expectations in an undesirable way and thus are likely to be recognized as deviant.

Goffman points out, however, that nearly any attribute (e.g., body size, skin tone, hair color, or eye shape) can become a source of stigma. Most of us have attributes that in some way violate prevailing appearance norms and make us susceptible to being labeled as deviant. As Goffman notes:

There are...norms such as those associated with physical comeliness, which take the form of ideals and constitute standards against which almost everyone falls short at some stage of his [or her] life. And even where widely attained norms are involved, their multiplicity has the effect of disqualifying many persons. For example, in an important sense there is only one complete unblushing male in America: a young, married, white, urban, northern, heterosexual Protestant father of college education, fully employed, of good complexion, weight, and height, and a recent record of sports....Any male who fails to qualify in any of these ways is likely to view himself—during moments at least—as unworthy, incomplete, and inferior....[26]

While Goffman's example focuses on the cultural ideals that apply for men in the United States, it illustrates that nearly all of us have traits, or combinations of traits, that fail to live up to the appearance norms of our society. As a result, we are potentially vulnerable to the threat of stigma and to the negative attributions that accompany it.

The Attribution Process: Imputing Motives and Negotiating Identities

After recognizing an act or feature as a rule violation, we try to determine what has caused it. We thereby engage in the process of **attribution**—a process in which we make inferences about the forces or motivations underlying an action or condition.[27] The inferences we make about a specific rule violation depend largely on whether we see it as accidental, forced, or freely chosen. If we regard a rule-breaking event as either accidental or coerced, we attribute its cause to external forces, which we see as mainly beyond a person's control. On the other hand, if we view this rule violation as freely chosen, we attribute its cause to internal factors, such as a person's motives or character traits. Imagine how you would react if someone bumped into you and knocked you off balance as you were entering a concert with your friends. If you determined that the person hit you accidentally or was pushed into you, you would probably let his or her actions pass, assuming that he or she didn't mean to cause you any harm. However, if you determined that the person

intentionally rammed into you just to get into the concert ahead of you and your friends, you'd be likely to infer that he or she was a "jerk."

Imputing Motives and Applying Stereotypes. When we attribute a person's rule breaking to internal factors, we are likely to call his or her basic nature into question, especially if he or she engages in risky conduct. We assume that his or her rule breaking reflects questionable motivations or personal qualities. Based on this perception, we are likely to attribute a deviant identity to him or her. This identity serves as a typification: a simplified and standardized category we use to make sense of the person's actions or attributes. In general, this typification leads us to see a rule-breaking individual in stereotypical terms. That is, when we categorize a person as deviant, we tend to see him or her in terms of a relatively simple and preexisting set of images we learn through socialization. These images are part of popular culture and are reflected in the contents of language and the mass media. Consider the case of people with a seemingly minor "deviant" trait: red hair. In our culture redheads are perceived in terms of several negative stereotypes.[28] As Druann Heckert and Amy Best have revealed, these stereotypes go way beyond any relationship to hair color and extend to character traits and ethnicity. The most common stereotypes that Americans have about redheads are that they are hot tempered, weird, clownish-looking, sun challenged, and Irish. Another prominent American stereotype about redheads applies to their sexuality and differs by gender. According to this stereotype, redheaded women are wild and sexy but redheaded men are wimpy and sexually unappealing, much like the Richie Cunningham character on *Happy Days*.[29]

Most importantly, these stereotypical assumptions guide many Americans' actions toward people with red hair, leading them to react to "redheads" primarily in terms of their "deviant" attribute. In the process, they transform this attribute into a **master status**—a status that serves as the primary basis, or essential characteristic, through which others define, evaluate, and respond to a person.[30] They thereby set up a self-fulfilling prophecy, evoking expectations and reactions that lead redheads (like others defined as deviant) to think and act in ways consistent with the stereotypical traits attributed to them. Heckert and Best found that many of the redheads they interviewed regarded themselves as hot tempered, zany, clownish, or wimpy, which revealed that they had internalized the stereotypes applied to them. Most of these individuals also reported that the stereotypes associated with red hair had made them the targets of negative treatment, especially by their peers when they were children. This negative treatment in turn led them to experience a lower level of self-esteem, feelings of undesirable difference, and a sense that they were constantly the center of other people's attention.[31]

Heckert and Best's findings illustrate how cultural stereotypes about certain statuses or characteristics, including seemingly minor and inoffensive ones, create expectations that impose constraints on the actions and interactions of those targeted, making it difficult for them not to internalize and live up to those expectations. In fact, regardless of whether they play out the deviant identity that is assigned to them, their actions or attributes may be interpreted as consistent with that identity and as reflective of who they are and have always been.

Avoiding or Resisting Deviant Labeling: The Role of the Accused in Attribution. While the process of attribution can powerfully shape the interactions, identities, and self-images of people accused of deviance, it is important to remember that the accused are not passive or powerless as this process unfolds. Indeed, they take steps to influence the attributions of others and to avert, deflect, or counteract stigmatizing typifications. In doing so, they draw on various strategies of stigma management and deviance disavowal. These strategies include normalization, neutralization, and destigmatization.

When individuals engage in the strategy of **normalization**, they try to avoid having a deviant label applied to their rule-breaking acts or attributes, usually by concealing these acts or attributes and maintaining a conventional self-presentation. *Passing* is probably the most common normalization technique used by stigmatized persons. When passing, individuals present appearances and make identity claims to suggest that they have attributes different from their actual statuses. For instance, people living with HIV/AIDS engage in "passing" when they conceal their diagnosis from others and present themselves as perfectly healthy. Of course, it is easiest for stigmatized individuals to pass as normal when their problematic attribute has a low degree of visibility and they have a fair amount of control over the information they present to others. They face a different situation, however, if their stigma is apparent and they interact regularly in public. Under these circumstances, they must devise more sophisticated, *covering* strategies to hide their "spoiled" identity. Typically this means developing and offering accounts that disguise this identity. For example, when people with AIDS reach the later stages of their illness and develop serious health problems, they sometimes choose to tell others that these problems derive from a less stigmatized illness, such as cancer, leukemia, or pneumonia.[32] By offering this cover, they can hide their health status from unsuspecting others and reduce or deflect the stigmatizing attributions directed toward them.

Yet, while strategies such as passing and covering are useful in averting or displacing stigma, they also have some drawbacks. When people conceal information about themselves, particularly from friends, partners, or relatives, their relationships become more strained and distant. Moreover, by adopting such an approach, they prevent themselves from receiving the understanding, acceptance, or practical assistance that unknowing others might provide if given the opportunity. In addition to these drawbacks, people with a stigmatizing attribute may feel anxious or ambivalent about the measures they have to take to cover it. They experience the stress and alienation so commonly felt by those who lead a "closeted" or "double" life.

Given the drawbacks of passing and covering, some individuals try to avoid stigma by carefully restricting their interactions or affiliations with others, thereby *insulating* themselves from negative attributions.[33] These individuals opt to interact as much as possible with a select circle of trusted associates, such as friends, lovers, family members, and, in some cases, members of support groups. They reduce contacts with people outside this circle because they are likely to be less tolerant or predictable. These individuals develop a small network of intimates who protect them from potentially threatening interactions and stigmatizing attributions. Within this supportive network, they feel little need to conceal their "deviant" attributes or identity. They thereby experience a measure of relief from the burdens of stigma management and information control.

In addition to using normalization techniques such as passing, covering, and insulation, people who are the targets of negative labeling often rely on the strategy of neutralization. When engaging in **neutralization**, they accept the attribution of deviance given to a rule-breaking act but offer accounts to explain why they should not be labeled as deviant for participating in this act. These accounts provide a reinterpretation of the rule-breaking behavior, neutralizing any attributions of wrongfulness associated with it or with its consequences.

As a number of interactionist researchers have revealed, people draw on six basic "techniques of neutralization" in their efforts to avoid or resist deviant labels.[34] These techniques include the following:

1. *The denial of responsibility.* When engaging in this form of neutralization, individuals offer excuses that acknowledge the wrongfulness of their actions but explain why they shouldn't be held responsible (see Chapter Six). Excuses are verbal strategies designed to communicate why admittedly untoward or undesirable conduct could not be avoided. Some of the more common excuses that people use to avert negative labeling include claims that a rule-breaking act, such as missing an exam, resulted from an accident ("I had a flat tire"), from biological factors ("I was sick"), from events outside their will ("My grandfather died the day before the test"), or from the behavior of others ("The professor didn't tell us that the exam was being given that day"). Each of these excuses suggests that under specific circumstances, individuals have "no choice" but to engage in rule breaking and thus should be regarded as blameless or even normal for doing so.

2. *The denial of injury.* When using this technique, people justify rule-breaking behavior by claiming it has not resulted in any real or serious harm to others. This claim rests on "the morality of consequences," or the presumption that actions should be seen as deviant or immoral only if they cause significant injury.[35] Examples of the use of "denial of injury" abound in everyday life. For instance, students who cheat on college assignments use this strategy when they justify their actions by claiming the assignments were so trivial or irrelevant that no one was truly hurt by their actions.[36] When using this type of justification, rule breakers argue that their actions were not intended to be harmful and therefore should not be categorized as deviant.

3. *The denial of victim.* When drawing on this technique, individuals admit that their rule-breaking actions caused harm but claim that the injured parties are not actually victims since any injury they incurred was retribution for injustices they had inflicted on others. In essence, when engaging in "the denial of victim" rule breakers see themselves as righteous avengers who are merely giving alleged victims "what they had coming" because of their own transgressions. While student cheaters are less likely to use this neutralization strategy than

others, one way in which they engage in the denial of a victim is by claiming their cheating is a way to "even the score" with a teacher who gave them an unfair grade.

4. *Condemning the condemners.* This form of neutralization involves challenging the moral superiority of those who question the motives or actions of rule breakers. The rule breakers reject the implied judgment of this questioning by condemning the people who seek to condemn them. In the process they try to shift the focus of attention from their own rule-breaking conduct to the motives and actions of those who would label them as deviant. For example, student cheaters "condemn their condemners" by pointing to the indifference or professional negligence of their instructors, as illustrated by the favoritism they have seen these instructors display when grading certain students, such as athletes, fraternity members, or attractive women.[37]

5. *Appealing to higher or other loyalties.* Another technique rule breakers use to neutralize deviant labeling is to claim that their acts are justifiable or even proper because they were done for a "higher purpose" or "greater good," such as loyalty to their friends, family, gang, or church. When relying on this form of neutralization, rule breakers contend that they had to give preference to the norms of their immediate group because these norms were more pressing, or involved a higher allegiance, than the norms of the society. Students who engage in cheating often justify their actions through invoking higher loyalties, claiming that they only cheated because they felt compelled to help a friend, roommate, or fellow fraternity/sorority member who was in need of their assistance. When offering this justification, the students do not challenge the legitimacy of the rules against cheating, but rather stress the greater moral obligation they felt to help someone they cared about.

6. *Claims of normality.* Finally, rule breakers may try to neutralize attributions of deviance by claiming that their behavior is normal or acceptable because "everyone else is doing it." While admitting that their actions technically violate a law, rule, or an ethical code, rule breakers argue that in practice it is not defined as an instance of deviance. Indeed, they contend that the rule against this conduct is ignored or unenforced, so violating this rule should not subject one to deviant labeling. In the case of student cheaters, this strategy is illustrated when they claim that "everybody else cheats too" and that "if I don't cheat, someone else will." In making the latter claim, these students imply that cheating is going to happen anyway so their involvement in it is of no moral significance.[38]

All of these neutralization techniques are examples of the broader process of "motive talk"—a process that is integral to the negotiation and attribution of deviance. As we noted in Chapter Six, when people engage in unusual or unexpected behavior, they are expected to offer accounts that explain this behavior and repair any breaches it has caused in the social order. Neutralization techniques are designed to serve this purpose, providing rule breakers with excuses or justifications they can draw on to explain their actions and counteract stigmatizing attributions. Through using these techniques, rule breakers convey that they understand and accord a degree of legitimacy to the dominant values of the larger culture. As they interact with conventional others, they do not try to challenge or change these values; instead, they propose that their failure to abide by these values is justifiable and should not make them subject to attributions of deviance. Thus, when engaging in neutralization, they show their own commitment to the societal values they have threatened through their rule-breaking behavior. They also try to convince others that it would not be appropriate to label them as deviant.

When individuals seek not only to avoid or neutralize the stigmatizing attributions of others but also to replace deviant identities with essentially normal ones, they engage in the strategy of **destigmatization**. As Carol Warren has observed, two of the destigmatization techniques that people draw on are *purification* and *transcendence*.[39] When participating in purification, individuals reverse the stigma imputed to them by exchanging a defective or less desirable self for a more valued identity. In most cases, this exchange takes place after a stigmatized person experiences a "rebirth" and forsakes his or her rule-breaking actions, replacing them with conduct that has a spiritual foundation, such as benevolent or self-sacrificial acts. Examples of this type of rebirth abound in the United States, particularly in evangelical churches and in "twelve step" groups such as Alcoholics Anonymous, Al-Anon, and Overeaters Anonymous. Individuals who engage in purification, through either sacred or secular conversions, commonly adopt a repentant stance regarding their rule-breaking conduct. They try to erase the stigma by offering apologies for their past mistakes and showing others that they have become new and better people.

By contrast, individuals who engage in transcendence do not erase or disavow a previous, defective self. Instead, they seek to "rise above" their stigmatized condition (e.g., physical disability or chronic illness) by displaying a pattern of conduct that is not expected of people having this condition. In some cases, they even strive to achieve a "supernormal identity," showing others that they can function at a more demanding level than "normal" people and that they can compete and excel at more challenging pursuits than their similarly impaired peers.[40] Some well-known examples of people who have transcended a physical disability and achieved a supernormal identity include Franklin Delano Roosevelt, Helen Keller, Elizabeth Barrett Browning, and Stephen Hawking. To realize a similar identity, along with the sense of value and transcendence associated with it, people living with a disability must demonstrate that they can succeed in pursuits that are ordinarily closed off to them. In essence, then,

they must convince others that they have an essentially normal or "better-than-normal" self.

For many people who have a stigmatized status, strategies such as purification and transcendence do not seem appealing or viable. As a result, they may turn to a third method of destigmatization: *distancing*. When using this strategy of stigma management, people try to counteract or disavow attributions of deviance by separating themselves from roles, associations, or institutions that imply undesirable identities.[41] For example, David Snow and Leon Anderson found that homeless individuals engaged in associational distancing by differentiating themselves from others who shared their status, as Tony Jones, a twenty-four-year-old homeless man, revealed when he said:

> I'm not like the other guys who hang out at the Sally [Salvation Army]. If you want to know about street people, I can tell you about them; but you can't really learn about street people from studying me, because I'm different.[42]

Snow and Anderson also discovered that homeless persons regularly took part in institutional distancing, as illustrated by their frequent griping about the agencies responsible for attending to their needs. The primary target of this griping was the Salvation Army. According to Snow and Anderson, many of the homeless who used this agency described it as a greedy corporation run by inhumane people who were "more interested in lining their own pockets than in serving the needy."[43] In support of this claim, the homeless recounted stories about Salvation Army workers who "looked down on them," "treated them like an animal," or stole donated groceries and goods. Most crucially, Snow and Anderson revealed that through denigrating the Salvation Army and other agencies that served them, the homeless offset the stigmatizing implications of their dependency on these agencies. Through this strategy, along with other forms of distancing, the homeless neutralized the centrality of their "deviant" identity and emphasized more valued parts of their lives and selves. Doing so enabled them to displace and resist the stigma that others ascribed to their homeless status.

In summary, people who are detected as rule breakers are typically active rather than passive participants in the attribution process. They draw on a variety of strategies—normalization, neutralization, or destigmatization—as they negotiate motives and identities with others. When successful, these strategies enable rule breakers to avoid or deflect stigmatizing attributions and to sustain valued identities. However, when these strategies fail, rule breakers are likely to be labeled as deviant and to have social sanctions brought to bear against them.

The Reaction Process: Sanctioning and Its Effects

To make sense of people's reactions to deviance, we have to remember that when they observe rule breaking, especially of a less serious nature, they often respond by ignoring it or acting as if "nothing unusual is happening."[44] This response is rooted in cultural and moral beliefs that emphasize the virtues of minding your own business, giving people a second chance, or letting officials deal with rule-breaking incidents. These beliefs are part of a larger set of societal guidelines that prescribe not only how and when individuals should respond to deviance, but also who is the most appropriate reactor in a given situation. Generally speaking, people feel more compelled to react to a deviant act or attribute when (1) it violates widely agreed-upon rules and threatens their sense of social order, (2) they believe their reaction will "do some good," and (3) they think that the rule breaker has failed to engage in appropriate kinds of remedial work. People are also more inclined to respond to deviance when they do not think it will be personally risky or embarrassing to do so.

Yet, as Howard Becker observed, the degree to which members of a group or society will react to a given rule-breaking event varies greatly.[45] First,

the degree of reaction varies over time. A person who is caught engaging in a rule-breaking act, such as smoking marijuana or selling sexual favors, may be responded to more harshly at one time than he or she would be at another. This is clearly illustrated in the case of law enforcement "drives" or campaigns against deviance. On some occasions the police decide to launch full-scale campaigns against specific forms of deviance, such as prostitution or the use of "meth" (methamphetamine). Obviously, it is risky for people to engage in these activities when such a campaign is in full swing. Their chances of getting detected and sanctioned as deviant increase substantially.

Second, the degree to which an act will be treated as an instance of deviance depends on who engages in it and who thinks they have been hurt by it.[46] Rules are commonly enforced more often against some individuals and groups than others. For example, as noted earlier, drug laws are applied differentially to African Americans than to whites. White drug users do not get as far in the legal process as their African-American counterparts, especially if the whites live in middle-class neighborhoods and the African Americans live in poor neighborhoods. The white, middle-class users are less likely to be monitored and apprehended by the police, and when they do happen to be apprehended, they are unlikely to be convicted and sentenced. By contrast, poor African-American drug users are much more likely to be monitored by the police, and when they are arrested, they are more likely to be convicted and sentenced. What this pattern of enforcement reveals is that the degree to which particular individuals are branded and sanctioned as deviant is often more of a measure of their social characteristics than their rule-breaking behavior.

Finally, the severity of the social sanctions directed toward identified deviants depends in part on the significance of the rules they have broken. If they have engaged in a minor rule violation, such as walking down the wrong side of a sidewalk, they will probably be the target of informal sanctions, such as staring, laughter, or ridicule. On the other hand, if they have engaged in a serious norm violation, such as murdering someone, they will probably be the target of formal sanctions, such as criminal charges and imprisonment. Before these formal sanctions are applied, however, an accused rule breaker typically has to go through a "public degradation ceremony." During this ceremony he or she is publicly transformed into a "deviant" and forced to accept this new and discrediting status. In many cases criminal trials and sentencing hearings serve as degradation ceremonies, but they are not the only examples. Psychiatric evaluations and medical examinations can also serve this function, especially when they impose a stigmatizing diagnosis (e.g., schizophrenia, syphilis, or terminal illness) on an individual.

The Effects of Social Reaction. The transformation of a person into a "deviant" has two types of effects on his or her life: objective and subjective.[47] Objective effects refer to the consequences that negative labels and corresponding sanctions have for a person's work life, economic status, political opportunities, social relationships, and community involvements. These consequences are far reaching for individuals who are formally labeled and punished as criminals. They are not only separated from their families and communities but also denied access to political rights and job opportunities, sometimes even after "serving their time." On the other hand, the subjective effects of labeling and sanctioning refer to how "deviants" think about themselves and their social worlds, especially from the vantage point of their stigmatized status. As we noted earlier, the processes set in motion by labeling and related social reactions tend to confirm and strengthen deviant identities. When people are defined as deviant, their other identities fade into the background. Their deviant identity overrides all their other attributes and serves to define who they are as persons. This commonly leads to **secondary deviance**, or deviance that results from the labeling process.[48] For example, if individuals become defined as criminals, they are apt to be

stigmatized and rejected by friends, relatives, and employers. They consequently have to turn to other criminals to find acceptance, moral support, and financial assistance. Once they become involved with these criminals, they are even more likely to see themselves as deviant and to engage in additional acts of rule breaking, thereby fulfilling the negative expectations of others. Ironically, then, a key consequence of labeling people as deviant is to structure them into deviant behavior patterns and careers.

As labeling theorists have observed, we regularly attribute secondary deviance, such as increased criminal behavior, to people's deviant statuses rather than seeing it as a consequence of the restricted interactions and opportunities that result from others' reactions. Often the individuals who get labeled as deviant apply this stigmatized identity to themselves and incorporate it into their self-concepts. (Reflect back to the discussion of the "looking-glass self" in Chapter Four.) This process of self-labeling, in turn, enhances the likelihood that they will seek out other deviants and engage in further rule breaking. Hence, people's self-identifications as deviant can have the unintended consequence of leading them to embark on a deviant career.

Challenging and Transforming Deviant Labels: Tertiary Deviance

Labeling theory has been criticized for offering an overly simplified version of the consequences of deviant labeling. Critics point out that people don't necessarily internalize the deviant labels applied to them and, even when they do, they don't automatically become involved in a deviant career.[49] In fact, many individuals are motivated to "go straight" after being stigmatized as deviant, as a result either of a brush with the law or of involvement in some kind of counseling or treatment program.

The problem with these criticisms is that they display a lack of understanding of the key tenets of labeling theory. Labeling theorists do not contend that the process of deviant label-ing automatically leads a person to internalize a stigmatizing identity and to engage in second-ary deviance. Indeed, because they are guided by the assumptions of symbolic interaction-ism, labeling theorists recognize that people are active agents who have the capacity to resist, deflect, or disavow the deviant labels attributed to them. Moreover, labeling theorists recognize that even when people are identified as deviant, they do not simply have to accept the negative social meanings attached to this identity. Instead, they can negotiate and reconstruct these mean-ings through their interactions with others. In some cases, they can even take part in efforts to challenge and transform these meanings, thereby entering a third stage of deviance, referred to as **tertiary deviance**.[50] When engaging in tertiary deviance, stigmatized individuals redefine their "deviant" acts or attributes as normal, laudable, or virtuous. They also take steps to transform their spoiled identities into socially desirable ones.

In recent decades it has become more com-mon for stigmatized individuals and groups to engage in tertiary deviance, as illustrated by the identity work of African Americans, gays and lesbians, people living with disabilities, and peo-ple who are overweight (see Box 7–2). Through banding together to form support networks and advocacy organizations, members of these groups have found ways to challenge the cultural norms and beliefs that discredit them. They have also inverted the meaning of their stigmatized sta-tuses, transforming them into sources of pride, social solidarity, and self-value.

To demonstrate how stigmatized individuals take part in tertiary deviance, we will describe some of the strategies that people living with HIV/AIDS draw on as they construct and nego-tiate the meanings of their illness. As Sandstrom revealed, most people with HIV/AIDS do not simply take part in efforts to avoid or neutralize stigma. Instead, they actively engage in processes of identity **embracement** and reconstruction that allow them to fashion, present, and sustain identities consistent with and supportive of favor-able images of self.[51] In doing so they effectively challenge and transform the stigma associated with their health status.

One of the ways individuals with HIV/AIDS transform stigma is by "coming out" publicly about their health status and engaging in AIDS-related activism. Through serving on the boards of AIDS service organizations, producing news-letters for people living with the disease, speak-ing in public education forums, and participating in rallies, marches, or lobbying efforts, they chal-lenge AIDS-related stigma and assert their right to define what it means to be a person living with HIV/AIDS. They also derive a sense of empow-erment and efficacy from the contributions they make in the "battle against AIDS." This in turn helps them to cope more effectively with the per-sonal ramifications of the disease.

Another way people living with HIV/AIDS transform stigma is by stressing the unexpected or hidden "blessings" that have resulted from their illness.[52] While acknowledging the difficul-ties and suffering evoked by HIV/AIDS, they also highlight the personal benefits they have derived from their illness experience—benefits they believe they might not have otherwise real-ized. For example, some individuals with HIV/AIDS emphasize how their illness has motivated them to make positive personal changes, such as improving their health practices, deepening their spiritual life, and reevaluating their values, goals, and priorities. Others stress how their illness has been a "gift" or "special opportunity" because it has enabled them to discover who their true friends are and to establish more caring relation-ships with these friends. Still others accentuate how their struggles with AIDS have led them to live more fully in the moment and to revel in the "wonder and beauty of the little things going on around them."[53] Through immersing themselves in such an intense present, they experience a renewed sense of joy and a revitalized self.

People with HIV/AIDS also highlight the benefits of their illness and realize valued identities through reassessing the importance of previously valued activities, such as sexual activity.[54] Persons with HIV/AIDS often experience declines in their sexual energy or activity levels as their illness unfolds. In turn, they may place greater emphasis on nonsexual involvements and relationships. Thus, rather than evaluating their desirability and worth in terms of their erotic activity or involvements, they may emphasize the new and deeper forms of expression, intimacy, and fulfillment they experience in nonsexual friendships. Some also stress the new images of self they develop and realize through these relationships—images of self as loving, thoughtful, and spiritually mature persons.[55]

By using a combination of the above strategies, people living with HIV/AIDS gain a measure of control and transcendence over the stigmatizing meanings associated with their health status. At the same time, they preserve or rebuild valued selves that help them cope more effectively with the daily implications of their unfolding illness. They thereby engage in processes of identity construction that enable them to overcome AIDS-related stigma and to become tertiary deviants. In doing so they often draw upon strategies and ideologies developed by other individuals and groups battling stigma, such as gays and lesbians, immigrant workers, and people living with disabilities.

In conclusion, what the phenomenon of tertiary deviance reveals is that people who get labeled as deviant are not necessarily tied to this label or the negative moral meanings it evokes. Rather, they can find ways to challenge and transform this label, particularly through banding together with others and developing counterstigmatizing ideologies and supportive social networks. These ideologies and networks not only undermine the prevailing societal meanings given to a deviant status, but also provide stigmatized people with the social and symbolic resources necessary to fashion revitalizing identities and to sustain a sense of dignity and self-worth. Tertiary deviance, then, is linked to subcultural identity work that enables stigmatized individuals to create symbolic resources that may not yet exist, to learn how to use these resources, and to find support for the valued identities they embrace and affirm.

Box 7–2 THERE'S NO SHAME IN BEING FAT:
THE COLLECTIVE DISAVOWAL OF STIGMA

In a comparative study of appearance organizations, Dan Martin revealed how the National Association for the Advancement of Fat Acceptance (NAAFA) enables its members to contest the stigma and shame associated with being fat in the United States. NAAFA is a human rights and self-help organization that encourages its members to "change the world, not your body." One of the ways NAAFA members do this is by making body announcements at organizational conferences or workshops. These announcements range from modeling clothes in an organizational "fashion show" to stating one's "true" weight publicly after reading the lower weight recorded on one's driver's license. In making such announcements, members display their fat bodies as shameless and avow a fat identity that is invested with at least a measure of dignity. NAAFA members also embrace and avow "fat identities" through various acts of public and private confrontation. Martin makes the following observation:

> Letter-writing campaigns and confrontations with public officials, as well as proprietors of businesses and services who engage in size discrimination, comprise part of the protest activities of NAAFA members. No social context is considered exempt from "fat activism." What is formulated in these activities, according to NAAFA members, is a way of life, an organized set of attitudes, and a mode of responding to many of the situations they face daily.

Beth: One time they [co-workers] were making cracks in the lounge about eating. Well, it was at lunchtime and, oh God, this one woman, who's always dieting, said "If we eat this, we'll all have to shop at Women's World [clothing store for large women]!" And everybody laughed. And I said, "Oh pardon me." I said, "Don't make fun of the places where I buy my clothes." I just said it in a nice, lighthearted tone. There was just dead silence. God, everybody at the table was embarrassed to death. I thought, "Hey Beth, good for you for saying that!"

Deborah: So I was shopping and...I found myself in front of this huge section of Slimfast products. And all of a sudden the idea came to me, "Gee, I don't need the entire [NAAFA business] card." So I just tore the bottom half of the card off, the part that had the NAAFA address, and left the upper part that said, "Do something about your weight, accept it!" And I just stuck it on the shelf, sort of like behind one of those little plastic place cards, and said, "There."

The contestation [of stigma and shame] emanates from the lived experiences of members who organize their lives around their organizational "fat" identity. This identity is viewed as relevant in all of the daily activities of NAAFA members, whether confronting fellow employees like Beth or grocery shopping like Deborah. According to NAAFA members, shame militates against the active initiation of individual and, hence, collective political practice. NAAFA sees social stigma as directly linked to the internalized oppression of shame. Shame contestation is thus a required component of identity politics where the aggrieved attempt to transform themselves by transforming both societal definitions of beauty and human value and the feeling rules that govern fat bodies.

Source: Daniel D. Martin, "Organizational Approaches to Shame: Avowal, Management, and Contestation," *Sociological Quarterly* 41(1), 2000, pp. 125–150.

LIMITATIONS AND EXTENSIONS OF LABELING THEORY

As Howard Becker stressed, the original goal of labeling theory was to expand the study of deviance so that researchers would consider the activities of all of the parties involved in its creation, which include not only rule breakers but also rule makers and enforcers.[56] Labeling theory has realized that goal, sensitizing analysts to issues such as who has the power to make the rules whose infraction constitutes deviance and who has the authority to apply these rules to particular people and label them as deviant. Labeling theory has also focused attention on how the process of deviant labeling can lead targeted individuals to engage in further rule breaking and to become involved in a deviant career. In doing so, labeling theory has made a distinctive contribution to social psychological analysis, highlighting how deviance is created and sustained at the level of *interaction*.

Despite its accomplishments, however, labeling theory has been rightly criticized for its failure to address concerns about the causes (or etiology) of deviance, or why individuals are motivated to engage in rule-breaking behavior in the first place. In responding to this criticism, labeling theorists have emphasized that they never intended to explain all aspects of deviance, particularly not its origins.[57] They have also contended that the sources of deviance are not distinctively different from the sources of "normal" behavior. Indeed, labeling theorists propose that deviance emerges out of the same motivations and interactive processes that underlie normal conduct. People who take part in deviance have the same kinds of goals and purposes as those who engage in rule-abiding activity. Yet, while agreeing with these points, some labeling theorists acknowledge that they need to address questions better about the etiology of deviance, especially since this is a central concern of rule breakers. These analysts propose that to develop a more comprehensive explanation of deviance, we have to take the etiological concerns and understandings of rule breakers into account.

Fortunately, some interactionist researchers have taken up this task. One researcher, Jack Katz, has insightfully illustrated how we can better understand crime by seeing it through the eyes of the people who engage in it.[58] Katz reveals how many forms of criminal behavior seduce the criminal through the sensual pleasures and psychological thrills they provide. A variety of crimes—ranging from shoplifting and stickups to cold-blooded murder—have positive emotional attractions for those who participate in them. While the criminals may recognize that what they are doing is morally wrong, their actual performance of the criminal act can be interesting, thrilling, and powerfully compelling. As Katz observes, criminal acts offer a seductive and "thrilling melodrama about the self as seen from within and without."[59] When engaging in crime, such as a robbery or a murder, criminals see themselves as addressing a challenge to their moral (rather than their material) existence. Through meeting this challenge they demonstrate their personal competence and establish a potent moral identity, such as "bad ass," con artist, or cold-blooded killer.

In addition to being criticized for its shortcomings in explaining the causes or etiology of deviance, labeling theory has been critiqued for its failure to see "the bigger picture" when analyzing the politics of deviance. Conflict theorists argue that labeling theory has focused too much attention on the activities of caretaking organizations and low-level bureaucrats in the creation of deviance. As a result, labeling theorists have made the mistake of attributing real political power to the low-level officials who are simply the most visible instruments of ruling-class power. According to conflict theorists, labeling theory

fails to recognize how the ruling class controls the larger structures and institutions that shape the smaller processes and interactions that result in deviance. For instance, the ruling class uses government bureaucracies (e.g., the Narcotics Bureau) to create laws against common crimes in an effort to maintain civil order in a capitalist society. Quinney proposed the following:

> [The] law is determined by the few, , , who dominate the political process. Although the law is supposed to protect all citizens, it starts as a tool of the dominant class and ends by maintaining the dominance of that class. Law serves the powerful over the weak; it promotes the war of the powerful against the powerless. Moreover, law is used by the state…to promote and protect itself. Yet, we are all bound by the law, and we are indoctrinated with the myth that it is our law.[60]

Labeling theorists respond to these arguments by pointing out that conflict theory, while offering impressive rhetorical claims, does not refute the key premises of labeling theory. As Kotarba asserted, the "implementation of political power must be observable at the interactional level unless you believe in the 'invisible hand' phenomenon."[61] And, while labeling theorists have focused primarily on how rules are applied on the most accessible levels of daily life, their framework can also be used to examine how rules are fashioned and implemented on more hidden, structural levels.

Labeling theorists also challenge the notion of a monolithic power structure (and ruling class) by pointing out how the processes of rule creation and enforcement reflect the complexities of power relations in our diverse and conflictual society. Laws and other social rules are not simply the creations of legislators, bureaucrats, or powerful interest groups who do the bidding of the ruling class. Members of all of these groups share some responsibility for creating new definitions of deviance—and, depending on the issue, they are more or less successful in getting their definitions translated into law. In recent years governmental bureaucracies have become increasingly powerful in the rule-making process, and they pursue organizational interests that sometimes conflict with the interests of economic elites. For example, the Environmental Protection Agency seeks to preserve clean air and water and therefore formulates regulations that designate certain corporations as deviant, much to the anger of their powerful owners.

Finally, while defending the merits of their approach for analyzing the politics of deviance, labeling theorists tend to agree that they should concentrate more attention on issues such as how laws, bans, and crime waves originate. In doing so, they can follow the lead of the many interactionist-oriented scholars who have examined the political and definitional dynamics involved in the construction of social problems.[62] Indeed, this area of interactionist work is best viewed as an extension of labeling theory to broader, macro-sociological concerns. Most important, it offers labeling theorists a useful template for analyzing how deviance is created through processes of claimsmaking, typification, and communication that unfold on both the institutional and interactional levels.

THE CONSTRUCTION OF SOCIAL PROBLEMS

Since its origins, symbolic interactionism has been linked to the study of social problems. In fact, interactionism emerged out of sociologists' desires to effect social and political reforms in Chicago during the early twentieth century. In recent years a growing number of interactionist studies have focused on troubling social and political issues, guided not only by the insights of labeling theory, but also by the "construction of social problems" perspective.

In studying social problems, interactionists ask: Why are some patterns of behavior defined as "problematic" while others, equally threatening, are "normalized"? Why do particular issues become regarded as social problems while others that seem equally or more significant get ignored? Who has the power to make their definitions of "problems" stick? Why, for example, is it legal to consume alcohol, a mood-altering substance that contributes to over 100,000 American deaths per year, while it is illegal to use other, apparently safer, mood-altering drugs? And, why does public concern about the use of certain drugs ebb and flow across time?[63]

As implied by the above questions, interactionists view social problems as socially constructed concerns rather than as objectively harmful conditions. In turn, they emphasize the *claimsmaking* activities and processes through which particular conditions become defined as a cause for public concern. Spencer Cahill nicely summarizes the interactionist approach to social problems in the following excerpt:

> Social problems are as much a matter of definition as other aspects of human reality. Many social conditions have negative consequences for someone. Some are simply not recognized by most people, others are considered personal rather than social problems; and still others are considered an unfortunate but inevitable fact of human life. Such social conditions only become social problems when they gain the attention of the public and policymakers as a particular kind of problem that can and must be addressed. In most cases, activists, such as Mothers Against Drunk Driving, or professionals, such as doctors and social workers, make claims that a certain social condition, such as alcohol-related traffic accidents or some forms of adults' treatment of children, is a serious problem requiring public concern and intervention. These "primary claimsmakers" also define the characteristics of the problem or just what kind of problem it is, such as "drunk driving" or "child abuse."[64]

Interactionist scholars have pointed out that almost any issue or behavior can become defined as a social problem. Yet they recognize that certain social and political conditions make it more likely for specific issues or actions to be defined as public concerns. For example, it is far more likely for a drug to become identified as a social problem if the following conditions are met.[65]

First, the media dramatize the use of the drug, particularly by claiming that it has grown to epidemic proportions, depicting it as highly addictive, and portraying the worst scenarios associated with its use as typical in nature. The media thereby become "secondary claimsmakers," generating or magnifying public alarm about the drug and putting pressure on lawmakers to deal with it.

Second, powerful interest groups, such as doctors, pharmacists, alcohol treatment professionals, law enforcement agencies, and/or churches, effectively claim for themselves, by virtue of their unique and specialized knowledge, the expertise and authority to define the drug as a problem. They also effectively claim that they have the best remedy to this problem (which, not so coincidentally, means that the public will need to grant them extensive resources). Of course, some of these claimsmakers offer competing arguments for how to best address the threatening drug problem, where to focus public attention and resources, and whom to give primary responsibility for implementing the solution. For example, law enforcement agencies are likely to stress the need for police departments to find more resources to monitor and arrest drug offenders, whereas the drug treatment industry is likely to emphasize the need for substance abuse programs to receive more funds.

Third, the drug emerges or becomes more widely used in a context of significant social or cultural conflict. For instance, the drug scare of the 1960s, which emphasized that marijuana was a "killer weed" and "dropout drug," was clearly prompted in part by public anxiety about youth participation in political struggles of the time, including battles over civil rights and the Vietnam war.

Finally, the drug becomes linked to a "dangerous class," or a group already defined as a threat, especially by powerful elites. As Craig Reinarman has noted, "It was not alcohol problems *per se* that most animated the drive for Prohibition but the behavior and morality of what dominant groups saw as 'the dangerous class' of urban, Catholic working-class immigrants."[66] Likewise, it was not merely problems associated with the use of cocaine that gave rise to the drug scare of the 1980s; instead, it was only when a smokable version of cocaine "found its way into the African-American and Latino underclass that it made headlines and prompted calls for a drug war."[67] By linking a drug to a group they view as disreputable or dangerous, elites can make them into handy scapegoats, focusing public concern on the drug use occurring within this group and diverting attention away from problematic elite activities, such as corporate crime or government corruption. In the process, elites can minimize public scrutiny of their actions and critical questioning of their legitimacy and power.

The Media and the Construction of Terrorism

In recent years, the construction of prominent social issues, such as the problem of terrorism, has become shaped by the "politics of fear" that is reflected in drug scares and the war on drugs. According to David Altheide, the **politics of fear** "refers to decision makers' promotion and use of audience beliefs and assumptions about danger, risk, and fear in order to achieve certain goals."[68] In utilizing this form of politics, leaders support attacking a target (e.g., crime, terrorism), stress the likelihood that citizens will be further victimized, advocate the restriction of civil liberties, and define dissent as being inattentive to citizen needs or even as unpatriotic.

Altheide emphasizes how the media plays a central role in promoting and perpetuating the politics of fear and in shaping definitions of reality, including definitions of terrorism. Based on his extensive studies of news accounts, Altheide reveals how mainstream news organizations enabled U.S. decision makers "to transform terrorism from an act into a condition and world view," to cast all Americans as its victims, and to engage in whatever military reprisals that national leaders deem necessary.[69] Indeed, media coverage of 9/11 emphasized the following themes:

- All Americans were victimized by the attacks, and, thus, they should all support the government's attempts to attack what it sees as the source of fear.
- The attacks were an assault on American culture, if not civilization itself, and they were caused by "the enemy's dislike of the United States of America, its freedom and lifestyle."[70] If anyone suggested that the cause might be more complex, they were ignorant or unpatriotic and they should be publicly condemned.
- Americans needed to "grant elites and formal agents of control all authority to deploy whatever measures they deemed necessary to protect citizens, take revenge, and prevent such an attack from reoccurring."[71] In a related vein, Americans needed to accept the expansion of government surveillance and security measures to enhance their personal safety and to ensure the success of the "global war on terror."
- Americans should deal with the grief resulting from the attacks by purchasing goods and services and by giving money to charitable organizations, such as the Red Cross.
- Drug use was not only criminal, it was an act that directly supported terrorism.
- Overall, the world had fundamentally changed and it required "new symbolic meanings…, social control practices, international relations, and, above all, a new rationale and perspective for" dealing with the pervasive and encompassing reality of terrorism.[72]

In many respects American news organizations essentially served as an arm of the U.S. government and, along with the Bush administration, they effectively persuaded Americans to support the curtailment of key civil liberties, the open-ended expansion of police and military authority, and the implementation of a preemptive war in Iraq, a nation that did not have any demonstrated link to the 9/11 attacks.

Most important, Altheide's analyses illustrate how media reports played a key role in shaping the "politics of reality" that surrounded 9/11. These reports contributed to major shifts in the social meanings of a variety of disparate acts and events (e.g., drug use, airport security checks, and patriotic rituals) that became symbolically linked with the "war on terror." In reshaping the meanings of these acts and events, media accounts gave rise to a new, preemptive foreign policy—a policy "skillfully implanted in a fertile womb of fear and victimization"[73] and guided by rhetorics such as "shock and awe," "preemptive strike," and "enhanced interrogation."

Ultimately, through his investigations of the social construction of terrorism, Altheide portrays the growing power that the mass media have in defining the reality of social problems and deciding how they should be addressed. Altheide also demonstrates how public understandings of contemporary social problems are informed by an overarching discourse of fear, which is enhanced by the perpetual images of fear displayed by entertainment media.

In concluding, interactionists highlight the fact that social problems are human products which emerge out of a political process—a process that involves struggles over conceptions of reality. Through this process claimsmakers, such as activists, industrialists, scientific experts, or the media, construct a condition as a growing concern that threatens a significant number of people, either directly or indirectly. They also offer their interpretations of the nature and causes of this problem and suggest related remedies. If their proposed interpretations and solutions receive significant media coverage and resonate with broader cultural understandings, the public is likely to accept them and subsequently incorporate them into taken-for-granted reality. For example, the vast majority of Americans view youth gangs, child abuse, and drunk driving as social problems. Yet these issues only became identified as public problems relatively recently.

Thus, they "are not mere reflections of harmful social behaviors, but products of effective claims-making, media exposure, and public policies."[74] In turn, we can see how the construction of social problems parallels the social creation of deviance. Like definitions of deviance, social problems are manufactured through the claimsmaking efforts of individuals and groups who draw on a vast array of resources, including symbols, organizations, media outlets, and material goods, to promote and apply their definitions of reality.

Most crucially, through examining claimsmakers, the mass media, and the processes that characterize the construction of deviance and social problems, interactionists offer revealing insights into the political and communicative processes that shape the "reality" of our everyday social worlds. In the next chapter we will explore these processes further, focusing on how, when, and why people engage in collective action and form movements to promote or resist social change.

SUMMARY

- In this chapter we have highlighted the key premises of the symbolic interactionist perspective on deviance, which serves as the foundation of labeling theory. The interactionist perspective challenges the notion that deviance is an objective quality of particular acts or attributes. Instead, interactionists adopt a relativist view of deviance, seeing it as a quality that people confer on particular acts and attributes based on the values, norms, and outlooks of the groups to which they belong. Deviance, then, is not an inherent feature of certain acts or attributes, but rather is a product of people's definitions of and reactions to these acts or attributes.
- Guided by an interactionist perspective, labeling theorists emphasize that deviance is a socially constructed reality that emerges out of a complex and overlapping set of processes. These processes include

banning, detection, attribution, and reaction. During the banning process, moral entrepreneurs strive to make and enforce rules that prohibit a particular behavior or condition. When successful, they convince the public to see the individuals associated with this behavior or condition as "deviants" in need of correction. The implementation of such a ban, however, only sets the foundation for the construction of deviance. To become defined as deviant, people have to be detected and recognized as rule breakers. This is far more likely to happen if they live in social circumstances where their activities are monitored regularly by the police or other deviance-detecting experts. It is also more likely if they possess a highly visible stigma, such as a physical or mental deformity, a blemished character, or membership in a discredited group. Yet even when people are detected as rule breakers, they are not automatically labeled as deviant. During the attribution process, they negotiate the meaning of their rule-breaking acts or traits and try to dissuade others from imputing deviant motives and identities to them. In this process they draw on a variety of "deviance disavowal" strategies, including normalization, neutralization, and destigmatization. When used effectively, these strategies enable people accused of rule breaking to avoid or deflect stigmatizing attributions and to preserve valued identities. However, when these strategies are ineffective, the accused are likely to have a deviant label and negative sanctions imposed on them.
- Once people are labeled and sanctioned as deviant, their other identities often fade in importance. Their deviant identity supersedes all their other attributes and serves to define them as persons. Since this identity is negative, it limits their options, pushing them away from conventional associations and pulling them toward "deviant" social circles where they can find acceptance, support, or financial

assistance. This, in turn, makes them more likely to internalize a deviant identity and to become involved in further rule-breaking conduct, thereby fulfilling the negative expectations evoked by the labeling process. A key consequence of labeling people as deviant, then, is the imposition of internal and external constraints that may structure them into a deviant career.

- While emphasizing how the labeling process may call forth further deviance, labeling theorists do not presume that this process automatically leads a person to internalize a discredited identity and to participate in a deviant career. Instead, labeling theorists recognize that people are active agents who have the capacity to negotiate and reconstruct the meanings of the deviant labels applied to them.

- Perhaps the most important contribution of labeling theory has been its revelation of the significant role played by rule makers and enforcers in the creation of deviance. By passing powerful bans and then applying these bans to targeted individuals and groups, rule makers and enforcers are intimately involved in the social production of deviance. Indeed, they have the power to define the parameters of morality and deviance and to subject people to stigmatizing labels and sanctions. As a result, rule creators and enforcers are crucial in the social enterprise of "deviance making." To understand deviance, one has to understand the outlooks and activities of these moral entrepreneurs.

- Drawing on the insights of labeling theory as well as a long tradition of studying social and political issues, a growing number of interactionists have examined the construction of social problems. In doing so, they have highlighted how social problems do not necessarily refer to objectively harmful conditions. Instead, they are socially constructed concerns that emerge in and through the political actions and struggles of various

"claimsmakers." To get a condition defined as a problem, claimsmakers must effectively communicate their ideas about its nature, causes, and remedies. In doing so, they must draw on a variety of resources, including symbols, organizations, expertise, money, and the media, to disseminate definitions of the problem that resonate with cultural understandings and offer acceptable remedies to the concerned public. In recent years these understandings and remedies are increasingly informed by a discourse of fear promoted by media images and reports.

GLOSSARY OF KEY TERMS

Attribution A process in which we make inferences about the causes or motivations that lead to an action or event. If we see a rule-breaking event as accidental or coerced, we attribute it to external causes, which we view as largely beyond a person's control. On the other hand, if we regard the rule violation as freely chosen, we attribute it to internal causes, such as a person's motives or character.

Banning One of the key processes involved in the creation of deviance. Through this process we, as members of the public, define a behavior or condition as bad, wrong, or immoral and view those associated with it as "deviants" who need to be punished, controlled, or corrected.

Claimsmakers Individuals or groups who make claims that a particular social condition or trend is a serious problem that requires public concern and intervention (see also **Moral Entrepreneurs**).

Destigmatization The strategy that we use when we seek not only to avoid or refute the stigmatizing attributions of others, but to replace deviant identities with essentially normal ones. Three major techniques of destigmatization are purification, transcendence, and distancing.

Deviance Acts or attributes that depart in an undesirable way from a group's norms and that provoke negative social reactions. Interactionists stress that the deviance of an act or attribute is relative; that is, it is determined by the interpretations and reactions of a social audience.

Embracement Strategies through which we express our acceptance of and attachment to an identity and find ways to reconstruct and present it so that it supports favorable images of self.

Labeling The process of classifying an act, attribute, or event into a larger category, such as "deviant." Labeling is an aspect of the naming process and an expression of the stereotyping pervasive in human perception.

Labeling Theory of Deviance An interactionist-based theory of deviance that stresses that powerful groups and persons can impose their notions of morality on others by defining certain acts or attributes as deviant and thus as deserving of negative sanctions. According to labeling theorists, if we are repeatedly defined as deviant on the basis of our actions or attributes, we are likely to internalize this label and regard ourselves as deviant. This, in turn, will encourage us to associate with others who are similarly labeled and to embark on a deviant career.

Master Status A status that serves as the primary basis, or essential characteristic, through which others define, evaluate, and respond to a person.

Moral Entrepreneurs Individuals or groups who crusade to translate their moral concerns into laws and to have those who violate these laws defined as "deviants" who need correction or punishment. There are two types of moral entrepreneurs: rule creators and rule enforcers. Rule creators are those individuals and groups who take the initiative to get rules formulated and adopted. Rule enforcers are those individuals, groups, or institutions (e.g., the police and courts) who are responsible for applying rules and ensuring public compliance with bans.

Neutralization A strategy in which we accept the attribution of deviance given to our rule-breaking act but offer an account that explains why we should not be labeled as deviant for engaging in this act.

Normalization A strategy in which we try to avoid having a deviant label applied to our rule-breaking acts or attributes, usually by concealing these acts or attributes and maintaining a conventional self-presentation. Some key normalization strategies include passing, covering, and insulating.

Politics of Fear According to Altheide, this form of politics refers to decision makers' promotion and use of audience beliefs and assumptions about danger, risk, and fear in order to achieve certain goals.

Primary Deviance The initial and often isolated violations of rules or laws that nearly all of us take part in. These episodes of rule breaking remain primary and are not subject to labeling as long as they are seen as incidental to our "real selves."

Secondary Deviance Deviance that is a response to the labeling process or to others' reactions to a person's initial or "primary" rule breaking. According to labeling theorists, deviance becomes secondary when, as a result of the assessments and reactions of others, we begin to see ourselves as deviant and act in accordance with that self-image.

Stigma A discrediting attribute or mark of disgrace that leads others to see us as untrustworthy, incompetent, or tainted. The common bases of stigma are physical deformities, character flaws, and membership in a tainted group.

Tertiary Deviance Redefining "deviant" acts, attributes, or identities as normal or even virtuous. When participating in tertiary deviance, we reject the notion that an act or attribute is discrediting and take steps to transform stigmatized identities into valued ones (see also **Embracement**).

QUESTIONS FOR REFLECTION OR ASSIGNMENT

1. Get together with three or four other students in class and assess the "deviance" of the

following acts and attributes, indicating the extent to which you agree or disagree that each act or attribute is deviant (5 = strongly agree; 1 = strongly disagree).

1.	Underage drinking	5	4	3	2	1
2.	Using cocaine	5	4	3	2	1
3.	Cohabitating	5	4	3	2	1
4.	Being an atheist	5	4	3	2	1
5.	Being gay or lesbian	5	4	3	2	1
6.	Price fixing by a company	5	4	3	2	1
7.	Forcing sex on someone	5	4	3	2	1
8.	Cheating on a test	5	4	3	2	1
9.	Dealing drugs	5	4	3	2	1
10.	Being obese	5	4	3	2	1
11.	Abusing a child	5	4	3	2	1
12.	Torturing animals	5	4	3	2	1
13.	Embezzling money	5	4	3	2	1
14.	Having AIDS	5	4	3	2	1
15.	Protesting against war	5	4	3	2	1
16.	Driving while drunk	5	4	3	2	1
17.	Being a victim of rape	5	4	3	2	1
18.	Illegally dumping toxic wastes	5	4	3	2	1
19.	Having sex before you are 18	5	4	3	2	1
20.	Being devoutly religious	5	4	3	2	1
21.	Robbing a bank	5	4	3	2	1
22.	Selling an unsafe product	5	4	3	2	1
23.	Being a racist	5	4	3	2	1
24.	Engaging in sex in public	5	4	3	2	1
25.	Ignoring a homeless child	5	4	3	2	1

After you have finished, ask each person in the group to identify which of the items they saw as "most deviant." Did you tend to agree with one another? Why or why not? What criteria did you use to judge this act or attribute as especially deviant? Do others use the same kind of criteria in assessing the deviance of various acts or attributes?

2. Draw a picture of a "criminal" and write a related description. What images come to mind for you? That is, what does "the criminal" look like? Who is he or she? What physical characteristics does he or she have? For example, what is his or her race and gender? Where does he or she live? What does he or she act like when interacting with others? What crime(s) has he or she committed? Where do you think your images of a "criminal" come from? How do they influence (and perhaps distort) your perceptions of individuals who are different from you?

3. Think of a time when you were labeled negatively by an authority figure, a parent, or someone else significant to you. How powerful was the label? Did it influence how others responded to you? Did it affect your perceptions of and feelings about yourself? Did you do something to try to counteract the label or its effects? Did you eventually overcome, transform, or shed the label? How and why?

4. Reflect on a mild stigma you have experienced in your life (such as the stigma of being a nondrinker, a nail-biter, an agnostic, an overweight woman, a bald man, or a person with acne). Analyze the role this stigma plays in your life, relating it to concepts discussed in this chapter. What is the nature of your deviance? What social reactions are generated by your behavior/attitude/appearance? In what situations? From which persons? How strong is this reaction? What do you think is the reason for this reaction—that is, what sort of threat does this deviance pose? Do you encounter stereotypes of your sort of deviance? What traits are linked with this deviance? What does being deviant feel like? How do you "neutralize," manage, or overcome your deviance? Why do you think you use these particular stigma management strategies? How effective are they?

5. Analyze a "deviant" behavior or person in one of your group contexts (e.g., a church group, fraternity, work group, or friendship circle), describing and evaluating it in terms of concepts discussed in this chapter. Why is the behavior (or person) you are analyzing viewed as deviant in your group? What rules are being violated? What social reactions are elicited by

this "deviance"? How strong are these reactions? What sort of threat or problem does this deviance pose to the group? Who is most actively involved in defining the behavior (or person) as deviant? What does the "deviant" person do to neutralize or counteract a deviant label? How effective are these neutralization or management strategies? What overall effect does this deviance (and the social reactions to it) have upon the group?

6. Using the Internet, conduct some quick research on the history of drunk driving laws (e.g., go to the following URL: http://en.wikipedia.org/wiki/Drunk_driving_(United_States)#History_of_drunk_driving_laws). Where and when did drunk driving laws originate in the United States? When and why did these laws become more prevalent in the United States? Which groups were central in getting these laws passed? How and why were they successful? What role did the media play in this process? Why is the legal blood alcohol limit set at 0.08 in most jurisdictions in the United States? What is it set at in other countries? What did the limit used to be in the United States? Why was it changed? Finally, do you see drunk driving as a major public concern? Would you have held the same view in the 1950s or 1960s? Why or why not?

SUGGESTED READINGS FOR FURTHER STUDY

Adler, Patricia and Adler, Peter. "The Cyber Worlds of Self-Injurers: Deviant Communities, Relationships, and Selves," *Symbolic Interaction* 31(1), 2008, pp. 33–56.

Altheide, David. *Terrorism and the Politics of Fear* (Latham, MD: Alta Mira Press, 2006).

Best, Joel. *Social Problems: Constructionist Readings* (New York: Aldine Press, 2003).

Goffman, Erving. *Stigma: Notes on the Management of Spoiled Identity* (Englewood Cliffs, NJ: Prentice-Hall, 1963).

Katz, Jack. *Seductions of Crime: Moral and Sensual Attractions in Doing Evil* (New York: Basic Books, 1988).

Mullins, Christopher. *Holding Your Square: Masculinities, Street Life, and Violence* (Devon, UK: Willan Publishing, 2006).

ENDNOTES

[1] See Jeannine Clark, "The Evolution of Nerd Disclipine," *Education Week*, Accessed August 18, 2008 at http://www.edweek.org/login.html?source=http%3A%2F%2Fwww.edweek.org%2Fsearch.html%3Fqs1%3DNerd%2BDiscipline; "School Officials Struggling With 'Nerd Discipline,'" *Waterloo-Cedar Falls Courier*, September 2, 1998, p. A5.

[2] Kai T. Erikson, "Notes on the Sociology of Deviance," *Social Problems* 9, 1962, pp. 307–314.

[3] David Newman, *Sociology: Exploring the Architecture of Everyday Life*, 7th ed. (Thousand Oaks, CA: Pine Forge Press, 2008), p. 220.

[4] John Hewitt, *Self and Society*, 6th ed. (Boston: Allyn and Bacon, 1994), p. 233.

[5] James Henslin, *Essentials of Sociology: A Down to Earth Approach*, 8th ed. (Boston: Allyn and Bacon, 2005).

[6] Stanley Eitzen and Maxine Baca Zinn, *In Conflict and Order*, 5th ed. (Boston: Allyn and Bacon, 2001), p. 177.

[7] Kai T. Erikson, "Notes on the Sociology of Deviance," (Note 2), p. 307.

[8] Howard S. Becker, *Outsiders: Studies in the Sociology of Deviance* (New York: The Free Press, 1963), p. 9.

[9] Patricia A. Adler and Peter Adler, eds., *Constructions of Deviance: Social Power, Context, and Interaction*, 3rd ed. (Belmont, CA: Wadsworth Publishing Company, 2000), p. 133.

[10] Howard S. Becker, *Outsiders: Studies in the Sociology of Deviance*, (Note 8).

[11] Ibid.

[12] Patricia A. Adler and Peter Adler, eds., *Constructions of Deviance: Social Power, Context, and Interaction*, (Note 9), pp. 133–134.

[13] See Joel Best, *More Damned Lies and Statistics: How Numbers Confuse Public Issues* (Berkeley, CA: University of California Press, 2004).

[14] Patricia A. Adler and Peter Adler, eds., *Constructions of Deviance: Social Power, Context, and Interaction*, (Note 9).

[15] This definition of banning draws on related ideas presented in David Matza, *Becoming Deviant* (Englewood Cliffs, NJ: Prentice-Hall, 1969), p. 146.

[16] The following discussion draws on information provided in "Legislators" "Think They Know What's Best for You," *Waterloo-Cedar Falls Courier*, February 7, 2000, p. A1; and Charlotte Eby, "Lawmakers Unleash Bills on Pet Issues," *Waterloo-Cedar Falls Courier*, February 20, 2005, p. B2.

[17] See Ronald Weitzer and Steven Tuch, *Race and Policing in America: Conflict and Reform* (New York: Cambridge University Press, 2006).

[18] William J. Chambliss, "Policing the Ghetto Underclass: The Politics of Law and Law Enforcement," *Social Problems* 41(2), 1994, pp. 177–194; Elijah Anderson, *Streetwise* (Chicago: University of Chicago Press, 1991).

[19] Edwin Schur, *Labeling Deviant Behavior: Its Sociological Implications* (New York: Harper & Row, 1971), p. 10.

[20] Richard Hawkins and Gary Tiedeman, *The Creation of Deviance: Interpersonal and Organizational Determinants* (Columbus, OH: Charles E. Merrill, 1975).

[21] Ibid., p. 78.

[22] Ibid., pp. 79–80.

[23] Alfred R. Lindesmith, Anselm L. Strauss, and Norman K. Denzin, *Social Psychology*, 7th ed. (Englewood Cliffs, NJ: Prentice-Hall, 1993).

[24] Erving Goffman, *Stigma: The Management of a Spoiled Identity* (Englewood Cliffs, NJ: Prentice-Hall, 1963), p. 4.

[25] Ibid., p. 3.

[26] Ibid., p. 128.

[27] Harold H. Kelley, "Attribution Theory in Social Psychology," in D. Levine, ed., *Nebraska Symposium on Motivation* (Lincoln: University of Nebraska, 1967), pp. 192–241.

[28] Edwin H. Pfuhl and Stuart Henry, *The Deviance Process*, 3rd ed. (New York: Aldine de Gruyter, 1993), pp. 126–127.

[29] Druann Maria Heckert and Amy Best, "Ugly Duckling to Swan: Labeling Theory and the Stigmatization of Red Hair," *Symbolic Interaction* 20(4), 1997, pp. 365–384.

[30] Howard S. Becker, *Outsiders: Studies in the Sociology of Deviance*, (Note 8).

[31] Fortunately, the cultural stereotypes associated with red hair are not as persistent or harmful as the stereotypes linked to other attributes, such as race or ethnicity. After reaching adulthood, the redheads in Heckert and Best's (see Note 29) study were treated less negatively by others and they felt more appreciative of their hair color, particularly the way it contributed to their sense of individuality.

[32] Kent L. Sandstrom, "Confronting Deadly Disease: The Drama of Identity Construction Among Gay Men with AIDS," *Journal of Contemporary Ethnography* 19, 1990, pp. 271–294.

[33] Ibid.

[34] See Marvin B. Scott and Stanford M. Lyman, "Accounts," *American Sociological Review* 33, 1968, pp. 46–61; Gresham M. Sykes and David Matza, "Techniques of Neutralization: A Theory of Delinquency," *American Sociological Review* 22, 1957, pp. 664–670; Alan Blum and Peter McHugh, "The Social Ascription of Motive," *American Sociological Review* 36, 1971, pp. 98–109.

[35] Edwin H. Pfuhl and Stuart Henry, *The Deviance Process*, (Note 28), p. 65.

[36] Donald McCabe, "The Influence of Situational Ethics on Cheating Among College Students," *Sociological Inquiry* 62, 1992, pp. 278–286.

[37] Ibid.

[38] Edwin H. Pfuhl and Stuart Henry, *The Deviance Process*, (Note 28), p. 69.

[39] Carol Warren, "Destigmatization of Identity: From Deviant to Charismatic," *Qualitative Sociology* 3, 1980, pp. 59–72.

[40] Kathy Charmaz, "Loss of Self: A Fundamental Form of Suffering in the Chronically Ill," *Sociology of Health Care and Illness* 5, 1983, pp. 168–195.

41 David A. Snow and Leon Anderson, *Down on Their Luck: A Study of Homeless Street People* (Berkeley, CA: University of California Press, 1993).

42 Ibid., p. 215.

43 Ibid., p. 219.

44 Richard Hawkins and Gary Tiedeman, *The Creation of Deviance: Interpersonal and Organizational Determinants*, (Note 20).

45 Howard S. Becker, *Outsiders: Studies in the Sociology of Deviance*, (Note 8).

46 Ibid.

47 Richard Hawkins and Gary Tiedeman, *The Creation of Deviance: Interpersonal and Organizational Determinants*, (Note 20).

48 Edwin M. Lemert, *Social Pathology* (New York: McGraw-Hill, 1951).

49 See Ronald L. Akers, "Problems in the Sociology of Deviance: Social Definitions and Behavior," *Social Forces* 46(4), 1968, pp. 455–464. See also Walter Gove, "Labeling Theory's Explanation of Mental Illness: An Update of Recent Evidence," *Deviant Behavior* 3(4), 1983, pp. 307–327; Bruce Link, Francis Cullen, Elmer Struening, Patrick Shrout, and Bruce Dohrenwend, "A Modified Labeling Theory Approach to Mental Disorders: An Empirical Assessment," *American Sociological Review* 54(3), 1989, pp. 400–423.

50 John Kitsuse, "Coming Out All Over: Deviants and the Politics of Social Problems," *Social Problems* 28, 1980, pp. 1–13.

51 Kent L. Sandstrom, "Confronting Deadly Disease: The Drama of Identity Construction Among Gay Men with AIDS," (Note 32). For a more detailed discussion of the concept of embracement, see David A. Snow and Leon Anderson, *Down on Their Luck: A Study of Homeless Street People*, (Note 36).

52 Kent L. Sandstrom, "Confronting Deadly Disease: The Drama of Identity Construction Among Gay Men with AIDS." (Note 32).

53 Kent L. Sandstrom, "Preserving a Vital and Valued Self in the Face of AIDS," *Sociological Inquiry* 68(3), 1998, pp. 354–371.

54 Rose Weitz, *Life with AIDS* (New Brunswick, NJ: Rutgers University Press, 1991).

55 Kent L. Sandstrom, "Redefining Sex and Intimacy: The Sexual Self-Images, Outlooks, and Relationships of Gay Men Living with HIV Disease," *Symbolic Interaction* 19(3), 1996, pp. 241–262.

56 Howard S. Becker, *Outsiders: Studies in the Sociology of Deviance*, (Note 8).

57 Ibid.

58 Jack Katz, *Seductions of Crime: Moral and Sensual Attractions in Doing Evil* (New York: Basic Books, 1988).

59 Ibid., p. 9.

60 Richard Quinney, *Critique of Legal Order* (Boston: Little, Brown, 1974), p. 7.

61 Joseph A. Kotarba, "Labeling Theory and Everyday Deviance," in Jack D. Douglas, Patricia Adler, Peter Adler, Andrea Fontana, C. Robert Freeman, and Joseph A. Kotarba, eds., *Introduction to the Sociologies of Everyday Life* (Boston: Allyn and Bacon, 1980), p. 99.

62 Joel Best, ed., *Social Problems: Constructionist Readings*. (New York: Aldine Press. 2003); Joel Best, ed. *Images of Issues: Typifying Contemporary Social Problems*. 2nd ed. (New York: Aldine de Gruyter, 1995); Joseph Gusfield, *The Culture of Public Problems* (Chicago: University of Chicago Press, 1981); Gary Alan Fine, "Scandal, Social Conditions, and the Creation of Public Attention: Fatty Arbuckle and the 'Problem of Hollywood,'" *Social Problems* 44(3), 1997, pp. 297–323; Joseph Schneider and John L. Kitsuse, eds., *Studies in the Sociology of Social Problems* (Norwood, NJ: Ablex Publishing Corp., 1984).

63 Kent Sandstrom, Dan Martin, and Gary Alan Fine, "Symbolic Interactionism at the End of the Century," in George Ritzer and Barry Smart (eds.), *The Handbook of Social Theory* (London: Sage, 2001), pp. 217–231.

64 Spencer Cahill, ed., *Inside Social Life: Readings in Sociological Psychology and Microsociology*, 3rd ed. (Los Angeles, CA: Roxbury Publishing, 2001), p. 269.

65 The following discussion draws on the incisive analysis of "drug scares" provided in Craig Reinarman, "The Social Construction of Drug Scares," in

Patricia and Peter Adler, eds., *Constructions of Deviance: Social Power, Context, and Interaction*, 5th ed. (New York: Wadsworth, 2005), pp. 139–150.

66   Ibid., p. 154.

67   Ibid., p. 154.

68   David Altheide, *Terrorism and the Politics of Fear*. (Lanham, MA: Alta Mira Press, 2006), p. 15.

69   David Altheide, "Consuming Terrorism," *Symbolic Interaction* 27(3): 2004, pp. 289–308.

70   Ibid., p. 291.

71   Ibid., p. 295.

72   Ibid., p. 304.

73   David Altheide, *Terrorism and the Politics of Fear*, (Note 69), p. 15.

74   Spencer Cahill, ed. *inside Social Life*, p. 270.

CHAPTER EIGHT

~

COLLECTIVE BEHAVIOR AND SOCIAL MOVEMENTS

During the 1880s, a powerful movement calling for an eight-hour workday emerged in the United States. On May 1, 1886, the American Federation of Labor and the Brotherhood of Locomotive Engineers issued a strike against employers who refused to support the eight-hour workday, causing 350,000 workers across the country to walk off their jobs. In Chicago, 40,000 workers went on strike. The result was that "every railroad in Chicago stopped running, and most of the industries in Chicago were paralyzed. The stockyards were closed down."[1] In response, local businessmen formed a "Citizens Committee" and plotted a strategy to break the strike and punish the strikers. The state militia and local police also stood ready to suppress any strike-related conflicts. On May 3, the strikers and their supporters gathered in front of the McCormick Harvester Works to fight with replacement workers, or "scabs," who had crossed the picket lines. As skirmishes broke out, the police fired into the crowd of strikers, killing four and wounding a number of others.

The strikers then organized a mass meeting to be held at Haymarket Square. When 3,000 people gathered to attend this meeting and hear a protest speech, they were confronted by 180 policemen, who ordered them to disperse. Suddenly a bomb exploded, wounding 59 police officers and killing 7. The uninjured officers reacted by firing on the crowd, killing several workers, wounding 200

others, and setting off what became known as the Haymarket Riot. This event proved to be a historic moment in Chicago labor organizing. In the end, four labor organizers were hanged for their alleged involvement in the bombing, although some evidence suggested that an undercover police agent had thrown the bomb in an effort to "set up" the organizers for arrest. The execution of these organizers provoked mass grief and anger, expressed in a funeral march that included over 25,000 people.[2]

In examining the events that surrounded the Haymarket Riot, we find organized movements, protest speeches, panicking crowds, and a funeral "demonstration," all of which are examples of collective action. **Collective action** refers to behavior that people engage in as a group and formulate as a response to problematic conditions, often in opposition to existing societal norms. Like other sociologists, symbolic interactionists distinguish between two key forms of collective action: collective behavior and social movements.

COLLECTIVE BEHAVIOR

When talking about group behaviors such as riots or panics, people often suggest that they are chaotic and unorganized in nature. Yet even in riots, where mobs of individuals cause mass destruction and seem to act mindlessly, we find at least a minimal degree of structure channeling behavior. In light of this, we believe that it is shortsighted to view collective behavior as unorganized. Instead, we propose that **collective behavior** is best conceptualized as relatively spontaneous activity that a group or crowd engages in, often in contrast with social norms, as they try to work out a joint response to an ambiguous situation. While this activity may seem unorganized, or perhaps even disorganized, this is clearly not the case. Collective behavior, like so many things, is organized in subtle but powerful social forms.

The social psychological study of collective behavior can be traced back over a century. The earliest approach to collective behavior, developed by Gustave Le Bon, suggested that crowds, by nature, are irrational. Le Bon proposed that crowds have a "group mind" and are subjected to contagious mass behavior or "mass hysteria."[3] This perspective made a certain amount of sense, explaining why individuals act appropriately and judiciously in their own personal affairs but become easily impassioned when joining a crowd. How do responsible people lose control so easily? Who is to blame? The assertion made by Le Bon was that there must be something in the social form itself that is responsible. Crowds do things that individuals do not do. Thinking of the crowd as a unit allowed social scientists to suggest that the crowd was, in effect, a different kind of being: an enlarged person or organism, but a human organism with a different set of values than the individuals who comprised it.

On closer inspection, however, Le Bon's theory of "group mind" failed to answer one critical question: *Where* was the new group mind located? After all, it was only individuals who made up the group. Something as mystical as the group mind is beyond the boundaries of empirical research. In response to this problem, researchers such as Ralph Turner and Lewis Killian developed an alternative perspective on collective behavior, known as **emergent norm theory**. This perspective suggests that crowds are not as uniform as they

appear. Rather, participants in a crowd may have very different motives for being present. Some may be looking to commit violence, while others are hoping to meet a romantic partner. Some may have joined intending to pick a pocket, while others desire to express a deeply held conviction. This approach to collective behavior suggests that new norms "emerge," or are created, as participants in a crowd interact with one another and negotiate the meaning of their current situation. Because a crowd situation is somewhat ambiguous, most participants are uncertain about both what they should be doing at the moment and what agenda they should pursue in the future. As a result, a few visible or outspoken members can define proper behavior by advancing a framework for action. Because the majority of the crowd may lack strong feelings about any particular course of action, the course followed is one proposed by those who assume a leadership role and suggest behavior that seems appropriate.

This emergent norm theory of crowd behavior is set squarely within the symbolic interactionist tradition. It assumes that a potential course of collective action will remain ambiguous and unrealized until it is defined through social interaction. Once definitions of both the situation and a plausible and relevant course of action are constructed, group members can formulate a response. This approach emphasizes that crowd behavior is something that participants in a group create, sustain, and modify through their ongoing interaction.

Emergent norm theory suggests that collective behavior is not a manifestation of the "contagion effect," caused by individuals who just happen to come together in the same place at the same time, nor is it caused simply by the convergence of individuals with similar backgrounds and interests. Unlike contagion or convergence theories, emergent norm theory contends that collective behavior is not inherently irrational or emotional. It also recognizes that crowds are heterogeneous and diverse. This theory proposes that participation in collective behavior does not necessarily violate widely accepted norms, but rather "situates" social actors in a new situation where conventional norms are defined as irrelevant for, or as obstructions to, the resolution of some problem. At the heart of emergent norm theory is the construction and acquisition of meaning, activities that occur through interaction. Consider those occasions in which you have been part of a crowd or large group. You were probably uncertain about what was expected of you or about what objectives you should seek, other than to be "where the action is."[4] The presence of others helped you to address and overcome that uncertainty.

A series of research studies demonstrates the principles underlying emergent norm theory. One of the earliest and most influential studies was conducted by the social psychologist Muzafer Sherif.[5] In his research, subjects were placed in a darkened room in which they were only able to see a tiny point of light. Because of the natural movements of one's eyes, the light in such circumstances appears to move spontaneously. This apparent movement is termed the **autokinetic effect**. For each individual the light appeared to move a different distance. When these individuals were placed into darkened rooms in groups and discussed the movement of light, group norms were created, and these norms were somewhat different for each group. Even though the norms diverged from the original estimates of the individuals, they placed substantial confidence in what their group had collectively determined. Quite simply, Sherif discovered that a norm—in this case, a single interpretation of a movement of light—emerged through group interaction.

Other studies have confirmed Sherif's observations that individuals will change what they see or believe as a function of what others suggest, even when they are not consciously responding to the demands of others. This process was demonstrated in a striking piece of research by Solomon Asch, a social psychologist, who showed subjects a "target line" and asked them to judge three other lines and select the one that was of the same length.[6] The exercise proved unproblematic when subjects were alone. Asch then had individual subjects respond in a group context where all the other participants were research confederates— individuals acting on behalf of the experimenter, unknown to the naive subjects. These experimental confederates provided objectively *incorrect* responses, identifying lines that were obviously of the wrong length when compared to the target line. Asch discovered that in approximately one-third of the trials the naive subjects followed suit, agreeing with their fellow subjects rather than providing the correct answer that was literally right before their eyes. The results demonstrate the process through which norms emerge, and also the power of sociability in producing conformity. In most cases, traditions that groups establish are judged as fundamentally correct and are the basis on which individuals judge others and judge their own actions.[7]

In making these points, we want to highlight that the interactionist perspective on collective behavior suggests that individuals in collective situations are thoughtful, even if they do not always know what they should be doing. While they may appear irrational or unduly emotional in their actions, the notion of the madding crowd has little bearing in fact. There is no evidence that crowds turn responsible individuals into conformist zombies or raging fanatics. Rather, even in such seemingly chaotic situations as riots, people formulate their actions in a meaningful way, organizing their behavior in terms of the norms and definitions that emerge through their ongoing interactions with others.

Riots

Crowds do permit, under certain circumstances, the expression of beliefs and actions that violate prominent cultural norms. This is certainly the case with **riots**, a form of collective behavior in which a large number of people assemble for the purpose of protesting a grievance and from which a violent disturbance may emerge. Throughout the history of the United States, many kinds of riots have occurred, but perhaps the most prominent and troubling kind has been the race riot. Race riots, which have been led by both whites and blacks, have occurred in virtually every major U.S. city over the last three centuries. Consider the events of 1741 when a Spanish vessel with an African crew sailed into the harbor of colonial New York. New Yorkers had planned to sell part of the crew in a slave auction. At the same time as the ship's arrival, mysterious fires began breaking out, damaging the governor's house and the king's chapel. Rumors swept through the city that captured blacks had set the fires in a quest for revenge. Some whites even believed that New York's black population was going to burn down the whole city. As a result of these beliefs, thirteen black men were burned at the stake; another seventeen along with four whites were hanged as well. This incident reminds us that the basic form of race riots has not changed over the past three centuries. Throughout the twentieth century race riots continued. Sometimes these riots were led by whites objecting to the intrusion of African Americans into what they considered to be "white space." On other occasions they were led by African Americans frustrated by the slow pace of progress and equality.

During the World War I era, most of the riots that took place in the United States were characterized by whites carrying out brutal attacks on blacks. One of the most dramatic race riots occurred in East St. Louis, Illinois, in 1917. East St. Louis was an industrial city experiencing profound changes as whites increased their union-organizing activities. In order to diminish the union's power, business leaders increased their efforts to recruit black laborers from the rural South to break strikes. Much to the dismay of white laborers, blacks were willing to work for considerably less money. Trouble began following a labor rally during which a series of white speakers denounced the attempts made by business leaders to "colonize the city" with cheap black labor. As the meeting dispersed, a series of rumors spread rapidly through the crowd alleging that blacks had been attacking white citizens. By the time the hostilities ended, nine whites and thirty-nine blacks had been killed.

Although riots may differ in their circumstances and expressions, they bear similarity to one another in their stages of development. Riots typically emerge as a result of problematic interaction between local authorities, usually the police, and an aroused community with its own set of unaddressed grievances. Consider, for example, what began as disruptive but nonviolent demonstrations during the 1999 World Trade Organization talks in Seattle, where global business leaders were meeting to create trade policies. The protesters in Seattle included students, union members, and environmentalists who were objecting to the exploitation of labor and the natural environment by wealthy global capitalists. The protests escalated into riot conditions as police fired "pepper spray" canisters into crowds of demonstrators. The crowds then responded by smashing windows with hammers and hurling objects at police.[8]

As conflicts escalate between authorities and an aroused community, riots are increasingly likely to arise. According to Ralph Conant, riots evolve through four identifiable phases.[9] The initial phase of all riots involves some precipitating event, an action or gesture that ignites the riot. In the dramatic race riot that took place in East St. Louis in 1917, the precipitating event was a rumor that blacks had physically attacked whites. In the race riot that occurred in Cincinnati during the spring of 2001, the precipitating incident was the police shooting of an unarmed African-American man. Of course, the acts or events that spark off a riot do not have to be as dramatic as a police shooting. They need only to be seen by an aggrieved community as typifying injustice, particularly a highly visible or longstanding injustice.

The significance of a precipitating event is that it motivates a large number of people to come together, albeit for different reasons. Some are motivated to join with an assembling crowd because they are curious or they want to be where the action is; others feel deeply upset about the precipitating event and want to provoke a riot as a "justifiable" retaliation; still others care little about the precipitating event but seek to use the crowd as a cover to engage in other deviant activities. As the crowd begins to grow and become agitated, local officials or community leaders often arrive at the scene and try to quell any acts of violence. Yet even as leaders attempt to engage in crowd control, local citizens swarm to the scene and the riot enters into a second, confrontation phase.

In the confrontation phase, various "keynoters," including those who want to instigate a riot, advance suggestions about the cause of the situation and the remedy that should be pursued. The outcome of this definitional process is crucial in determining whether or not a riot actually emerges. During this process, instigators begin to articulate the rage felt by members of the crowd, competing with each other as they suggest possible courses of action. At the same time, other keynoters, such as church and neighborhood leaders, may suggest that the crowd cool off and disband. As this process unfolds, the police usually arrive and seek to impose order by dispersing the crowd. While crowd members may abide by the instructions of police and disperse, they may also choose to become more angry and violent, particularly if the police act in ways that elevate hostile keynoters into prominent positions.

Along with the police, the mass media and civil authorities play a crucial role in defusing or inflaming an emerging riot situation. If the media sensationalize the event, tensions will be heightened, making it more difficult for civil authorities to respond. These authorities, however, will not be rendered helpless. If they listen to crowd complaints and suggest a visible and responsive means for addressing them, crowd members will be less likely to engage in violent behavior. On the other hand, if the authorities choose *not* to interact with the crowd and rely only on the police to represent them, crowd tensions are likely to reach a crescendo, setting the stage for major eruptions of violence.

The third phase of riot formation, known as the carnival phase (because of the carnival-like atmosphere once rioting has begun), is marked by crowds reassembling away from their original gathering place once police intervene. When they reassemble, a new norm quickly emerges: destroy property. As this norm takes hold, older persons tend to drop out of the crowd, allowing young people to take over and direct the action. The hurling of objects, taunting of police and shopkeepers, setting of fires, and destruction of cars set the stage for looting.[10] The police, in turn, tend to respond by firing teargas, rubber and "beanbag" bullets, or live ammunition. In some cases, they also beat rioters with their night sticks. When engaging in these behaviors the police precipitate the return of older adults, who try to defend the younger rioters from what they see as unnecessarily brutal police conduct.

Overall, the "carnival" phase of a riot is marked by a structure in which rioters destroy symbols of domination and exploitation, including statues and icons, local businesses, police cars, and even police stations. As this destruction unfolds, the crowd's initial ambivalence regarding the precipitating event is resolved by a new set of emergent norms. These norms establish that the precipitating event was unjust and required revenge in the form of looting and property destruction.

The fourth and final phase of a riot is marked by a siege. A siege occurs as local authorities decide to suppress rioters through overwhelming force. This decision results in the polarization of authorities and rioters and a complete breakdown of communications between them. As communications come to an end and a warlike situation arises, authorities escalate the level of violent repression, often seeking additional police or military support from the state and federal levels of the government. A clear-cut example took place during the 1992 rioting in Los Angeles. To end the violence engaged in by rioters, city officials ultimately resorted to calling in the troops of both the California National Guard and the U.S. National Guard.

To summarize, we have illustrated how riots, like other forms of collective behavior, are not disorganized acts. Rather, riots emerge and unfold through processes of interaction and communication. Indeed, the form and direction of riots are shaped by the ongoing interactions that take place within an aroused crowd and between this crowd and relevant authorities.

Rumors

Although collective behavior often consists of overt, physical behaviors, it also includes verbal communications, such as gossip and rumors. Indeed, many of the race riots mentioned in the previous section were intimately connected with rumors. Rumors served to spark the anger that led to the rebellions and provided the underlying beliefs that made hostility plausible.

The reality is that rumors surround us. Their content is as diverse as their style and the conditions under which they are performed. We use the term **rumor** to refer to information that is neither substantiated nor refuted and that is driven by a search for meaning, clarification, and closure.[11] A rumor is typically presented as something that could be believed whether or not it is true. In other words, a rumor represents a truth claim. Rumors may in some instances turn out to be true, while in other instances they may turn out to be totally false. Further, some rumors may be factually incorrect in the specifics of their claim but reveal fundamental truths about the nature of the cultural order. Judging the truth of some rumors is simple, while assessing the validity of others is nearly impossible. If a rumor claims that a particular individual is pregnant or has AIDS, the claims can be readily checked through standard scientific tests. But consider the case of the rumors that have proliferated around the assassination of President John F. Kennedy. Can we say for sure who did or did not kill Kennedy, and whether there was a conspiracy involved? A similar point might be made for the assassination of Reverend Martin Luther King, Jr., a topic on which there is still considerable disagreement and rancor. While we should not dismiss the possible truth or falsity of a rumor, we need to recognize that it may be equally important to learn whether people assume it to be true or false. As a result, we need to ask about the conditions that make a particular rumor *plausible* for its audience. Judgments about the plausibility of a rumor represent a complex combination of evaluations of how well the content fits a set of cultural beliefs, along with evaluations of the teller. What people believe about a rumor and its teller reflects how they perceive themselves, their associates, and the conditions under which they live.

Although both the context and content of rumors can vary widely, rumors do share some common sociological features. The telling of rumors often occurs when people face uncertainty, as illustrated in the famous 1969 rumor that Paul McCartney had died. On October 12, 1969, Russ Gibb, a disc jockey at a Detroit radio station, talked on the air with a listener by the name of "Tom," who made the following claims: if you play the Beatles song "Revolution Number 9" backward, the lyrics normally heard as "number nine, number nine" are heard as "Turn me on dead man!" Moreover, if you listen closely to the song "Strawberry Fields," you can hear a voice (allegedly John Lennon's) say, "I buried Paul!" Two days after Gibb's interview with Tom, the University of Michigan newspaper, the *Michigan Daily*, ran the story "McCartney IS Dead." This story, written by Fred LaBour, claimed: "Paul McCartney was killed in an automobile accident in early November, 1966, after leaving EMI recording studios tired, sad, and dejected."[12] The story by LaBour included a photo of an automobile accident that displayed the body of a victim whose head had been decapitated. The story also claimed that McCartney had been replaced by a "double." Within a matter of weeks, the news of McCartney's alleged death had traveled the entire globe—quite an astonishing feat in the days before the Internet!

Why was this rumor believed? By 1969 the Beatles had begun to break up. They had also gone into seclusion, meaning that fans had little access to information about them. This provoked a situation of great uncertainty—a situation that was ripe for the emergence and dissemination of a rumor. Rumors can result from uncertainty sparked by the complete absence of information, by conflicting reports, or by confusion about what actions to take in light of recently received information. When people lack clear or official information, they rely on informal networks as an alternative source of information. With respect to the rumor of Paul McCartney's death, Beatles fans relied on information disseminated informally through word of mouth and "verified" by a student newspaper.

Ironically, even when Paul McCartney and the representatives of the Beatles' record company pointed out that the rumors of his death were absurd, they were not believed. Fans saw the record company as covering up the truth so that they could continue to sell Beatles albums.[13] As in the case of other rumors, even when information becomes available from official sources, it will be believed only if people regard these sources as credible. When people view official sources as suspect or untrustworthy, they become increasingly likely to seek information from informal or unofficial sources.

Although the content of rumors varies considerably, the transmission of rumors is characterized by three processes: leveling, sharpening, and assimilation. In a classic experiment, psychologists Gordon Allport and Leo Postman asked a subject to view a picture and then relate details about it to another subject in seclusion in an adjacent room.[14] This second subject then relayed the information he or she received to a third subject, and this process was repeated through seven subjects. As Allport and Postman observed this "chain" of information transmission, they noticed that with each successive telling of a story a **leveling** process occurred; that is, some details of the original communication were condensed or dropped out. This leveling process was accompanied by a process of **sharpening**, in which individuals highlighted or exaggerated some of the key details of the original communication to make them easier to remember. For instance, if they had to describe the details of a fight that broke out in a dorm, they would transform the original description of a "small gash on the face" into a "big, bloody gash across the forehead." Finally, Allport and Postman found that as a story is repeated, a third process, which they called **assimilation**, takes place. When engaging in assimilation, tellers modify or alter details of a story so that these details fit into their preconceived biases or expectations, perhaps adding racial or social class details so the rumor "makes sense" to its audience.

As we noted earlier, the power of rumor to provoke mass violence and hysteria is clear. There is an extensive literature on what is called "mass psychogenesis illness," or hysterical contagion. This collective psychosomatic illness is rooted in beliefs about nonexistent or unobservable toxic agents. Episodes of the illness often occur during periods of stress, in which groups believe they smell a strange or unpleasant odor, which they then assume to be poisonous. Occasionally tiny bugs are said to cause the maladies. Nausea, dizziness, shortness of breath, weakness, and headaches are the primary symptoms of these contagions. The symptoms potentially relate to any number of different kinds of toxic agents and are so general that their specific cause is difficult to determine. One person starts the contagion, but that individual is soon not alone. The symptoms spread rapidly among people as the word circulates that there is poison in the air.

A particularly dramatic case involved the "Phantom Anesthetist of Mattoon." Mattoon is a small town in southern Illinois. A resident of the small town came to believe that a prowler had opened the door to her bedroom window and sprayed her and her daughter with a gas that paralyzed them. Although the local police arrived quickly, they could find no trace of the supposed intruder. The next day, the local newspaper headline on page one read "Anesthetic Prowler on the Loose." During the next weeks, reports followed quickly of prowlers and gassers. Yet despite the massive police effort and some additional "sightings," a perpetrator was never found. But the belief was real. One newspaper wrote:

> Groggy as Londoners under protracted area blitzing, this town's bewildered citizens reel today under the repeated attacks of a mad anesthetist who has sprayed a deadly nerve gas into thirteen homes and knocked out twenty-seven victims.... Seventy others dashed to the area in response to the alarm, fell under the influence of the gas last night.... All skepticism vanished and Mattoon grimly conceded that it must fight haphazardly against a demented phantom adversary that has been seen fleetingly and has so far evaded traps laid by city and state police, and a posse of townsmen.[15]

In time this episode ended as mysteriously as it started. Calls to police eventually stopped and no anesthetist was ever discovered, in Mattoon or elsewhere. Of course, we cannot prove that no prowler existed, but no evidence reveals anything other than the presence of rumor in this situation.

This instance should underline the importance of rumor. In this light it is significant that U.S. Marine General Smedley Bulter once claimed, with some hyperbole, "I'd rather fight an entire army than battle an idle rumor." At least in fighting an army, one knows where one stands. The 1968 report of the National Advisory Commission on Civil Disorders, established by Lyndon Johnson in response to the race riots of the 1960s, recognized that rumors significantly aggravated civil tensions and disorders in more than 65 percent of the cases it studied.

Although it is useful to focus on rumor and its content, it is also important to note from an interactionist perspective that rumor is the outcome of social processes and situations. As Tamotsu Shibutani noted in his important book *Improvised News*, a rumor is an essential part of collective sense making. Shibutani emphasizes that rumor is a "form of communication through which men and women caught together in an ambiguus situation attempt to construct a meaningful interpretation of it by pooling their intellectual resources.[16] From the interactionist perspective, rumor constitutes a form of collective problem solving, permitting people to cope with life's uncertainty and guide their behavior. In essence, rumor is another example of the interactive and definitional processes through which people seek to find meaning in events.

The perspective that one adopts toward rumor often depends on the type of rumor one examines. When one studies riots, panic, natural disasters, or wartime rumors, it is only natural to see rumor as undesirable. Likewise, if one analyzes how rumor is used for economic enrichment, one is also likely to see it as objectionable. The New York Stock Exchange embraces this view, enforcing a rule that forbids the spread of rumors on the floor of the stock market even when fraud is not intended. As you can imagine, a rumor of a quarterly loss for a company might significantly affect the value of a stock, as would hearsay about a major government policy or an assassination attempt. Rumors may involve intentional deception as well as misguided beliefs. Here the role of government propaganda comes directly to mind, especially, but not exclusively, during wartime. The false claim that the Iraqis had removed premature Kuwaiti babies from their medical respirators was designed to inflame the citizens of Kuwait and the United States prior to the first Gulf War, and it was highly likely that at least some of the government agents who spread the rumor knew it was false. In a similar vein, President George W. Bush's false claim that Saddam Hussein tried to purchase uranium from Niger was designed to increase public support for military intervention in Iraq in 2003. In both cases, government officials used rumor and propaganda to demonize the enemy.

By contrast, some rumors appear to promote solidarity and shared concerns. Rumors can enable a community to discuss ongoing anxiety and emerging events by focusing on a common issue. In such a case, people engage in collective problem solving. Although the outcome of this discussion might have negative consequences, at least people are talking to each other. One problem that often arises in the case of racial rumors is that the communities in which they are spread are insufficiently diverse: whites are unlikely to share claims about blacks with African Americans, just as African Americans are unlikely to tell whites what they know about white practices and institutions. This is what symbolic interactionist David Maines refers to as "racialized pools of knowledge." In these circumstances, frequently characteristic of interracial contact, the potential benefits of problem solving are short-circuited by the segregation of talk.

Although there are many forms of collective behavior aside from rumor, rumor is in many ways an ideal topic for interactionist social psychology. Rumor by its very nature involves the creation of meaning through interaction. In rumor one sees how the natural world is given shape and organization through the construction of individuals. It often seems that rumors are grounded in thin air, but they are actually based on what individuals regard as plausible. Further, rumor connects to interactionist theory in that it reveals the power of a definition of the situation. Individuals who come to believe that a rumor is accurate will act on that belief. Their actions have consequences. Thus, even if they are not based in fact, the assumptions behind rumor, like any definition of the situation, can prove to be consequential.

Panics

The early part of the twenty-first century has produced a variety of natural and human-made disasters that have captured public attention, particularly through heart-rending media images of people scrambling for safety or pleading for help.

These disasters include the World Trade Center bombing, which killed more than 2,500 people in New York on September 11, 2001; the Indian Ocean tsunami that killed thousands of people in Thailand, Sri Lanka, and Indonesia in December 2004; and Hurricane Katrina, which flooded major portions of the southeastern United States, including the city of New Orleans, in September 2005. Each of these disasters strained the human capacity for collective action and resulted, at least for a time, in psychological terror, social disorganization, and collective panic. People commonly experience terror and panic when confronted with a direct and imminent threat to their physical survival. When they see no way to counteract the mortal peril they are facing, the typically respond by fleeing or trying "to get away from it."[17] In cases where a large number of people are confronted with such a threat, a mass panic is likely to ensue.

Panics can also take place in circumstances where people define a threat to their physical safety as real, even if it is actually poses a minimal danger. Within such situations, rumors and miscommunication between segments of a crowd may serve as triggers to a panic, leading people to redefine their situations as imminently dangerous. This type of scenario was clearly illustrated in the crowd behavior that occurred in Iraq on August 31, 2005. A large crowd of Shiite Muslims were walking in a demonstration march to a nearby Muslim neighborhood when rumors of a suicide bomber set off a mass panic. Earlier that day, Iraqi insurgents had fired upon Shiite marchers who were waiting for the demonstration to begin. Thus, the marchers were sensitized to the possibility of another attack. As they reached a footbridge that slowed the crowd's progress to a halt, rumors began to circulate about the presence of a suicide bomber. In describing the march, Associated Press reporters observed:

> Tensions were high...when the procession jammed a pedestrian bridge that spans the Tigris River and joins the Sunni Muslim

neighborhood of Adhemiya. Several survivors said rumors of a suicide bomber spread through the crowd on the bridge. In the ensuing panic, hundreds of Iraqis—mostly women and children—were trampled to death and scores of others died when they were pushed off the bridge or jumped into the river 30 feet below to escape suffocation."[18]

According to the British Broadcasting Corporation (BBC), the resulting death toll included "at least 965 confirmed deaths, making the incident the single biggest loss of Iraqi life since the U.S.-led invasion in 2003."[19]

In analyzing such a tragic event, symbolic interactionists draw upon the insights of Ralph Turner and Lewis Killian, who suggest that four primary factors characterize mass panics.[20] First, situations become potentially panic producing when the physical setting, such as the pedestrian bridge in Adhemiya, contains only one or two escape routes. Turner and Killian refer to this as partial entrapment. Entrapment only emerges as a meaningful definition of the situation when people seek to escape from the setting. Under other conditions, a crowd may have access to the same number of exits but are not fully aware of the constraint this imposes or do not see the exit situation as important. This feature of the setting only becomes significant to members of the crowd when they experience a perceived threat, such as the threat of a suicide bomber. A perceived threat is likely to produce a mass panic if it is "regarded as being so imminent that there is no time to do anything except to try to escape."[21] Obviously, when a crowd of people think a suicide bomber is about to trigger an explosive device in their midst, especially on a small bridge, they will feel an impulse to flee. When a third factor, the partial or complete breakdown of the escape route, characterizes a setting, people's perceptions of threat and entrapment become heightened. They see that their path to escape is blocked, obstructed, unidentifiable, or unclear and, consequently, become more fearful.

For instance, the Shiites on the pedestrian bridge saw that their escape route was blocked by a mass of other people, and this provoked intense feelings of anxiety. Finally, a crowd's surge forward toward the presumed route of escape is precipitated by another key situational factor: front-to-rear communication failure. As a crowd moves in a specific direction, those in the back of the crowd infer that their exit to safety must still be open, albeit somewhat restricted. Unfortunately, they cannot communicate effectively with those near the exit, who could tell them that the path to escape is completely blocked and they must proceed more slowly to maximize everyone's safety. When coupled with evidence of movement, lack of front-to-rear communication in a crowd leads those people far away from an exit to misperceive the situation and rush to escape. As a result, those closest to the obstructed exit are crushed, smothered, or trampled to death. This outcome was tragically illustrated in the deaths of the 965 Shiites on the bridge in Adhemiya.

Panics do not always or necessarily occur because members of a crowd sense impending destruction. In some cases they are triggered by a milder threat that elevates the level of urgency felt by crowd members, such as when they think they are being deprived of a valued experience or resource. This scenario unfolded at a concert performed by the British rock band, *The Who*, on December 3, 1975, in Cincinnati, Ohio. Six hours before the concert was scheduled to begin, fans began gathering outside of Riverfront Coliseum. The Coliseum staff planned to open the doors to fans at 6 o'clock so that they could enter well before the band came on stage. However, the band arrived late and the crowd was left waiting outside for a longer time than expected. Then, at 7:30 p.m. two Coliseum doors were opened while technicians were testing *The Who's* sound system, The crowd heard the amplified sound of the acoustics test and mistakenly thought the concert had started. Most of the 7,000 waiting fans held general admission tickets for "unreserved" seating and hoped to get close to the front of the stage. When they heard the music and saw the two open doors, these anxious fans rushed forward, smashing down a locked door, shattering glass, and stampeding over hundreds of people. In describing the panic scene that emerged, some fans observed:[22]

> It was like a movie, first it was fun and then it got crazy...you could see people near the door waving to their friends like the doors were open, and if your wanted to be near the front, you had to run.

> I didn't even move my feet....One moment I was maybe 200 feet from the door and the next thing, I was stacked up like kindling. I don't know, but I'd bet there were six or eight people under me.

> It was unreal simply unreal....People were yelling. Everybody was stoned. The firemen put this girl down near us. It took a few moments, but then it dawned on us. She was dead.

According to media reports of the crowd's behavior:

> The wild melee lasted only a few minutes. When it ended, eleven people ranging in age from 15 to 22 were dead, suffocated in the crush. "Most of the people who died were very small," said Fire Chief Bert Lugannani. More than twenty others were injured, and the white concrete outside the 18,000-capacity area was piled ankle-high with purses, coats, and eyeglasses.[23]

This tragic event can be explained in part by Turner and Killian's model. The crowd experienced a sense of constraint and perceived a threat; that is, they felt constrained because they were being denied access to the Coliseum, and they felt threatened by the prospect of missing a part of a concert they highly valued. The crowd was also characterized by a front-to-rear communication failure, which helped to precipitate the mad rush to the two open doors. Yet some elements of this panic demonstrate the need for refinements of Turner

and Killian's model. The crowd's behavior at the *Who* concert shows that *restricted access* to a setting, much like partial entrapment in a setting, can serve as a facilitating condition for a mass panic, particularly when it is coupled with a sense of urgency and threat. In fact, the condition of restricted access better describes what we observe across a variety of panics than the condition of partial entrapment. Restrictions of access that contribute to panics can include the limited availability of escape routes in a setting or limited entrée to a highly valued social scene, such as a rock concert.

Regardless of the terms we use to identify its key features, panics provide evidence of the challenges and paradoxes people face in everyday life because of their capacity to use and share symbols. The use of significant symbols, such as "FIRE!" or "CONCERT STARTING," can enhance people's safety or pleasure or, almost as easily, precipitate a panic. Most crucially, interactionists emphasize that panics, like other forms of collective behavior, are not simply unreflective or spontaneous responses to a given stimulus; rather, they are rooted in and emerge out of processes of interaction and social definition. The social psychological dimensions of panics are revealed in the definitions of reality and group communications, which give rise to panic behavior and shape how it unfolds. Social definitions and group communications are also important in preventing panics. Airlines, railways, bus companies, and other organizations clearly try to ward off panics during disasters by training employees and the public about how to respond to crises rationally and effectively. Some organizations, such as the Federal Emergency Management Agency (FEMA), spend much of their time formulating blueprints for collective action in advance of disasters so that social order can be maintained or quickly restored after a disaster takes place. Of course, as demonstrated in the case of Hurricane Katrina, these organizations do not always have the resources or leadership necessary to deal with major disasters and their social and psychological consequences.

SOCIAL MOVEMENTS

Throughout American history, a remarkable array of social movement organizations have existed, from the radical International Workers of the World to the corporate National Association of Manufacturers, from the Animal Liberation Front to the Women's Christian Temperance Movement, from the Michigan Militia Corps to the Rainbow Coalition. Some movement organizations seek to promote change, while others oppose that change. Sometimes after change occurs, as after the 1973 Supreme Court decision that legalized most abortions, the roles of opposing movement organizations switch. Now "pro-choice" organizations are fighting to maintain government policy, while "pro-life" organizations are fighting to change it. Should the Supreme Court ever decide to overturn *Roe v. Wade*, these movement organizations will quickly reverse the positions they currently adopt in regard to whether official policy should be changed.

When we use the term **social movement**, we are referring to a collection of individuals who organize together to achieve or prevent some social or political change. Obviously, social movements differ considerably in their structure, tactics, ideology, and goals. Some social movements are organized with a rigid hierarchy, while others have a more democratic or nonhierarchical structure. The tactics used by social movements vary widely and can include activities such as persuasion, letter writing, voter registration, civil disobedience, and violence. Successful movement activists continually adjust their strategies to changing political conditions, taking advantage of political opportunities when they arise. Thus, some revolutionary organizations, such as the Irish Republic Army or the Palestine Liberation Organization, may renounce terrorism when they see it as in their interest to do so; other groups may become frustrated working in a political sphere and choose to become more militant, such as some antiabortion groups and offshoots of the militia movement. Evidence suggests that within the United States, groups engaging in more forceful action, such as violence or disobedience, are generally more successful in responding to repressive treatment than are meek organizations.[24] Moreover, radical groups serve a valuable purpose for less militant groups addressing similar concerns because they make these groups appear more reasonable and mainstream to the public and to civil authorities.

How Do Social Movements Emerge, and Why Do People Join Them?

Social scientists have proposed numerous theories to explain how social movements emerge and why people become involved in them. Many of these theories assume that people participate in social movements because of some form of individual or collective pathology.[25] Early studies of activism, for example, attributed involvement in a social movement to some kind of personal deficiency. Biologically based theories argued that the "neuromuscular machinery" of movement participants differed from that of nonparticipants, making them physiologically abnormal.[26] In a similar vein, psychiatric theories proposed that people became involved in social movements because of their emotional deficiencies or deep-seated frustrations, rooted in unresolved childhood struggles against parental authority.

Deficiency models of collective action have emphasized the psychological "abnormalities" of movement participants, arguing that people are led to join social movements because of unmet emotional needs, such as the need for a charismatic authority figure. In contrast to these deficiency-oriented explanations, other sociologists emphasize the social conditions that lead people to form and join social movements, highlighting the existence of strain in society. When a strain is recognized, groups typically try to deal with it. This strain has two key sources. On the structural level, the major institutions in society grow weaker and function less effectively, often because of events such as war, economic crises, natural or technological catastrophes, or rapid social change. On the psychological level, a gap emerges between what people expect to achieve and what they are actually likely to achieve. When this gap becomes too wide, people experience a sense of relative deprivation. This in turn provokes feelings of stress and discontentment, motivating them to become involved in movements for social change.

Critics of strain theory point out that deprivation "only provides a cognitive state that *might be* conducive to, but is not sufficient for, movement participation."[27] One of these critics, Virginia Hine, has pointed out that experiences of deprivation and degradation do not influence whether or not individuals join a movement or actively participate in it. Drawing on her research on the Pentecostal Movement, Hine concluded that social strain is only a facilitating condition for movement participation; it does not cause such participation.[28]

According to interactionist scholars, such as Louis Zurcher and David Snow, the two most important factors to consider in explaining how and why people join social movements are (1) the relationships they have with others who already belong to the movement and (2) the ideology of the movement.[29] People are more likely to become involved in a social movement when they are part of a preexisting social network that includes movement members. These social networks provide an established system of contact and communication through which individuals can be recruited into a movement. Yet these social networks are not sufficient in and of themselves to induce people to join a social movement organization. Potential recruits must also be offered an ideology that blends with their existing beliefs and helps them make sense of their current situation—that is, an ideology that offers a guide for action, an explanation of existing problems or injustices, and a picture of the world as it is and as it could be.[30]

Zurcher and Snow's ideas about the bases of social movement participation are generally associated with what is known as **resource mobilization theory**. In critiquing strain theory, resource mobilization theorists point out that, at any given time, a level of deprivation and suffering exists in society that is sufficient for mobilizing a social movement. Frequently, however, this deprivation and suffering does not result in the rise of a movement. Why? According to resource mobilization theorists, it is because a social movement cannot emerge and spread until a committed group of individuals is willing to acquire and use resources on its behalf. In the broadest sense, these resources need not be material objects but can also include mobilization of the press, utilization of members' social networks, and deployment of political symbols and rhetoric. If a group cannot effectively mobilize these resources, they are not likely to have much success in forming or sustaining a movement.[31]

Strategies and Bases of Movement Recruitment

Sociologists have observed that people are often induced to join social movements through a process of bloc recruitment, or recruitment of entire groups of people who belong to the same social network.[32] This process was evident in the protest activity that followed the rioting in Cincinnati discussed earlier. Gauging the actions of the mayor, the police, and the business community as unresponsive to the needs and concerns of the city's African-American community, "a group of about 75 Cincinnati clergy, representing a cross section of churches and faiths, called for a general boycott of the city's annual feast, Taste of Cincinnati."[33] Several days later, the clergy organized a boycott of Mayor Luken's prayer at the festival, as described in the *Cincinnati Enquirer*:

A group of Cincinnati ministers said Tuesday they will not be praying with Mayor Charlie Luken at Taste of Cincinnati this weekend. Instead, they will join a boycott set up by the newly formed A Group of Concerned

Clergy....Meanwhile, A Group of Concerned Clergy has threatened more boycotts in the summer if city officials do not address race issues quickly. The clergy group is demanding that the city allocate 50 million dollars to fund Cincinnati Community Action Now, change how the police chief and civil servants are hired, grant subpoena and investigatory powers to the Citizens Police Review Panel and outlaw racial profiling. Sunday night, the three co-chairmen of Cincinnati Community Action Now met with the ministers for three hours, attempting to discourage a boycott. The effort failed.[34]

Bloc recruitment can be powerful in that it uses preestablished social networks to create organization. It is not any individual or string of individuals that gives a social movement power but rather the collective action of sets of individuals. When a group takes action, that action has more influence than the actions of a similar number of isolated individuals.

So, how important are preestablished social networks for recruiting people into social movements? In studying the recruitment strategies of Cesar Chavez and the United Farm Workers, Craig Jenkins found that they had success among seasonal workers who harvested crops in the same region but not among migrant workers who traveled from region to region. Jenkins explained that this was because seasonal workers had ongoing interaction with other long-term residents in the same community. The sharing of housing and locale by the workers enabled them to establish meaningful social relationships and a strong sense of solidarity before movement organizers ever entered the community.

While many sociologists have focused a great deal of attention on the importance of social networks in recruiting participants for social movements, other theorists have highlighted the social psychological importance of "ideological" appeals made by movements.[35] For example, Hans Toch has suggested that the Nazi Party was effective in recruiting members in Germany because of the appeals they made, particularly through their leader, Adolf Hitler. According to Toch, "Appeals are psychologically relevant commodities. They are features of the movement which tie into the susceptibilities of people."[36] Appeals are most effective in recruiting movement members when they cater to a wide array of needs and orientations and offer a redefinition of prevailing social and personal problems.

The factors that Toch highlights in explaining why people join social movements are echoed in the interactionist analyses of John Lofland, who studied recruits of the "Moonie" movement (the Unification Church of Sun Myung Moon).[37] Lofland noted that almost all of the Moonie recruits had suffered from a series of interpersonal strains prior to joining the movement, which led them to experience a life problem. This life problem in turn caused them to feel estranged from the roles they conventionally played, such as their work and family roles. They also suffered from an inability to put their "problems in living" out of mind. In fact, they were unavoidably consumed by these problems. Although these factors made people susceptible to recruitment, Lofland found that they did not necessarily cause potential recruits to join the Unification Church. A more influential factor was whether they saw themselves as religious seekers who were receptive to finding spiritually oriented solutions to their problems.

According to Lofland, recruits were also induced to join the Unification Church through a process of intensive interaction that led them to develop strong emotional ties to other members. Veteran members of the church built close ties with potential members by first *picking up*, or making contact with them, which usually involved a casual, friendly invitation to dinner or some other social event. The veteran members then engaged in *hooking*, or emotionally engaging their targeted recruits through a series of compliments, thereby encouraging them to be favorably disposed towards the movement. Finally, veteran members would achieve *encapsulation*, absorbing the attention of recruits by involving them in group activities that limited their outside contacts and their access to alternative ideas and perspectives.

Yet, while Lofland's model of conversion offered a number of interesting insights, it needed further refinement. David Snow and Cynthia Phillips provided this refinement in their illuminating study of how people became members of a Buddhist movement, Nichiren Shoshu, which was imported to the United States from Japan.[38] Like the Unification Church, the Nichiren Shoshu movement (NSA) seeks to change society by changing its individual members, allowing them to experience personal rebirth and happiness. However, unlike the Unification Church, NSA does not see Christ or some variant thereof as "the way" to personal and social transformation. Instead, they believe that the key to happiness and change lies in the repetition of a chant, the *Nam-Myoho-Renge-Kyo*.

Snow and Phillips found that converts to Nichiren Shoshu did not necessarily or invariably experience life problems or see themselves as religious seekers prior to joining the movement— although some did, most did not. Given these findings, Snow and Phillips argued that it was questionable to explain people's involvement in a movement in terms of prior problems or motivations. Rather it was more accurate to contend that once people join a religious movement, they tend to reinterpret their past and "discover" past strains or problems. They also learn to see their membership in their religious group as a solution to those strains or problems. Thus, the problems they emphasize when explaining their conversion may actually be a product of the conversion process itself.[39]

In contrast to Lofland, Snow and Phillips also found that it was not particularly important for NSA converts to break off or weaken their ties with others who did not belong to the cult. In fact, Snow and Phillips observed that individuals who converted to Nichiren Shoshu generally developed stronger bonds to people outside of the movement, particularly if they were family members, co-workers, or friends. One reason for this, Snow and Phillips suggest, is that NSA is a noncommunal movement and it does not seek or demand complete loyalty from its members. Another reason is that NSA is not seen as "revolutionary" or especially "peculiar" by the broader public, so members do not have to distance themselves from outsiders.

While Snow and Phillips's study challenged Lofland's model of conversion in some important respects, it also offered empirical support for his contention that emotional bonds and intensive interaction are necessary elements of conversion. Guided by interactionist insights, all of these analysts agree that networks are a crucial part of religious conversion and, more broadly, of movement recruitment and participation. Networks provide a foundation for movement recruitment and participation because they encourage the development of strong emotional bonds and facilitate intensive interaction. Emotional bonds are important because they make the message of a movement more credible to members and potential recruits, offering them social support for embracing beliefs that conflict with the surrounding culture. Intensive interactions are important because they normalize the movement's ideals, goals, and practices. Through spending time regularly with other members and hearing them talk about the movement and its beliefs, participants come to see it as quite normal or ordinary.

Ideology, Identity, and Commitment

As noted above, ideology is an important element in the emergence and success of social movements. An **ideology** consists of a set of interconnected beliefs, shared and utilized by members of a group or movement, that offer explanations and solutions regarding social issues.[40] An ideology provides a movement with a cognitive map that articulates the nature of the grievances that members face, focuses blame for these grievances, and justifies relevant political action. Of course, it is not ideology *per se* that articulates grievances but rather the movement spokespersons who develop and utilize it. These spokespersons look for moments when they can express and apply ideology in an inspiring way, thereby encouraging people to redefine their situation and support movement activity. This was illustrated by one of the leaders of the Black Lung Movement, Dr. Robert Wells, who ended his meetings with miners by crumbling up dried sections of diseased black lungs and telling them that this material was just like a slice of their own lungs.[41]

In a similar vein, members of a Cincinnati group known as MOMS (Mothers of Murdered Sons and Daughters) organize demonstrations in which they give speeches and display simulated tombstones with the names of the local black youth who have been murdered. In their speeches, MOMS members stress that violence is a manifestation of white repression and describe how murder reshapes the lives of affected families and the larger community.[42] Much like Dr. Wells's crumbling of a black lung, the demonstrations of MOMS members serve as "ideological articulating events"—actions which express the ideology of the movement, evoke emotion, and make grievances apparent. When successful, these events challenge prevailing definitions of reality and encourage people to question the conduct and claims of established authorities.[43]

Overall, ideologies serve a variety of important functions for social movements and their members. As interactionists Ralph Turner and Lewis Killian have observed, ideologies:

1. Act as a "map" or prescription which tells movement participants how to look at events and people.
2. Simplify reality and thereby eliminate the basis for troublesome doubts about whether the attainment of movement goals will actually foster movement values.
3. Place the movement and its goals in a moving time perspective, offering an account of the past history that led to the present sorry state of affairs.

4. Often depict a relative utopia that is to be attained.
5. Translate self-interest into an ideal by identifying it as the general welfare.
6. Identify a limited set of individuals who are engaged in a deliberate conspiracy to pursue their own sinister interests against that of the general welfare.
7. Specify the character of the movement so that it can be assimilated into members' self-conceptions as they identify with the movement.[44]

All of these elements are accomplished as movement members draw on a common rhetoric or "party line" that boldly communicates movement ideology in a clear and understandable way.[45] The creation of a party line serves two important purposes. First, it provides movement members with preformulated answers that they can easily remember, thus helping them to feel more comfortable and confident as they spread the word to others. Second, it offers members ready-made and effective ideological responses to objections that might be raised by their opponents. Through providing a sense of confidence and effectiveness to participants, the party line of a movement generates conviction among them and increases their capacity for risk taking. In the process, it fosters a deepening of their commitment to the movement. As movement members communicate this commitment to others, they generate charisma that helps them bring in new recruits.[46]

Luther Gerlach and Virginia Hine found that commitment was heightened not only as new recruits adopted the party line, but as they engaged in "bridge-burning acts." Bridge-burning acts are actions through which a complete alteration and realignment of identity takes place, leading to changes in a participant's belief system and self-image.[47] An example of this type of activity occurred in the Black Power movement. According to Gerlach and Hine, many participants in this movement experienced police beatings and arrests as bridge-burning acts. Even though movement participants anticipated beatings and arrest, they continued to march in demonstrations. This action resulted in a stronger commitment to Black Power ideology as movement members embraced the positive view of black identity that it championed. In general, movement ideology is important for participants in constructing the meaning of events such as beatings and arrests because it enables them to define these experiences in a way that supports the movement's perspectives and goals. In addition, movement ideology is useful for participants in constructing a collective memory; it serves as a means through which participants can preserve experiences of commitment, transformation, and movement success while also transmitting these experiences to potential recruits.

Gerlach and Hine's analyses of movement participation highlight concepts central to interactionism, including symbols, meanings, interaction, and identity. In recent years many of the insights offered by Gerlach and Hine have received greater attention in symbolic interactionism because of the emergence of frame analysis, an interactionist approach that focuses on the importance of social movement ideology. Frame analysis emphasizes the importance of the discourses, or frameworks of meaning, that movement participants draw upon as they define and make sense of situations, a topic we consider in the next section of this chapter.

EMERGING DIRECTIONS IN INTERACTIONIST ANALYSIS OF SOCIAL MOVEMENTS

In the following discussion we consider two areas of social movements analysis in which interactionists have taken the lead. In addressing the first area, frame analysis, we highlight the symbolic processes through which movements recruit members and encourage their continued commitment. In discussing the second area, the culture of social movements, we examine the importance of meanings, symbols, and stories for social movements. In doing so, we consider the various types of symbols that characterize all social movements. We also describe some of the narrative forms used by movement members as they challenge authorities, address perceived injustices, recruit and motivate others, and create group culture.

Frame Analysis and Alignment

Since the late 1970s interactionist scholars have argued that successful social movements engage in a process of framing meaning. In making this argument interactionists have drawn on frame analysis, an approach developed by Erving Goffman. According to Goffman, a frame is a set of definitions of situations that are "built up in accordance with the principles of organization which govern events—at least social ones—and our subjective involvement in them."[48] Social movement frames are those definitions constructed and maintained by movement participants through which experience, interaction, and communication are structured and rendered personally meaningful. For social movement organizations to be effective, they must facilitate a process of **frame alignment**. In other words, they must find ways to link their ideology with the attitudes of potential recruits, the public, members of the established order, or other movement groups.[49] Frame alignment occurs as individuals construct frameworks of meaning that draw on the ideas and beliefs of the movement so that collective action makes sense on a personal level. After all, personal involvement in a social movement involves a commitment of time and resources as well as risk and may be difficult to justify if others are already doing the work, even if one agrees with ideals of the movement. It may seem simpler and more advantageous to be a "free rider," or someone who reaps the benefits of the movement, while not expending his or her own time and resources on it.[50]

By offering useful frameworks of meaning, movements can provide individuals with justification for involvement. Interactionists suggest that social movement participants constitute agents of meaning for colleagues, opponents, and their audience. According to interactionists David Snow and Rob Benford, movement participants produce **collective action frames,** which can be defined as emergent action-oriented sets of beliefs and meanings that inspire and legitimize movement activities and campaigns.[51] Collective action frames are developed and designed to help prospective movement members "understand what happens around them, identify sources of their problems and devise methods for addressing their grievances," notably methods that involve collective action.[52]

One element of a collective action frame is what William Gamson and his colleagues call an injustice framework, or the "belief that the unimpeded operation of the authority system, on this occasion, would result in an injustice."[53] Gamson, Fireman, and Rytina offer a telling account of how an injustice framework inspired participation in social movement activity when describing what happened at the University of California in 1964. In the fall of that year, eight students at Berkeley were suspended by the administration for violating a campus ban on political activity. The next day students gathered in front of Sproul Hall, the administration building, to protest the suspensions. A student named Jack Weinberg arrived before the rally to set up a "political" table in front of Sproul Hall, an action that was strictly forbidden. Weinberg was subsequently confronted by the acting dean and arrested by the police. The ensuing events are described here:

> Weinberg, following classic civil rights tactics, did not either assist or resist the arrest, requiring that several officers carry him to a nearby police car. The police were careful to avoid provocative roughness in making the arrest in front of the now sizable crowd of students attracted to the scene. Within about 30 minutes students had seated themselves in front

and back of the police car containing Weinberg and the arresting police officers. In another moment there were more than 100 students sitting on the ground around the police car, effectively immobilizing it, and their numbers continued to grow.... The police car was held for more than 24 hours while negotiations were carried on by various faculty and student intermediaries.[54]

The negotiations resulted in a short-lived truce—within a few days, students and administrators became embroiled in a major conflict, prompting a large mass of students to take over Sproul Hall. This in turn led to the arrest of 750 students, giving birth to the Berkeley Free Speech Movement.

In analyzing the emergence of this movement, Gamson, Fireman, and Rytina contend that as the students at Berkeley interacted with the administration, they created and became influenced by two primary frames of meaning. First, as they witnessed the arrest of one classmate (Jack Weinberg) and the suspension of eight others, they started to believe that the actions of the administration would continue to result in injustice; that is, they developed an injustice framework. Second, and more crucially, they linked this frame to a larger collective action frame, thereby defining their situation as one that required a collective response in the form of movement activity. It was their embrace of a collective action frame that led students to surround the police car holding Jack Weinberg and, subsequently, to take over the administration building. Although students might have adopted an injustice frame in assessing their situation on campus, this frame alone did not lead them to participate in the protests and sit-ins that rocked the university. They had to define their situation as one that would be best addressed and resolved through engaging in collective action. In essence, they had to engage in what interactionists call **frame bridging,** a process in which individuals move from a frame where they share common grievances and orientations, but do not express them, to a frame where they see personal involvement in collective action as the answer to their problems.

The process of developing and embracing a collective action frame occurs through the creation of narratives, discourses, and stories. People not only create images, but also tell stories that portray these images. These stories convey the justice of the movement and the triumph of movement members over the suffering, punitive action, and grievances that they have experienced. The point of storytelling is to develop shared concepts, phrases, and ideas that will stir the emotions and thinking of others, leading them toward collective action. When movement activists have successfully brought about such responses, they have forged what is called **frame resonance**—a deep connection between the movement's frame of meaning and the experience, emotions, and cognitions of its members and/or potential recruits.[55] For example, Mitch Berbrier has investigated a new movement known as "white separatism."[56] Berbrier found that, in contrast to white supremacists, white separatists use a "racialist" master frame that claims to be "hate-free." This frame presents the injustices suffered by whites as equal in magnitude to those of ethnic and racial minorities, and the heritage of whites as equal in value. The white separatist frame includes the concepts of love, pride, and "heritage preservation" and is offered to prospective movement members as evidence of the group's ethnic credentials and lack of animosity. According to Berbrier, this frame resonates broadly with the values of conservative whites, allowing them to veil their racist beliefs and to ignore the harmful consequences of these beliefs.

Box 8-1 COLLECTIVE ACTION FRAMES: FROM PROTEST TO MOTHERHOOD

In 1973 International Telegraph and Telephone (ITT) donated $1 million to the Central Intelligence Agency to have Salvador Allende, Chile's first democratically elected president, assassinated.[1] When foreign corporations like Anaconda Copper repeatedly underpaid workers and exported their profits back to shareholders in the United States rather than reinvesting in the Chilean economy, Allende declared that the companies' assets would be controlled by the state. In response, the CIA engineered a coup d'état, installing Augusto Pinochet, a right-wing dictator who used death squads to suppress labor unions and quiet political opposition.

Research on Chilean politics (1953-1978) by Rita Noonan demonstrates that activists in the women's movement faced many dangers and obstacles as Pinochet came to power that were nonexistent before the coup.[2] For the women's movement in Chile to survive, it had to maintain a collective action frame that had frame resonance with former activists but also Pinochet's fascist regime. During this period the "progressive feminist frame" of the women's movement—a frame that emerged as Chile became more democratic under Allende—was replaced by a "maternal frame" that emphasized traditional values of family and motherhood. Because the ideology of women's rights was reframed by feminists as "motherhood," which mirrored forms of political discourse used within Pinochet' regime, progressive groups were able to continue pushing for change in support of women and families.

Research such as Noonan's, which connects the analysis of social movements to the forms of talk that people use as they frame issues, clearly fits with the interactionist tradition. As we have highlighted throughout the book, symbolic interactionism looks at how individuals and groups, through communication, create, sustain, and transform meanings. Within social movements, the creation of sets of meanings, or "frames," is a decisive factor in mobilizing people to join together to change their social conditions.

1. Anthony Sampson, *The Sovereign State of ITT* (New York: Stein and Day, 1980).
2. Rita K. Nonan, "Women Against the State: Political Opportunities and Collection Action Frames in Chile's Transition to Democracy," in Doug McAdam and David A. Snow, eds., *Social Movements* (Los Angeles: Roxbury Publishing), p. 25.

The Culture of Social Movements

Perhaps more than any other group of theorists, symbolic interactionists have argued that social movements both challenge and *create* culture. While movement organizations such as the Animal Liberation Front, Democracy Now, and the White Aryan League actively contest dominant culture, they also generate culture, both through their daily interactions and through the symbols and stories they share. John Lofland has argued that "symbolic objects are an important part of social movement culture vested with great emotion. As such, symbolic objects hold special meaning for people."[57]

Logos, Martyrs, and Places. Social movements become associated with what Lofland calls "identifiers"—unique logos and symbols that serve to represent the nature and goals of a movement. Some well-known movement logos include the peace symbol of the antiwar movement and the white hoods of the Ku Klux Klan. Yet these logos are only one type of movement identifier. Individuals themselves may also serve as symbols of a movement, as illustrated by charismatic leaders such as Mohandas Gandhi, Martin Luther King Jr., and the notorious Adolf Hitler. More commonly, individuals who suffer extreme persecution, or martyr themselves for the cause, become symbols of social movements. Examples include Joan of Arc, Che Guevra, and, more recently, Nelson Mandela, the icon of the antiapartheid movement in South Aftrica. These martyrs earn esteem and become identifiers of the movement not simply because of their rhetorical skills or dynamic personalities, but primarily due to their personal sacrifice for the movement's beliefs, goals, and members.

As Lofland observed, artifacts, events, and places can also serve as special symbols for movements. Posters, buttons, protest signs, and souvenirs from past demonstrations may represent successful campaigns or important moments, invoking a sense of nostalgia among movement members. Moreover, artifacts that conjure up memorable moments may be placed on display at key events, which also commemorate special times or occasions. One such event for members of the labor movement is May Day, or International Workers' Day, celebrated on May first of every year. This occasion commemorates the event outlined at the beginning of this chapter—the 1886 Haymarket Massacre, which resulted in the death of several Chicago laborers who were protesting in favor of an eight-hour workday.

Because events are situated in time and physical space, places can also become notable symbols of a movement. For example, the mall area in Washington, D.C., where hundreds of thousands of people gathered in 1963 to hear Martin Luther King, Jr.'s "I Have a Dream" speech, became a powerful symbol of the Civil Rights Movement. Similarly, Wounded Knee, South Dakota, became a defining site for the American Indian Movement after several of its members battled FBI agents there for seventy-one days in 1973. Both of these places became imbued with reverence and emotion by movement participants and, in turn, became solidly anchored in their group culture and narratives.

Movement Narratives. Interactionists have recently expanded their analyses of social movements by including "narratives (stories, tales, anecdotes, allegories) in their discussions of framing"[58] As Gary Alan Fine has noted, frames are expressed and made concrete through the use of narratives. However, narratives differ from frames in some respects, particularly in how they engage audiences, represent and organize reality, and construct collective identities. As Francesca Polletta points out, these "differences are a function of narrative's dependence on emplotment, point of view, narrativity, and a limited fund of plot lines."[59]

Most important, Polletta reveals how narratives shape the development of social movements in several significant ways. For example, when a movement initially emerges, narratives are often used to explain the discontent as something that has inexplicably caught fire, "exploded," or burst forth "like a fever" from a previously unprepared and unaware group of people. While this story of the movement's origins is not always true, it becomes useful strategically in mobilizing public support for what is portrayed as a spontaneous grassroots campaign. Narratives also serve the purpose of explaining how and when protest begins and how and when individuals transform into movement "activists." In fact, in movements where "the goal is self-transformation as much as political reform," personal story telling itself may become a sign of activism.[60]

Narratives also take on a prominent role in when movements experience defeats, reversals, or strategic failures. To overcome setbacks and the organizational crises they provoke, movements must develop narratives, or "fortifying myths," that can explain what has happened and recast failures as trivial, fleeting, or as victories in disguise.[61] In making this point, Polletta emphasizes how the United States Knights of Labor, a movement that included 750,000 workers, collapsed in the aftermath of the 1886 Haymarket riot, largely because they "were unable to tell a story that could blame anyone but themselves when things went awry."[62] By contrast, the British "new unionist" movement that arose in the same era sustained itself by developing narratives that enabled its members to make sense of and reframe the defeats they experienced and to feel that the moral rightness of their cause would ensure them long-term victory.

While Polletta's research examined the nature of movement narratives and the role they played in shaping the development and success of movement organizations, Gary Alan Fine has investigated the specific types of narrative used by social movements and how they create and sustain group culture. In his pertinent analysis, Fine observed that social movements are essentially "staging areas" for behaviors where actions and forms of talk are judged and encouraged or discouraged.[63] For example, "strategy sessions" serve as staging areas for brainstorming as social movement leaders and participants plan for police actions such as tear gassing, arrests, or searches and seizures. As movement organizers advance a call for violent action or nonviolent resistance, they are surrounded by an audience of other activists who evaluate their performance as well as the appeal of their stories.

As Fine highlights, the processes of movement organizing, protesting, and strategizing are filled with stories of injustice. These stories exist as "bundles of narrative" through which movement participants create rituals, identities, and other symbolic referents. On a broader scale, the narrative used by movement members is important because it serves as the vehicle for "constructing shared meanings and group cohesion and it contributes to organizational identity."[64] It also serves as the medium through which the actions of the movement and its adversaries are interpreted.

Fine identified three categories of narratives that movement organizers use to construct a sense of injustice and encourage movement participants. The first category includes atrocity tales, or stories that convey a sense of injustice emerging from some kind of negative personal experience. Fine refers to this category of tales as "horror stories."[65] Horror stories tell tales of stigma and public degradation, revealing details in which activists and other movement members are persecuted for their beliefs, their movement activities, or their movement identities. The story of Emmett Till, an African-American teenager from Chicago who was killed in Mississippi during the 1950s, provides a powerful historical example of a horror story that motivated members of the Civil Rights Movement. After allegedly "cat calling" at a white woman, Till was seized by a group of white men who beat him, bound him with barbed wire, and threw him into the Tallahatchie River with a cotton gin fan tied around his neck.[66] To draw attention to this brutal violation, Emmett Till's mother held his funeral on September 3, 1955, with an open casket, displaying his disfigured face and body to protest his treatment at the hands of whites. Within the Civil Rights movement, like other movements, telling a horror story of this kind and sharing related experiences of injustice fosters higher levels of commitment. It also promotes higher-risk activism and a stronger sense of collective identification.

A second kind of narrative used by movement organizers and participants is the "war story." This type of story, which can be a form of what Poletta calls a "fortifying myth," talks about hard times to show the resiliency, creativity, and perseverance of activists as they fight back, communicating the "underlying message that the movement is just and the participants are moral actors."[67] A third kind of movement narrative, the "happy ending," highlights the successes or victories resulting from the work of movement participants. In the happy ending, "the speaker surprisingly benefits from movement participation, or changes occur for the better." This form of narrative thus provides "a morale boost and directly reinforces movement

involvement."[68] In many cases, it tells of activists successfully outmaneuvering authorities, creating huge turnouts at demonstrations through creative public relations work, or stifling police by getting arrests overturned in court. Ultimately, a "happy ending" narrative serves the dual purpose of offering movement participants hope while also demonstrating the movement's effectiveness to sympathetic bystanders, thereby enhancing the prospect of recruiting them.

To summarize, movement organizers and participants draw on various narratives to make sense of their experiences, to explain the rise of their movement, to motivate themselves and others, to sustain a sense of hope and solidarity in the face of setbacks, and to shape their unfolding actions. Their story telling can be a fluid process, changing in response to shifting demands or desires. For instance, when speaking at a movement event, organizers may begin by telling "horror stories" to appeal to potential recruits only to follow with a "war story" designed to motivate movement members by highlighting their skill and persistence in battling against unjust authorities. In wrapping up their narrative, organizers may emphasize a "happy ending" to show members and potential recruits that they can outfox their adversaries and realize the social changes they desire. Most important, through telling and retelling these types of narratives, members of a movement construct and sustain its culture. They also fashion a collective identity that not only provides them with a basis for self-definition, but also enables them to build solidarity with others who share their interests, understandings, and experiences.

Box 8-2 SOCIAL MOVEMENTS AS DRAMAS OF POWER

Drawing upon observations of the antiapartheid, labor, and nuclear disarmament movements, Rob Benford and Scott Hunt offer a dramaturgical analysis of power in social movements.[1] They contend that social movements both construct and contest definitions of power relations through four primary techniques: (1) scripting, (2) staging, (3) performing, and (4) interpreting. According to Benford and Hunt, social movements are essentially dramas in which organizers must direct action, movement actors must give performances, and performances must project an image of power.

Much like directors in the theater, movement organizers must take up the task of scripting. That is, they must develop a script or plan, identify key actors, and coordinate action by giving directions and outlining expected behaviors. Through creating scripts for action, movement leaders not only provide direction to followers, but also supply them with an alternative vision of power relations and a rationale for changing the way things are. A key aspect of scripting involves the attribution of motives to a cast of characters. Typically people and groups who are antagonistic to the movement are characterized as villains while movement participants and their supporting cast members are typified as benevolent, just, and good. These typifications are offered to a broad public audience through vocabularies of motive that supply justifications for movement action.

When engaging in staging, movement organizers promote events and gain publicity for movement issues and successes by mobilizing symbols that are likely to elicit support from the public. A notable example is the mass demonstration held in Seattle in November 1999 during the meetings of the World Trade Organization (WTO) meetings. In a protest of WTO policies, antiglobalization activists surrounded the convention center, effectively shutting down the meetings for a day. One of the groups participating in the demonstration included approximately 300 children, dressed in colorful turtle costumes and protesting fishing practices which kill off approximately 150,000 sea turtles each year. In staging the event, activists sought to dramatize troublesome environmental, labor, and trade issues and to evoke public concern about WTO policies that contributed to these problems.

The staging of movement events provides opportunities for performing. Benford and Hunt use this term to refer to the demonstration of power to an audience through some movement action. The gathering of thousands of protestors in Seattle, including labor leaders, environmental activists, social justice advocates, students, teachers, and indigenous rights activists, and the closing of the convention center where WTO representatives planned to meet proved to be an effective performance. However, while activists at the protest shared the antiglobalization movement's definitions of the WTO, organizers of the event were unable to ensure dramaturgical discipline, that is, the maintenance of self-control among all movement participants so that the movement's definition of the situation could be sustained. Throughout most of the day of November 30, protestors blocked intersections and key areas of downtown Seattle. Although the protests were nonviolent, the police responded by beating and gassing protestors. In response, a small group of anarchists began to fight back, hurling bricks, bottles, and other material at the police, turning over garbage cans and damaging property, breaching the movement's definition of the event as an organized and peaceful protest.

While little remedial work could be done to restore the original definition of the situation, organizers still sought to frame the day's events in meanings favorable to the movement. Benford and Hunt refer to this activity as interpreting. "Interpreting" ultimately means defining events and action in terms and images that facilitate the adoption of an injustice framework by the public, by movement constituents, and/or by potential recruits. This may demand making adjustments in a performance of movement participants so that it embodies meanings and definitions that are important to the movement. By highlighting the brutality of the Seattle police rather than the activity of anarchists in the crowd, organizers at the WTO demonstration attempted to frame the actions of most protestors as peaceful, police as violent, and the actions of rioters as a natural response to that violence. In doing so, movement activists hoped to evoke audience sentiment for the cause of the movement and for the protestors being beaten.

1. Robert D. Benford and Scott A. Hunt, "Dramaturgy and Social Movements: The Social Construction and Communication of Power," *Sociological Inquiry* 62, 1992, pp. 36–55.

CONCLUSIONS

We hope that we have demonstrated that symbolic interactionism offers a compelling and important perspective on collective behavior, social movements, and more broadly, social life. As outlined in this chapter, interactionism has clearly contributed many concepts and lines of research that have added to sociological understandings of how and why people engage in collective action. Moreover, as we illustrated in previous chapters, interactionism has enhanced sociological understandings of language, emotion, the self, interaction, inequality, social organization, and postmodernity

Most crucially, we hope that we have shown you that symbolic interactionism offers a unique and, in some senses, "radical" perspective on social life—a perspective that might not have been so evident before you took the class. This perspective stresses that nothing can be taken for granted. Meaning, it points out, is not inherent in things; rather, it emerges out of people's responses to things. Even a seemingly simple object, such as dust, can have multiple meanings. It can stand for a child's right to play, a bachelor's incompetence as a house cleaner, or a corporation's neglect of its workers' health. We hope that as you have read this book you have started to question some of those meanings you previously took for granted and that you have learned that things which may have appeared simple are really not so simple. We also hope that you have come to appreciate the insights of the symbolic interactionist perspective and how it can help you understand yourself, other people, and the larger social world.

Ironically, symbolic interactionism started as an oppositional movement in the 1960s, challenging the assumptions of the functionalist perspective that dominated sociology at that time. Like other movements, it must deal with broader changes and trends that pose threats to its future success and viability. The first trend that threatens symbolic interactionism is its increased incorporation into the body of mainstream sociology. In some respects, interactionism has become the victim of its own success. Because of the insights it has offered, interactionism and its core concepts have increasingly become absorbed into mainstream sociological theory. In turn, interactionism is losing its distinctive "voice"; that is, its voice is becoming integrated with, and largely indistinguishable from, the chorus of other voices that make up the discipline. This trend has become evident in the analyses that can be found in many prominent sociological books and journal articles. Indeed, as David Maines has observed, a number of leading social theorists draw heavily on interactionist ideas and assumptions, even though they are often unaware that this is the case.[69]

The second threatening trend affecting interactionism is the growing diversity and division emerging among its practitioners. Interactionism has a long history of being open to innovation, and, as portrayed throughout this book, it continues to emerge in new forms, blending creatively with a variety of other sociological approaches. In the process, interactionism has become increasingly diverse. Although this diversity has been beneficial in many respects, especially in fostering creativity, it has also led to fragmentation—a trend that threatens to undermine the viability and coherence of symbolic interactionism in the future. As proponents of the perspective become more diverse in their beliefs, interests, and practices, it will become increasingly difficult for them to share a common mission or identity.

In the end, the future direction and successes of symbolic interactionism will be determined largely by the central mission that its practitioners pursue. We suggest that this mission should be to blend scholarship and citizenship in ways that "merge values, research competence, education, and practical politics" in efforts to construct more just and egalitarian communities.[70] Guided by this goal, interactionism can live out the aims of the early pragmatists, creating and applying knowledge that helps people to address the problems they face and improve their social circumstances, particularly by reducing exploitation, oppression, and other unjust practices. We will continue in our efforts to apply interactionism for these purposes, and we hope that you will join us in this endeavor.

SUMMARY

- Collective action refers to any behavior that people engage in as a group to rectify some problematic condition. Symbolic interactionists distinguish between two key forms of collective action: collective behavior and social movements. In spontaneous forms of collective action—what sociologists call "collective behavior"—new norms emerge which allow for social behavior that would otherwise not be accepted. Whether the collective behavior is a panic, a riot, or a rumor, symbolic interactionists emphasize that in each case some minimal degree of social organization is present.
- The perspective that underscores how new norms are created in a situation is called "emergent norm theory." This approach

argues that people in a crowd create new norms as they negotiate the meaning of the current situation. Because crowd situations are always somewhat ambiguous, most people are uncertain about what actions are appropriate for themselves as well as for the group. When people are faced with such uncertainty, a few visible participants may be able to instigate action by passionately advancing suggestions that seem appropriate to the crowd. Emergent norms are also evident in a variety of collective behaviors, such as riots, rumors, and panics.

- In contrast to collective behavior, social movements are more highly organized and last for a much longer period of time. Social movements do share at least one characteristic with collective behavior such as riots: they are socially constructed in ways that express grievances and discontent. In social movements the expression of grievances is highly organized and mobilized through networks. What is defined as a grievance ripe for mobilization and protest is not inevitable, but a function of interests, resources, political opportunity, and active organizing efforts.
- Recent work in the area of social movements demonstrates that resources (such as people, places to meet, money, and access to media outlets) and preestablished social networks are key ingredients. Social networks are particularly important because they serve as the mechanism through which new members to a social movement are recruited. Networks are often formed along lines of kinship, friendship, personal interests, and shared ideologies.
- An ideology consists of a set of interconnected beliefs that are shared and used by members of a movement with a blueprint for political action. Social movement researchers have observed that demonstrations and protests are commonly used by movement activists as "ideological articulating events," times in which such actions are taken for the purpose of expressing the ideology of

the movement, evoking emotion, and making grievances transparent. For new initiates into a movement, these moments may also be "bridge-burning acts," actions which facilitate a complete transformation of identity on the part of a participant, solidifying changes in their personal beliefs and self-image.

• Symbolic interactionists have made several unique contributions to social movement theory, including the areas of frame alignment theory, social movement culture, social movement narratives, and the construction of collective identity. Frame alignment refers to the social processes through which a social movement's frame of meaning is linked to the personal meanings of an individual, facilitating their entry into the movement. "Frame resonance" is achieved to the degree that organizers present the frame through which people recognize their own experiences and begin to identify with the meanings that it contains. Each social movement typically has its own unique culture, which is made up of special symbols, places, stories, and identities. Narrative analysis of social movements reveals that there are different types of stories that movement participants create and use, including horror stories, war stories, and stories with happy endings. The narratives that people develop are also employed to identify themselves with a movement and to fashion a collective identity.

GLOSSARY OF KEY TERMS

Assimilation — The process that occurs during rumor transmission in which the original details of the story are modified or transformed so that they fit into the tellers' preconceived biases or expectations.

Autokinetic Effect — The change in perception due to the natural movements of our eyes that makes light appear to move spontaneously.

Collective Action — Action that people engage in as a group and formulate as a response to problematic conditions, often in opposition to existing societal norms.

Collective Action Frame — Action-oriented sets of beliefs and meanings that not only explain and justify but also inspire social movement activities and campaigns.

Collective Behavior — Relatively spontaneous social action, often in contrast to social norms, taken by a large number of people who have gathered to work out a joint response to an ambiguous situation.

Collective Identity — A group identity that members of a social movement create for themselves, which becomes subjectively meaningful for all members of the group.

Emergent Norm Theory — A perspective that sees a crowd as a diverse and heterogeneous group of people who, in the face of ambiguous stimuli or circumstances, develop a group norm that establishes a framework for action and provides a sense of uniformity.

Frame Alignment The process through which movements align their ideology with the attitudes of the potential recruits, the public, members of the established order, or other movement groups.

Frame Bridging A process in which we move from a frame where we share common grievances and orientations with others, but do not express them, to a frame where we see personal involvement in collective action as the answer to our problems.

Frame Resonance A deep connection between the movement's frame of meaning and the experience of actual or potential recruits, which stirs their emotions and cognitions, predisposing them to mobilization.

Ideology A set of interconnected beliefs and their associated attitudes, shared and utilized by members of a group or movement, that offer explanations and solutions regarding social issues.

Leveling The process during the repeated telling of a rumor in which some of the details of the original communication drop out.

Panic Episodes in which members of a crowd respond to an immediate threat with highly charged emotional behavior that increases rather than reduces the danger faced by themselves or others.

Resource Mobilization Theory A theory of social movements that stresses that access to resources is crucial to an aspiring movement and that social movements can only grow when a committed group of individuals is willing to acquire and use resources on its behalf. These resources include not only material items like money and equipment, but also symbolic goods such as leadership skills, recruitment networks, and media savvy.

Riot A form of collective behavior in which a large number of people assemble for the purpose of protesting a grievance and from which a violent disturbance may emerge.

Rumor A piece of information that is neither substantiated nor refuted and is driven by a search for meaning, clarification, and closure. From the interactionist point of view, rumor constitutes a form of collective problem solving that enables people to cope with life's uncertainty and guide their actions.

Sharpening   The process in which some of the original words and phrases initially used in telling of a rumor are highlighted and given additional emphasis as the rumor is retold.

Social Movement   A collection of individuals who organize together to achieve or prevent some social or political change.

QUESTIONS FOR REFLECTION OR ASSIGNMENT

1. What are the key differences between collective behavior and social movements? How could you tell the difference if you were conducting a field observation and found a mass of people congregated outside the county courthouse?

2. Through what phases do riots progress? In what phase might authorities best intervene so that a riot is prevented? If a riot broke out in your city and you were asked to give advice to the mayor's office, what steps would you recommend? Why?

3. What are the four basic features of a mass panic? If you served on a stadium board and were commissioned to develop policies that would prevent the emergence of a panic inside or outside of the stadium, what would you recommend?

4. Imagine that you wake up one morning to find that all the electricity is out in your dorm. Your roommate then informs you that he or she heard that all university classes have been canceled. What conditions would lead you to suspect that your roommate is spreading a rumor? About an hour later, you hear another dorm resident say that classes have been canceled for the next three days and that students might have to vacate the dorm. Would you be likely to believe this? Why or why not? How can you explain the changes that have taken place in the message being transmitted throughout your dorm?

5. You are a tenant in an apartment complex that is in a perpetual state of disrepair. The heating system in the buildings has failed, and the weather is unusually cold even though it is still early fall. Within the complex are elderly people who have lived in their apartments for a long time, families who are recent tenants, and single people whom you occasionally meet. You decide to start a tenants' rights movement in the building. How would you begin? What resources would you need to mobilize? Why?

6. As you try to build your tenants' rights organization, you find that some people are afraid that they may hurt the landlord's feelings if they confront him about the bad conditions in the complex. What kinds of "frames" and "frame alignment" strategies might you propose to convince them to engage in collective action that will rectify the problem? What kinds of narratives would you use to encourage them to join and stay in the organization?

7. After reading this book, what do you see as the major insights offered by symbolic interactionism? How has this perspective helped you to understand yourself, your interactions, and your everyday social worlds?

SUGGESTED READINGS FOR FURTHER STUDY

Benford, Rob and Scott Hunt. "Identity Talk in the Peace and Justice Movements," *Journal of Contemporary Ethnography* 22(4), 1994, pp. 488–517.

Fine, Gary Alan. *Difficult Reputations: Collective Memories of the Evil, Inept, and Controversial* (Chicago: University of Chicago Press, 2001.)

Fine, Gary Alan and Patricia Turner. *Whispers on the Color Line: Rumor and Race in America*

(Berkeley, CA: University of California Press, 2001).

Lowney, Kathleen S. "Wrestling with Criticism: The World Wrestling Federation's Ironic Campaign Against the Parents Television Council." *Symbolic Interaction* 26(3), 2003, pp. 427–446.

McAdam, Doug, and David S. Snow. *Social Movements: Readings on Their Emergence, Mobilization, and Dynamics* (Los Angeles: Roxbury Press, 1997).

McPhail, Clark. "The Crowd and Collective Behavior: Bringing Symbolic Interaction Back In," *Symbolic Interaction* 29(4), 2006, pp. 433–464.

ENDNOTES

1 Howard Zinn, *A People's History of the United States: 1492–Present* (New York: Harper Perennial Press, 1995), p. 264.

2 Ibid., p. 266.

3 Gustave Le Bon, *The Crowd: A Study of the Popular Mind* (New York: Macmillian, 1897).

4 Erving Goffman, *Interaction Ritual* (Garden City, NY: Doubleday, 1967).

5 Muzafer Sherif, *The Psychology of Social Norms* (New York: Harper & Row, 1936).

6 Solomon Asch, *Social Psychology* (Englewood Cliffs, NJ: Prentice-Hall, 1952).

7 Gary Alan Fine, "Working Cooks: The Dynamics of Professional Kitchens," *Current Research on Occupations and Professions* 4, 1987, pp. 141–158.

8 David Postman, Jack Broom, and Warren King, "Clashes, Protests Wrack WTO: Police Use Tear Gas Against Blockade," *Seattle Times*, November 30, 1999, p. A1.

9 Ralph W. Conant, "The Phases of a Riot," in Ralph H. Turner and Leis M. Killian, eds., *Collective Behavior* (Englewood Cliffs, NJ: Prentice-Hall, 1972).

10 Ibid.

11 Ralph L. Rosnow and Gary Alan Fine, *Rumor and Gossip: The Social Psychology of Hearsay* (New York: Elsevier, 1976), p. 4.

12 Ibid., p. 14.

13 Ibid., pp. 14–20.

14 Gordon W. Allport and Leo J. Postman, *The Psychology of Rumor* (New York: Holt, Rinehart and Winston, 1947).

15 David M. Johnson, "The 'Phantom Anesthetist' of Mattoon: A Field Study of Mass Hysteria," *Journal of Abnormal and Social Psychology* 40, 1945, pp. 175–186.

16 Tamotso Shibutani, *Improvised News: A Sociological Study of Rumor* (Indianapolis, IN: Bobbs-Merrill, 1996).

17 Ralph H. Turner and Lewis M. Killian, *Collective Behavior* (Englewood Cliffs, NJ: Prentice Hall, 1957), p. 95.

18 Hannah Allum and Tom Lasseter, "Baghdad Bridge Stampede Kills Hundreds of Shiites," *Duluth News Tribune*, September 1, 2005, p. 13A.

19 British Broadcast Corporation, September 20, 2005, web page, World News, http://news.bbc.co.uk/1/hi/world/middle_east/4199618.stm.

20 Ralph H. Turner and Lewis M. Killian, *Collective Behavior* (Note 17), p. 84.

21 Ibid., p. 95.

22 Allan J. Mayer and Jon Lowell, "Cincinnati Stampede," in *Newsweek*, December 17, 1979, p. 52.

23 Ibid., p. 52.

24 William A. Gamson, "Violence and Political Power: The Meek Don't Make It," *Psychology Today* 8, 1974, pp. 35–41.

25 Virginia Hine, "Deprivation and Disorganization Theories of Social Movements," in Eli Zaretsky et al., eds., *Religious Movements in Contemporary America* (Princeton, NJ: Princeton University Press, 1974), pp. 646–661.

26 Thelma Herman McCormack, "The Motivation of Radicals," in Barry McLaughlin, ed., *Studies in Social Movements* (New York: Free Press, 1969), pp. 73–84.

27 Louis Zurcher and David Snow, "Collective Behavior: Social Movements," in Morris Rosenberg and Ralph Turner, eds., *Social Psychology:*

Sociological Perspectives (New York: Basic Books, 1981), p. 454.

28 Virginia Hine, "Deprivation and Disorganization Theories of Social Movements," (Note 25).

29 Louis Zurcher and David Snow, "Collective Behavior: Social Movements," (Note 27).

30 Ibid.

31 For representative works of the resource mobilization perspective, see Bruce Fireman and William A. Gamson, "Utilitarian Logic in the Resource Mobilization Perspective," in Mayer N. Zald and John D. McCarthy, eds., *The Dynamics of Social Movements* (Cambridge, MA: Winthrop, 1979), p. 844; John D. McCarthy and Mayer N. Zald, *The Trend of Social Movements in America: Professionalization and Resource Mobilization* (Morristown, NJ: General Learning Corp., 1973); and Charles Tilly, *From Mobilization to Revolution* (Reading, MA: Addison-Wesley, 1978).

32 McCarthy and Zald's findings suggest that federations of movement organizations develop out of preexisting nonmovement local groups with concentrations of adherents or isolated constituents. Mayer N. Zald and John D. McCarthy, *Social Movements in Organizational Society: Collected Essays* (New Brunswick, NJ: Transaction Books, 1987).

33 *Cincinnati Enquirer*, "Clergy Urge Boycott of Taste of Cincinnati," Saturday, May 19, 2001, p. A1.

34 Kevin Aldridge, "Some Churches Won't Join Prayer at Taste of Cincinnati," *Cincinnati Enquirer*, May 23, 2001, p. A1.

35 On the importance of persuasive appeals, see the following sources: Hans Toch, *The Social Psychology of Social Movements* (New York: Macmillan, 1965); Charles J. Stewart, Craig Allen Smith, and Robert E. Denton, *Persuasion and Social Movements* (Prospect Heights, IL: Waveland Press, 1984); Barrie Thorne, "Protest and the Problem of Credibility: Uses of Knowledge and Risk Taking in the Draft Resistance Movement of the 1960s," in Jo Freeman, ed., *Social Movements of the Sixties and Seventies* (New York: Longman, 1983), pp. 101–116; Luther P. Gerlach and Virginia Hine, *People, Power, Change: Movements of Social Transformation*

(New York: Bobbs-Merrill, 1970). On the role of agitators in social movement, see Herbert Blumer, "Social Movements," in Barry McLaughlin, ed., *Studies in Social Movements* (New York: Free Press, 1969), p. 829; John Lofland, *Protest: Studies of Collective Behavior and Social Movements* (New Brunswick, NJ: Transaction Books, 1985).

36 Hans Toch, *The Social Psychology of Social Movements*, (Note 35), p. 16.

37 John Lofland, *Doomsday Cult* (Englewood Cliffs, NJ: Prentice-Hall, 1966).

38 David Snow and Cynthia L. Phillips, "The Lofland-Stark Conversion Model: A Critical Reassessment," *Social Problems* 47(4), 1980, pp. 430–447.

39 Ibid.

40 Gary Alan Fine and Kent Sandstrom, "Ideology in Action: A Pragmatic Approach to a Contested Concept," *Sociological Theory* 11(1), 1993, pp. 21–38.

41 Bennett M. Judkins, "Mobilization of Membership: The Black and Brown Lung Movements," in Jo Freeman, ed., *Social Movements of the Sixties and Seventies* (New York: Longman, 1983), p. 39.

42 This information was collected in an interview with the lead MOMS organizer, May 23, 2001.

43 Daniel A. Foss and Ralph Larkin, *Beyond Revolution: A New Theory of Social Movements* (South Hadley, MA: Bergin and Garvey, 1986), p. 72.

44 Ralph Turner and Lewis Killian, *Collective Behavior*, 2nd ed. (Englewood Cliffs, NJ: Prentice-Hall, 1972), pp. 269–272.

45 Luther Gerlach and Virginia Hine, *People, Power, Change*, (Note 28), p. 161.

46 Ibid., p. 110.

47 Ibid., pp. 137 ff.

48 Erving Goffman, *Frame Analysis* (Garden City, NY: Anchor Books, 1974), pp. 10–11.

49 David A. Snow, E. Burke Rochford, Steven K. Worden, and Robert D. Benford, "Frame Alignment Processes, Micro-mobilization, and Movement Participation," *American Journal of Sociology* 51, 1986, pp. 464–481.

50 Mancur Olson, *The Logic of Collective Action* (Cambridge, MA: Harvard University Press, 1965).

51 David A. Snow and Robert D. Benford, "Ideology, Frame Resonance, and Participant Mobilization," *International Social Movement Research* 1, 1988, pp. 197–217.

52 Rita K. Noonan, "Women Against the State: Political Opportunities and Collection Action Frames in Chile's Transition to Democracy," in Doug McAdam and David A. Snow, eds., *Social Movements* (Los Angeles: Roxbury, 1997), p. 254.

53 William A. Gamson, Bruce Fireman, and Steven Rytina, *Encounters with Unjust Authority* (Homewood, IL: The Dorsey Press, 1982), p. 14.

54 Ibid., pp. 19–20.

55 David A. Snow and Robert Benford, "Ideology, Frame Resonance, and Participant Mobilization," (Note 51).

56 Mitch Berbrier, "Half the Battle: Cultural Resonance, Framing Processes, and Ethnic Affectations in Contemporary White Separatist Rhetoric," *Social Problems* 45, 1998, pp. 431–450.

57 John Lofland, "Charting Degrees of Movement Culture," in Hank Johnston and Bert Klandermans, eds., *Social Movements and Culture* (Minneapolis: University of Minnesota Press, 1995), pp. 188–216.

58 Francesca Polletta, "Contending Stories: Narrative in Social Movements," *Qualitative Sociology*, 21(4), 1998, pp. 419–446.

59 Ibid.

60 Ibid., p. 430.

61 Ibid.

62 Ibid., p. 432.

63 Gary Alan Fine, "Public Narration and Group Culture: Discerning Discourse in Social Movements," in Hank Johnston and Bert Klandermans, eds., *Social Movements and Culture* (Minneapolis: University of Minnesota Press), 1995, pp. 127–143.

64 Ibid, p. 133.

65 Ibid., p.135.

66 Davis W. Houck and Matthew A. Grindy, *Emmett Till and the Mississippi Press.* (Jackson, MS: University of Mississippi Press, 2008).

67 Luther P. Gerlach and Virginia Hine, *People, Power and Change: Movements of Social Transformation* (New York: Bobbs-Merrill, 1970), pp. 99–158.

68 Gary Alan Fine, "Public Narration and Group Culture," (Note 63), p. 136.

69 David Maines, *The Faultline of Consciousness: A View of Interactionism in Sociology* (New York: Aldine de Gruyter, 2001).

70 Ibid., p. 240.

AUTHOR INDEX

~

SUBJECT INDEX

~

CPSIA information can be obtained at www.ICGtesting.com
Printed in the USA
BVOW080243270612

293480BV00002BB/1/P